P9-BZR-399

Gardening in the Mountain West

by Barbara Hyde

Designed and Illustrated by Daina D. Penn

Barbara J. Hyde, Inc.
2831 Mountain View
Longmont, Colorado 80503

Dedication

This book is dedicated to the Master Gardeners of Cooperative Extension. Because of their experience, selflessness, initiative, skill, patience, and persistence, they have had a major impact on the level of horticultural excellence now achieved by the gardeners of this nation.

Designed and illustrated by Daina D. Penn
Cover photograph of author's garden by Robert Pollock

Library of Congress 92-094319
Hyde, Barbara
Gardening in the Mountain West — 1st edition.
Includes bibliographical reference and index.
ISBN 0-9635224-0-X $15.95

Printed in the United States of America by
Associated Printers
P.O. Box 8115
Longmont, Colorado 80501

Table of Contents

Part 1
A LANDSCAPE TO FIT YOUR NEEDS

Part II
CULTURAL PROCEDURES

PART III
CHOOSING PLANTS TO FIT YOUR PLAN

Part IV
THE GARDEN NECESSITIES

Volume II (1994)

The Progress of a Gardener

Acknowledgements

I owe a great debt of gratitude to a great many people, a few of whom are: my children for their encouragement and support, Kerrie and Kurt Badertscher, Dr. Kenneth Brink, Marjorie Burman, Anthony and Judy DeCino, Dr. James Feucht, Zelma Jennings, Carl Jorgensen, William G. Macksam, Marie Orlin, Daina D. Penn, Andrew Pierce, Robert Pollock, Inez Prinster, R. Stefan Ringgenberg, Scott Skogerboe, Dr. Roger B. Swain, Rosemary Verey.

Introduction

This is a how-to book, the first of two volumes. It was written with the premise that there are many long-time residents as well as newcomers in the Mountain West who, as gardeners, have difficulty with the soil, water, and climate differences in the area.

Constraints on a reader's time are too great today to expect that all readers will read this book from beginning to end. More likely, each chapter will be read as the need arises. Therefore, there are repetitious passages for which I beg your indulgence. For example, soil preparation directions are repeated for each grouping of plants because the neophyte gardener might assume that soil preparation was unnecessary. Some cultural direction and plant protection procedures are repeated as well to assure success, not to add length to the book.

Horticulture is a swiftly changing science. Each gardener is urged to communicate their successes with other gardeners and particularly with the media so that we may all learn together.

Part I

A Landscape to Fit Your Needs

CHAPTER 1

Landscape Planning

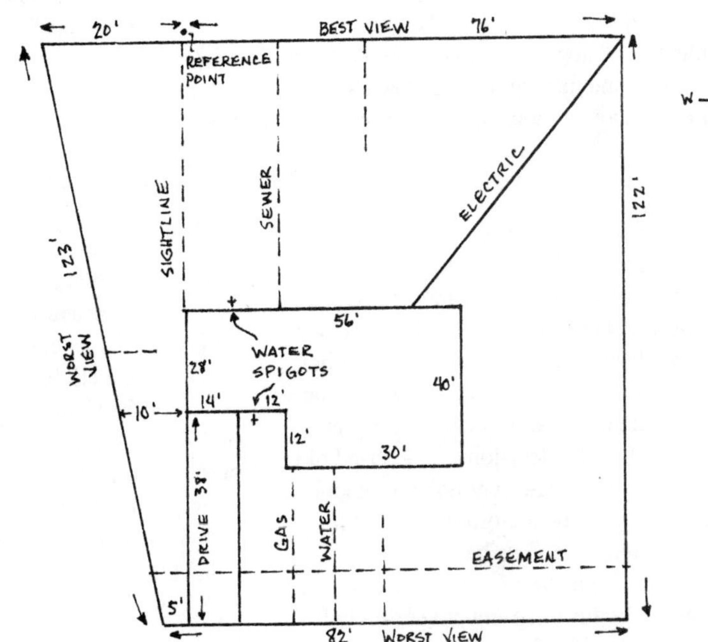

Buying a new house or renovating an old one is always a traumatic but exhilarating experience. At first you are concerned only with the inside, but gradually you begin to look out the windows and venture outside to view the vast emptiness of an unimproved lot, or in the case of a renovation, you may be looking at weeds, clutter and a coal shed. A feeling of hopelessness may ensue, but optimism usually returns when you begin to picture tall trees, lawn, shrubs and flowers, and perhaps, a vegetable garden or a swimming pool. Why do we risk a deflated bank account, blisters and sprains to achieve this picture? Psychiatrists have a name for it. They call it "the primal association." It means that even if you have been born and reared surrounded by asphalt, concrete, glass and steel, there is a pre-history, primitive part of you that associates with a green scene. You need plants around you to be totally comfortable. For centuries slave masters, prison wardens, and physicians have known that they would have a more manageable slave or prisoner, or a healthier patient if gardening was allowed or encouraged. You can let fly with dreams unbounded knowing it is good for your mental health! Of course, fresh air, sunshine and exercise don't harm your state of well-being either.

■ *The primal association, a pre-history, primitive part of you that associates with a green scene . . . you need plants around you to be totally comfortable.*

Survey Your Needs

Before the task ahead overwhelms you, sit down with your family and discuss what each one wants from this landscape. Do you spend a lot of time at home? Do you entertain a lot and would you like to entertain outdoors? Do you like to work outdoors? Do you like outdoor sports that may be played on a small lawn? Do you

■ *The need for a paper plan will be obvious if you are short on time.*

like all flowers, or do you have a specialty flower, such as the rose, that you would like to cultivate in earnest? Do the children and dog or other pets need a space for rough and tumble play? Does a shady patio with a hammock show up often in your dreams? Be realistic in your survey, for it is easy to change a plan on paper.

If You Are Renovating

You may be relieved to learn that it is best to wait a full year before renovating a new/old or tangled landscape - that is, one that has been in place for many years, but is new to you. You will be amazed at the season changes that will take place that will temper your decisions. A gnarled old tree that you wanted to remove immediately may become a glorious sight in its autumn foliage, and its bare limbs a charming silhouette in a snowy winter scene. A bonus of spring-flowering bulbs may appear in the place you planned an asphalt pad for basketball. You may not be aware that your neighbor's ear-splitting woodworking shop lies just beyond the fence of your newly planned patio. The spruce tree you planned to remove because it swats you in the face as you exit the front door is much needed to shade west-facing windows and is worth the cost in moving it. All of these examples demonstrate the mistakes you could make if you rushed the renovation of your landscape. A year of waiting may save some valuable elements or mark others for destruction. For certain, the changes you make will be wiser next year.

The Paper Work

There are those who boast that everything "just fell into place" or there are those who admit they made mistakes before everything fell into place. The need for a paper plan will be obvious if you are short on time.

You can waste time measuring the perimeter of your lot, then the outline of your home, or you can measure by the connect-the-dots method.

If you are inclined toward the latter, buy or borrow a measuring tape, fifty feet or longer. Place an eight-by-eleven inch sheet of paper on a clipboard and draw a rough sketch of the shape of your lot and the outline of your home on the lot. Go outdoors, preferably with a partner, to begin more precise measurements. Stand at a corner of your house with the tape in hand while your partner strings the tape all the way to the nearest corner of your lot. Mark this measurement with a dot on your sketch at the coinciding point on your drawing and make a note of the distance. Repeat this process all the way around your house. If your house has an L-shape or an H-shape, or any other shape, you will measure at each corner to the boundary in a straight line. If the boundaries of your lot are not parallel, or if your home is not parallel to at least one boundary, enlist the aid of your partner to hold a rake or broom handle upright on the property boundary as you sight along the house wall toward the handle; then measure the distance from the rake handle along the boundary line to the nearest corner. This measurement is your reference point. Find the sightline on the illustration. Measure the location of all permanent features as well. Mark them on your rough sketch.

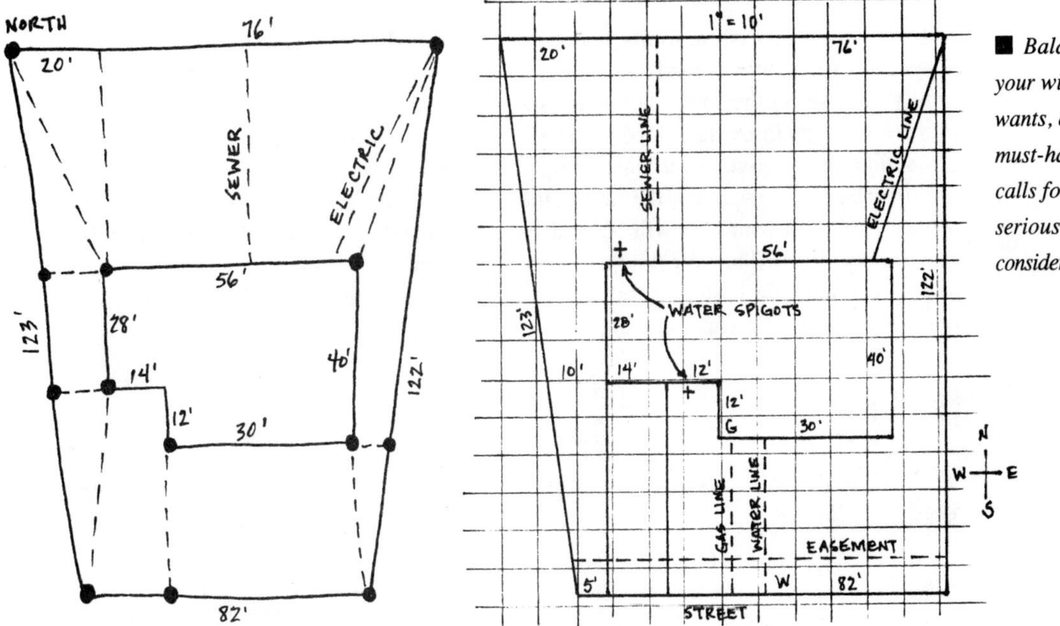

■ *Balancing your wishes, wants, and must-haves calls for serious considerations.*

Locate the house on the rough sketch by measuring in two directions from a corner point and mark with dots on your sketch. Measure the house along the foundation as a check against your connect-the-dots method. Also measure the depth of the eave as a note for future reference. Go inside and transfer these measurements to a sheet of graph paper, using a scale of one inch equals ten feet; Connect the dots, and you will have drawn to scale your lot and the placement of your house on the lot.

Sketch in the permanent features as shown, such as the gas and water connections, location of underground telephone cables, location of windows, drive, or walks. Sketch in with a dotted line the utility easement if there is one. This easement gives your municipality the right to remove any permanent plantings in order to excavate to reach the gas, water, sewer, or electric lines. You will find the measurement on your abstract of title or on the description of your property on your mortgage.

Draw dotted lines to show the direction of the best view, the worst view, and the prevailing winds in summer and winter. You may have to ask the neighbors for this latter information.

Balancing your wishes, wants, and must-haves calls for serious consideration. Each family must select the combination of uses that best suits its individual desires. The more thought you give toward analyzing family needs for now and in the future, the more meaningful your plan will be, and the more likely you will be to follow it. Even though you may not wish to install all the features of your landscape plan immediately. PLAN NOW for everything you contemplate doing now and in the future. Budgeting the development of a landscape over a period of years is a common practice, but to achieve a unified appearance years hence, the total development must be planned in advance. Use the check list below and add any other specific uses your family suggests.

Check List

Check those that apply to your family's needs and desires.

______ Place for ____ trash cans
______ Wood storage for fireplace

Clothesline:

______ rectangular, ____ feet$_2$
______ carrousel, ____ feet$_2$
______ Off-street parking for __ cars

Parking:

______ Parking space for trailer, motor home, boat, over-snow vehicle
______ Drives, service walks
______ Garage
______ Carport
______ Hobby and crafts shop

Patio for:

______ barbequing
______ relaxing
______ entertaining
______ people
______ dancing
______ other:

Night-Lighting:

______ spot lights for areas:

Low-voltage lights for (areas):

Family Activities:

______ basketball ____ sandbox
______ croquet ____ shuffleboard
______ badminton ____ exercise bars
______ horseshoes ____ playhouse
______ swings ____ other (list)

Garden for:

______ annuals and perennials
______ vegetables ____ fruits
______ salad greens ____ herbs
______ other (list)

Water Features:

______ reflection basin ____ swimming pool
______ fountain, waterfall __ lap pool
______ vegetable wash basin and spigot
______ lilypool ____ birdbath(s)

Garden Work Area:

______ greenhouse ____ potting bench
______ root cellar ____ sunpit
______ tool storage ____ soil bins
______ coldframes ____ compost bins

Pet Needs:

______ doghouse ____ dog run
______ restrictive fence ____ other (list)

Is there need to provide for:

______ mail delivery ____ milk delivery
______ grocery delivery
______ concrete, fill dirt,heavy equipment delivery
______ birdhouses ____ birdfeeders

Are there any plant(s) to which any member of the family is allergic?

CHAPTER 2

Designing for the Mountain West

USDA Zone of Hardiness Map

In designing your landscape you will be influenced by your heritage, the architecture of your home, the climate, your recent past, and the terrain of the area.

Whether you know it or not, you will be influenced by your ancestral heritage. Did your forebears come from central Europe, the Orient, England, Spain or South America? Even though your people may have lived on these shores for many generations, there are subtle influences handed down that you may not be aware of. You may want to emphasize your heritage in the design of your landscape.

Matching the architecture of your home with the style of your landscape is not as important as one might think. However, there are a few inconsistences you want to avoid. For example, the white picket fence would be at odds with the California ranch-style home; the modern xeriscape[1] would be out-of-place leading to the front entry of the Georgian styled home.

The climate of the Mountain West is more varied than any other climate in the United States. And there is no doubt that the Mountain West can expect some violent weather events from time to time. The variety is part of the fascination in living in this area. Check on the climate if you are new to the area, however. The local weather station or a neighbor who is native to the area will be glad to give you the dates of the first and last frosts, the lowest temperatures of winter and the highest in summer. Wind speeds and the months of the highest wind speeds are also important. The Department of Agriculture has a map showing zones of hardiness for all areas of the country, but they can be relied upon only in a general way. The individual microclimates of each landscape have far more influence than an arbitrary line drawn through a map. For example, a white birch

[1] *Xeriscape is a trademark of the National Xeriscape Council.*

tree planted on the wide-open prairie of eastern Colorado would be marked for sure death, but the same tree planted in the shade of a mix of tall deciduous trees and evergreens would become a healthy, vigorous tree. A shrub of doubtful hardiness in your area might be given a good chance of survival with a planting site in the protection of, but beyond the root competition of, nearby trees or shrubs where temperatures will be warmer in winter and cooler in summer.

Your recent past will figure heavily in the design of your landscape. If you are newly arrived from New England, the landscapes of that area, even after three centuries, still favor square corners and symmetrical borders. If you are a native Californian, you may be accustomed to featuring many plants growing in containers. Landscapes in the Mountain West represent a meeting place for the influences of the past, but the climate itself dictates the distinctive quality. The terrain of your plot of ground and its climate will dictate both design and the choice of plants you will grow.

In addition to the extreme variety, the climate of the Mountain West is set apart from the climates of all other parts of the country by the low amount of precipitation, very low humidity, clear skies and bright sun in both summer and winter, cool nights in summer and deep fluctuations in temperature in winter.

The immensity of our soaring mountains automatically dominates any landscape. Learn to select the best of all the influences upon you and not copy a plan blindly.

No attempt will be made here to repeat the concepts and principles of landscape architecture. Many books are available on the subject. Landscape architecture is a combination of beauty and utility. Some contend that if a landscape is designed for utility, it is automatically beautiful. You may not agree with this theory, but striving to combine the greatest amount of beauty with a maximum of usefulness will create a landscape you will be proud of.

It is possible to be your own landscape architect, but count on making some thoughtful decisions, and perhaps a few mistakes. But also count on having a great feeling of accomplishment when the final effect is nearly like the landscape of your dreams.

If you change your mind midstream, no law says you have to stick with it. Search out a qualified landscape architect and ask him or her to finish the job.

When you have completed the plan yourself, but if you are unsure that mistakes have been made, make an appointment with your Cooperative Extension Agent for horticulture and ask him or her to critique the plan for you. If the Cooperative Extension office in your county does not have a person on staff who is qualified to critique, they may send your plan to the state land-grant university where your plan will be evaluated by the teaching staff.

The Cooperative Extension Agent for horticulture in your county will critique your plan before you make your final drawing.

Matching Use Areas

You will find that matching the use areas to the entry that corresponds to the activity in that area will make both your home and your landscape more useful. For example, matching the kitchen entry to the utility area or garage will eliminate tracking through the living room from the vegetable garden. Likewise, the patio may become an extension of the living and dining rooms in summer, thus expanding the space.

The role of the so-called public area - the area adjoining the street - is changing. The price of land is too high for a homeowner to maintain a showpiece front lawn for the pleasure of the viewing public. You may want the privacy of the front area shielded by small flowering trees and shrubs and low-maintenance ground covers. In addition, fast-moving traffic in the street beyond makes it necessary to have a space to turn your cars around in your own driveway so that you may enter the street more safely. Guest parking, also, is no longer a luxury.

Make Some Trial Designs

Using sheets of tracing paper secured by tape to your plot plan, make some trial designs. Use the voice of experience listed under "What Works and Why" to guide you in your design efforts. Read "Modifying the Climate Around Your Home" before you begin adding planting areas. After you have several designs, submit them to members of your family for approval. Don't be surprised if consensus takes some time.

When you have arrived at a design of the general areas: public, family, and utility, use colored pencils to give each area a different color. Color the planting areas green to guide you in selecting plants later on. Remember to transfer to your plan the arrows for the direction of the best or worst views and the direction of prevailing winds in summer or winter. Lightly pencil in the words "tall, medium or low" to guide you in choosing plants that will not block the good views, but will block the unsightly views.

What Works and Why

HOUSE PLACEMENT

Whenever possible, the house should be placed with a corner rather than a side facing south. This will eliminate the two greatest planting problems around a conventionally placed house that is square with the lot lines - the too-shady north side and the hot and sunny south side. With this diagonal placing of the house, there will be a little sun on every side and not too much on any; thus allowing a much higher selection of ornamental plants.

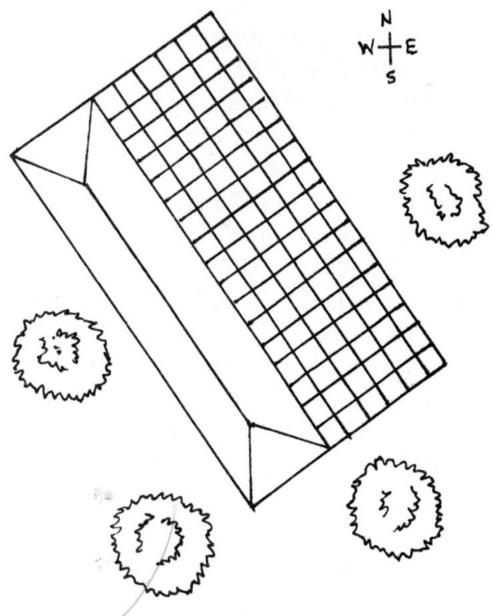

The best aspect for the home is one in which a corner, not a side, faces south.

PATIOS AND DECKS

Patios constructed by subdivision contractors are often the size of a postage stamp. Astonishingly, the outdoor living area should be *twice* the size of your living room. In your outdoor living room, the sky is the ceiling, the trees and shrubs are the walls. Outdoor spaces will seem cramped if you are unable to move the furniture about to suit the number of persons using the area at the moment.

A north-facing patio will be coolest in summer, while a south-facing one will be useful in both late winter and late fall. If possible, have one of each.

Patios and decks should be designed and constructed so as to be flush with the door sill. Nothing is so jarring as an unexpected step down as you walk from the house to the patio. The patio will seem to be more an extension of the home if they flow as one at the same level.

THE OVERHEAD GRID - DO YOU NEED ONE?

The quality of sunlight at high noon in the Mountain West can be a blistering experience. We welcome its warmth in winter, but summer sun at high altitude is dangerous and uncomfortable. The overhead grid for your patio or above west-facing windows gives a dappled pattern that tempers those rays enough to make them bearable to those sitting beneath. The construction techniques will be found in any of the many booklets sold at bookstores and garden centers.

The overhead grid shields in summer, but allows welcome sunlight in winter.

FENCES

Fences have an advantage over hedges in not taking up as much space, but if they are at the height needed to give as much privacy as possible, the effect that might be claustrophobic.

If the restrictive covenants* of your subdivision allow, consider placing a fence across the front of your property, taking the utility easement into consideration, if there is one. Angling the fence will give it less of a bastion effect, as will a clipped hedge. The hedge will lessen the visual height also.

* *See Glossary*

Fence angles give shadow patterns.

BERMS

If restrictive covenants in your area do not permit fences, consider a berm. A berm is a man-made hill, usually about three feet high, extending across the streetside of the property, undulating here and there and with boulders seated to resemble a mountain scene. Plant drought-resistant evergreens and deciduous shrubs at the top in natural groups. Rock-alpines can be tucked among the boulders, Berms screen out dust, odors, traffic noise, and unattractive views. They can also become a good windbreak when the evergreens reach maturity.

DRIVES, WALKS AND TURNAROUNDS

The drive leading from garage to street need not be straight, but curving drives and walks must have a reason for curving. For example, a major tree or a broad shrub planting would be reason to curve a walk or drive, but have pity on the beginning driver who must negotiate a curve while backing the car. Designing a curving walk or drive for reasons of quaintness is of questionable value.

On the other hand, a curve in a drive that becomes a turnaround is a major convenience and safety factor in the landscape that must contend with a major collector street beyond. An easy way to determine placement of a turnaround is to back your longest car out of the garage and put it in a tight turn on soft ground. The tire tracks become the pattern for the hard surface to follow. If your drive is already paved, scatter flour to determine the angle for the added construction of a turnaround. See page 10 for illustrations.

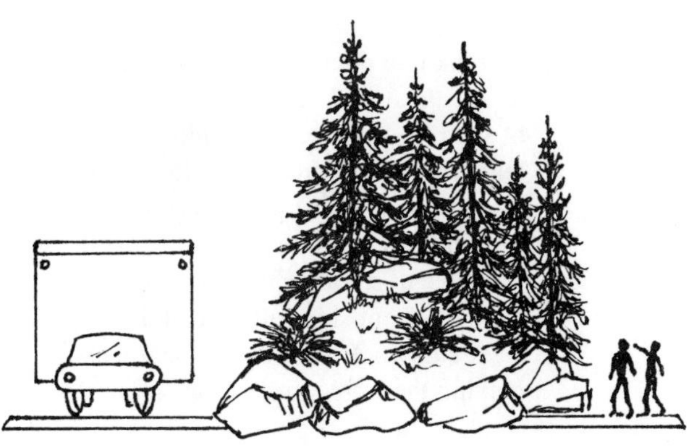

Berms are naturalistic screens.

■ *Turn-around angles and guest parking.*

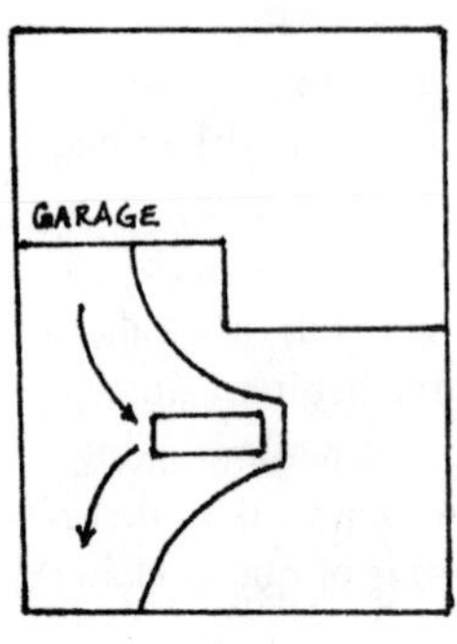

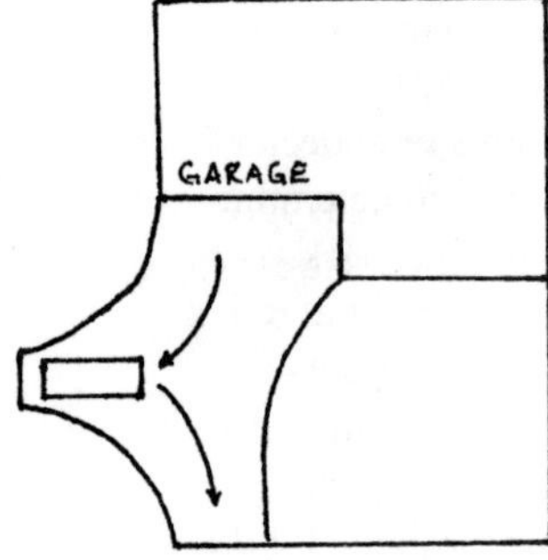

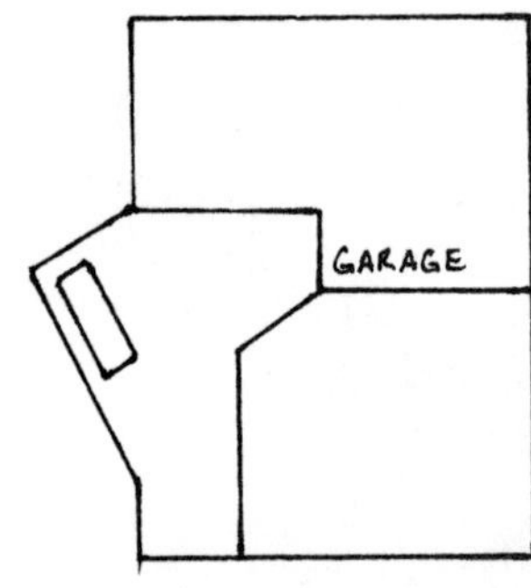

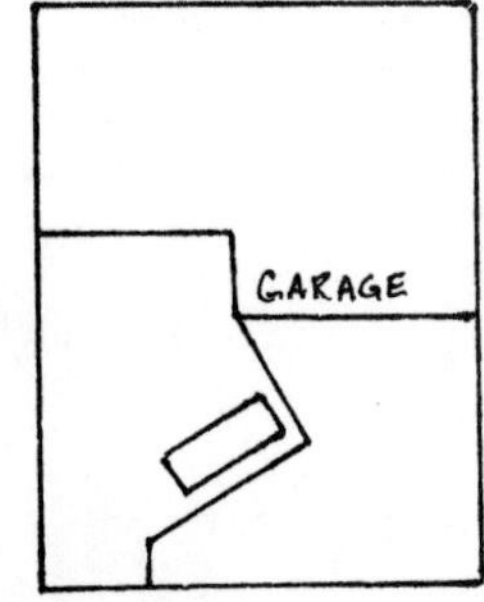

Guest parking is a convenience.

Plan two spaces for cars in a guest parking place. If three more cars can park in your drive, the parking is usually adequate.

The width of the drive is determined by the width of the garage opening, with some space added to make alighting from the car more convenient.

The width of a walk adjoining the drive or of a walk leading from the front walk to the door should be at least four feet. This width accommodates two people walking side by side. A walk that is narrow as a shoestring might lead approaching visitors to think that poor-spirited people live inside. The walk and entry are the measure of your hospitality. We seldom see a walk leading from the front walk to the entry because today most people arrive by car - even the mailperson; so it is logical to use the drive as a walkway when approaching from the front sidewalk. In addition, a front walk cuts the front area into segments, making the front yard appear smaller.

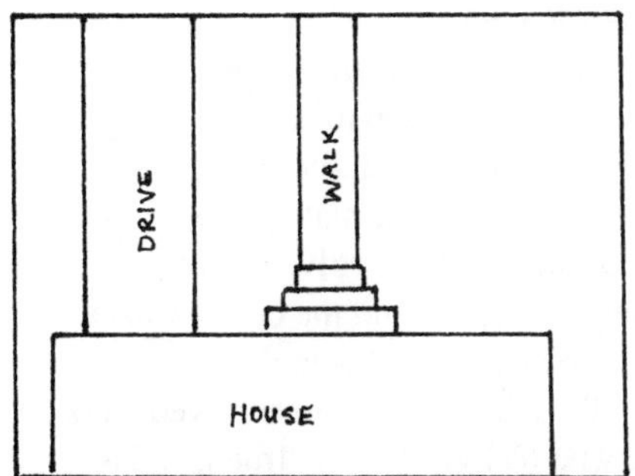

A front walk cuts the area into segments, making the front yard appear smaller.

A NOTE OF DANGER

There is an inclination to plant small evergreens at each corner of a drive or at each side of a walk that leads from the street to the entry. These plants can become death traps, for they grow far higher than a child is tall. A child darting out into traffic is hidden by these shrubs until it is too late for the oncoming driver to stop. These shrubs are a barrier where no barrier should be. They visually chop the property into segments as well.

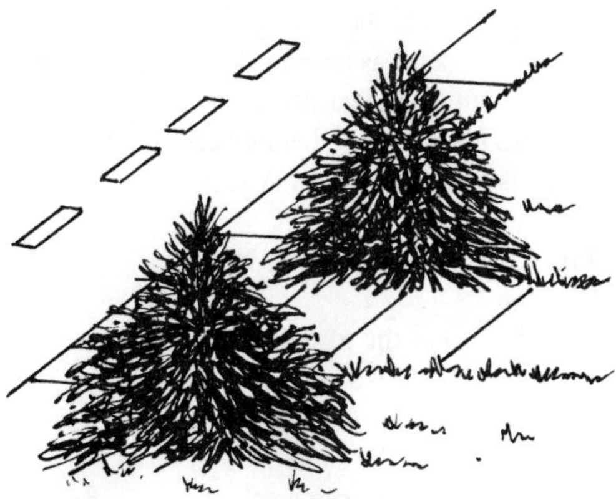

Shrubs at drive or walk entries create danger for children.

Radiated Heat

Turf adjoining areas of paving or asphalt demands five times the amount of water needed by the remainder of the lawn. More attractive than burned-out grass is a strip at least five feet wide planted with ground covers that grow no higher than six inches, or, if needed, a privacy screen of shrubs and flowering trees can occupy this area. A mulch of pole peelings*, bark chips, or gravel will complete the planting and save water.

The Sides of a City Lot

The area at each side of the average property in a city will vary in width, according to the restrictive covenants of the city, town, or subdivision. Often it is no wider than five feet, thus eliminating any possibility of plantings. Fabric weed-barrier laid down with a topping of gravel; then paving stones or blocks seated into the gravel is adequately attractive and serves the purpose of getting from the back yard to the front yard or serves as a hard surface to set up a ladder when washing windows.

If you have the luxury of more than five feet in width, this can become a display area of container-grown plants or a hobby collection. Your friend, the dog, would appreciate this space as well.

Steps

Steps can be much more than a connection between two levels. Landscape designers learned centuries ago that steps could express the mood and tempo of a landscape. Their design can assure you of a safe passage, put you in a leisurely mood, make you hurry, or arouse your curiosity. To prove this, take every opportunity to study steps before making a final decision on design. The material chosen for step construction also affects design.

* *See Glossary*

Outdoor steps have different riser/tread relationship than indoors.

Too often outdoor step design is left to the general contractor who uses design dimensions for indoor, rather than outdoor steps. The result is a set of steps that is too narrow and too steep. The riser and tread relationship literally makes or breaks the success of steps, for a poor design can be an ankle breaker. There are few rules than cannot be broken with satisfactory results except this one:

Twice the riser plus the tread equals twenty-six inches.

For example, if you want a four-inch riser, you will need an eighteen inch tread. 4 + 4 = 8 + 18 = 26 inches

A four-inch riser is a common dimension in outdoor steps, and it is generally accepted that if a four-inch change in grade occurs in your property at any point, a four-inch riser and two treads placed flush with the ground at the two levels is safer and easier to maintain than a sloping walkway or grassed slope. In addition, the step becomes a design element, much like a sculpture.

Garden Rooms

As more gardeners visit Great Britain, more thought is given toward imitating their designs of garden rooms. These enclosures around the stately homes of knights and nobility evolved from the kitchen gardens within the courtyards of castles. When siege was laid upon the castle, the inhabitants who survived were those who had vegetables, fruits, and a stable of pigs and milk cows within the defensible walls. These walls also proved to be ideal protection from cruel winds coming off the North Sea.

As gardening came to be the oneupmanship pastime of the Victorian era, the walls were extended to become flowery bowers or topiary display rooms, one leading from the other.

Yankee ingenuity has improved upon this concept by adapting it to the garden design of both the city and country dweller. The high masonary or stone walls of England are expensive adjuncts in this country, but they may become worth their cost if they block out the sight and sound of the city or the blast of the blizzard in the country. The walls are especially useful as a heat trap in early spring and late fall for the garden in the most northern portion or at the high elevation portions of the Mountain West.

The Condominium or Townhouse Garden

The patio of the townhouse or condominium is usually a contractors afterthought. The air-conditioning condenser is often housed in the same area, its roar a nuisance for the whole area.

If you can surmount the air-conditioner problem, your patio can become another room in summer and on sunny days in winter.

If there is a high board fence around your patio, investigate the redwood lattice panels found in most lumber yards. They are easily attached to the board fence if furring strips are nailed first at intervals, and the lattice nailed or screwed to the furring strips.

The lattice fence then becomes the wall of your patio "room" and a palette to create a picture that makes it your own. There can be bright, colorful morning glories or the delicate tracery of ivy climbing your lattice. Perhaps a fountain trickling from a lavabo mounted on the fence appeals to you. Any adornment of the fence, from the endearing to the eclectic, will disguise its height and stark design.

If you are faced with the hard glare of a concrete pad for a patio floor, and an edict from the homeowners association that it cannot be defiled, defile it anyway with a harmless and removable covering of brick or concrete pavers set about half-inch apart. Sweep coarse sand between the brick or pavers and plant some creeping thyme in the cracks if there is sun. If the area is shady, collect thumbnail size pieces of moss to press into the sand in the cracks, and it will soon take hold and spread if light moisture is applied frequently.

There is often planting space for one tree in the townhouse/condominium patio. If puttering in this little patio is relaxing to you on a summer evening, the chances are strong that you will water a tree to death. The solution is to plant a tree that can withstand your mothering. There are few plants that fit the bill. A willow might get its roots into the plumbing, but our native alder, *Alnus tenuifolia*, is ideal for all areas of the Mountain West. It's dark red bark is marked with lenticel stripes. It often forms charming multi-trunks, and the serrated foliage turns brilliant yellow in fall.

CHAPTER 3

Placing the Elements of Design; Finishing the Plans

Before you begin the design of the planting areas around your home, work toward modifying the climate as well as giving your home the surrounding plants that will make it attractive.

■ *. . . that is what makes gardening a challenging hobby.*

The Mountain West has its heat waves in summer and cold spells in winter, and both are capable of causing stress to people and plants. However, fluctuating temperatures caused by winter sun and a sudden drop in temperature at sundown are the worst enemy of a plant and the most common cause of winterkill. In spring, summer, or fall, high or low temperatures can be accompanied by strong winds that suck moisture out of plant tissues.

By locating plantings and structures at strategic points, you can create a more suitable climate for some of the desirable non-native plants you've wished you could have. You may have a yen for rhododendron and azaleas or bamboo and bananas. These plants are a possibility when pockets of protection are offered by structures or other plantings. Gradually acclimatizing a plant to your microclimate will increase the chance of that tender plant surviving. It is a risk, granted, but that is what makes gardening a challenging hobby. Most often the area that will be the most successful for the tender plant will be found on the east of your home, or northeast of another planting or structure.

Major Shade Trees

You modify climate greatly when you plant large shade trees. Locating them on your plan is critical. In the front of the home framing trees on either side of the home will enhance the picture and form a frame with your home as the center of interest. The two trees or groups of trees need not be directly opposite each other; in fact, it makes for a more interesting picture if one is placed forward of the other. You may want to consider placing one so that a window is shaded in July, as well.

Locate a shade tree to shade a window during summer's heat.

In placing framing trees on your plan, draw a space around them for planting small shrubs or shade-loving flowers. This eliminates root competition for the tree from turfgrass, the danger of striking the tree with the lawn mower, and the possibility of over-watering the tree. The amount of water needed to keep the grass green is too much for a young tree.

An island planting of a shade tree, small shrubs or shade-loving flowers assures the tree of safety from the mower, overwatering, and root competition.

A small flowering tree framing the front entry is a charming addition if the architectural style of the home is compatible with this off-center addition.

A tree to shade the outdoor living area is a must. Remember to plant it far enough away from the patio or deck so that its roots will not grow underneath. Under a deck, roots do not receive enough water. Roots may rupture the patio brick or stone, and lack of air to the roots may cause the tree to die.

If properly located, the patio tree will shade and cool the patio in summer, and after the leaves have fallen, you can sit in the warm sun on a winter day.

When you finish your design and begin to choose the plants for the design, choose a patio shade tree that does not fruit. Sweeping up fallen or smashed fruits is a very tiresome task.

■ . . . *choose a patio shade tree that does not fruit.*

The Foundation Planting

The practice of completely concealing the foundation of the home with shrubbery comes from the era when architects did not seriously consider the appearance of a house from the outside and left exposed concrete foundations, blank walls, or irregular angles that became the landscape architect's nightmare job to hide or beautify. A foundation planting is still important, but it is no longer necessary to conceal the entire foundation. Think of the house as the Thanksgiving turkey on a platter. The parsley around the bird doesn't keep it from sliding off the platter, just as the foundation planting does not anchor the house to terra firma - it just gives it a finished appearance.

Pointed evergreens at opposite ends of the front of the home will do more toward giving your landscape an outmoded look than any other. They are obsolete. They act as an exclamation point at the end of a

■ *The winsome little shrub in a one-gallon pot at the nursery may grow into a monster in three years!*

sentence. "This house ends here," they proclaim. The opposite effect is demonstrated, however, if yours is a two-story home and groups of pointed evergreens are planted at either side. Select rounded shrubs that have an ultimate height of two-thirds the distance from the ground to the eave. This shape will give the easy transition from the ground line to the vertical line. The shrubs can be evergreen or deciduous.

Shrubs with a round silhouette break the vertical line of a corner.

Groups of evergreens form the transition between the horizontal and vertical plane of a 2-story home.

You will choose the plants for the foundation planting from the lists in Part II with care taken to note ultimate height of your choices. One of the pitfalls in foundation planting is the tendency to overplant. The winsome little shrub in a one-gallon pot at the nursery may grow into a monster in three years! Plan for enough space between each of your selections so that they will "close" within three years. This means the branches of each will grow to touch its neighbor; then, unless the plant is extremely vigorous, there is probability the entire planting will not overwhelm the house or overgrow its allotted space. Drive or walk around established neighborhoods to note how plants look at maturity. With care not to block the view from a window, the height at maturity of a foundation shrub should be the same as above - two-thirds the distance from ground to eave, and with a good mix of evergreen and deciduous species.

A low grouping around the entry will allow optimum viewing of your entry door and will extend a welcome to your visitors. Later on, as you choose plants, keep in mind that changes of texture in foliage in summer will add interest even when flowers are not present, while branch structure and "twigginess" will enhance the winter silhouette. Visualize how each plant will look as a companion to another at each season, and don't forget winter.

As you draw the foundation planting on your plan, check first on the eave depth of your house. For the safety of your foundation, don't try to grow anything under the eaves, not even a ground cover plant. Building contractors advise that a strip four feet wide all the way around the house should be left free of shrub vegetation or turf to protect from water seeping down to damage the foundation concrete as well as to allow for working room when painting the house or washing windows. Lay down a fabric weed barrier in this area under the eaves and cover it with four inches of gravel. It will then be maintenance free. An added benefit of this gravel covering - a burglar will be wary because one footstep on this gravel is a loud scrunch!

A Windbreak

As you continue to modify the climate of your property with plantings, include a modest windbreak if yours is a city property, and a generous one if you live in the country. Wind is efficient in scouring away stagnant, polluted air, but in the velocities common in the Mountain West, it is a feared and damaging element of our weather. Hail is probably the most dreaded weather event for a gardener, but wind is a close second. Wind sucks moisture out of plants, leaving them in a weakened condition, and sometimes they never recover. A cold wind in April just as plants are emerging from dormancy is common. A hot wind in early May is always a certainty when new leaves are still susceptible to scorching.

A windbreak in the city landscape is a group of three to five tall evergreens planted in the area of prevailing winds. However, if the direction of the prevailing winds is also the direction of your best view, you are located on the horns of a dilemma. The choice is yours, but the view is with you every day, while the wind is not.

If your patio is located "in the teeth of the gale", take heart for there is a way to enjoy the view and temper the breeze. Glass panels attached to strong posts will give you protection from all but the strongest winds. For areas where gale force winds (above 75 mph) are common, consider clear plastic panels secured in strong frames.

Glass panels temper the breeze and don't block the view.

■ *If your patio is located "in the teeth of the gale", take heart for there is a way to enjoy the view and temper the breeze.*

A windbreak for the country home or farmstead is a necessity. Livestock and crop values will often depend on a good windbreak. In the post-dust-bowl years, thousands of windbreaks were restored or planted to become climate modifiers, wildlife refuges, and a beautiful part of the rural scene. Unfortunately, many of these are dying from old age, neglect, or the greed of the property owner who removes the windbreak to plant more crops.

The rural windbreak is no longer planted in multiple rows like marching soldiers. Only the first windward row (the tallest) is planted in a row. Planting the inner portion in groups of three to five to seven plants is a better way to baffle the wind. See Chapter 10, "Windbreak Care."

In the Mountain West, irrigation and weed control in the windbreak will make the difference between success and failure.

The Pet and Utility Area

The utility area and pet run are best located near the kitchen, garage, or utility room door.

Pets are regarded as members of the family, sleep on the sofa, and are seldom relegated to a pen. Experts say that having a pen and shelter that is shaded in summer and warmed in winter is a benefit to the animal if used for a specific time period each day or at night. Having dutifully written this, it is fortunate that pets can't read.

You may have enough space in your garage for the trash containers and tools, bu most families fill their garages with autos, auto-related paraphernalia, and sports equipment.

The utility area can be very attractive and inviting, with a place for every tool, a potting bench, soil storage bins, pot storage in graduated sizes, and a space for at least three compost bins. A cold frame is a necessity for a serious gardener.

A greenhouse, hoop house, or sunpit need the benefit of southern winter sun and a little shade in summer. Invest in one of the many booklets available in the design of these structures and see Chapter 20 "Mountain Homes."

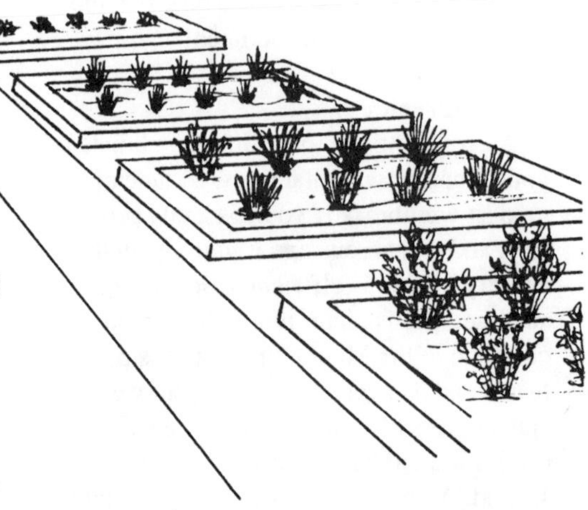

Terraced raised beds for vegetables on a slope.

The Vegetable Garden and Fruit Orchard

■ *. . . you may dream of the ambiance of lying beneath a blooming or fruiting tree.*

In the Mountain West, we are fortunate that our altitude gives us a higher quality of sunlight than at a lower elevation. We can get by with six hours of sun for both vegetables and fruits. This means, however, that the sunlight must be afforded the plants in the months of May through September, except for raspberry, which will thrive under only four hours of sunlight from May through September.

A level space for both fruits and vegetables is desirable, but if such a space is not available, consider terracing an area, using raised beds.

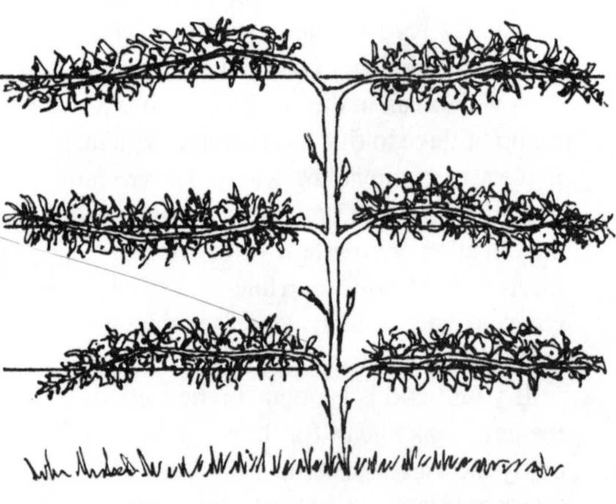

Fruits espaliered on a fence take little space.

While the vegetable garden should be located as close to the house as possible, the fruit orchard can be farther away, such as behind the tree-and-shrub border of the backyard. Dwarf fruit trees are more convenient to take care of and bear fruits earlier than standard sizes, but you may dream of the ambiance of lying beneath a blooming or fruiting tree on your chaise lounge. A standard fruit tree can be pruned to allow walking beneath. The first scaffold limbs of dwarf fruit trees are only two feet from the soil level; therefore, they are more like large shrubs.

Fruit trees can also be grown espaliered on a wire fence on the perimeter of your property. When they are mature, the fence can be removed and the trees will become the fence. See Chapter 9 "Pruning" and Chapter 7 "Plant Protection."

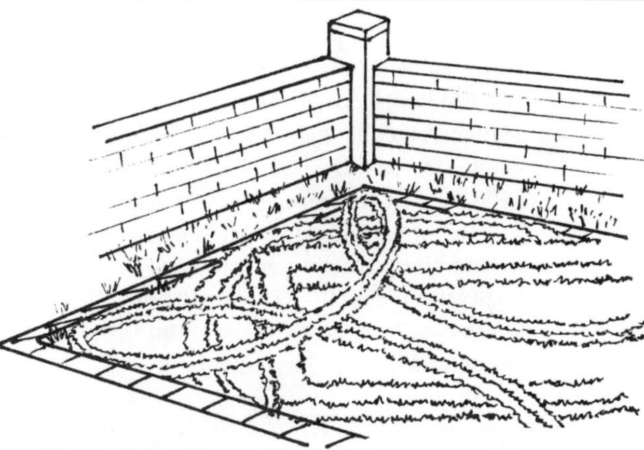

The traditional knotted herb garden.

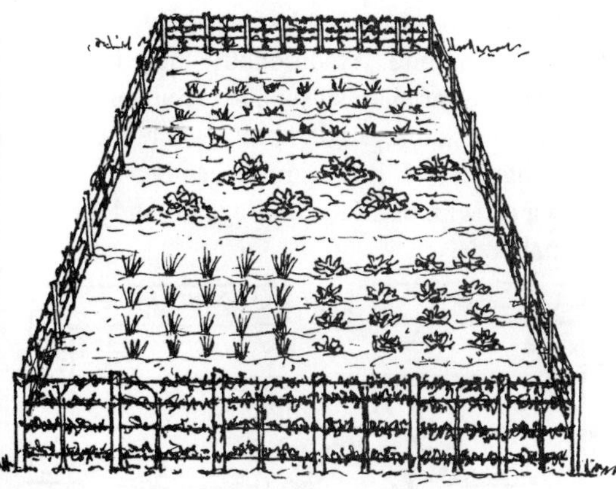

Espaliered fruit trees can become a perimeter fence.

Herb gardens can follow the designs of ancient monastery gardens of the Middle Ages, forming a design of circular knots. Or they can be utilitarian to give you a good harvest from a few plants. Whatever your preference, do a little research at the library before you consider them as a design element.

Fruits, vegetables, and herbs will pay for themselves many times over if the gardeners involved have only a modicum of dedication.

The Shrub and Flower Border

Planting a wide border of small flowering trees and evergreen and deciduous shrubs will give you privacy and protection, and most of all — beauty. This is the area where your gardening skills will be acquired, honed and tested. A broad planting, at least ten feet wide for the average property, located around the perimeter of your property will include small (less than twenty-five feet) flowering trees, tall, medium and low evergreen and deciduous shrubs. Flowers will round out the planting. If flowers are not in your future, the border can be faced down with low-growing shrubs.

A straight or gently curving line for this border will be more attractive and easier to maintain than an intricate, wiggly line.

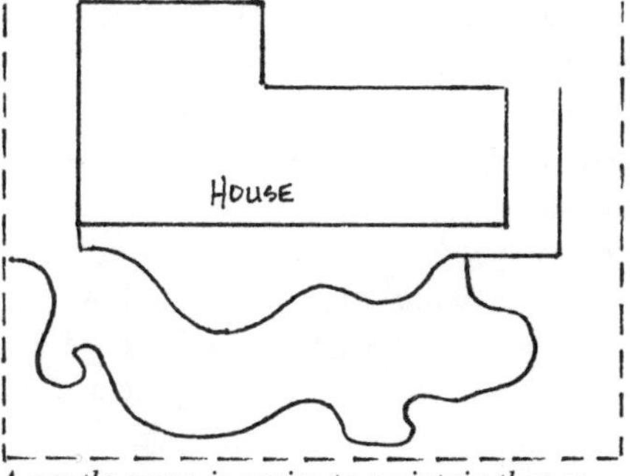

A gentle curve is easier to maintain than a wiggly one.

If you have the opportunity and space, use another island of planting, such as one shown in the illustration under Major Shade Trees with a few small shrubs or low-growing flowering ground covers. Locate it in an area that will interrupt your view when you stand on your patio to survey your domain. This small aura of mystery will fool the eye, and your property will seem larger than it is.

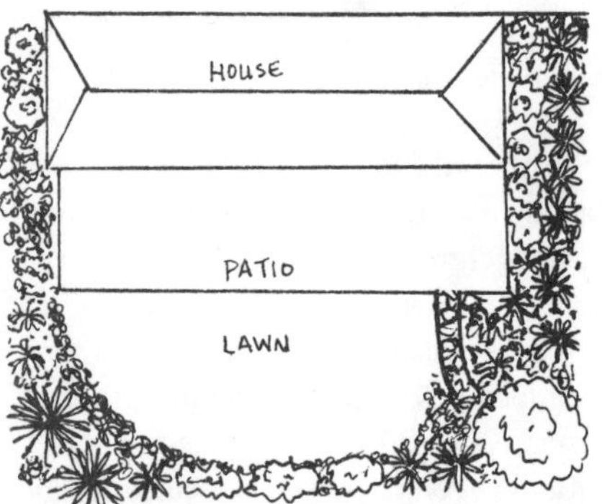

Mystery of "what's around the corner" will make your landscape seem larger.

The Specialty Gardens

■ *Its value in the landscape as a reflective surface is unique. . .*

The water garden, waterfall, and bog garden look more natural and logical if they are located at the lowest point on the property, provided this area receives at least six hours of sunlight per day. See Chapter 19 "The Water Garden."

The swim pool or lap pool needs a location in full sun where there are no deciduous trees to drop their leaves into the water. Evergreens will give the swim pool a suitable setting. A grape arbor can provide shade for swimmers not seeking the sun. Since the lap pool is a shallow, long, rectangular pool that is used only for swimming laps, it is does not require a special setting. Its value in the landscape as a reflective surface is unique, however. Locate it where it will reflect a beautiful old tree, a gazebo or summer house.

Roses are loved by everyone, and rhododendrons are the challenge of every aspiring expert gardener.

If you plan to grow either on a large or small scale, locating a space for them on your plan now will give you a headstart on success.

The formal rose garden can be incorporated into a plan in an area that receives at least six hours of sunlight each summer day. The formal design that is ages old is still the most practical for caring for each plant, for one can walk all the way around each bed to prune, pick blooms, spray, weed, and admire. Traditionally, there is a small center of interest, such as a fountain or piece of statuary, at the point where the beds intersect. Climbing roses can be grown on wire or lattice treillage around the formal beds.

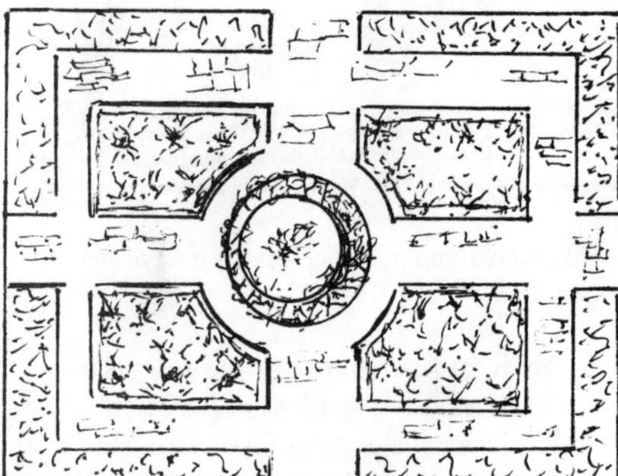
The formal rose garden is still the best way to view their beauty from all sides.

Floribunda roses are grown often with the perennials and shrubs in a border where they will bloom ceaselessly all summer.

Shrub roses and antique variety roses are moving up in popularity because they are almost disease and insect free, and because their exquisite fragrance cannot be matched in the new introductions. They make graceful, tall or medium hedges about five feet high and five feet across, yet their formidable thorns make them a good crime barrier, for not even a cat can get through them. Songbirds favor rose hedges for their nesting, and many shrub rose varieties will produce colorful fruits, known as hips, that are sought after by wildlife in winter. See Volume II for rose culture.

Rhododendrons and azaleas require some shade from summer sun and do best where root competition is not severe. In many parts of the Mountain West, these conditions can be found on the north side of your home. Since they must be kept moist, a hose bib nearby is also a convenience. See Chapter 18, "Azaleas and Rhododendrons."

How Much Turf Is Enough?

Kentucky bluegrass lawns are becoming an embarrassment no one wants to talk about except in negative epithets such as, water hog, guzzler, or contaminator of ground water (because of chemicals that are sometimes used), While it is true that water is the most important natural resource of the Mountain West, and it is equally true that turfgrass is a water user, there are some truths about turfgrass that we cannot ignore. Turf, even a small plot, lowers high summer temperatures and adds needed humidity in our dry climate - enough, sometimes, to make summer heat bear-able. Turf sets the stage for the home, giving it a more settled appearance. Turf can become the playing surface of childhood that keeps the family recreation on a close-knit basis. Lastly, turf, if managed properly is still an economical, easy-to-care-for surface in the home landscape.

Some restraints should be followed in the use of turf, however. Leave the broad sweeping vistas of turf to the nearby city park or golf course. No city or country home landscape needs more than one thousand square feet of quality turf surrounding the home. Use the latest in turf research to your advantage. Drought-tolerant varieties of Kentucky blue grass are now commonplace; rye and fescue grasses add even more choices of drought tolerance.

■ *Leave the broad sweeping vistas of turf to the nearby city park or golf course.*

You have drawn all the features on your plan that will meet your needs and those of your family: patios or decks, fences, berms, drive, walks, turn-around; utility area, vegetable garden, fruit orchard, islands of shade trees, the flowering-tree-and-shrub border, foundation planting, windbreak, and specialty gardens. The remainder will be planted in turf. First, however, use your scale ruler to add up the number of square feet that will be in turf. If it adds up to more than one thousand square feet, look for ways to cut it back. For example, a little walkway of concrete or stone pavers around your flower and shrub border will serve as a mowing strip and dry footing as you stroll around viewing the blooms. Shaving a little turf off here and there adds up, and will make a difference in your water bill.

Turf used for playing games is always a possibility in any family. Use the table below to judge the total areas that will be needed for the games your family will play.

The Space Required for Games:

Game	Space
Archery	90-200' x 15'
Badminton	17 x 44 singles
	20 x 44 doubles
Basketball	50 x 84
Boccie	10 x 60
Box Hockey	4 x 10
Croquet	30 x 60
Deck Tennis	14 x 40 singles
	17 x 40 doubles
Handball	20 x 34

Hopscotch .... 5 x 12.5
Horseshoes .... 5 x 25
Marbles .... 10' diameter
Shuffleboard .... 6 x 52
Table Tennis. .... 5 x 9
Tether Ball. .... Circle 6' in diameter
Volleyball .... 30 x 60

If you live in the country, you may want to play games that take more space:

Soccer .... 100 x 200
Touch Football. .... 120 x 240
Softball .... 45' diamond

The admonition remains for the country landscape that does not need more than one thousand square feet of quality turf around the home to set it off and provide climate control. The flowering-tree-and-shrub border can be extended to fifteen to twenty feet in width with the remainder of the property in pasture for animals or as rough grass for touch football or soccer.

■ *Groundcovers are often touted in books and magazines as the answer to all the non-gardeners problems.*

The Pros and Cons of Groundcovers

There are certain areas where turfgrass is a mistake and groundcovers are the answer.

1. Under a maple tree. Maple roots are notoriously near the soil surface. The competition for water and nutrients is steep. The tree usually wins. An attractive shade-tolerant groundcover, such as Baltic ivy (*Hedera helix 'Baltica'*) or Periwinkle (*Vinca minor*) will also mask the protruding maple roots.

2. On a steep slope where plying a lawn mower is hazardous. The roots of the groundcover will prevent soil erosion as well.

3. In areas where there will be no foot traffic. Groundcovers are often touted in books and magazines as the answer to all the non-gardeners problems, but, instead, they present stealthy little problems that soon become annoying. For example, they are catchers of litter. You may not think the wind blows much in your area until you are faced with a groundcover clotted with facial tissues and drink cups.

Groundcovers cannot withstand foot traffic to any degree of reliability. The catalog may tell you that creeping thyme can be trod upon, while the real truth is - maybe once in awhile. Groundcovers are a high-maintenance feature because they are difficult to keep weeded. A plan that will eliminate weeding is a drip irrigation system that is laid down with a fabric weed barrier over the top; then groundcover plants are planted through x-shaped cuts in the fabric. A mulch of pole peelings will mask the fabric and protect it from puncture. If information seems negative about groundcovers, keep in mind their advantages listed above. A moderate amount of turfgrass will require less care. See Chapter 16 "Groundcovers, Alternatives To Turfgrass."

Choosing the Plants

Now you are ready to choose the plants and place them on your plan. Consider the colors as an extension of those you have used inside the home. You chose them because you liked these colors, and you will like the same colors in your landscape. Use the plant lists to give you a succession of bloom and still look good in the winter scene. Make your choices of plants according to their ability to tolerate the conditions of each location, sun, shade, dry, wet. etc., and to fit the needs for height and width at maturity. Also, note colors and textures of foliage at different seasons.

Transfer your choices on your plan in pencil from your collection of tracings.

At this point you may wish to once

again ask a professional to critique your plan as referred earlier. Call your county Cooperative Extension office and ask that the agent in charge of horticulture critique the plan. If he or she is not trained in this field, it can be sent to the state university for a critique by the teaching staff.

Your Plan On Paper

After your plan has been critiqued, you are on your way to a permanent plan. Make templates* from the outlines of trees and shrubs in the illustration so that you may draw them to scale on your permanent plan.

Finish your plan by adding the name of the owner(s) of the property, the address, the date, compass direction of north, the scale of the map (example: 1"=10'), and your name as the one making the plan.

At this point it is wise to consider waterproofing your plan. You will be using it outdoors, remember, and a working drawing takes a beating. Lamination is often available at a printshop. You will want to make one or several copies for the sake of safety.

You are on your way toward the satisfying goal of landscaping your own property. The muscle-work that lies ahead will test the fortitude of everyone in the family, but could it be worse than papering the kitchen?

■ . . .
could it be worse than papering the kitchen?

* *See Glossary*

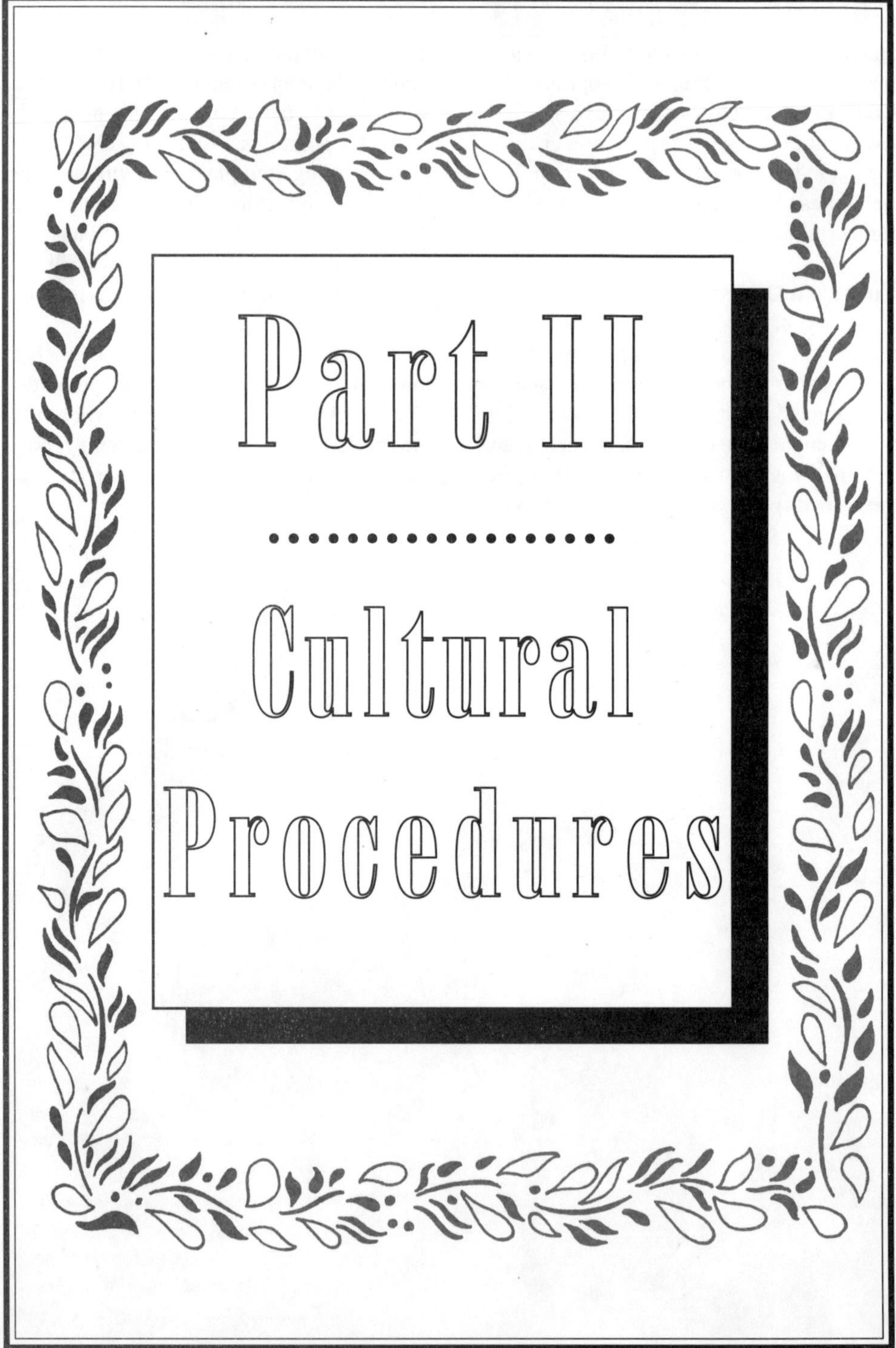

Part II

Cultural Procedures

CHAPTER 4

Soil, How to Make it and Keep it

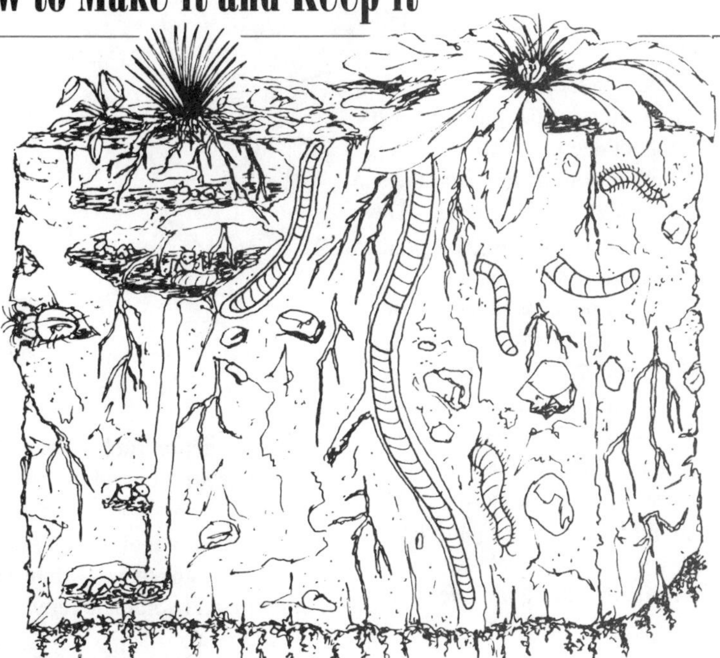

Soils in the Mountain West are nothing to rave about. In geologic time, they are young - meaning that they are recently derived from the parent material rock, such as granite or sandstone. All the factors of climate work together in the Mountain West to break down the ever-present rock to give us soil: the variable winds, deep temperature fluctuations, moisture constraints, steep slopes, the plants and animals living here, and geologic time. Most mountain soils are not soils yet, but a gritty material that will weather gradually as eons pass to finally become soil. As the parent material is weathered, it first becomes sand; then a slightly smaller particle, silt; and finally the smallest of soil particles - clay.

Weathering of parent rock is very slow. Rainfall averages annually only six inches in the Southwest to twenty inches in mountain valleys. This, compared to forty inches annually east of the Mississippi River, has its advantages and disadvantages. The good news - Mountain West soils are abundant in micro-nutrients needed by plant life. The bad news - Mountain West soils are alkaline, often highly alkaline.

Frost wedging is important in soil formation. Melting snow, as it drips into crevices and cracks of boulders and cliffs freezes and expands to break down the rock into smaller and smaller pieces. The freezing at night and thawing in daytime is a powerful force.

Plants and animals have a part in soil formation as they live a few days or a few years; then die and break down into organic acids and carbon dioxide. As rain or melting snow percolates down through the soil, the water carries with it the particles of organic matter, acids, carbon dioxide, and oxygen, thus enabling billions of microscopic organisms, plants and animals to live beneath or on the surface. Their life functions continue to add more organic matter.

The degree of slope comes into the soil-forming picture as hilltops are likely to be well drained and conducive to different plants than the valleys. Soil washes down the slope to collect deeply. The angle of slope and direction the surfaces face the sun have much to do with micro- climate. Have you noticed that spruce and fir grow on the cool north-facing slopes of mountains, while pines and junipers are found on the warm, south and west-facing slopes?

Time and the parent material type give us the soil in the valleys as little trickles become rivers and roaring torrents to carry sand, silt, and clay down to the valleys. As you can surmise, soft sandstone wears away faster than granite. If you are a gardener, either old or new, you enjoy observing these forces of nature going on quietly all around you.

Construction Site Rubble

■ *At no other time will you have control over the soil on your property as you do before planting begins.*

If you have some authority over the construction site of your new home, make sure that the top soil is saved. No matter how unproductive it looks, it is better than subsoil. If weeds were seen growing on it previously, it is a promising sign. Too often, however, topsoil is sold by the developer to pay for street lights, paving, and gutters. There is no law preventing this practice in most states. Saved topsoil should be covered with cut brush or a large tarp in windy areas.

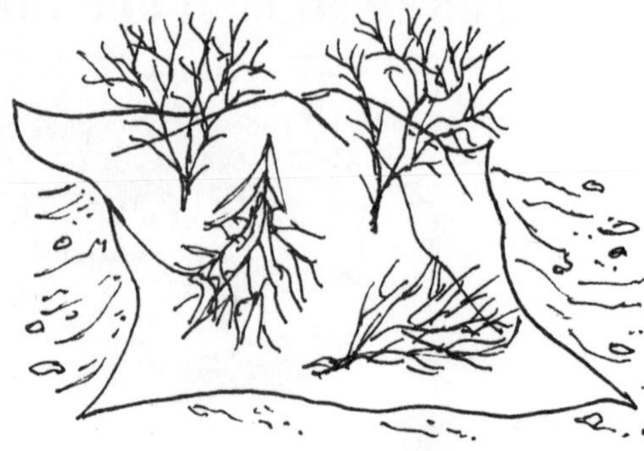

Saved topsoil is covered with cut brush or a large tarp.

Construction rubble left on the property, or, worse still, buried in some unobtrusive place, is the sign of a poor builder. If left in its buried site, it almost invariably leads to the turf fungus disease "Fairy Ring." Digging and complete removal of it is the only answer.

Making and Keeping Soil

At no other time will you have control over the soil on your property as you do before planting begins. Skimping now will lead to makeshift measures in years to come that will never result in a good soil that will grow vigorous, healthy, trouble-free plants.

It is not as monumental a task as one might think. The nutrient-absorbing roots of trees and shrubs reach only about eighteen inches below the soil surface; therefore, you need to amend the soil to a depth of eighteen inches; then forever after bask in smug satisfaction of having done the right thing.

The Advantages of Making A Good Soil

If you have been left with sterile-looking, gray-brown sub-soil, take heart. The one advantage of sub-soil is that it does not contain weed seed. The much-maligned clay particle is not all bad. It has the ability to hold water, a distinct advantage in the arid West. Another advantage of all western soils is that they almost always contain all the mineral nutrients needed for good plant growth, but not all may be available to plants because of a high (alkaline) pH. In the eastern part of the country the high amount of annual precipitation washes these mineral nutrients away and it is a costly nuisance to replace them each year. The high amount of precipitation also plays a big part in making eastern soil acid. While the dry soils of the Mountain West are alkaline, they lack only organic matter and water to become productive. The Mississippi River is known as the Lime Line because soils east of the river must be "limed," that is, agricultural lime must be added to raise the pH to neutral. Many transplanted easterners bring their gardening practice of liming the soil with them - to the everlasting detriment of their western soil. When lime is applied to an already alkaline soil, fertility is seldom achieved ever again.

The macro-nutrients needed by plants are: nitrogen, phosphorous, and potassium. The secondary nutrients are: calcium, magnesium, and sulfur. The micro-nutrients needed are iron, manganese, zinc, copper, cobalt, boron, chlorine, and molybdenum. Phosphorous and iron are often deficient in western soils in a form that is available to a plant. The addition of organic matter will change the pH and make these elements available to the plant.

Nitrogen, the growth nutrient, is most often in short supply in all soils because plants use a lot of it and use it quickly. Organic matter is a source of a small amount of nitrogen.

Before amending the soil you have been left with, get a soil test from the laboratory of the state university nearest you. The Cooperative Extension office will have soil test bags with complete directions on how to dig the soil for the test. The report will show how much and what kinds of amendments will be necessary. Almost all soils in the Mountain West have been mapped. If yours is a large country property, go to the office of the Soil Conservation Service to consult one of their maps to learn the soil types on your property. Their experts will aid you in amending and conserving soil.

■ *Almost all soils in the Mountain West have been mapped.*

Amendments that are recommended on your soil test report will almost always list a shortage of organic matter and nitrogen. Phosphorous is usually present in sufficient amounts, but not in a form available to plants. If any amendments are needed in the remaining elements, the amounts are so small that no great expense or time is involved in adding them at cultivation time.

How Much and How Deep

The recommended amount of organic matter to spread on top of your soil is eight inches! Spreading eight inches of organic matter in the form of weathered manure, fortified dried leaves or sawdust on all the soil of your property that is to be under cultivation sounds like a big job. But take it slow and do it right. Using your plan, measure and stake areas, such as a drive, walk, fence, patio, etc., that will be under asphalt or concrete or some other hard material. Attach twine between the stakes so that you can see them while you are plowing, yes, plowing the organic matter into the soil. Not many gardeners who read this book own or are proficient in plowing. It may take some searching of the yellow pages and newspaper classified ads to find a farmer who does custom plowing. If you don't find one, put an advertisement in the classified pages of a nearby country newspaper. The operation may take less than one hour, and you may be able to purchase the organic matter in the form of weathered manure from the same farmer who plows for you.

Plowing organic matter into the soil will fracture the subsoil for a lasting amendment.

■ *If it appears that you will be up to your knees, literally, in the manure, be assured that a weathered manure is dry, fluffy, and virtually odorless.*

The type of organic matter for this deeply plowed portion of your land is important. Weathered manure is animal manure that has been piled out-of-doors for a year or more. Harmful salts as well as almost all the nutrient value have leached away with rain and melting snow. Yet, its gradual and further breakdown will promote slow but steady plant growth. The organic matter will also add aeration and water-holding capacity to your soil. Why so much? Because this is a once-only operation. This is the last and the only time you will have the opportunity to change the texture of the soil deeply. If it appears that you will be up to your knees, literally, in the manure, be assured that a weathered manure is dry, fluffy, and virtually odorless. The plow will mix it with the soil to a depth of eighteen inches. After the plowing operation, make haste to settle the soil by sprinkling with water. You have added air to the soil, which, in moderation, is a good thing, but that same air can cause oxidation of the organic matter you worked so hard to incorporate. Sprinkling with water will eliminate some of the air and eliminate the danger of oxidation. One cubic yard will cover 40 ft_2 of soil 8 inches deep. Dump trucks come in various sizes. The most common holds 12 cubic yards.

Fortified Leaves or Sawdust

When available, chopped, dried leaves and sawdust are excellent sources of organic matter that contain few weed seeds. For every ton of dried leaves or sawdust, it is necessary to add from 75 to 100 pounds of ammonium sulfate or its equivalent and mix it well. This small amount will add back the nitrogen lost through decomposition.

Creating Topsoil

The next operation is the addition of still more organic matter, but this time it is four inches of high-quality compost or sphagnum peatmoss and fifteen pounds of Triple-Super-Phosphate per one thousand square feet spread over the surface and tilled in with a rotary tiller. You may want to do this operation yourself with a rented tiller. You are adding phosphorous at this time because it is an element that is in short supply in a form that is plant available and it does not move readily in the soil. Tilling it in will make it available to plant roots immediately.

You now have a deeply prepared soil that probably has a rough surface. Let it settle for a day or two before sprinkling it with water to settle it further, and to avoid the oxidation of the organic matter. (See above).

There will be the short-cut gardener who will prefer to prepare the soil each time a plant is planted, but the results will never be as satisfactory as a one-time soil preparation that will last the lifetime (and more) of all the plants you choose.

If You Are Renovating

When renovating a landscape, your soil rejuvenation efforts will be, by necessity, piece-meal. Preparing a planting hole will sometimes be torture as you encounter roots, rocks, and old construction rubble. It is a temptation to cover the whole thing with two feet of topsoil and start over. This would result in suffocation and death of the trees and shrubs that were included in the higher price when you bought the property. If you decide to destroy a sparse, weedy ;awn, see Chapter 21 "Lawn is the Stage." This will give you the opportunity to redesign corridors of turf and islands of trees and shrubs that will spell the difference in health and vigor of both as well as lower maintenance costs. If you decide upon amending the soil each time you plant, see Chapter 6 "Planting Procedures." One third of the soil from each planting hole soil will be discarded and replaced with weathered manure, compost or sphagnum peatmoss.

If Time Is On Your Side, Choose a Cover Crop

Also known as green manure, a cover crop is an alternative to the method of adding organic matter to the soil. Winter rye is a common seed planted in tilled soil in early fall at the rate of one to two pounds per one thousand square feet or about ninety pounds per acre. It has the advantage of being able to germinate at soil temperatures of thirty degrees. Before the stalks can set seed, they are tilled in deeply to rot over the winter. The problem is that soils in the Mountain West cool rapidly in August and the cover crop does not break down, but remains in a green condition to tangle the tines of the tiller the following spring. The remedy is to allow the cover crop a full year to break down. Usually tilling several times will hasten the breakdown. Other cover crop seeds are legumes such as buckwheat, cow peas, and red clover.

If you have a country property with poor, sparse soil, or a city property where time is no consideration, put in three successive crops of winter rye and legumes as cover crops, allowing three full years for breakdown. The reward is a rich, loamy, enviable soil that will rival the drop-in-a-seed-and-step-back-quickly soils of Iowa.

What the Soil Does Not Need

VITAMINS

Vitamins are manufactured by plants, but plants don't use them in their life processes. This fact was proven many years ago, but vitamins, especially B1 are still seen for sale at garden centers and nurseries. Californians are especially reluctant to let go of this obsolete practice.

GYPSUM

Gypsum is calcium sulfate. Soils in the Mountain West are almost all derived from calcium-bearing rock. If you apply gypsum to your soil, you are adding more calcium - more of what it already has an abundance of. Gypsum is useful only on a sodium soil, also known as "black alkali." Your soil test may but rarely advise the use of gypsum.

ROCK PHOSPHATE

Organic gardening publications decry the use of phosphorous in the form of Triple Super Phosphate, claiming it is not organic, and, therefore, harmful to the soil. Triple Super Phosphate is rock phosphate which has been treated with phosphoric acid to make it available to the plant. Rock phosphate is mined in Florida and South America. Soil scientists tell us that if rock phosphate is placed on western soils, it will never become available to plants because the organic acids are not strong enough to break it down.

BONE MEAL

Bone meal contains a little nitrogen and some phosphorous, but it isn't what it used to be. Long ago, bones, blood, entrails, fur, hide, horns, and whole carcasses were ground up, dried, and sold as bone meal. Now these materials are steamed to recover many other products that are sold separately. Bone meal is still of some value, but not much.

SOIL CONDITIONERS

"If it sounds too good to be true, it probably isn't" is a good axiom to remember. There are snake-oil salesmen and charlatans in the gardening trade as there are in any endeavor. Soil conditioners contain detergent. Detergent makes water wetter so that it penetrates more deeply. You can accomplish the same feat as a costly soil conditioner by adding a teaspoon or two of detergent to a bucket of water and pouring it over the soil.

■ *Fertilizing shade trees, flowering trees, shrubs, and even tree fruits is seldom necessary.*

PLANT GROWTH HORMONES

Here are products that sound like a scam, but aren't. They are synthetic or natural powders that are highly useful in plant propagation, but they should not be added to backfill soil when planting. There is evidence that they could seriously impede growth.

PEP-UPS AND START-UPS

Nurseries and garden centers sometimes will suggest you purchase starter fertilizer products at the same time you are purchasing plants. They are not necessary, and may, in fact, burn newly formed, tender roots.

WORMS

The presence of the old familiar "fishing" worms in a soil are known to announce that the soil is a good one. You may buy them, if you wish, but they will come unbidden to a good soil. An overabundance of night crawlers, those extra-long worms you see on the sidewalk after a heavy rain, are not so welcome in a soil because they create a lumpy surface. They are present in soils of lawns that are heavy with organic matter. Nevertheless, they are nature's best aerator, for their burrows open a heavy soil to air, and they mix organic matter with subsoil as they travel from the surface to the subsoil.

CHEMICAL FERTILIZER

There is no need to till in granular fertilizers at the time you are doing overall soil preparation. If you are preparing the soil in the fall, the fertilizer would be wasted by natural leaching of winter moisture, and if applied at planting time in spring, it could cause harmful burning of tender roots. Fertilizing shade trees, flowering trees, shrubs, and even tree fruits is seldom necessary. If you fail to note a normal growth rate of about six inches (depending upon species) of growth rate per year, fertilizer can be used. See Chapter 6 "Planting Procedures."

SAND

The recipe for concrete is: Clay + Sand + Water = Concrete Adding sand to your soil will give you problems that will plague you forever. The sand particles cling to the clay to make an impossibly stiff soil. Pea gravel is added to rock garden soils to great advantage, but organic matter is also added at the same time to add water-holding capacity to a quick-draining, gravel-laden soil.

TOPSOIL

The problem of finding good topsoil will exist until there is a law regulating what topsoil is. If you are contemplating buying topsoil, ask the dealer to bear the cost of having the so-called topsoil tested at the state university soils laboratory. His agreement to this impartial test will add to his stature with his customers.

FRESH MANURE

Each time reference is made to manure, you will notice, it is prefaced by the word "weathered." Fresh manure is high in salt - a plant-killing compound. Until the salts have been leached away by rain and snow for a year or more, the manure is dangerous to use. An exception is in composting. The millions of organisms in the compost pile will quickly render the salts harmless, and as soon as the temperature of the compost has gone down and the pile cools, the manure is sufficiently aged to be usable. Take care not to overwhelm the compost pile with too much fresh manure. Use only an amount equal to the amount of green material, such as grass clippings.

WOOD ASHES

Wood ashes are alkaline. Therefore, they are of some benefit to soils back East, but in the Mountain West where soils are already alkaline, wood ashes are harmful. Keep a small amount in a container to sprinkle where slugs are feasting. The ash is irritating to their skin and they will move on.

The Mighty Mulches

The word "mulch" may be unfamiliar to you. It is a layer of organic or inorganic material on top of the soil. Now that you have literally *made* your soil, you will keep it by mulching. Mulching is akin to composting and you will become a mulcher and a composter when you achieve the title "gardener."

■ *. . . you will become a mulcher and a composter when you achieve the title "gardener."*

The greatest benefit of mulch in the Mountain West is to save water - the West's greatest natural resource. Mulch blankets the soil to catch and hold moisture, and to reduce evaporation and runoff. Weeds are suppressed by mulch so that they don't compete for the soil nutrients. The soils of the Mountain West are often heavy. Rain, when it comes, is hard and in large droplets, sealing the soil to penetration and later baking and crusting. With a mulched soil, the precious rain soaks in and none is wasted to erosion and runoff. Anyone who has seen a flash flood has witnessed the power of water to demolish everything in its path.

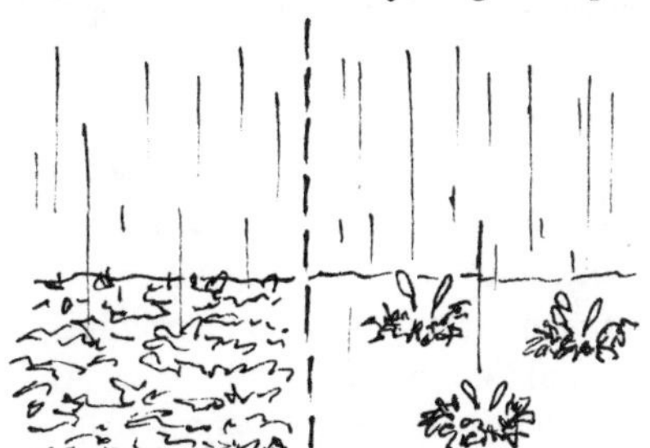

Rain on a mulched and unmulched soil.

Temperature fluctuations are a plant's worst enemy. With a mulch, a sudden heat wave is hardly noticed by a plant. When nights cool in August, mulched soil is slow to lose its growth-pushing warmth. Winter mulch similarly maintains an even soil temperature, retarding the freeze-and-thaw cycles that heave shallow-rooted plants out of the ground.

As an organic mulch decomposes, compounds are produced that filter down and bind soil particles into aggregates known as "crumbs." Both sandy and clay soils are thus given a spongy, granular structure, well aerated, draining easily but capable of storing large amounts of moisture in its pore spaces.

Good Soil under a mulch - the livliest community in the world.

Just under a mulch is the liveliest community in the world. Myriad types of organisms multiply fantastically to carry on the decomposition of the organic mulch. These mobilize not only minerals but also growth-stimulating hormones. Earthworms, too, increase in the cool, moist, food-rich conditions under mulch. As stated above, the earthworms come unbidden. An earthworm's soil enriching abilities should not be underestimated. An earthworm digests its own weight in soil daily, and its castings contain five times the nitrogen, seven times the phosphorus, and eleven times the potassium found in the material it consumed.

■ *. . . its castings contain five times the nitrogen, seven times the phosphorus, and eleven times the potassium found in the material it consumed.*

An organic mulch can also absorb and buffer the mistakes gardeners make. The soil is said to be a great forgiver, but perhaps it is the mulch that is most charitable, for it can absorb and hold an herbicide or excess fertilizer and reduce it to carbon dioxide, which is vital in a plant's food-making process.

WHEN A MULCH IS HARMFUL

Mulched seedlings may come down with damping off disease. A tree or shrub with mulch applied too heavily directly next to its trunk may become infected with crown rot. Too much mulch (five or more inches) around shallow-rooted plants, such as evergreens, will have a suffocating effect. Measure the mulch every season to make sure you are not adding too much. At high altitudes, mulch that kept soils from freezing deeply in winter should be drawn away in spring so that the sun's warmth can penetrate. A mulch that is more than five inches deep may cause roots to reach into it and to wander around, rather than reaching deeply into the mineral richness of the soil.

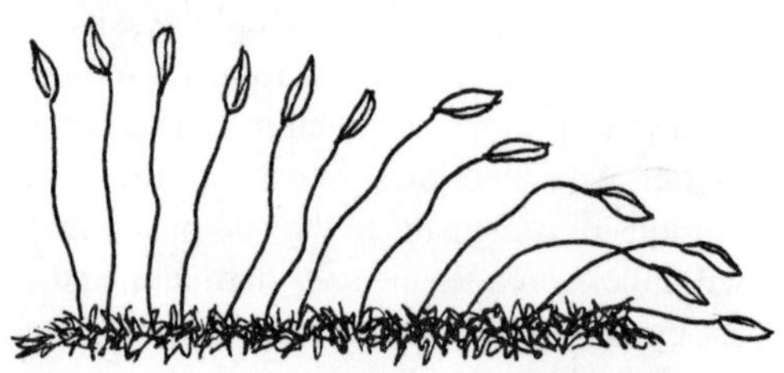

Too much mulch can cause seedlings to topple with damping-off disease.

But, despite some disadvantages, the soil that you have so carefully made will wear out like a piece of cloth if you don't preserve it and replenish it with mulch.

ORGANIC MULCHES

Bark Chips: These are nearly round nuggets, often of redwood, that are very slow to breakdown, but quick to blow away.

Buckwheat Hulls: A mulch highly-touted in slick magazines; very rich dark brown color, long lasting. Since buckwheat is seldom grown in the Mountain West, these are expensive. A two-inch depth is adequate, but must be renewed each year.

Coconut Fiber: Good dark brown color; long-lasting; seldom found in the Mountain West.

Coffee grounds: Rich color, high in nitrogen and some trace elements. If you don't like coffee, you won't like the smell.

Compost: The best; excellent even in half-rotted chunk form at mid-summer.

Corncobs: Best if chopped in walnut-sized pieces. High in sugar which stimulates aggregation organisms; light in color, and should be fortified with nitrogen using directions above for sawdust or leaves.

Cornstalks: Very good if shredded, or whole as a topdressing of finer mulch in the vegetable garden in winter.

Excelsior: Light color; excellent as packing around tender plants in winter. Very flammable.

Hay, Field Grass, Weeds: If cut before they go to seed, these can be allowed to dry and serve well to mulch large areas, such as the tree-and-shrub border of a country property.

Leafmold: Especially good for wild-flower meadows or shade plantings.

Leaves: Shredded oak leaves especially good for acid-loving plants, such as rhododendrons. Cottonwood, aspen, linden, willow, and green ash break down into alkaline compost , which is not desirable.

Manure: Best well-weathered and strawy; for liberal (one pound per square foot) use on the vegetable garden and roses, lightly in other areas. Often full of weed seeds.

Peatmoss: Mountain peat is alkaline and undesirable; Sphagnum peat is a living moss, acid, very desirable, and expensive.

Pine and Other Needles: Acid; should be composted for best use; as a dry mulch they break down slowly or blow away.

Pole peelings: The shreddy slivers of lumbering operations. Knits together; does not blow; attractive in color.

Sand: Can be useful mixed with peatmoss to mark where bulbs are planted, but it quickly disappears.

Sawdust: Fortify with nitrogen. Apply two inches deep; light in color, but weathers to deep brown. Avoid old sawdust from deep piles that has fermented.

Snow: Nature's finest. Colorado's champagne powder contains the finest insulating quality of air spaces between light-weight flakes. Free winter protection.

Spent Hops: More available as number of breweries and brewing pubs increase. Light in color, but effective.; fire resistant; therefore, good for mountain homes.

Spent Mushroom Compost: Earthy color, usually regarded as a fertilizer with 1-1-1 percentage of N,P,K.

Straw: Good general mulch, cheap; lasts longer but is more flammable than hay.

Wood Shavings: Cedar shavings repel many pests; needs fortification with nitrogen. Good color.

INORGANIC MULCHES

Aluminum foil: Repels aphids, thrips and other insects; reflected light said to increase yield on many crops.

Asphalt Building Paper: Effective and long-lasting; unattractive.

Carpet: Old carpet of man-made fibers excellent in between rows in the vegetable garden, berry patch. Breaks down slowly and can be added to as it dissolves into the soil.

Fabric-weed barrier: Spun-bonded man-made fibers excellent for water, air penetration and preventing weeds. Easily torn or blown away if not covered with a second

■ *Mountain peat is alkaline and undesirable. . .*

mulch of pole peelings or gravel.

Fiberglass Matting: Very effective and permeable to air and water; glass fibers repel pests; often used in container plantings.

Gravel, marble chips, mineral clay chips, crushed stone: Decorative, especially good for rock plants; avoid marble on acid-loving plants; use dark-colored types to attract heat; light colored to radiate heat.

Newspaper: Use 3 to 6 sheets thick, and cover with an organic mulch for appearance and to speed decomposition.

Perlite: Sheds water; good for cacti and succulents. Sterile. Blows easily.

Plastic Films: Many types, for weed control and soil temperature regulation, not for long-term use.

Rocks and Stones: decorative and effective except for weed growth between them; hold heat in spring and fall to warm soil; can be placed in interesting patterns, and used right up to the trunks of trees where organic mulches would encourage rot and rodent attack. Cobble rock (the river biscuits of the Mountain West) do not conduct heat.

Vermiculite: sterile; useful as a top dressing for seedlings; good insulator; holds water well.

The White Crust

In poorly drained areas of the Mountain West there will often be found a white powdery crust on top of the soil in low areas. There is an alkaline substrate that is floating the substance to the surface. Providing drainage will solve the problem. Dig shallow trenches that lead to a curb and gutter if you are in the city, or to a dry well if you are in the country. The salts will gradually drain away. Adding organic matter that is acid, such as sphagnum peatmoss, will change the pH of this soil and aid in draining away the salts.

You may not have had a good soil originally on the property you purchased, but following the directions of making the most of the basic soil you have with amendments will bring you results for years to come.

Buying Fertilizer

Flowers, vegetables, turfgrass, and small fruits (berries) will need supplemental fertilizer from time to time, even though you have already prepared the soil on all of your property. All of the seventeen nutrients elements needed for normal plant growth must be balanced in the correct proportions. Of these, carbon, hydrogen and oxygen are supplied by air and water, so they aren't generally thought of an part of a fertilizing program. Too much or too little of even a single nutrient can throw a plant's metabolism off kilter or make other nutrients unavailable, resulting in a plant that grows poorly or one that may be more vulnerable to insects, diseases, or environmental stress.

Supplemental fertilizers can be a great benefit, but they are no substitute for building up your soil with organic matter, which in the long run will decrease the need for supplemental fertilizer.

If you are confused that fertilizer is often referred to as "plant food," the two terms are inter-changeable, although strictly speaking, the sun is the only source of plant food. Its energy, through the process of photosynthesis, allows the plant to make the nutrients needed for growth. Nonetheless, mineral nutrients still play a big role in the photosynthetic process.

You have the soil test results from Cooperative Extension that were made before you amended the soil. The same test should be run about every three years -

more often if there are symptoms of nutrient deficiency. Using a home soil test kit is likely to be less accurate and may mislead you to make soil additives that are incorrect or unnecessary. Your Cooperative Extension will have booklets that contain colored photos of leaves with symptoms of nutrient deficiency. These are easily compared with leaves from your own plants, and can be very reliable in prescribing the need of a particular plant nutrient that is deficient in your soil.

Fertilizer Choices

Fertilizer is sold in three forms: dry granules, solid pellets, tablets or spikes; and liquids or soluble powders.

Granular fertilizers are composed of small particles that fall with a specified size range. Generally speaking, the lighter in weight the fertilizer, the more expensive it is, but granular fertilizers are least expensive overall. They are most often used on lawns and as a side-dressing on vegetables.

There are both slow and quick-release granular fertilizers. The particles of a slow- or controlled-release granular fertilizer have been coated with a polymer or other plastic that reduces the speed with which the nutrients become available. Most of the nutrients of a quick-release granular fertilizer are available soon after application and may last a season or less, depending on length of growing season, temperature and soil type.

Slow-release fertilizers are often more expensive, but require less frequent application. They provide a steady supply of nutrients without surging an overdose of nitrogen that might burn tender roots. Read the label to determine slow or quick release types of fertilizers.

Solid spikes or tablets of fertilizer are the most dangerous to use. Thrust into the soil, and without enough water to dilute their effects, they can become a quick death for plants because roots are burned away.

Liquid fertilizers are sold as concentrates or powders that you mix with water. They are applied as a spray to the soil or to foliage, or you mix them in a bucket and dump measured amounts on each plant.

Chelated fertilizer also can be mixed with water for spraying on foliage in early evening to quickly correct a deficiency symptom, especially for iron. Chelation is a process in which a non-nutrient compound is joined to an element, such as iron, to increase its availability. Please note, apply on a cool evening.

Complete and Incomplete Fertilizers

All-purpose fertilizers are often known as "complete," that is, containing nitrogen, phosphorous, and potassium, and they may also contain iron or other essential nutrients. Incomplete fertilizers will contain only one or two of the macro-nutrients, such as ammonium sulfate, which contains only nitrogen and a little sulphur, or bonemeal, which is essentially only phosphorous.

Reading the Label

The label contains, most importantly, contains one set of numbers that, by law, must be in prominent printing - the analysis. This is usually three numbers (sometimes four) that guarantee that the percentage by weight of nitrogen (the first number), phosphorous (the second number), and potassium (the third number).

Nearly all labels contain the brand name, fertilizer grade, guaranteed analysis, source of nutrients, net weight and the manufacturer's name and address. Many include information about the types of plants the fertilizer is good for, directions for application, as well as cautions about use.

The label is not as deep and mysterious as one might think.

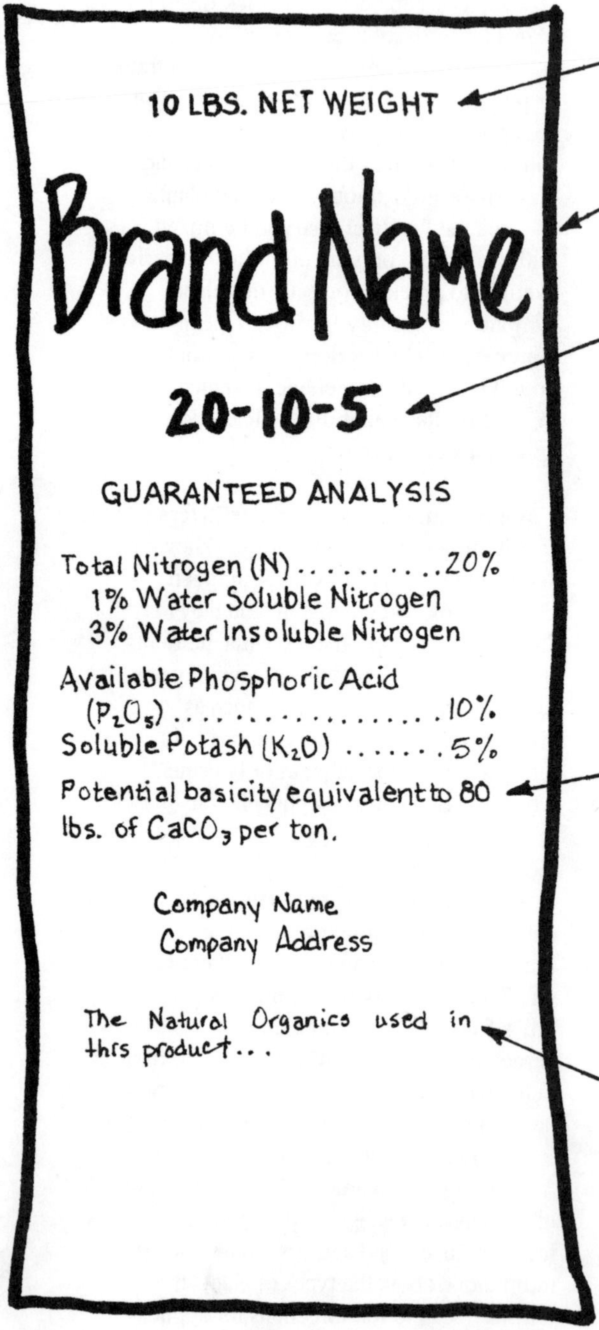

10 LBS. NET WEIGHT

Brand Name

20-10-5

GUARANTEED ANALYSIS

Total Nitrogen (N) 20%
1% Water Soluble Nitrogen
3% Water Insoluble Nitrogen

Available Phosphoric Acid (P_2O_5) 10%

Soluble Potash (K_2O) 5%

Potential basicity equivalent to 80 lbs. of $CaCO_3$ per ton.

Company Name
Company Address

The Natural Organics used in this product...

Net weight — this number is the total weight of the fertilizer bag.

Brand name — this is the product name for a fertilizer - usually a copyrighted trade name.

Fertilizer grade — In addition to the percentage of the primary nutrients - nitrogen, phosphorous, and potassium - the guaranteed analysis lists the percentage of all other nutrients; the breakdown of water-soluble and insoluble components. The remaining percentage of the fertilizer is made up of combinations of non-nutritive chemicals to provide bulk and prevent caking.

Potential acidity or basicity — fertilizers that contain ammonium nitrogen can acidify the soil. The label will show the amount of calcium carbonate that would be required to neutralize the decrease in pH resulting from the application of one ton of this fertilizer. In the Mountain West, we welcome a material that acidifies soil.

Derived from — this portion of the label may describe the source of each of the organic ingredients in the fertilizer. Examples might be: poultry waste, animal tankage, dried blood, or fish waste.

Fertilizers don't pose the same risk that many pesticides do, but granular fertilizers in particular can irritate the lungs, skin and eyes upon contact. In addition, misuse can cause the product to leach into ground water or can drain into streams that are sources of drinking water.

Organic fertilizers will have the sources of organics on the label, such as animal tankage, cocoa tankage, cottonseed meal, bone meal, blood meal, etc.

Organic or Inorganic

Misconceptions about organic and inorganic fertilizers are rampant. The plant must turn the organic fertilizer into inorganic elements before it can use these nutrients. This fact is inescapable, but nevertheless not what the organic gardener wants to hear. The controversy would dissolve if the two proponents of the inorganic and organic fertilizers would concentrate on making the best possible soil and and creating the best possible growing conditions for each plant in their care. A balance of both types of fertilize will achieve the best results.

Fertilizer Application Rates

If you are in the dark about how much dry fertilizer to apply to an area, you must first measure the area to determine the square footage. Length multiplied by width equals square feet. Nitrogen is usually the key factor in determining the amount; therefore add a zero to the nitrogen number on the fertilizer bag. This is always the first number. Then divide 1,000 by that number. The result is how many pounds of fertilizer you will need to place one pound of actual nitrogen on 1,000 square feet.

Add a zero to the fertilizer nitrogen grade number to determine how many pounds of fertilizer to apply to 1,000 ft_2.
example: fertilizer grade - 20-10-5
20 + 0 = 200
1,000 ft_2 divided by 200 = 5 lbs.

Exchange of Gases

There is growing evidence that an exchange of gases may be as beneficial as fertilizer. Every year trees, shrubs, and vines are fertilized unnecessarily and roots are often burned so that a plant fails to recover. Make holes in the soil by sinking an iron bar at intervals into the soil in the root run of the woody plant; then rock the bar back and forth. This enlarges the hole and allows gases to escape from the soil and oxygen to enter. No, you won't notice an odor, but dramatic results have been observed as a result of this simple procedure.

Organic Fertilizers Available in the Mountain West

FERTILIZER	%N	%P	&K	AMT TO USE POUNDS PER 100 ft_2	REMARKS
Blood, dried	13	1.5	0	3	
Bone meal, raw	4	22	0	5	A little N, P mostly insoluble.
Bone meal, steamed	2	27	0	5	P more available.
Cottonseed meal	6	2.5	2	3	Very acid.
Fish scrap	9	7	0	3	Not to be confused with fish emulsion.
Guano, bat	6	9	3	3	
Guano, bird	13	11	2	2	
Hoof & Horn meal	14	0	0	2	
Manure:					
cattle	.5	.3	.5		No amounts can be given because moisture content varies.
chicken	.9	.5	.8		
horse	.6	.3	.6		
rabbit	.9	.6	.6		
sheep	.9	.5	.8		
swine	.6	.5	.4		
Peat, reed or sedge	2	.3	.3		Alkaline.
Sewage, activated	6	5	0	4	Milorganite.
Sewage sludge	2	1	1	5	Do not use raw.
Wood ashes	0	2	6	5	Very alkaline.

CHAPTER 5

Composting

There's a certain lure in the word "compost." It conjures up deep, dark, woodsy-smelling stuff that creates magic in the plant world, making you rich and/or famous. That's almost the truth. It can be deep - usually about four feet. It is usually dark. If it has been made right, it does smell woodsy. The rich and famous part may follow.

As we've already learned in Chapter 4 "Soil, How To Make It and Keep I,t" the soils of the Mountain West are young in geologic time, and, because of arid conditions, lacking in organic matter. In fact, the organic matter is the magic elixir that is the "fixer" of Mountain West soils. Organic matter adds air to the heavy clay soil and water-holding capacity to the sandy soil. Our soils have all of the mineral nutrients that are needed, but they are sometimes not available to plants because of lack of organic matter. Add the organic matter - compost, in this case, and the tied (unavailable) nutrient is released from nutrient jail and ready to go to work for you.

We are nagged relentlessly from all sides about the need to recycle. Composting can make you a proud recycler, salve your conscience, and give you back a product that is remarkably useful in gardening. You can seldom buy high quality compost, though there are many products in bags at your nursery that claim to be compost. Compost is very fragile. It doesn't last long. It would simply vanish if it were bagged up in quantity, and the nursery selling it would soon have bags of dark powder, and not much of that!

■ *Add the compost, and the nutrient is released from nutrient jail and ready to go to work for you.*

Containers

So you must make it yourself, and let us get started. If you have a utility area that is partly shaded, you are in luck, for this is ideal for three compost bins - 1. for compost in progress, 2. for finished compost, 3. for oak-leaf compost.

Why do you need an oak-leaf compost bin? Chances are, sooner or later, you will hanker after some acid-loving plants, such

The contents are almost too easy.

as rhododendrons, azaleas, mountain laurel, gardenias, and any number of others that require acid soil. Oak leaves are tough and waxy. They don't break down easily in our dry climate, but eventually they make a rich compost that is ideal for mixing with garden soil to create a suitable soil for acid-loving plants.

The bins can be made from anything handy, or no bin at all - just three piles. However, since most gardeners are neat-niks to some extent, it is wise to have a corral of some sort. A favorite is snow fence. Since this is a common item sold in rolls in almost every Mountain West community, it's easy to come by. A roll is twenty-five feet, which can be cut in three equal parts. The wood slats held together by wire are ideal for allowing air to enter the compost pile, and the height of the slats is four feet, another ideal. A common cause of compost failure is making the pile less than four feet deep. Apparently, the weight of the pile at four feet keeps the ingredients in close enough contact that the decomposition process proceeds at the correct speed. In compost-making there are no absolutes, and not much data is available. Everyone out there has a different idea on how it should be done. The following directions are from experience, but feel free to improvise totally on your own.

Many compost containers are available - from the Cadillac-priced tumblers and domed plastic edifices that resemble college campus beer kegs to home-made scrap lumber bins. All will work well if you, the gardener, give the composting process a little help.

Ingredients

The contents are almost too easy. Most compost-making begins in the fall when autumn leaves are available in huge quantities. In fact,leaves should be the basic ingredient in all compost piles.. In summer green weeds (those that have no seed heads) are available. Twigs, garbage, and animal manure are optional. Soil and water are not, for you need at least a shovel of soil to add the millions of mirco-organisms that will start the decomposition process, and the water is needed to cool the heat of decomposition to an acceptable level. Without water, the pile can actually begin to smolder.

Grass clippings are an occasional possibility, but you should not be collecting clippings each time you mow. There is a time or two during the summer season when grass clippings may be available, such as the mowing of your lawn after you return from vacation. If you didn't arrange for lawn care while you were away, the lawn is ankle-deep, and collecting clippings is in order. Clippings should be mixed with soil before adding to the compost bin, for they can become as a thatched roof, preventing rain or water from your hose from entering the pile. They are also a notorious place for the breeding of house flies.

Acceptable Leaves

Not all leaves make good compost[1]. Some are too leathery, being filled with cellulose and lignin, and when they break down, they make a compost with an alkaline reaction. We already have more than we need of alkaline soils in the Mountain West.

[1] *Research of James Borland*

Avoid using these leaves in compost:

Cottonwood	Poplar
Aspen	Linden
Willow	Green Ash

The best leaves for compost-making are:

Maple	Fruit-tree
Oak	Pine Needles

If you have other trees in your yard, place a few fallen leaves in your kitchen blender with a little distilled water. Blend them to a soupy mix; then test with a bit of drugstore litmus paper. The result should tell you whether the leaves will produce an acid or alkaline compost. Blue is acid; pink is alkaline.

If the leaves from your trees are not the right kind, there is nothing preventing you from raking leaves at local cemeteries, schools, universities, churches and public libraries. As long as you explain your mission to the caretakers, chances are good that you will be welcomed with shouts of joy. It takes about eight packed-tight plastic garbage bags of leaves to fill a snow-fence bin four feet tall. The leaves will break down faster if they are chopped, but maple and fruit tree leaves break down quickly, and this is seldom needed. Oak leaves are slow, and, as stated above, should have their own separate bin. If you are a lover of gardening gadgets, now is the time to indulge in one of the best. The leaf-chopping devices that are on the market are very efficient. Most have a hopper shaped like a bushel basket and legs that fit down over a common size trash barrel. You fill the hopper, turn it on, and the whirling nylon strands whip the leaves into shreds, neatly dropping them into the trash barrel. Lacking a gadget like this, you can pile your leaves in rows on the lawn and run over them with the lawnmower, which does a good job of chopping, but doesn't do your mower much good.

The ideal situation is to gather fallen leaves in autumn as you mow the lawn. Most power lawn mowers have a vacuum action. The blades chop the leaves, which are then sucked into the bag, along with grass clippings. The green grass clippings raise the carbon/nitrogen ratio and the composting process will be very fast if the weather is mild. After each mowing, add a little water to the pile as you dump the grass and leaves contents from the mower bag into the compost bin.

■ . . . *chances are good that you will be welcomed with shouts of joy.*

Garbage and Manure

Those who live in the country will want to add kitchen garbage to their compost piles. It saves wear and tear on the septic system. Those in towns and cities may face an ordinance against such a practice. The compost containing kitchen waste is superior because the micro-nutrients from the soils of other areas - even those of other nations have been added. For example, banana peels from Costa Rica, nut shells from the Middle East, citrus rinds from Florida or California, and coffee grounds from Brazil.

Animal manure, preferably fresh, is also a good addition, but not one likely to be welcome in a city compost bin. Cattle, horse and sheep manure is good. Even better is poultry, which is considered "hot." But best of all is rabbit. Weed seeds are almost always present in all but rabbit manure. These gentle creatures are fed little nutrient pellets that are free of weed seed. Rabbit manure, high in nitrogen, is quick to break down in a compost pile.

The city ordinances against animal manures are difficult to understand. When mixed with the other ingredients in a compost bin, there is no odor unless the pile is too wet or too dry.

Manure from dogs and cats is not acceptable. There is danger of intestinal worms that might not be killed by the heat of the decomposition process.

Topping Off the Pile

Topping off a compost pile gives a great feeling of satisfaction. You have mixed together all the ingredients as the season progressed, and now the bin is full.

The next step is important. Use the hose to wet it down till a squeezed handful is spongy. This is needed to insure the right environment for the micro-organisms and to prevent the heat of decomposition from cooking them.

The last ingredient is a topping of soil to hold in the heat and moisture. A few shovels of any ordinary soil will do. It doesn't have to be topsoil. Subsoil is also full of mineral nutrients.

If you are interested, you may wish to place a thermometer into the pile. A long candy thermometer works well. The temperature will build up quickly to a peak; then cool gradually.

Use a fork to remove the contents of the pile onto a tarp, making a windrow. Replace the pile by beginning with the former top of the pile.

Turning

■ *If you don't have the time, strength, or inclination. . .*

If you don't have the time, strength, or inclination to turn the pile, don't feel guilty. The compost will cook on its own with no further help from you. If you do get the urge for exercise, spread a plastic tarp beside the pile. Use a spading fork, or an old-fashioned pitch fork, if you have one, to remove the contents, making a long windrow on the tarp. To put it back, begin at the end of the windrow that contains the top of the former pile, and you will have turned the pile.

If you are using one of the tumblers as a container for compost, read the directions before beginning to fill the tumbler, for the best results are obtained by filling the tumbler all at once. This means four cubic feet of organic matter. Not many home landscapes can furnish that much at once. Stockpiling it nearby is not a tidy operation. Handling it twice is necessary to collect it, pile it; then fill the tumbler. Turning the tumbler on its cradle is easy, and the composting process is very speedy using this device.

Questions

Composting was known in the Mountain West in times of the Anasazi. Early white settlers also practiced composting to boost the fertility of thin, sandy soils of the alluvial plain or the poor cold soils of the mountains. Many early practices included additions, devices, and fetishes that may be valid today. Some examples of questions you may have are:

Will I need a broomstick stuck in the center of the pile?

A piece of perforated pipe might make more sense today. The plastic or metal pipe has holes at intervals. When stuck into the center of the pile, it will allow air to enter the pile and heat to escape, even at the center. Air prevents the decomposition process from becoming anaerobic, meaning without air. The anaerobic decomposition process will still result in good compost, but it is slower. It also emits a powerful odor whereas aerobic decomposition is odorless.

Is the addition of limestone necessary?

This question comes from a person who has composted in the East or Southeast where soils are acid. The soil you add to the compost pile will be our native alkaline soil, which contains enough lime to counteract the acidic reaction of the composting process; therefore, the limestone is not necessary.

How often must the pile be turned?

Never, if you are not so inclined. There will be a few undecomposed leaves on the outside of the pile, but the remainder will be undistinguishable. Turning the pile from time to time will make it break down faster.

How will I know if the pile is too hot?

You won't know that heat is present unless you have a thermometer or stick your hand into the pile. If you have placed a perforated metal pipe in the center, the pipe will feel warm to the touch.

How will I know if the pile is too dry or too wet?

You will notice a strong odor. If it is too dry, it will be the sweet odor of putrefaction. If it is too wet, the odor will be sour.

Does compost attract animals?

Rarely, but this is another reason for a pile constructed within the confines of snow fence or some other device. If you live in the country and add garbage that contains meat scraps, dogs or cats could be attracted, but not for long because the decomposition process takes care of it quickly. Mice are sometimes attracted in the fall, as they seek out a warm home for the winter. If this happens, however, you will also find the neighborhood cats sitting in a patient circle around the compost, and the mice are soon eliminated.

■ *. . .you will also find the neighborhood cats sitting in a patient circle around the compost.*

Does compost attract insects?

As mentioned above, house flies are attracted to grass clippings, but the problem is eliminated if the clippings are mixed with soil before being added to the pile. Centipedes are sometimes found in a pile when it is opened, but they are short-lived. Earthworms will be attracted in great numbers, which is another benefit of compost. You don't have to purchase them. They come unbidden to digest and turn the compost for you, leaving their nutrient-rich castings.

What yield can I expect?

The average household of four can expect about two cubic yards of compost

■ *Some people would never think of starting a compost pile without adding a pair of old woolen trousers.*

per year. The four-foot high bins of snow fence as described will break down to finished compost that is only two feet high.

When can I expect finished compost?

If you start in the fall when leaves are abundant, you can expect finished compost by June 15 of the following year if you turn it only once on about April 1. If you are using one of the sophiticated tumblers and it is midsummer, you can expect finished compost within two to three weeks.

Will the compost continue to "work" all winter?

Yes, the pile seldom freezes, and if it does, it is only the top portion, and only for a few weeks. In areas of heavy snowfall, a clear plastic sheet placed over the top will conserve heat and prevent too much moisture from penetrating the pile when the snow melts.

Are there any ingredients especially good for adding to the compost?

Some people would never think of starting a compost pile without adding a pair of old woolen trousers. The chemistry of this is fairly sound, but not necessary. Wool, after all, is organic, and we can add almost anything organic to the pile. This means old latex paint, hair, dead fish, Christmas fruit cake, wormy apples, cotton rags, and many other items. Sugar in any form is especially good, such as home-canned peaches that have turned unappetizingly dark, or strong-flavored honey that no one in the family will eat. Think of organic matter as *anything that has lived*, and let that be your guide.

Are there any ingredients that should be avoided?

Cigarette butts should be avoided. Filter tips will not decompose, and the tobacco virus present in all cigarettes is especially harmful to tomato plants and turfgrass.

How should I apply compost?

By the teacup-full, by the bucket-full, by the wheelbarrow-full. Begin applying it as a mulch in and around the vegetables and flowers as the season warms. Scratch it in a little to keep it from blowing away, for it is very light weight. By fall you will want to spade it lightly into the soil. Save some to add to the soil for your indoor plants that you are re-potting. Give a special gardening friend a bucketfull for Christmas!

What is mushroom compost?

This is a compost you *can* purchase where mushrooms are grown commercially. It is usually made from fresh cattle or horse manure mixed with straw. Some has been tested and found to be l-l-l, which is one percent nitrogen, one percent phosphorous, and one percent potassium. This is *hotter* than you can expect your home-made compost to be. Compost is not high in nutrients. It is a soil amendment, not a fertilizer.

What is vermicomposting?

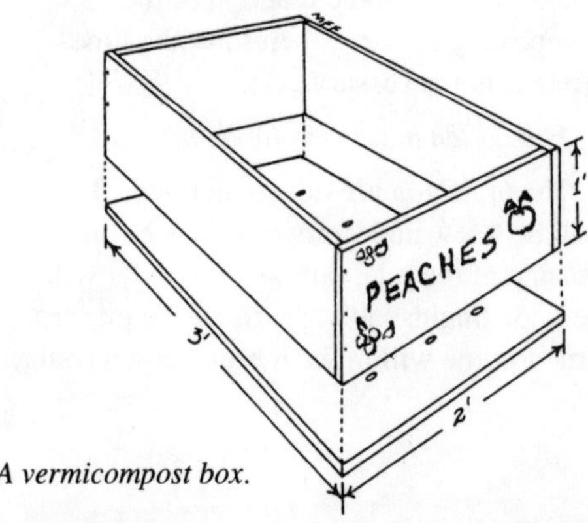

A vermicompost box.

It is a method of composting kitchen waste using redworms (ordered by mail) as the living agent of digestion. A box of a size similar to a peach box is filled with shredded cardboard or newspapers; moisture is added; kitchen waste is added until the breakdown process is begun. Worms are then added and the process is self-contained after that. The castings are collected every two or three months for use in the garden. The box can be kept anywhere in the home, for the temperature required is the same as most homes. There is no odor. Start-up cost is about twenty dollars for a pound of redworms.

Can you give any specific reasons why compost is so beneficial?

The results obtained are much too impressive to be explained by the nutrients it contains, its moisture retention, or its cation exchange capacity. There is no doubt that compost contains organisms that secrete antibiotics that protect plants against disease and the onslought of harmful insects. Acids formed during the decomposition process dissolve and make available some of the great store of minerals in the topsoil and subsoil. But above all this, it produces plants of extraordinary vigor and productiveness. THINGS GROW IN IT!

Suggested reading:

"Worms Eat My Garbage", Appelhof, Flower Press, 10332 Shaver Rd., Kalamazoo, MI 49002, 1981.

Order form for redworms is included with the booklet.

CHAPTER 6

Planting Procedures

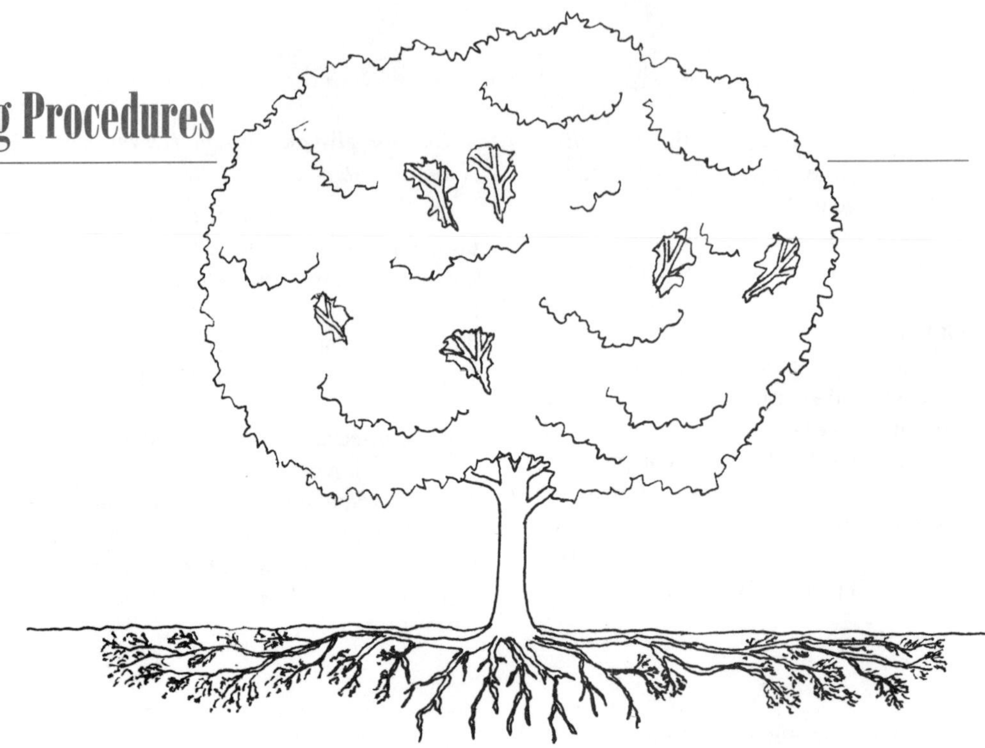

Anchor roots directly beneath the trunk hold the tree in place, but nutrient-absorbing roots in the top eighteen inches of soil range far beyond the dripline.

How To Plant a Bare-Root Tree or Shrub

Methods of culture change as we learn more about the physiology of plants and about the stresses that they can tolerate and those they cannot. Until recently it was thought that we were doing a tree a kindness by removing all of the soil from a deeply dug hole, discarding it, and bringing in all new soil or a soil mixed from sphagnum peatmoss and new topsoil. Now research shows that a tree will make a more sustained adjustment to its environment if it must make do with thc soil at the site. In addition, it is now known that the tree roots that absorb the nutrients are only about eighteen inches deep and in a wider circle beyond the dripline* than previously thought. There are a few anchor roots directly under the trunk.

■ *. . . it must make do with the soil at the site.*

Digging the holes the day before or several days before you plant gives both you and the tree or shrub advantages:

1. The fatigue factor can set in and you will skip a step in preparing the holes.
2. By digging the holes the day before you plan to plant, you can add the very beneficial step of filling the planting holes with water twice and allowing it to drain away. This will soak the surrounding soil so that roots will penetrate quickly.

If you have prepared all of the soil of your property according to direction in Chapter 4, there will be no need for the following pre-planting soil preparartion. Simply dig the hole and proceed according to the direction for bare-root or container planting.

* *See Glossary*

Always dig a planting hole with verticle sides.

To prepare a planting hole for a bare-root tree or shrub, dig a wide, shallow hole with straight sides and a flat bottom. Build a hill inside the hole wide enough to accommodate all the roots when they are spread over the hill, and high enough so that the trunk will be at the same level with the soil surface as it was when growing in the nursery. There is usually a dark mark on the trunk to give you this measurement. Set the soil aside on a tarp. Carry away one-third of the soil to be used elsewhere, (such as in compost-making), and mix the remaining two-thirds with sphagnum peatmoss, compost, or weathered manure. The organic matter will give the tree or shrub a lifetime supply of aeration if the soil is clay, and water-holding capacity if it is sandy. The organic matter will break down slowly to become a source of nutrition.

After spreading the roots over the hill, make sure that none are crossing or broken. If one root is longer than the hole is wide, cut it. Twisting it around to fit the hole will lead to a *girdling* root. One root crossing another eventually girdles both roots, which then die. Fill the hole halfway before allowing the hose to run into the hole slowly. This will eliminate air pockets. Don't mash down the soil with your feet!

Finish the backfill, once again watering slowly. Complete the planting process with a mulch of pole peelings, gravel, or dried grass clippings. The mulch will keep the soil at an even temperature, hold the moisture deeply and prevent crusting and cracking.

■ *Don't mash down the soil with your feet!*

You probably won't need to water again for two weeks. Use a long screwdriver to plunge into the soil within the planting hole. If it shoves in easily, no need to water.

Planting a Container-Grown Tree or Shrub

If you are planting a container-grown tree or shrub, the hole is dug and backfill soil mixed as described above, except that there is no need to build a hill within the planting hole. Small baskets or plastic pots must be removed before planting. Cut all wires, ropes, wood, and plastic at the top of the root ball of large trees after you have positioned the root ball in the planting hole. Before the backfill begins, remove all the wires, ropes, and plastic wrap from the top HALF of the root ball. Cut all remaining wires so that they are no longer holding the root ball. Burlap is cut and as much as possible removed after the plant is positioned in the planting hole. Examine the roots of all container grown plants before the backfill begins. If they are visible and encircling the root ball, the plant is root bound. Use a sharp knife to score or nick the roots vertically. This will "break the habit", so to speak, of the roots encirclement. They will then form new root hairs at the point of the knife nick.

Backfill quickly, for exposed roots, especially of evergreens, dry out fast. The mulch over the soil surface is especially important for evergreens.

Setting Stakes and Guy Wires

If you live in a windy area, you may wish to guy or stake trees or tall shrubs for one season. Set the stakes or guy wires as illustrated, keeping guy ropes loose enough so that the tree will be allowed to sway a little. This has proved to be beneficial to root development. Remove the stakes, wire or ropes at the beginning of the second season. The tree will be weak and dependent on the support if it is left longer.

Balled and burlapped evergreen is positioned properly.

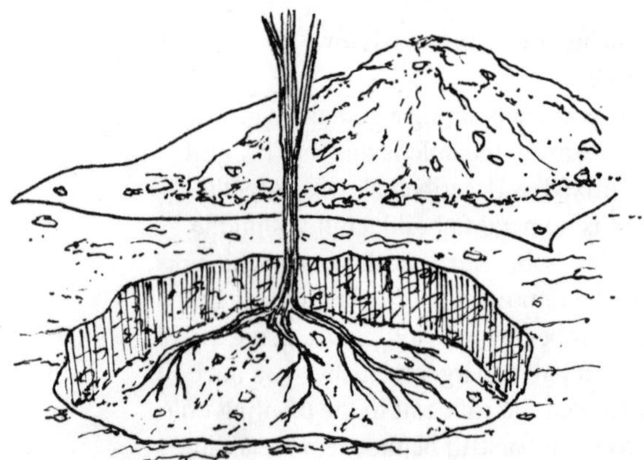

Roots are spread over planting hill. Trunk level is noted by dark line that shows the depth it grew in the nursery.

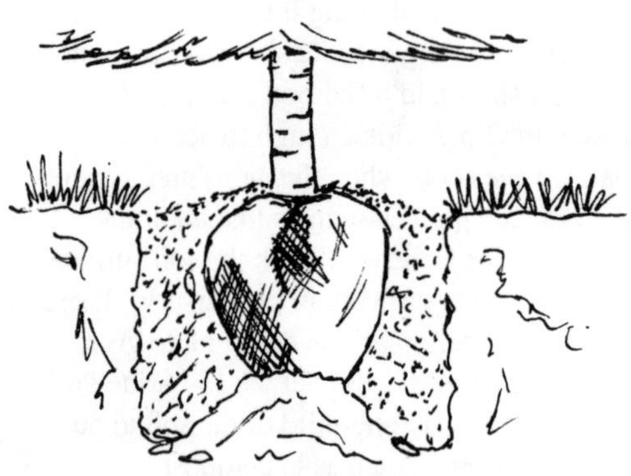

Sculpted pedestal for proper planting if planting site is in clay soil. Hole is straight-sided.

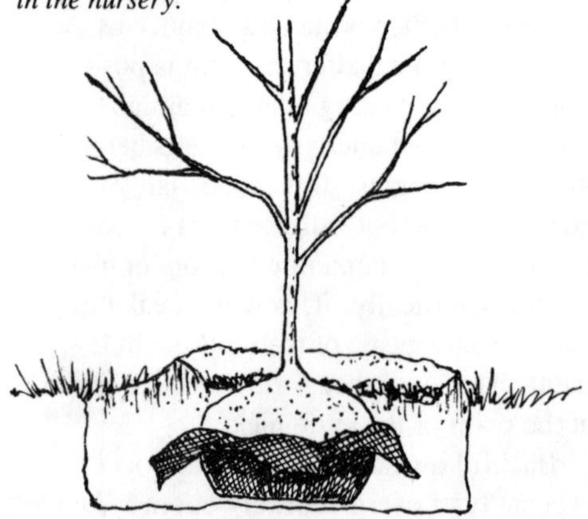

Large container-grown plants have ropes, wires and baskets removed from the top half of the root ball.

Butterfly the roots of a shrub grown in artificial media.

Stake a tree in a windy area.

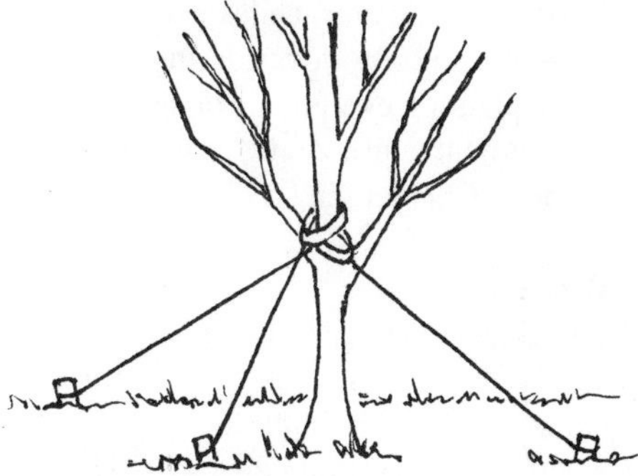

Guy a tree that will be buffeted with changing wind directions.

The Exceptions

When heavy clay soil is encountered in digging the planting hole, and when soil preparation has not been complete over the entire property as described in Chapter 4, a sculpted mound is left inside the hole, rather than removing all of the soil. This hard-packed mound serves as a pedestal to rest the soil ball of a container-grown plant so that the weight of the ball will not allow it to settle below the soil surface where water will collect. More trees die from overwatering than underwatering. Clay soil holds large amounts of water. If the soil ball stands securely atop the sculpted mound, danger of overwatering is minimal.

Shipping cost increases have forced nurseries in the areas where grower nurseries are located (Texas, California, etc.) to find light-weight growing media, such as vermiculite or sawdust. When you purchase a container-grown tree or shrub, lift the plant out of the pot to examine the roots and the media in which it is growing. You may find a solid mat of roots in an unfamiliar media. These plants are planted with a technique known as "butterfly." After the planting hole has been dug and backfill prepared, lay the plant on its side, slice through the rootball vertically by two-thirds, using a sharp knife with a serrated edge. Spread the two halves of the rootball to straddle the planting hill within the planting hole. See illustration. Push it down firmly while backfilling around it. Fill the hole halfway before settling the soil with water in a gentle stream. Finish the backfill and water again. Mulch with the material of your choice. Planted in this manner, the plant will immediately put out new roots where the cut was made, venturing into new soil instead of continuing to wind around.

Pruning After Planting

■ *Pruning to match tops with supposed root loss is now an obsolete practice.*

Pruning to match tops with supposed root loss is now an obsolete practice. We cut out only weak, spindly branches and those that are crossing another branch. We are also careful not to "limb up" a tree by removing lower branches so that walking underneath would be permitted. The lower limbs aid in increasing the diameter of the trunk.

A tree that is not 'limbed up' will have increased girth.

Providing Drainage For Pines

Pines are not tolerant of "wet feet" (standing water around the roots). They cannot withstand overwatering for long and will soon succumb. If you have a pine located in an area where water may drain near the roots, see "Plant Protection" for flooding.

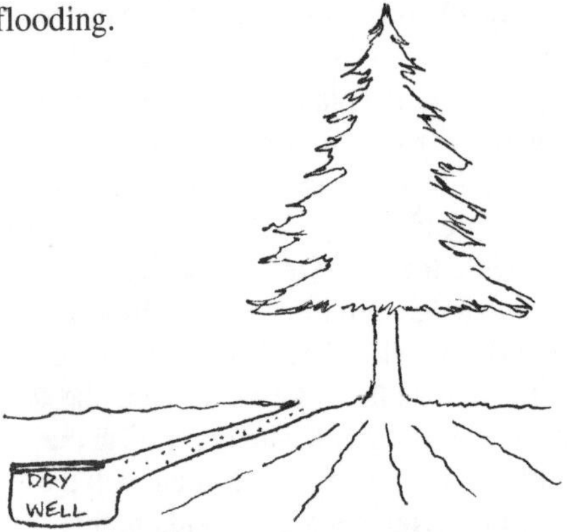

Trenches lead excess water away from the roots of a pine.

Guidelines for Fall Planting of Trees and Shrubs

If you are willing to take the risk of fall planting[1], there are bargain prices as an incentive. Keep in mind that the plants you buy have been growing all summer at the nursery and may be root-bound. See previous section for directions in planting root-bound stock.

Plant in August, if you have the opportunity. Roots will have time to become established before soils cool to the point that root growth stops - about the first of October in a zones 4 and 5. In Zone 3, it will occur when your soil thermometer reads forty-five degrees.

To give the fall-planted tree or shrub the best chance, follow all the planting directions above, but mulch more heavily - to a depth of six inches. This will postpone the freezing of the soil and allow more time for root establishment. Water well just prior to the freezing of the soil in your area - usually about Thanksgiving time, and water monthly when there is no snow cover during winter. If you are planting evergreens or small shrubs, follow the directions for winter protection in Chapter 7.

Fertilization

No fertilizer is added to the planting hole or to the backfill. Nor is the plant fertilized at any time during the first three years. After three years, examine the tree or shrub closely. If it has not made the amount of growth characteristic with its species, it can be fertilized with a 10-10-10 formula at a rate of one-fourth pound for each inch of girth measured at the height of your shoulder. For shrubs, one-fourth pound for each is sufficient. Scatter the fertilizer on the soil within the root run of the tree or shrub. No need to dig it in. Apply water until the fertilizer granules are dissolved and no longer visible. Additional fertilization should not be needed. Stimulating a plant unnecessarily only leads to a soft, watery, wand-like growth that is unnatural and unhealthy which will lead to susceptibility to disease , insects, and breakage. Organic mulches break down slowly to give woody plants needed nutrients without use of chemical fertilizers.

[1] Research of Dr. Bert T. Swanson, Jr., Associate Professor, Dept. of Horticulture, Colorado State Univ., conducted from 1971 until 1975. Published August 1975 in Progress Report. Research of Dr. Phillip Carpenter, professor of landscape horticulture at Purdue Univ., "Is Fall for Planting", September, 1987, Horticulture magazine.

Transplanting a Large Tree

Some subdivisions and business parks have a restrictive covenant that requires that large size trees and shrubs be planted. In other situations, a homeowner buys a large tree because he knows he won't be living in the home for more than a few years and he doesn't want to wait for a tree to grow to maturity.

TIMING

Early spring almost always assures success in transplanting a large tree because soils are cool and the tree does not have to expend energy in supporting leaves. Energy is concentrated on restoring root growth. Summer is the worst possible time for large tree transplanting. In the Mountain West we enjoy the lack of humidity in summer, but for a large transplanted tree, hot, dry air makes recovery from transplanting shock very difficult.

EQUIPMENT

Tree spades are large mechanized scoops that dig a cone-shaped hole; then dig the same size root ball around the tree to be transplanted. The tree with its root is then carefully transferred to the hole. Results are mixed and controversial. There is evidence that a large backhoe is equally useful in digging the hole and digging the tree. Regardless of which machine is used, take precautions to make sure the tree's branches and trunk are protected during transport. The sides of the hole should be fractured with an iron bar to break up soil of the slick sides. In addition, mix a slurry of water and sphagnum peatmoss to add to the hole. As the tree is lowered into the hole, the slurry sloshes up the sides of the hole to become a buffer to the cut roots within the root ball. The new root hairs that form can push into the moist peatmoss easier than into the hard, slick clay. As they enlarge, they will thrust into the clay.

After completing the backfill, water the newly planted tree slowly with a deep-root watering device to force out air pockets. No fertilizer is necessary. Staking is needed for a year. See staking directions above.

Large evergreen trees or shrubs are transplanted in the same manner described above. Junipers of any species are high risk subjects for transplanting.

■ *Early spring almost always assures success in transplanting a large tree. . .*

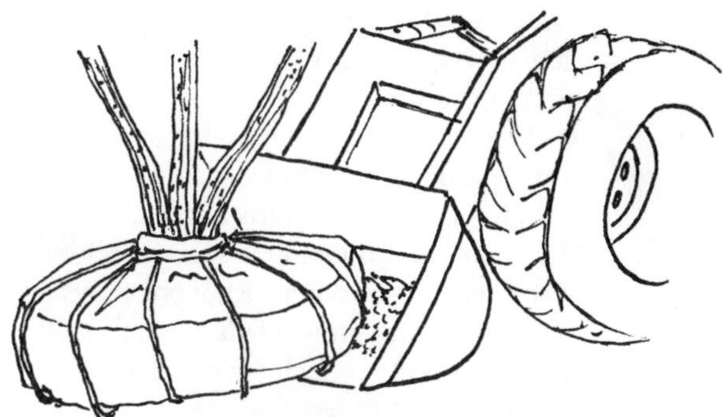

Transplanting a large tree is a job for a professional - with your supervision.

Transplanting a Large Deciduous Shrub

Even when transplanted in very early spring, a large shrub, such as a lilac, will likely go into an irreversible shock. Cutting the large shrub back all the way to three-inch stubs is a shocker, but it is a successful technique. This method also eliminates the gargantuan task of digging and removing a large shrub.together with its root ball. In early spring before leaves unfurl the shrub, once topgrowth is removed, can be lifted (using the cut stubs as handles) and soil shaken from the roots. It is then planted by the method described for bare-root planting in its new location. The root quickly re-establishes an sends up a forest of new shoots. Be ready with pruning shears to select three or four of these shoots to become the framework for new topgrowth, eliminating all others. Large shrubs transplanted in this manner will often bloom the second year.

Moving the Difficult Shrubs

Moving a large deciduous shrub, such as a boxwood, oakleaf hydrangea, bridalwreath spirea, or a broadleaf evergreen rhododendron - if you should be so fortunate as to possess a large rhododendron in the Mountain West - is a risk that can be tempered by taking two or three seasons to accomplish the task.

Early fall transplanting is the best season for these difficult-to-move plants. This means late August or early September. Begin by root pruning two seasons before the contemplated move. Root prune by sinking a trench around half the roots . Dig the trench wide enough for your feet to fit comfortably, and deep enough so that you encounter no more roots. When a root is encountered, cut it cleanly with a sharp shovel or with loppers. A chewed root that you have tried to sever with a dull spade will never recover, and can become a point of disease entry. After the trench is completed, fill it with the soil dug from it; water well and keep it watered well during winter. The following season, root prune the other half and fill the trench once again. At the third digging, dig the entire root ball. New roots will have formed within the trench boundaries so that encasing the ball in burlap is not too difficult. Rope the ball securely for its move to the planting hole. Prepare the planting hole as described above. Slide the rootball on a child's sled, a heavy tarp, or a makeshift slide that will involve as little lifting as possible. Invite as many friends over as you can muster to aid with the project. Promising similar aid in return is a good ploy. Rolling the bound rootball from sled to its new location is a possibility, and far easier on both you and the plant than dragging. Your planting hole should be straight-sided and flat-bottomed, and no deeper than the rootball you have fashioned. As you ease the plant into the hole, position it so that it faces the same direction it faced previously. Remove the burlap by peeling it down on one side; then backfill quickly with enough soil to hold the shrub in place. Rock it over enough so that the burlap can be pulled from underneath. Backfill with the soil dug from the hole, mixed one-third by volume with good quality sphagnum peatmoss. Water well, leaving a small dike around the plant to hold water. Do not water again until a small depression is finger-tested for moisture. More newly transplanted plants are killed by overwatering than underwatering.

Take three seasons to prepare a difficult-to-transplant shrub ready for the move. Root prune one-half during two growing season; transplant in the third spring.

Planting Herbaceous Perennials

Contrary to directions for woody plants, many herbaceous perennials are benefited if planted in the fall. Cool weather gives their roots extra stimulus, and they are ready to bloom the following spring.

Almost without exception, the fall-blooming perennials are best planted or transplanted in early spring. The spring-blooming perennials are transplanted in early fall.

Use the same techniques described for bare-root planting of woody plants, cutting back all topgrowth if planting in the fall. Don't be alarmed if new growth starts immediately, only to be toppled by the first frost. Mulch the flower border well with evergreen boughs after the soil freezes.

Planting Bearded Iris, Oriental Poppies, and Peonies

German or Bearded Iris (*Iris x germanica*) are planted or transplanted just after their bloom period in June. Dig a wide, shallow hole and set the rhizomes on small mounds of soil within the hole so that their roots are on either side of the mound and the fan of foliage is toward the outside of the hole. Fill in just to cover the rhizomes.

Cut the fan of foliage to three or four inches. Water gently so as not to disturb but to soak well the mounds of soil under the rhizomes.

If you are transplanting iris, dig the entire clump and set aside on a tarp. Use two spading forks to pry the clump apart in the center; then work with fingers to snap off the rhizomes separately. Discard the woody rhizomes in the center that have no attachment to a fan of foliage, for they will not bloom again.

If these iris are to be grown in the perennial border, they will get more than their liking of water; therefore, cover only the roots and not the rhizomes as they sit on the mound of soil. The uncovered rhizomes will become bronzy in color, but the clump will be healthy.

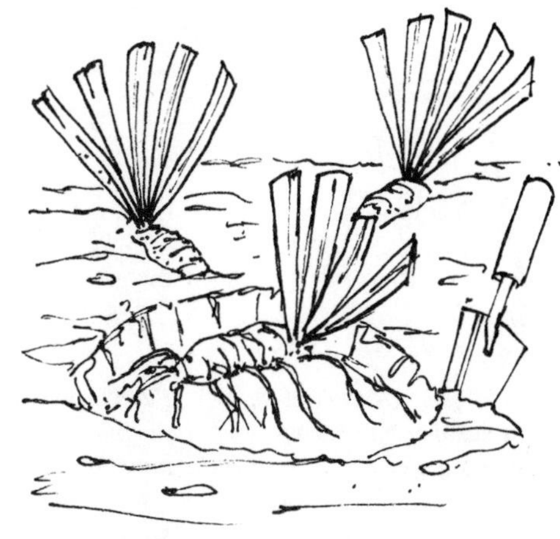

Planting German iris in July is the simplest of all transplanting procedures.

The delicate Oriental Poppies (*Papaver orientale*) are part of perennial borders everywhere, but their planting and transplanting is a procedure that is somewhat difficult. The foliage of poppy dies down in midsummer to an unsightly brown, which is why it is often planted near a daylily which will have enough overhanging, strappy leaves to hide the poppy as it goes dormant. The plant will begin to make new foliage in early September. At this time lift the entire clump carefully and tease out the individual plantlets from the clump. They are very brittle. Set three to five plantlets into the new planting hole vertically as deep as they were growing previously. Gently backfill and mark with a stake.

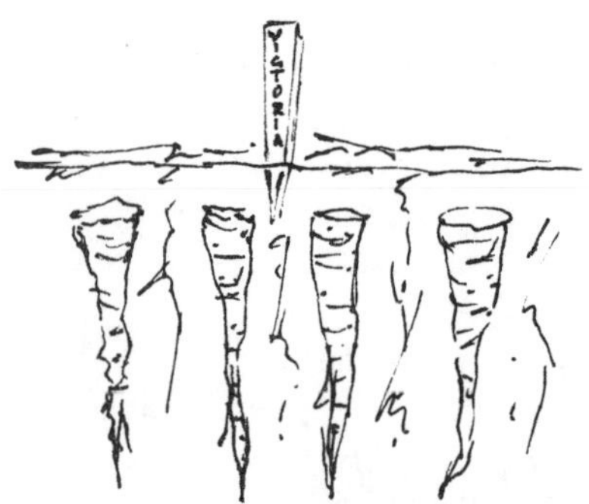

Brittle roots makes dividing and transplanting Oriental poppies in late summer an onerous task. Each broken root usually grows.

Peony root is supported while backfilling soil in the planting hole so that topmost node will be only one inch below the finished grade.

The roots of Peony (*Paeonia lactiflora*) are planted in September. They are long and woody with small pink nodes on each side that are called "eyes." Prepare a deep planting hole with a backfill of at least one-third organic matter, such as weathered manure, compost or sphagnum peatmoss. Hold the peony roots in place with one hand while backfilling with the other so that the topmost "eye" will be at least one inch but not more than two inches below the soil surface. This is an exacting procedure that seems out of character for the big sturdy plants that have survived in abandoned farmsteads for a century, but if the topmost eyes are too deep, the plant may not bloom for years or not at all. Water carefully after half the backfill is in place to force out air pockets and to prevent too much settling, for at this point you can pull it up a little if it has settled beyond the one-inch/two-inch rule. Complete the backfill and water again. The best support for stems is a circle of chicken wire laid over the top of the plants just as the shoots are emerging in spring.

Planting Annual Flowers

DIRECT SEEDING

There are groups of annuals that resent transplanting, no matter how carefully done. The gardener is apprehensive about planting seeds directly in the soil for fear that lack of time or inclination will spell sure doom. While this prediction may come true, try direct seeding for a few sure-fire species, and you may come around to this method for many others.

Soil preparation must be complete. Digging a trench in hard-packed soil and scattering seeds is a waste of time. Turn the soil over in the area and mix with compost, peatmoss or weathered manure, and smooth it so that no soil particle is larger than a pea. Read the package directions very carefully about how deep the seed should be planted. Use a hoe or spade to open trenches slightly deeper than the depth the seed is to be planted. Scatter the seeds thinly, for sowing too thickly means a risk of non-germination because of over-crowding and a thinning job later on. Cover the seeds the recommended depth and firm the soil with the back of your hoe. Sprinkle with a gentle stream of water until soil is thoroughly soaked; then mulch with dried grass clippings or straw. Never allow the soil to dry completely after sowing. Check on it daily. Usually ten or more days pass before germination is complete. Thin the seedlings after they have their first pair of true leaves* to the distance apart recommended on the seed packet. The following is a list of annuals that grow best if seeds are planted where the plants are to grow. Try one of these each year and you'll become a fan of direct seeding. See ANNUALS, FILLERS FOR FOCUS OF COLOR for further directions on direct seeding of annuals.

Annuals That Resent Transplanting

Alcea rosea	HOLLYHOCK
Clarkia spp.	SATIN FLOWER
Cleome spinosa	SPIDER FLOWER
Convolvulus spp.	MORNING GLORY
Cosmos spp.	COSMOS
Ipoemea spp.	MORNING GLORY
Lathyrus odoratus	SWEET PEA
Layia elegans	TIDY TIPS
Lobularia maritima	SWEET ALYSSUM
Mirabilis jalapa	FOUR O'CLOCK
Nemophila spp.	BABY BLUE EYES
Papaver spp.	POPPY
Phacelia campanularia	CALIFORNIA BLUEBELL
Salpiglossis sinuata	PAINTED TONGUE
Trachymene caerulea	BLUE LACE FLOWER
Tropaeolum spp.	NASTURTIUM

Planting Container-Grown Annuals

The six-pack of annuals is found in every supermarket and nursery in spring each year. Thousands are planted successfully, but there are tips that will insure better topgrowth and blooms.

Most often the roots have greatly overgrown the miniscule space given them in the six-pack. Use the "butterfly" method described above in planting container-grown shrubs. It works equally well for root-bound annuals. Mulch the annual bed with compost or dried grass clippings to keep the soil evenly moist and prevent shock.

* *See Glossary*

CHAPTER 7

Plant Protection

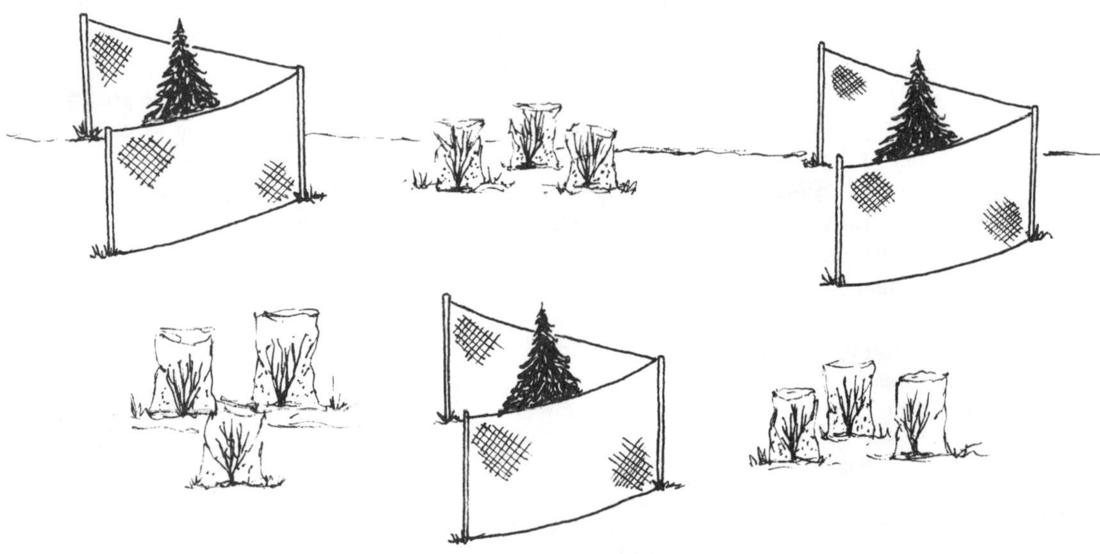

The vagaries of weather are probably no worse in the Mountain West than in any other area. To a gardener it may seem that we are *put upon* more often than is our share when weather becomes the judge, jury, and executioner of our efforts. If we take stock of our assets, we find that number one is the unmatched quality of sunlight. Our higher altitude gives us a closer vantage point to Ole Sol, thus giving unheard of brilliance to flower colors as well as the ability to get good plant growth with less sun than would be required in the east or on the west coast. Fewer cloud layers in the Mountain West have been noted since explorers first came. Though Montana and New Mexico carry off the honors for the brightest of blue skies, all skies in the Mountain West enjoy this wondrous phenomenon. As we examine all the weather factors and the methods to protect plants against them, watch for the "silver lining." Only vandalism and hail have no redeeming features. If only a way could be found to pit one against the other! In alphabetical order so as not to show preference, let's look at the weather bug-a-boos of gardening:

Flood

The word "flood" conjures up thoughts of trenches and dikes, perhaps sandbags. All of these are appropriate, but *flood prevention* is like the disaster prevention departments of government - unpopular. We are uncomfortable with a feeling of foreboding, but, as gardeners, we should deal with it and be done with it. Excess precipitation is, in some areas, an annual occurrence and in other areas, an unheard of happening. In the Mountain West we prepare for flood by heading for high ground or making "high ground" within the boundaries of our own property.

TREES AND SHRUBS

Only a few native trees and shrubs can withstand root inundation for longer than twelve hours. The cottonwoods and willows and spruce trees that line our stream banks are adapted to withstanding long periods of root inundation because the water in which they are growing is moving and it carries oxygen. Standing, stagnant water over the roots of these natives will kill them just as quickly as it will the delicate exotic plant in your garden.

If yours is an area that is flooded regularly, begin with a plan to manufacture high ground. Construct raised beds. They don't have to be inordinately high. Six inches is adequate to drain water away quickly in the sudden flood of a summer storm. Border the raised beds in which trees and shrubs are planted with stone, landscape timbers or railroad ties. A word of caution: Don't even consider building raised beds around trees and shrubs already growing on your property. The sudden weight of added soil will smother the roots and they will quickly die. Instead, install permanent trenches filled with gravel to drain away unwanted water. They may seem unsightly at first, but they will spell the difference for the health or death of your landscape.

If you are faced with an occasional flood, when flood waters begin to invade your property, it's time to don the rubber boots to sally forth to do battle. Quickly dig shallow trenches that will lead water away from the root run of trees and shrubs. A few shovels-full of soil to make a dike will often divert enough water to prevent soil from being saturated. It's better to dig into turf to furnish sod squares for dikes than to allow the flooding. The turf is easily replaced. The trees and shrubs will quietly die.

■ *. . . it's time to don the rubber boots to sally forth to do battle.*

EROSION CONTROL AND CHECK DAMS

If you live in a hilly area and flood water is coming toward your property, look closely for signs of little rivulets that have occurred previously. In these areas make check dams by placing a shovelful of soil *across* the rivulet. Use small stones to pack against the sides of your little dam. Children, who love to play in the water anyway, will be fascinated if given this task. Keep on hand bundles of fagots or twiggy cut brush in an out-of-the-way place to use as erosion control when the flood is in progress. Push the twiggy branches into the rivulets with the twigs on the uphill aspect. They will catch soil and debris to further slow down the water flow.

Erosion control using twiggy branches and check dams.

FRUIT TREES

The cherry trees are the most vulnerable to flooding. They will wilt and die within eight hours of flooding. Plum trees are only a little more able to withstand a flood. Apple, peach, and pear should be trenched, but haste is not as imperative. Of the small fruits, elder, raspberry, currant, and gooseberry are tolerant of flooding, but strawberries and grapes are not. As you are likely to be working in a downpour, use this information as a priority list.

GRASS

Buffalo grass can withstand several days of inundation - a point to remember when planning a landscape in an area of regular flooding. All of the other turf grasses are vulnerable to flooding as well as intolerant of the covering of silt that washes over them. If yours is a lawn with a slight slope, trench it quickly to drain to a lower area. If yours is a lawn that is almost flat, begin with a shallow trench, deepening it gradually till it empties into a quickly-dug well about two feet deep and two feet wide.

VEGETABLES

Many gardeners grow vegetables in raised beds, but their beds may not be edged in weather-proof material. Soil will quickly erode and wash away. Invest in some landscape timbers to edge your beds. Line the valleys created by your raised beds with 20 mil plastic sheets topped with straw or dried grass clippings. These paths will become fast-moving water courses during the flood, but the excess water will not harm the roots of your vegetables.

WATER GARDEN

It is important to trench flood water so that it does not enter your lily pool. If your property is flooded regularly, consider a lily pool constructed above ground with a seat-cap around the top edge. If your pool is at a low spot on your property, water will run toward it with great speed. Have in mind a plan where trenches should be dug to divert the flood water, for if it drains into your pool, fish will almost certainly succumb to the silt-laden invasion. Water lilies will be harmed as well if silt covers the crowns of the plants.

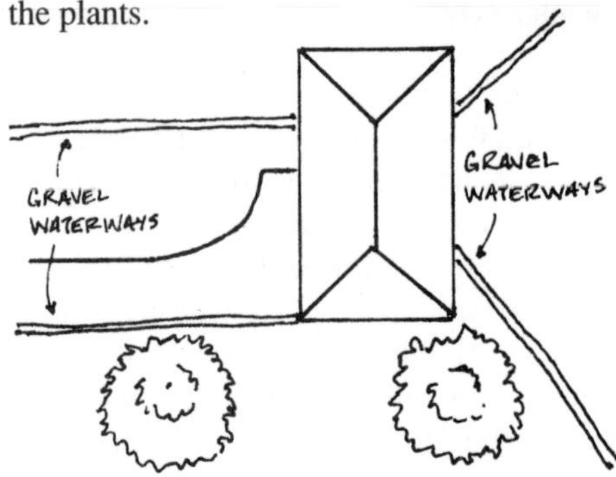

Trenches filled with gravel across your property will permanently discharge flood waters without damage.

Raised beds for vegetables will protect from floods. Pathways become temporary waterways.

AFTER THE FLOOD

When the weather event is over, the first thing that comes to mind is to get out there to survey the damage. Good idea, but don't dare even step one foot on the soil. Compaction is the biggest danger now. Soil texture can be destroyed forever by the compacting of your footsteps. Use two or more lengths of one-by-six lumber to make a movable path. Take up a length and lay it down ahead of you as you move along. Carry with you as you walk a crowbar or length of rebar. Push the bar into the soil at intervals within the root run of trees, shrubs, and flowers. These holes may look insignificant but will release moisture to be evaporated and allow much needed oxygen to enter the holes.

To rid the lawn of a silt layer, it would seem that adding more water is an insult, but that's what has to be done. Use the hose to swoosh the silt away as quickly as possible. If you have a helper and own a squeegee, the helper can squeegee the silt away as water from the hose is applied.

Flower and vegetable foliage flattened by a flood will dry quickly if lifted and propped against a quickly placed twig. The soil stuck to leaves will drop away when dry. Your objective is to open the stoma on the undersides of leaves quickly so that normal respiration of the leaves can return.

Soil structure is harmed by heavy downpour and saturation, causing the finer particles of soil to float to the top so that, after the sun comes out and drying begins, the surface is baked, crusted, and then cracked. Use a scuffle hoe, drawn lightly over the surface of the soil, to break up the crust. This operation only takes a few minutes, but will spell the difference between success and failure of plants to thrive after a flood.

Dealing With Drainage From a Neighboring Property

The cause of the gradual demise of a favorite plant can often be traced to the sneaky invasion of water coming from the middle-of-the-night sprinkler system of a neighbor. If no amount of complaint or cajolery brings results, defend yourself with an installation of perforated pipe. Perforated plastic pipe is available in various diameters. It has small holes along one side. Dig a shallow trench along the length of your property adjoining the offending neighbor and make the trench of increasing depth so that it will drain harmlessly into the gutter at the street or into a barrow pit if yours is a country property. Lay the perforated pipe with the holes upward. Cover the trench and pipe with clean gravel. Put a cap on the top end of the pipe so that you can uncap it to flush out silt with a strong stream of water from the hose once a year.

■ *Soil structure is harmed by heavy downpour and saturation. . .*

Frost

A gardener is always keeping "a weather eye" out for late spring and early fall frosts. Clear skies at evening are dreaded signs that earth's heat will rise into the atmosphere and the temperature drop just before sunrise will be low enough to end the tender growth of spring or the growing season in fall.

TREES AND SHRUBS

Insulation with old bedspreads and blankets is hardly possible for our large trees and shrubs. We rely, instead, upon water and wind. The energy expended in the freezing of water is often enough to protect the new growth on a tree or the bloom of a fruit tree in spring. Turning the sprinkler hose on trees and shrubs is hazardous, for ice is heavy and can quickly destroy what it is protecting. Usually the frost danger is over as the air warms after sunrise and the ice melts away.

FRUIT TREES

Frost damage to fruit trees is stealthy and long-lasting. A flower bud may survive frost, but as the developing fruit gains in weight, it may drop because the stem was too weakened by frost to hold it.

The permanently installed framework of PVC pipe is a multi-purpose thwart to weather. The framework, installed at planting time around dwarf fruit trees is draped with floating row cover (tied down at corners) as a protection against frost in spring and fall, and against insect invasion in summer. In winter it can be draped with heavy plastic and packed inside with excelsior to protect against extreme cold and heavy snow. The latter has not proved to be an infallible method in Canada, but newer materials will appear on the market.

Armies of smudge pots once lined the orchards of Western Colorado and Southern Utah in early spring. Smog from burning tires blanketed the valleys. Wind machines are more prevalent now, but the insurance policy against frost is the only sure defense against crop loss for the commercial grower. For a single backyard tree, the smudge pot is still available, and the box fan may stir the air enough to push cold air from around the tree, for cold air sinks; warm air rises.

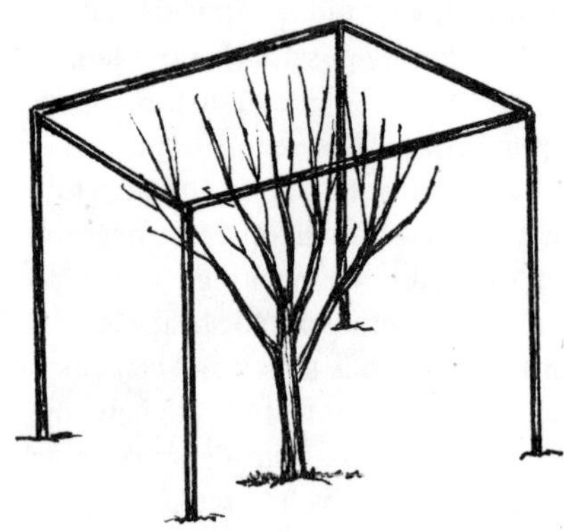

PVC pipe makes a framework for multi-purpose protection for dwarf fruit trees.

■ *Avoid early fertilization of roses.*

USING A BOX FAN

Moving air is also a protection for frost, but you do not summon the wind unless you own a wind machine. An ordinary box fan that you use in the house in the summer can be placed outdoors the night before the expected frost; then turned on just before dawn. It will keep air moving enough to prevent frost damage to coveted plants. Planting your tree and shrub border with enough thought to air drainage will give you protection from frost in spring and fall as well as prevent fungal diseases such as powdery mildew. Density in the form of twigginess is usually a virtue for the sake of privacy, but give a thought to air drainage as well. Open spaces in the foliage will allow air to drain through enough to prevent light frost.

ROSES

The rose garden in spring is especially vulnerable to frost, for if canes are green and foliage beginning to unfurl, permanent damage can occur. A cache of cardboard boxes, blankets and old bedspreads will always be part of a gardeners tools, but they are being replaced sometimes by light-weight spun-bonded materials called "floating row cover." This material is sold in lengths sufficient to cover a hybrid tea, floribunda, or grandiflora rose.

Avoid early fertilization of roses. The weak cane attachment that results from early or over-fertilization is especially vulnerable to low temperatures. The floating row cover can be counted upon to keep a protected plant seven to ten degrees above the temperature outside the cover. If, however, the temperature drop is accompanied by heavy snow, the old cardboard box is still the answer.

VEGETABLES

The cold-hardy vegetables, such as parsnips, Brussels sprouts, cabbage, broccoli, and cauliflower are improved in flavor by a light fall frost. Even pumpkins and squash are not harmed by it, though their vines are quickly blackened. The use of the sprinkler on a cold spring or fall dawn is a high risk in the vegetable garden, and many gardeners resort to the bed-spread-box routine.

The bedspread-box routine is a common defense against frost in the vegetable garden.

If Number 9 wire or plastic irrigation pipe is placed as a half circle over the vegetable rows, it will serve as a frame to hold the floating row cover against frost in spring and fall. Nylon or wire poultry netting can be substituted in summer to prevent damage from birds, vandals, animals and hail. Winter will see the frame doing duty again to hold heavy plastic sheets to keep out the cold.

Hoops of plastic pipe or wire are ready to hold spun-bonded cover for protection from cold, heat, insects; poultry netting for protection from hail.

Hail

Hail is the most dreaded weather event for a gardener. It comes with almost no warning, and the sight of shredded torn plants is devastating to the new gardener.

TREES AND SHRUBS

The experienced gardener knows that after a hail storm a quick survey of the most badly damaged is in order. Don't bother with the piles of shredded leaves on the ground yet. Look, instead, for scarred limbs and twigs that are left hanging. Cut these off cleanly. Cut back behind a badly scarred limb, for this is the potential entry point of insects and disease.

FRUIT TREES

Pick hail-damaged fruit and discard it, or if it is far enough along toward ripening, chop and dry it for winter bird food. Hail-damaged fruit almost always drops or, if it remains on the tree, is the target for insects or disease. Damaged plants are always more vulnerable.

■ *Hail-damaged fruit almost always drops. . .*

WATER GARDEN

Lily pads are punctured quickly by hail and will not recover. Wait, however, until they begin to turn yellow; then cut them off at the soil line in the planting buckets. Fertilize each plant and new pads will appear soon.

VEGETABLES

Many new gardeners walk away from a hail-damaged plot. Experienced gardeners know the potential of those plants to recover. Flattened foliage should be lifted and rinsed off with the hose, taking care not to compact soil if hard rain has accompanied the hail storm. Onion foliage should be left to recover, no matter how bad it looks. Corn leaves will also recover, even though split in several parts. When only stubs are left of the entire garden, assess the potential against how much growing season is left. With only six weeks till frost, for example, corn won't have time to recover and produce. With nine weeks, however, there is a good chance. Remember the roots are still undamaged and ready to grow! Till up the rows that won't have enough time to grow and produce. Plant them to quick producers, such as turnips, radishes, scallions, lettuce, spinach, or snap peas.

If you live along the Front Range of Colorado, you live in Hail Alley. This area is world famous for the frequency of hail storms. Weather scientists come from all over the world to study the phenomena. Use the wire or irrigation pipe hoops described previously to permanently support poultry netting with close interstices. It's easy to toss aside while tending the plants or harvesting. Most of the hail will hit the wire and be sliced into harmless pieces. A few hail pellets will fall through an interstice cleanly to damage the plant below, but it's the price we pay for the risk we take as gardeners.

Heat

We are lucky in this department. Searing heat is experienced only in the low-altitude portions of the Mountain West. There are some procedures for minimizing damage:

TREES AND SHRUBS

The trees and shrubs that have been watered deeply are not harmed by a hot spell. The greatest danger is to those mature trees that are surrounded by turfgrass. The shallow, frequent watering to keep the grass green does not soak deeply enough to benefit the trees and shrubs. Their root systems gradually die away. With a diminished root system that cannot pump water fast enough to support foliage during a dry, hot spell, the plant flags and dies quickly. The gardener usually suspects a disease, but, instead, it is a cultural error.

Growing trees and shrubs in islands in the turf or in tree-and-shrub borders will avoid the drought problems at root depth. Use a deep-root watering device to water a tree or shrub located as a specimen in the lawn.

TURFGRASS

Deep watering is needed to prevent damage to turf during a hot spell, but application should be at night or in early morning to avoid evaporation and wasting water. The old wives tale that night-watered grass will succumb to disease is not true. If it were, golf courses and municipal parks would not exist. Standing with a hand-held hose used to be thought of as only an exercise in cooling yourself on a hot evening, but now this method is recommended for those small dry spots that may need more water. First, however, sink a spading fork into these spots at intervals to relieve the compaction to make the soil accept more water.

FLOWERS AND VEGETABLES

Misting with the hose during the heat of the day will prevent wilting and damage to such drought-prone plants as lettuce, tuberous begonias, caladiums, ferns, and bog plants.

Seedlings will live through a heat wave if a polymer gel* has been mixed with the soil. It allows the seedling roots to draw on the water supply held by the gel as needed. They don't have to wait for you to notice their distress.

Ice

Preplanning will prevent ice damage. Haven't you seen a shrub that has been planted directly under the eave of a home

** See Glossary*

that is damaged when ice tumbles off the roof? Keep in mind that you can channel snow and water accumulation that freezes into a solid mass on your roof by structural changes in the house, such as increasing the size of the gutter in areas of accumulation.

TREES AND SHRUBS

The Mountain West is not subject to ice storms such as those that occur in the East and South. The occasional storm of heavy wet snow that turns to ice is a danger to all trees and shrubs. In early fall cut six-inch wide bands of nylon netting - the kind used for bird protection of fruit trees - into lengths that can be wound around an evergreen native juniper*, Arbovitae, and other upright-growing plants. The netting is almost invisible and will hold the wand-like branches close to the trunk so that ice will not harm it, nor will heavy snow accumulate to spread the branches into a permanent unnatural shape.

Pruning offers the greatest protection against breakage. Prune in early spring so that limbs are not directly above one another. Snow will fall harmlessly to the ground through the limbs to the ground, rather than alighting on them. This practice is especially essential in the high altitudes of the Mountain West where deciduous trees of any age are seldom seen because of ice and heavy snow damage. Select species that can withstand the climate. See Chapter 20 "Mountain Homes" for species to select.

Building structures over tender plants is standard procedure in New England, Minnesota, and Wisconsin. The eyebolt makes it easy to take these structures apart for storage in summer.

VEGETABLES

When snow accumulation turns to ice and storms are following storms in March, the month of heaviest snow accumulation, we look to the wire or plastic pipe hoops over vegetable rows to prevent damage. If heavy 20 mil clear plastic sheets are draped and secured over the hoops in early December, the slick surface allows the crystallized snow to slide off. The warmth created by the plastic in March will bring rhubarb and asparagus to life.

Lightning

Nothing is more heart-wrenching than to lose a tree to lightning. If one or more of your trees are the tallest thing on the horizon in your neighborhood, they are prime targets for a lightning strike. Once again, your insurance agent is your first ally because the damage caused can be real and devastating. The second ally is prevention! Call a qualified expert to install lightning rods in the target trees. This is not as expensive a process as one might think, and in no way disfigures the tree.

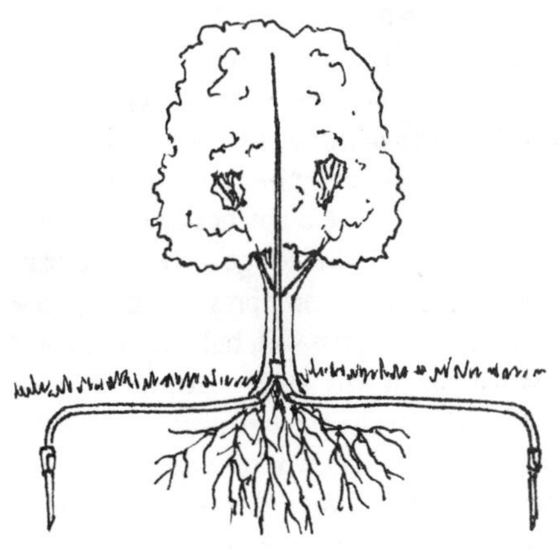

Lightning rods installed in a target tree are not disfiguring.

** See Glossary*

Vandalism

Because vandalism is seated in mental anguish, it is difficult to plan ahead for the attack. We do know that the larger caliper trunk size of newly planted trees are less likely to be vandalized than the slender sapling. Peeling of bark so as to girdle a tree is a common vandal act. When the girdle is complete, it is possible to bridge-graft. Your Cooperative Extension office has pamphlets giving direction for bridge-grafting. Trees wrapped for winter protection may afford some protection against vandalism.

Chemicals, either sprayed or dumped, on your property are a possible vandal's attack. If you see spray drift of an unknown material approaching your property, protect yourself first. Make a decision as to whether you want to venture outdoors to do battle. If you do, put on long pants, shirt and jacket with long sleeves, hat, goggles, and a face mask. These masks cost less than one dollar and everyone should have one on hand. Then make haste (after calling the authorities) to spread plastic sheets over exposed soil surfaces. Most people won't have sufficient plastic sheets on hand to cover their entire property. Have your priorities in mind. Cover the most expensive plants and most difficult to replace. Then place a power nozzle on the hose and hose down foliage as best you can. The plastic sheets won't prevent all the run-off from entering the soil, but will dilute it to the point that it will be less harmful.

If you arrive home and suspect from the odor and from the sight of wilting foliage that herbicide or other harmful chemicals have been sprayed or dumped on your property, your only recourse may be to replant. If your neighbor poured soil sterilant on his property. near your boundary, there is definite danger that the chemical will travel through the soil to affect your trees, shrubs, flowers, vegetables, turf, etc. As quickly as possible, dig a trench thirty inches deep along the boundary line and insert heavy 20 ml plastic sheets vertically in the trench. The best tool for this job is a mechanized trencher that is often available from a rental shop. The plastic may prevent the chemical from seeping into the root run of your trees and shrubs, but do not expect this method to be fool-proof. Many of these chemicals are known to remain in the soils for twenty years. The average length of time, though not always true, is three years.

Soil laboratory tests for herbicides are exorbitant in price. You can test your own soil for the presence of herbicides. Gather some of the suspected soil and place it in a flower pot. Gather some soil from an area known to be free of herbicides (such as the potting soil you use for house plants) and place it in a flower pot. Plant two or three bean seeds in each pot, water and place in a warm place. The first leaves to expand after germination are the cotyledon leaves and are usually the same in both pots. Give both pots six hours of sunlight. If the second or third set of leaves on the suspect soil pot begins or curl and twist, your suspicions are confirmed.

Wind

Wind doesn't have a whole lot of uses in the gardening scheme of things, especially when velocities over one hundred miles per hour are a common occurrence in the Mountain West. The wind direction that damages plants will come from different directions in each geographical area. Learn from neighbors or the local weather station where the strongest, coldest, hottest, driest winds come from in your area before planting. No season is immune from wind.

IF YOU LIVE IN THE COUNTRY, make use of manufactured snow fence. It comes in twenty-five or fifty-foot lengths and is exceedingly effective in preventing drifting of wind-driven snow. Be prepared, however, for a pile-up of a large drift just beyond it; therefore, it should be placed about fifty feet from the area you are trying to protect from drifting snow.

TREES AND SHRUBS

Trees and shrubs, in themselves, become the protector of our property against wind, as you learned in Part I. However, the species of those that can take the brunt of the wind are planted on the windward side, and the planting is of mixed deciduous and evergreen species. Our mountains make their own weather. The westerly chinook winds are dry. Moisture-laden clouds coming from the Pacific are quickly squeezed of their moisture as they pass over chains of mountains, with each succeeding mountain range receiving less and less moisture. The east-facing or south-facing slopes are those in the shadow because they are the last to receive precipitation; thus the term *rain shadow* was coined, for they are the dry areas. The up-slope you hear of on TV weather broadcasts is the result of moisture-laden clouds formed over the Gulf of Mexico dumping their load when they reach the high plains, foothills, and mountains, thus creating the monsoon in summer and the heavy snows of winter. Winds from the north in advance of a low pressure area from the north are dreaded, for they signal an "Arctic Express" - the white-out blizzard that can be devastating for the traveller, stockman, and gardener.

See Part I and Chapter 3 for windbreak location and Part II, Chapter 10, "Windbreak Care."

TURFGRASS

New plantings of turfgrass are especially vulnerable to wind. Once the seeds have dried, they seldom germinate. Straw is often used to mulch a new seeding, and it blows to Kansas with the first breeze. The solution is unsightly, but effective. Use cut branches from pruning shrubs or trees to hold down the straw. The brush will also offer enough shade to keep the seedling grass blades moist, and become a barrier to foot traffic.

VEGETABLES

It took a Wyoming gardener to demonstrate how to use a single row of grain to thwart the wind. In the land of never-ceasing wind, we see vegetable gardens interspersed with curious rows of wheat, barley, or whatever grain seed was at hand at planting time. The tall grain plants bow gracefully in the wind to protect the tender lettuces or peas. The grains often are harvested and ground by hand for kitchen use. And are you aware that a vegetable garden in a windy area has very few harmful (or beneficial,for that matter) insects? The little dears can't hang onto a plant long enough to do any damage!

■ *It took a Wyoming gardener to demonstrate how to use a single row of grain to thwart the wind.*

Winter

This is the season that tries the patience of all gardeners. Greenhouses, sun porches, solar rooms, and sunny windows offer a little respite from the doldrums of not being able to be outdoors, but they are no substitute for being outdoors grubbing in the garden.

Dreaming over catalogs will launch some ideas of growing a plant of doubtful hardiness in your area.A new introduction or an old favorite of by-gone days when you lived in another area will beckon you to risk growing it in this area. Farmers and gardeners are the gamblers of the world.

If you have a protected spot on the east or southeast side of your home or another structure or beyond the root run of a group of evergreens, why not take a chance? You may find success the first growing season, only to have the plant succumb to the winter. Try again, and this time prepare for winter with some novel, some tried-and-true methods of plant protection that are worth the effort.

TREES AND SHRUBS

If the plants you have in mind to grow are offered in small size, by all means buy them. They can acclimatize better than a larger size. Also, if the plants you want to grow are offered from nurseries in an area almost as cold or colder than your area, buy them. Plant carefully with the protection of nearby structures or evergreens in mind. A planting site facing directly south or close to the side side of a building will warm too quickly in late winter.

FROST CRACKS

In the northern-most parts of the Mountain West, as well as in the high mountain valleys during winter, tree trunks and branches may freeze solid. On a warm day in January or February the trunks may thaw on the southwest side, and at sunset when the temperature drops suddenly, there will be heard loud cracks as the trunks split open lenthwise in splits several inches or as much as twelve inches in length. Research of Dr. Alex Shigo shows these splits are directly related to previous wounds in the trunks. Sometimes the splits will close with equal suddenness, but more often the crack remains open. Bolting the tree is not thought to be a successful treatment, and further research will be needed to deal with this phenomenon.

WITHHOLDING FERTILIZER

Trees and shrubs that have been fertilized in midsummer put on a soft, succulent growth that cannot harden into tough woody tissue before fall. With a sudden drop in temperature they may freeze back to the ground. They may recover from the root the following spring, but plants grafted at the root will come up an unexpected species. It is unwise to fertilize trees and shrubs unless characteristic growth patterns are not achieved.

HARDENING OFF

Heavy watering will also keep a tree or shrub unprepared for winter. In late August and early September gradually withdraw water until the first sign of fall foliage - the first yellow or red leaf. This may seem a dangerous procedure, for high temperatures often occur in early September. If the tree or shrub has received normal care during the summer, it will be better prepared for winter if it is hardened off in September.

PROTECTION METHODS

In early November use commercial tree wrap to wrap trunks of trees and single-stem shrubs. The angle of the sun is low on the horizon, drilling into the thin bark of the tree. The temperature on the south side of a trunk in January on a sunny day can be eighty degrees at one P.M., but it can drop quickly to twenty degrees at sundown. This deep fluctuation in temperature is prevented when tree wrap keeps the trunk evenly cold, not warm. Remove the tree wrap in early April. Apply it again each fall until the tree has established a thick bark, usually within five years.

Set a sprinkler to run several hours around trees and shrubs once a month in winter when snow is not present. Before winter sets in, rough the soil around a newly planted tree or shrub so that moisture will soak in deeply.

Immediately after Christmas collect discarded Christmas trees to stand upright around the tender shrubs.

Construct a three-legged burlap screen to place on the windward and southern side of a newly planted evergreen. Also consider the use of excelsior bats. Excelsior is an old-fashioned material made of thinly shaved wood from soft-wood trees, such as aspen. It is sold by the yard as batting. It is encased in nylon netting and available where evaporative air conditioners are sold. To prepare a shrub for protection with excelsior, use soft twine to draw shrub branches together. Place a length of excelsior batting upright around the shrub or small tree. It allows air circulation and natural precipitation to fall through, but insulates against the wind. Prop boards around the batting to form a teepee, lashing them together with rope or heavy twine. Many Zone 6 trees and shrubs are seen thriving in the Mountain West, but with winter protection.

The excelsior bats placed on both sides of a tender vine or espalier fruit tree growing on a fence will bring them through the winter. The idea is not to keep it warm, but evenly cold - but NOT TOO COLD!

In lieu of the excelsior bats, once again use soft twine to draw shrub branches together. Cut the bottom from a large plastic bag and slip it over the shrub. Lightly pack inside dried leaves that are unsuitable for compost, such as cotton-wood, aspen, linden, or green ash. Secure the top back on loosely with tape. Cut some circles in the sides of the enclosure for entry of air and your plant is ready to face the winter, though, admittedly, it's not a pretty sight!

If the above methods are too much for your aesthetic senses, and if you're a "craftsy" person, weave a wattle fence. See Chapter 18 "Azaleas and Rhododendrons." You will see these being used as winter protection for plants in Williamsburg, Virginia, the nation's gem of historic preservation. Our founders used what was at hand - willow stems - to weave a pliable, miniature fence that could be erected around or in front of vulnerable shrubs.

A basket turned over a plant is still an effective way to protect tree peonies, Nandina, summer-flowering spireas, dwarf evergreens, and many others. Include a few moth balls to drive away mice. It is always a surprise to lift the basket in April to find a bright green, ready-to-go plant that has benefited from only a small amount of protection.

FRUIT TREES

Getting fruit trees ready for winter involves cultivating grass and weeds away from the tree trunks, for voles and mice are likely to chew the bark. If the soil is bare, the rodents are easily seen by their predators, owls and hawks, as well as by the family pussycat. We don't take chances, however, for these hunters may miss their mark. Each trunk is encircled with hardware cloth, which is not cloth but a heavy wire mesh. Push it into the soil several inches so that digging is also thwarted. The wire should stand away from the trunk far enough to prevent the rodents from reaching through with their sharp incisors.

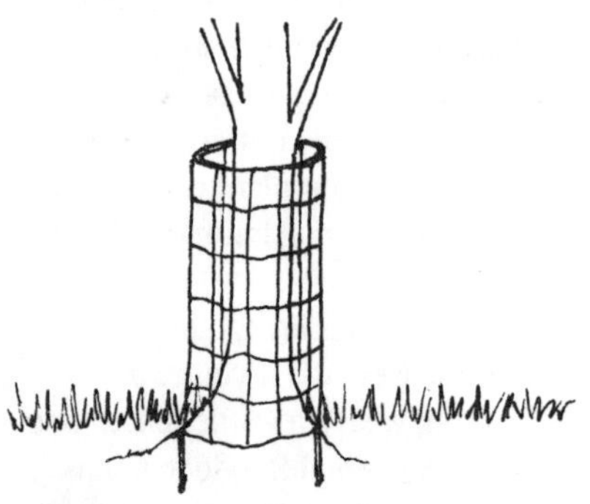

Hardware cloth encircles fruit tree trunks to prevent rodent chewing damage in winter.

ROSES

Roses now enjoy the luxury of specially manufactured protectors. Collars of corrugated white plastic now encircle them, fastening with snaps. The collars can be rolled and stored in summer. Fill the enclosure with soil, however, for to fill it with dried leaves, bark chips, or grass clippings would attract mice to nest. The moth ball trick is only mildly effective in rose protection. Mice are also a fond of chewing rose canes; so don't take a chance. Use soil as a filler for the rose protectors.

TURFGRASS

Approaching winter is the season to lower the mower blades so that turfgrass goes into winter a little shorter. It is also the time when trees begin to lose leaves. As your mower bag is put in place after being stored for the summer, you will catch lawn clippings mixed with shredded leaves. This is a treasure trove of potential compost at each mowing and vacuuming of leaves with your mower. This mixture of coarse and fine debris is the stuff of which top quality compost is made. When you gather this harvest, mix it with fresh manure (rabbit is especially good), and watch it warm up and begin working. This season-end making of compost is one of the most pleasurable garden tasks. It's the beginning of next year's successes.

VEGETABLES

Winter protection in the vegetable garden is a labor of love for the die-hard vegetable gardener. Most gardeners are ready to hang up the hoe for the season when winter approaches, but winter vegetables, such as Brussels sprouts, parsnips, kale, carrots, turnips, beets, and celeriac are given a loose, but thick mulch of straw to protect the soil from freezing so that these vegetables can be harvested even after real winter has arrived. Cinder blocks placed on either side of a vegetable row and topped with a sheet of plywood will protect it without too much bother. When you want to dig some vegetables for dinner, lift the plywood to slide off the snow load, and unfrozen soil will be found beneath, making digging easy.

CONTAINER PLANTS

Large potted plants summering outside should be brought in to be put to sleep for the winter. These include Lantana, Cape Plumbago, Fuchsias and Pelargoniums. Turn them on their sides and shove them close together under a greenhouse bench or in the sunpit where temperatures will remain just above freezing. Oleander and citrus trees can go into the garage or unheated porch where they will receive almost no water. As spring approaches, bring them out for repotting, heavy pruning, and a drink of very warm water; then give them no more water until leaf buds begin to swell. Increase watering as growth resumes. Fertilize when leaves are fully expanded.

PERENNIALS

As perennials die down in fall, cut them back to leave stalks about three inches high. These stems will not spring back to life next spring, but they will serve as anchors for evergreen boughs and netting. As winter approaches and leaves are falling from trees, leave those that fall on or blow into the perennial border. The air spaces left between the leaves will act as insulation. Collect discarded Christmas greens to lay over the beds, topping it all with nylon trellis netting if you live in a windy area, for wind will dislodge your careful efforts without a doubt. You can also push u-shaped metal tent stakes into the soil at the border's edge. Then thread nylon rope in criss-cross fashion across the border to hold down the evergreens.

Don't be in a hurry to remove mulch and boughs in spring. Remove only a little each week as spring advances so that plants will harden to frosty nights in spring and not be harmed.

MUD SEASON

The thawing of saturated soil creates the mud season in the Mountain West. Farmers, miners, and townsfolk have had to deal with it since the days of the early pioneers. Their method was to construct walks of boards across the low areas where mud was deepest. This is still a sure-fire method that gets rid of the problem with the least amount of damage to the soil. Soil structure and texture are fragile. Compacted mud dries into an impermeable mass that destroys fertility.

Mud slide, also known as mass wasting ,is one of the most dangerous phenomena known. Whole hillsides have been known to give way with the mud traveling at incredible speed. While there are occasional survivors of avalanches of snow, there are seldom survivors of mud slides. If your home is newly constructed on a hillside, be prepared with small concrete-lined waterways across the hillside to direct water on both sides, Secure the services of an engineer to direct you in compacting the fill dirt and terracing the slope to minimize the likelihood of disaster.

MIDWINTER THAW

Early in February temperatures often warm suddenly, melting snow and thawing the top few inches of soil. Roots of trees and shrubs and clumps of perennials are rudely heaved out of the ground. If they aren't quickly tamped back down again, the roots dry out and the plant dies. Buds on trees and shrubs from warmer climes may begin to swell and grow. This is because their genetically numbered hours of chilling required to keep them dormant are completed. Only winter cold keeps them dormant. When the weather suddenly turns spring-like, the plant bursts forth. The devices described and illustration are ideal to prevent this untimely growth.

HEAVY SNOW LOAD

Though we usually regard snow as the best of insulators for plants, when a heavy wet snow arrives or if dry snow is followed by rain, which then freezes into an immensely heavy and impervious cover, it is the worst of all disasters. This covering breaks limbs from fruit trees and smashes shrubs and roses.

The best prevention against this type of damage to a shade, evergreen, or fruit tree is the forked limb - either a natural one or one you've made from scrap lumber. Before winter arrives, forked limbs, sharpened to thrust them into the soil easily, are placed so that the fork is supporting the limbs most likely to be damaged. Keeping a collection of these limbs (usually gathered from prunings) in an out-of-the-way place is a real advantage for use when fruit trees are also heavy with fruit.

After the big snow, however, you'll be the first to rush outside to lift limbs with a soft broom to allow the heavy load to drop. Remember to lift from underneath, Don't smack the broom on top of the heavily loaded limbs.

Scoring the icy layer of snow with a hoe is said to promote earlier thawing, but it may be no more than good exercise for the housebound gardener.

Tip pruning evergreens in early summer when new growth is but one inch long will cause them to form new compact branchlets at the tips so that the tight growth that will not allow snow to pile up on the limbs.

All of the methods of plant protection will be improved upon as new devices hit the market. You will improvise as the need arises. Let everyone know about your successful improvisations!

CHAPTER 8

Learning to Apply Water

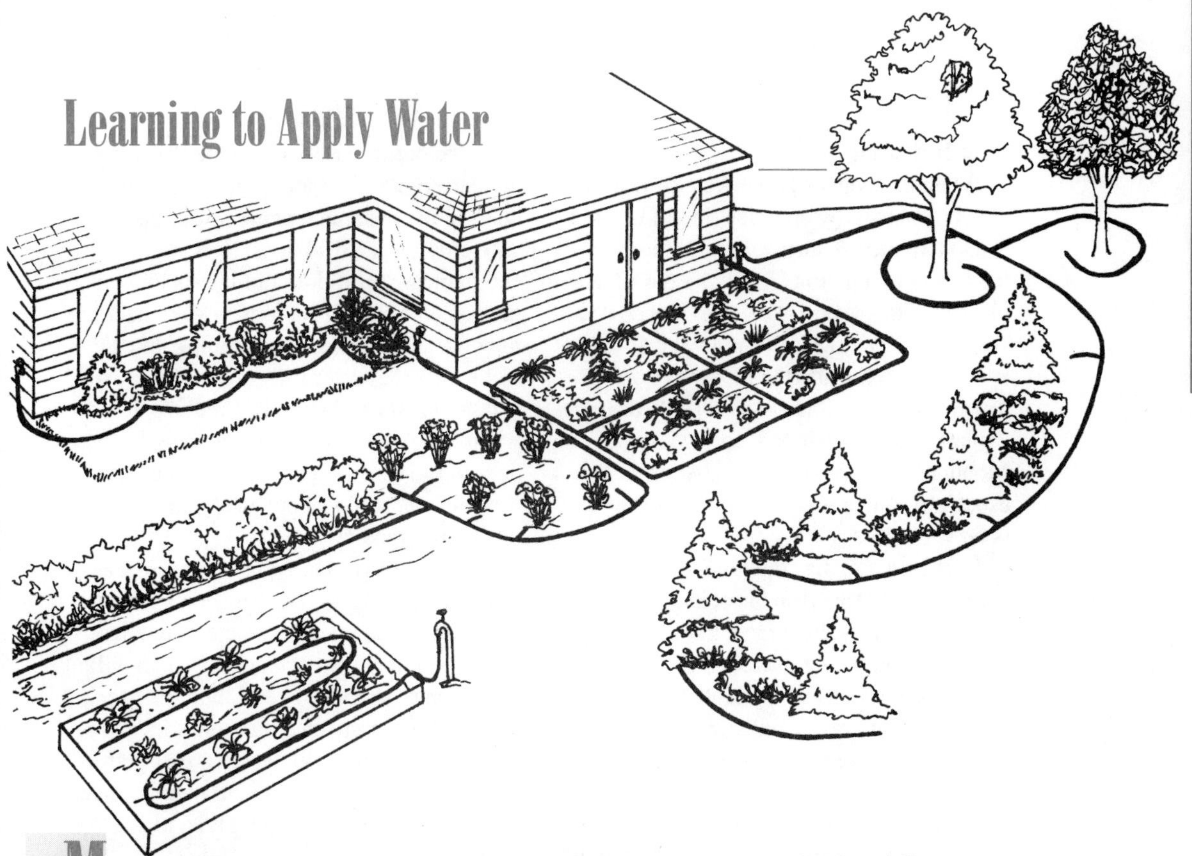

Many newcomers to the Mountain West have never purchased or operated a hose. Water fell from the sky where they came from and no thought was given as to a lack of it. In fact, most concerns were how to get rid of it.

If you have the usual trees, shrubs, flowers, and perhaps a vegetable and herb garden, a small orchard, and some groundcovers, you have need for at least three of the five kinds of irrigation we use on home properties in the Mountain West. If you live in the country, you may use all five.

When the Mountain West was first settled, it became apparent that settlers would have to find a way to lead the water in rivers and creeks to their property. Companies were formed to dig intricate canal systems. The community with a water engineer in their midst quickly prospered. Since the water in rivers and creeks was at a seasonal ebb and flow, depending on the snowpack in the mountains during the previous winter, the rights to the water became a commodity sold as shares of stock. These shares were issued by the companies that ranchers and farmers formed as they dug canals and ditches. Water rights were bought and sold along with the property to which they pertained. Unfortunately, the hoped-for water did not always materialize or a water-user would abuse his right to the water according to his number of shares, and the hapless downstream user had no water when his turn came. The same dilemma faces farmers and ranchers in the Mountain West today. If you are a newcomer buying a country property, avail yourself of a local real estate agent, lawyer, or banker who will know how many shares of water you will need to properly cultivate the land you plan to buy.

■ *It leaks water from pores all over its surface.*

Drip Irrigation

When the state of Israel was formed, it was surrounded by enemies- it still is - and it was a matter of survival that it learn to feed itself as a nation. To make the desert bloom, so to speak, Israelis developed a system of watering fruits and vegetables and grains that made the most of every drop of their precious water. Thus, drip irrigation was developed, and we in the Mountain West have capitalized on it. It is especially suited to windy areas, for there is no water loss.

Drip irrigation has three main components - head hose, drip hose, and emitters. The head hose is the largest in diameter and is laid out along one edge of the area to be watered, usually at the high end, if there is one, so that gravity will aid in the flow. The drip hoses are smaller in diameter and attached to the head hose at intervals where you want the rows of vegetables or the plants in a border to be watered. Placement depends upon what plants are being watered. Inserted in the drip hose are various types of emitters that deliver the water in amounts of one half to two gallons per hour. Some emitters are designed to spray a small pattern; others are designed to fog or mist the plants. Some head hoses, drip hoses, and emitters are designed to be installed underground. All are well designed to cause the water to percolate downward into the roots of the plant with the least amount of evaporation or erosion.

Leaky hose is a simpler form of drip irrigation. The hose is made from discarded auto tires. It is usually sold in fifty-foot lengths to snake up and down vegetable rows, through a flower border, or along a section of groundcovers. It leaks water from pores all over its surface. It is exceedingly efficient for rock gardens, for it can be buried just beneath the soil surface and left in place season after season. It can be used in the same manner as the the above-described drip hose. It is very economical, but it does not last as long as the conventional drip hoses. Leaky hose is not efficient when placed running down a slope. All the water runs to the bottom end, and the plants at the top end receive no water. Take care, also, when using leaky hose not to overload it with a high pressure of water, for it blows out easily and is difficult to repair.

Study the different types of drip irrigation before making your decision as to which type you want, but, be assured, an investment in a drip irrigation system will save money and water for a long time to come. Most companies that sell drip irrigation systems will design a system for you free of charge if you send them a scale drawing of your property and the plants you are growing.

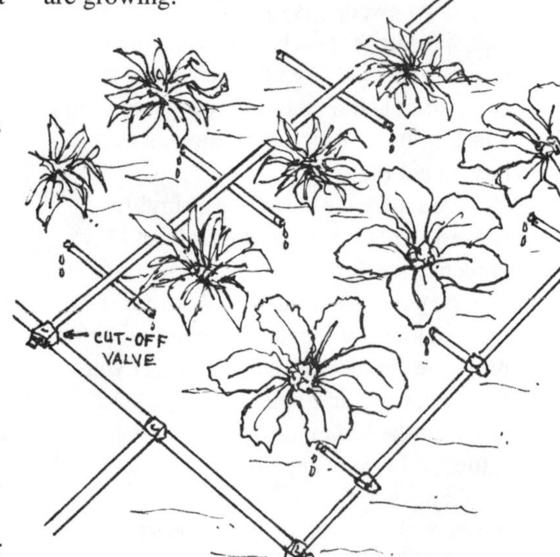

A vegetable garden will have a drip system with drip hoses that have cut-off valves so that each row can be watered according to its need.

Flood

Flood irrigation has been used since the Mountain West was first settled, and it is still an efficient way to apply a large amount of water in a hurry. Its success depends upon soil type and crop type. The best soil type for flood irrigation is clay loam. The clay particle will hold water well until it is available again - sometimes a long interval in a dry year, and the loam portion of the soil will keep it from crusting and baking in the sun. The crop type that can withstand flood irrigation is variable. Delicate little seedlings cannot stand the lack of oxygen before the water seeps below the root line. Almost all others, if far enough along in development, will benefit. Root systems under flood irrigation have been measured and found to be far longer and healthier than those under any other type of irrigation. This is because the water draws the roots down deeply as it makes its way through the soil profile, and because it drags oxygen along with it. To a plant root, a dose of oxygen is like wine. Proliferation of roots at a deeper than normal level leads to less need for water and happy gardeners all around!

To flood irrigate requires a series of permanent or temporary dikes. A lawn, for example, will have permanent dikes all the way around. Vegetables will be grown in beds that are lower than the paths between them. Fruit trees may have either permanent or temporary dikes, depending upon the necessity to set up ladders to harvest the fruits.

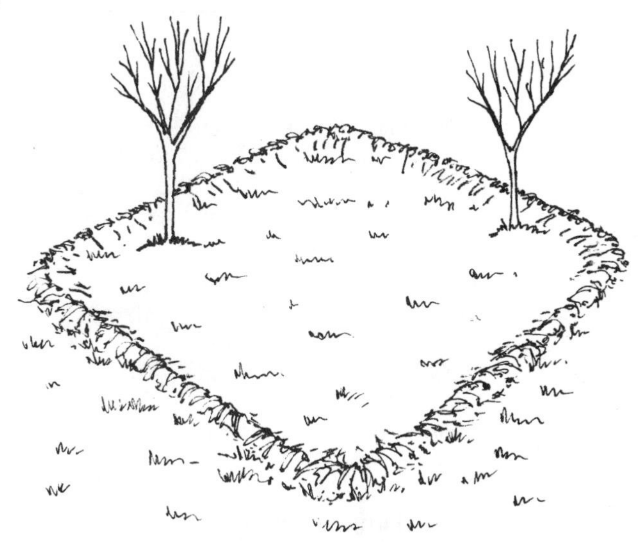

Permanent dikes around a lawn that is flood irrigated.

Vegetables that are flood-irrigated are grown in beds that are below the level of the paths.

■ *Soil texture is easily destroyed if you forget this one rule.*

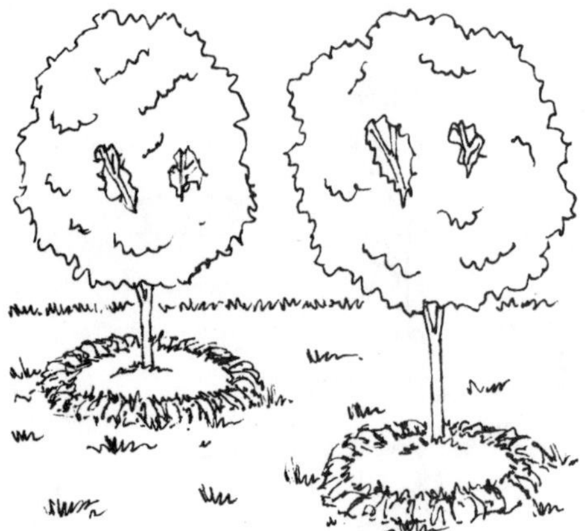

Temporary dikes hold water around dwarf fruit trees.

Flood irrigation water should be applied in early evening, with all the water that is to be used applied within one hour. The water should no longer be visible on the soil surface within four hours. Then, it is imperative that there be no traffic on the surface until it is dry enough to hold your weight without any sinking. Soil texture is easily destroyed if you forget this one rule. Except for a lawn, using a three-pronged cultivator hoe to stir the surface soil as it dries is useful in keeping down weeds as well as preventing crusting.

Furrow

Furrow irrigation is centuries old, developed in China and in the Middle East. The vineyards of the early Roman empire were watered using furrows. Today we seldom see true furrow irrigation, except on the small home vegetable garden or fruit orchard.

The canal systems throughout the Mountain West are more than a century old, and we seldom see a new one dug because all water rights have long since been sold. Old canals are being lined with concrete, gunnite, plastic, or butyl rubber, however, with great savings of water the result. Weeds dry up and die from lack of seepage water. Not only is water saved in the lined canal, but seepage of water is a problem if your land lies under an unlined canal or its smaller counterpart, the ditch.

Each canal or ditch has its ditch rider, who is a person commissioned by the ditch company to parcel out the water according to the number of shares owned. The ditch rider has control of the head gates on the canal or ditch. This is a device that opens or closes a wood or metal gate to allow the water to flow or cease to flow into your property. In days gone by and still in use in some areas, the water flowed into a *head ditch*, which was a ditch, usually two-and-one-half feet wide and one foot deep. It spanned the width of your property. More likely to be in place now is lightweight portable, gated pipe, which acts as the head ditch. Once again, weeds are at a minimum when there is no seepage water.

From the head ditch or gated pipe smaller ditches lead to areas to be watered. Water runs by gravity flow through each of these, and can be run even further into still smaller ditches, called creases. As the water completes its run through all of the system, if there is any left, it is collected in a waste ditch, which may lead to a neighbor's property. Not a drop is wasted, you see.

Portable pipe is attached and gates opened to allow water to flow into small furrows or creases. This type of water management is especially useful for the home orchard.

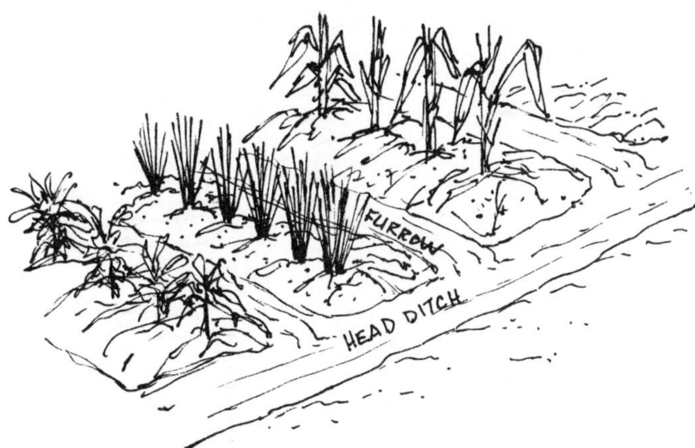

Furrow irrigation for the home garden is useful and thorough. Head ditch is filled with water. Furrows are then opened one at a time to allow water to run through until it is "black across the row." Furrow is closed with a metal gate or a shovelful of soil, and water will move through the next furrow.

The amount of water run through each furrow depends upon soil type, but the irrigator will judge when a plant has had enough by looking at the soil between the furrows. When the soil is wet, it is dark; therefore, the saying "black across the row" found its way into the vocabulary of every farmer, orchardist, or gardener in the Mountain West, and this descriptive saying continues to serve the purpose today. As each furrow darkens with saturation, the farmer/gardener places a shovel full of soil and mud to close the furrow. The head ditch is then opened for waterflow and the next furrow is opened. Furrow irrigation is the most difficult to manage and takes the greatest amount of time.

Siphon

Siphon irrigation is a sophisticated form of furrow irrigation, and easier to manage. After the head ditch fills with water, metal tubes are filled with water and inserted with one end in the head ditch and the other in the furrow. As long as the furrow is lower than the head ditch, the water will be pulled by the siphon principle from the head ditch to the furrow, with none of the need to shovel mud and soil to stop the flow of one furrow or to open another. As many siphon tubes can be set as there is head of water to keep them filled.

■ *. . . the saying "black across the row" found its way into the vocabulary.*

Siphon irrigation is used for many commercial row crops, but is seldom seen on the home property. However, it could be used to great advantage to water pasture around the home located in the country.

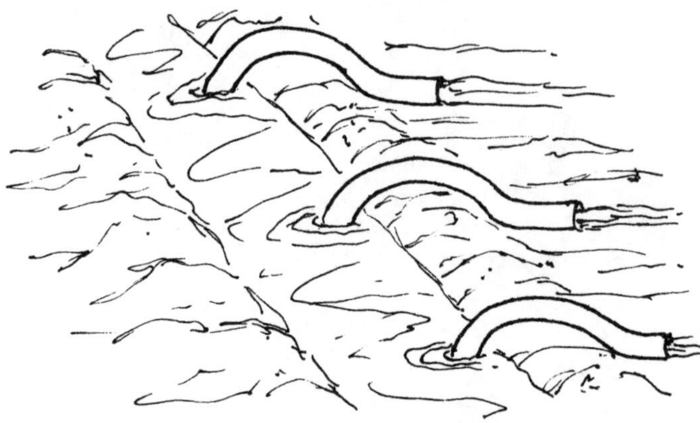

Siphon tubes are filled with water and inserted in the head ditch. The siphon principle will pull water from the head ditch as long as the furrow is below the head ditch level.

■ *Over-watering is the sin of all sins in the Mountain West.*

Sprinkler

This is the type of irrigation familiar to almost everyone. For lawns the best advise is to install the most sophisticated sprinkler system you can afford, for they are designed to save water. Check the references of the installer and beware of fly-by-night dealers in bargain hardware. Computerized timers are commonplace, and are not as complicated as one might think. They are easy to override in the event of rain, and many can sense rain and turn themselves off without your presence.

Make sure the installer has a plan of your land, drawn to scale, with all of the features you plan for the future. Nothing will dismay you more than having to deal with an under-designed system when you add new features, such as a rose garden.

Using sprinkler heads that allow watering of turf without wetting flower borders beyond is an added safety for the flowers, for many diseases are easily carried by water droplets.

Size of water droplet and height of application is important. The larger the water droplet and the lower the arc of application, the more efficient the system. More water is lost to evaporation by a fogging system shot with an arc high in the air than any other.

An old myth that refuses to die says that watering at night will spread disease. The theory behind this is sound. Water droplets that are slow to dry may be carriers of disease, but most parks and all golf courses are watered at night, and are almost never beset by lawn diseases. In the Mountain West, the humidity is seldom high in summer, and the danger of disease is low.

Sprinkler irrigation is efficient on a well-aerated lawn, but there is a danger in using it in the unmulched flower border, fruit orchard, or vegetable garden. As droplets of water strike bare soil, the resultant puddling causes the finest of particles in that soil to rise to the surface. The soil then becomes a different texture in a layer at the top, with symptoms of baking and crusting. With no organic matter in the top layer to hold moisture, it dries out. The gardener, seeing this drying, waters again with more of the same result, while the soil in the lower portion of the soil profile becomes more and more water-logged. The mulching of the soil will prevent the problem, as will the use of drip irrigation instead of sprinkler irrigation in the areas of flower border, fruit orchard, or vegetable garden.

Overwatering

Overwatering is the sin of all sins in the Mountain West. Gorging the soil profile with water drives out oxygen, and plants are quickly killed. Overwatering also leads to a dependency of water, as well as a predilection to insect and disease attack. Bugs like soft, succulent, well-watered foliage, as do deer, elk, pocket gophers, etc.

Trees and shrubs on a Spartan regime of water will be somewhat smaller in stature and with smaller, tougher, more leathery leaves, but they are more likely to withstand hardship. Symptoms of overwatering are the same as those of underwatering - wilting caused by lack of oxygen. Use your trusty long screwdriver to determine the problem by shoving it into the soil. If it is easy to shove, chances are strong that the soil is overwatered.

Gray Water

In the arid Mountain West the day may come when the use of gray water is sanctioned. Gray water is water that has already been used for washing in the bathroom (either sink, shower, or tub) or the laundry water. There are methods to save this water in heavy plastic pillows, or it may be piped directly to the garden. The problem at present is that it is illegal. San Luis Obispo and Santa Barbara, California are the only communities that sanction the use of gray water. Since many Mountain West soils are already tight with high alkalinity and clay, the use of gray water is a risk because it can be laden with alkaline salts and unsafe bacteria. Check with your local health department before contemplating using gray water.

Spring

As the frost leaves the soil, there are many cracks that open. Some are only a fraction of an inch deep; others may be as much as six inches deep. As long as there is moisture to fill these cracks before soil down deep dries out, the cracks are beneficial, for they allow air to penetrate deeply and gases trapped in the soil all winter to escape. However, it is wise to stroll around your domain on a sunny day in late winter closing cracks with your booted feet. Just the act of pressing your foot on the crack will close it and prevent loss of a shallow-rooted plant that has struggled to make it through the winter, only to succumb to the spring! Use your long screwdriver to tell you when to begin watering in spring. When it shoves in easily, no need to water yet. When it shoves in hard, begin watering.

As you will learn in Chapter 6 "Planting Procedures," fertilization of trees is not necessary in the Mountain West. However, fracturing a clay soil and aerating a sandy one will be beneficial. Use a tool designed for this task or use a heavy pry-bar to sink deeply into the soil. Rock it back and forth before withdrawing it. Do this around all trees, shrubs and in the orchard. The soil will then accept water throughout the season and there will be a satisfactory gas exchange between oxygen and carbon dioxide as roots penetrate the fractured clay.

Use of Polymer Gels in Planting

A compound is available that is of great benefit when planting soils that hold water with difficulty. A polymer gel is a white flaky granule that is similar in looks and action to the unflavored gelatin we use in molded salads and desserts. One teaspoonfull is added to a quart of very dry soil and mixed thoroughly. The result gives the plant the ability to draw out moisture from the soil that is normally held by tension to soil particles. Research is underway to determine the validity of using this material in the culture of golf greens and container-grown plants, thus cutting labor and water costs. For the home gardener, using a polymer gel in the potting soil of container grown plants relieves the gardener of at least half the tedium of watering. Soil in pots stays moist twice as long. The gel

■ *. . .many Mountain West soils are already tight with high alkalinity and clay. . .*

■ *Young trees and shrubs quickly succumb to the amount of water it takes to keep a bluegrass turf green.*

appears to last about one season, but further tests must be made for accuracy in all aspects of the use of this material.

Summer

As the season advances into summer, scheduled watering becomes the norm. Watering bluegrass turf every third day when it does not rain is practical in the Mountain West. Many years of research* has determined our previous thoughts that watering long and deep once a week was erroneous. Watering a moderate amount every third day will produce the best bluegrass. Small dry spots occur in every lawn, which brings up another practice we thought a fallacy has proved true. The cartoon showing the corpulent gardener cooling himself in the evening by holding a hose, spraying the lawn is not too far off. Those little dry spots benefit from the hand-held hose, and saves the practice of watering the entire lawn to make the little dry spot green up! If it fails to green up, use a spading fork to aerate the soil in that spot.

Trees, shrubs, flowers, and vegetables will benefit from a drip irrigation system. Mature trees and shrubs that are located in the turf will suffer from the shallow watering of sprinkling. Young trees and shrubs quickly succumb to the amount of water it takes to keep a bluegrass turf green. With oxygen driven out of the soil by too much water, the young trees and shrubs quickly die. Use the deep-root watering device to water the mature trees and shrubs located in turf once a month. Remove turf around young trees and shrubs to form an island so that you can better monitor the amount of water reaching them.

Fall

This is the season that we slack off on watering trees, shrubs, vines, hedges, roses, and perennial vegetables, such as rhubarb and asparagus. The hardening off process takes place within each cell of the woody plant. By withholding water so that a plant becomes slightly stressed, we prepare it for winter. Continuing to apply copious amounts of water right up until the hard freeze keeps the plant in a soft, succulent condition that will winter-kill without doubt. Use the first sign of fall foliage color to tell you that it is okay to begin watering once again.

Winter

The gardener newly transplanted from the East is certain the gardener in the Mountain West is out of his mind when he is seen watering turfgrass, trees, and shrubs during winter. The fact is that without water during winter, we would lose most of our exotic flora. A few native plants might make it through, but even they suffer from the bright, cold sunlight in daytime, and the sudden, swift temperature drop at sundown.

Use a low-arc sprinkler to water trees, shrubs, and turf in the early part of the day when the temperature is above freezing. Use the Thanksgiving holiday at a reminder that the soil should go into the winter sopping wet. The soil often freezes about a week after Thanksgiving.

After Thanksgiving water once a month when there is no snow on the ground, except for March. In March the Mountain West receives the second greatest amount of annual moisture, and your efforts, at last, can be relaxed. Use the sprinkler because it is most convenient, but use the deep-root watering device at intervals about two feet apart all the way around the dripline of

* *Dr. Jackie Butler, Colorado State University, 1983-86*

large trees. The device should be left in place only thirty seconds before moving on to the next point. Shoving the device into the soil before the TV football game begins and running out to change it during half-time will destroy roots, not save them. The force of water is too great to be left in place for any length of time.

Lack of winter watering is the cause of the demise of many trees and shrubs. The lack of water diminishes the root. The plant has the strength to leaf out in spring, and often it blooms as well, but as the dog days of July arrive, the diminished root cannot pump water fast enough and the tree or shrub begins to show yellow, chlorotic foliage, and may succumb quickly. It may hang on another year or two, but its life expectancy is short.

Applying water in the Mountain West is an art that is learned gradually. Begin by having a high regard for this precious resource and you will soon think of ways to save water, spurred on by the receipt of your first water bill!

CHAPTER 9

Pruning

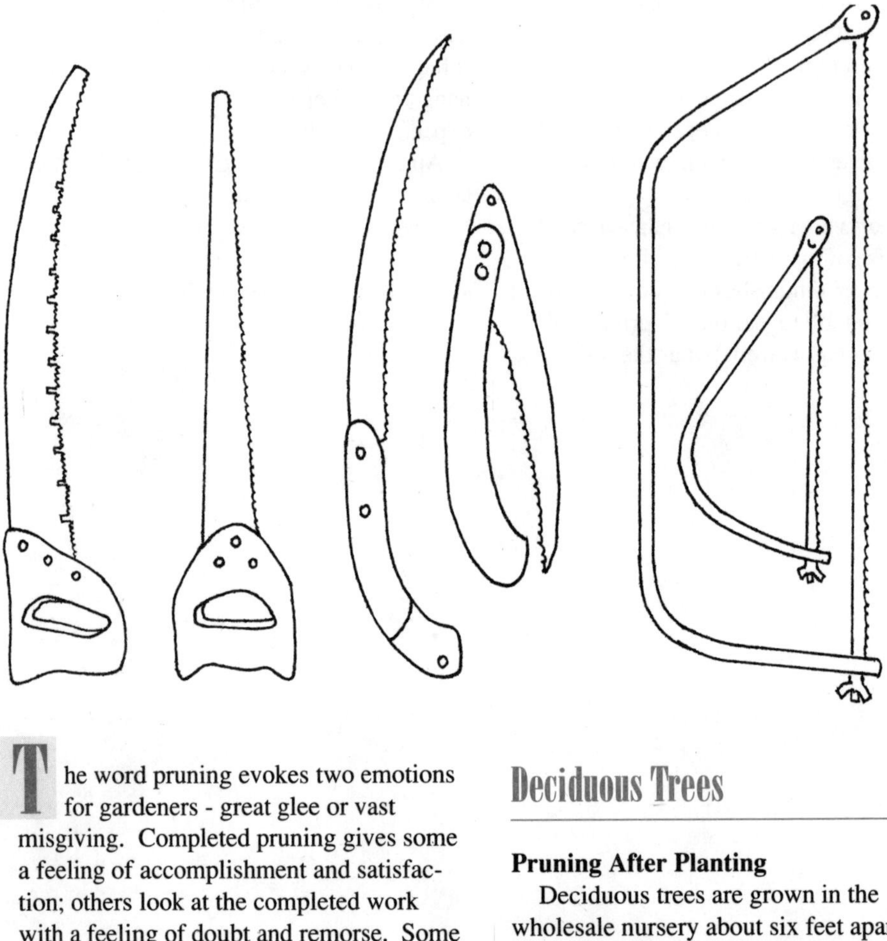

The word pruning evokes two emotions for gardeners - great glee or vast misgiving. Completed pruning gives some a feeling of accomplishment and satisfaction; others look at the completed work with a feeling of doubt and remorse. Some are cutters, some are not.

The management of a woody plant - one with bark-covered stem(s) - is different for each plant genus and each plant species within the genus. Now, if that statement is not enough to make you uneasy, let us state that there are several extant schools of thought on pruning. One is outraged by the theory that a tree must be managed; the other's philosophy is one of, "I will be the boss of this tree." There is a middle road.

Deciduous Trees

Pruning After Planting

Deciduous trees are grown in the wholesale nursery about six feet apart. It is normal for the saplings to put on branches close to the ground. Low branches aid in increasing the girth of the trunk as well as in forming the "taper"*. In the late fall these are removed and new "feathers," as they are called, grow again the following spring to aid, once again, in increasing the diameter of the trunk.[1] When the trees are dug and sold to the wholesale nursery, they will be bare-root or B&B*. When the "feathers" grow in the retail nursery, they

[1] *William Flemer III, Princeton Nurseries, Princeton, New Jersey*

* *See Glossary*

are often removed to allow trees to be stored or planted in closer proximity or because the public demands a tree with a clean trunk.

When you purchase a tree in spring (See Chapter 6, "Planting Procedures"), choose the one with branches low on the trunk, one with top growth that has no crossing limbs, and one without a limb directly above or below another. This is a tall order, but there is bound to be one that fills the bill. If, after planting, your tree develops feathers, leave them to give your tree a thicker trunk in less time. As the tree matures, the "feathers" will drop and others will not form.

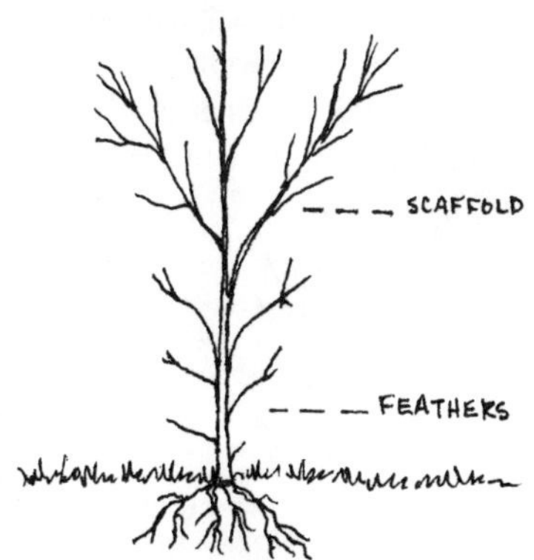

The best choice in a nursery tree.

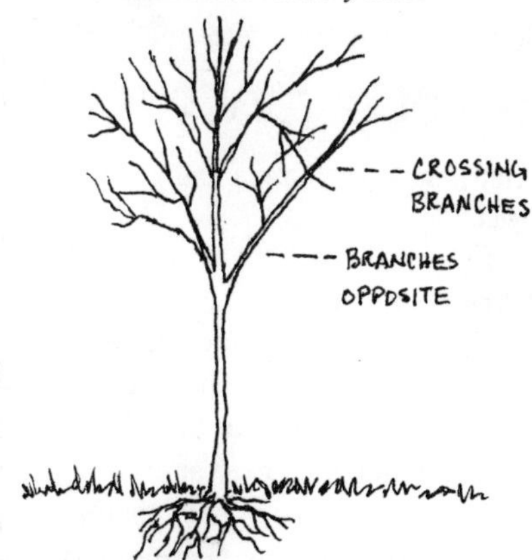

The worst choice. (labels for scaffold limbs, crossing wood, feathers.)

Direction of the Lowest Limb

High-altitude sun is a real danger to a deciduous tree in winter. The sun's arc in the sky is low on the southern horizon at this time of year, drilling its strength into the trunk of a tree. The temperature on the bark can reach 80° at 2 P.M.; yet at 4 P.M. when the sun goes down, the mercury can plummet to 20°. Therefore, it makes sense to plant your new purchase with its lowest limb pointing southwest. Even though the limb is void of leaves in winter and early spring, the limb will cast a shadow on the trunk, thus protecting it from the harmful rays that would cause sunscald (deep pits in the bark). This is your first scaffold branch.

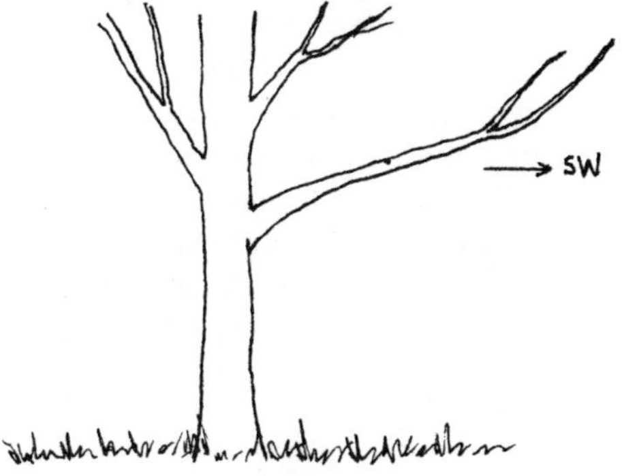

The first scaffold branch.

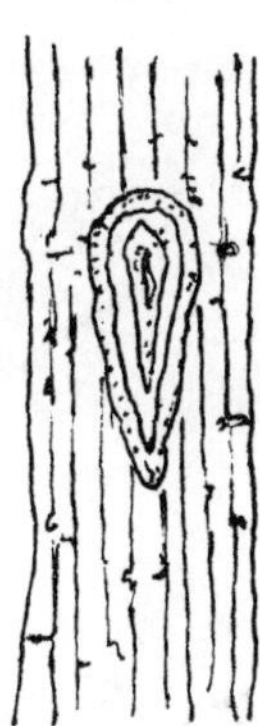
Sunscald is a sunken pit on the southwest side of an unprotected trunk.

You have saved your scaffold branch but as the tree grows, the normal urge may be to prune it off to (1) give it a better appearance, (2) to better mow around it, and (3) to allow you to walk under it.

To counter these arguments:

(1) If two trees are compared - one with the lower limbs removed and one with the lower limbs left to grow, the girth of the tree with lower limbs left to grow will be doubled that of the other.

(2) After reading Chapter 6 "Planting Procedures" you will see the reasons for not planting a tree as a specimen in the lawn. Therefore, you won't have any need to mow around it or prune off lower branches. Turfgrass is a tremendous force of competition for woody plants. It steals water and nutrients, and, in some species of grass, emits an allelopathic* substance that hampers the growth of the tree. Trees growing in an area free of turf will grow faster and the tree will be healthier than a specimen tree growing surrounded by turf.

The healthiest tree will be found growing in an island planting.

(3) Walking under a tree becomes unimportant since you won't be mowing under it. If it is growing in an island or border with a pole-peeling mulch*, it will be growing fast. As the tree reaches maturity, you will prune the tree for the convenience of walking under it, if necessary.

Necessary Pruning at Planting Time

It is an obsolete practice to "head back" limbs, which means cutting them back by half, or to decapitate the leader - the topmost upright growing branch. The only major limb that might eliminated at planting time is one that forms a narrow crotch. It poses a danger in a few years because it is a weak connection to the trunk and will, most surely, break in a storm. After a weak crotch is removed, no other pruning at planting time is necessary except to remove weak, spindly growth and any branches that are crossing another. The tree needs all the leaves it can muster to manufacture nutrients for growth. Why chop off limbs?

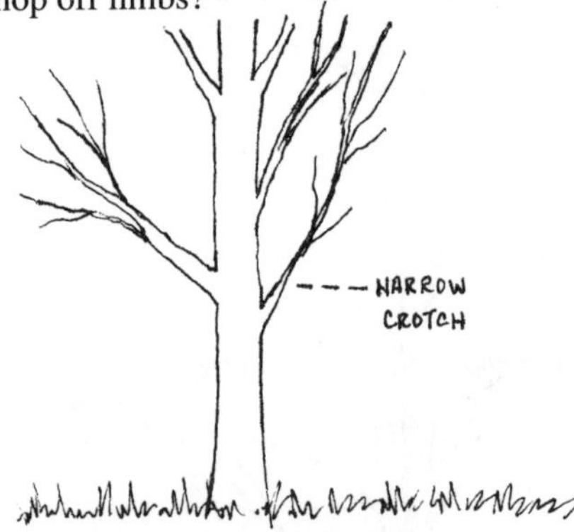

The narrow crotch; weak and spindly growth to be removed.

If You Are Renovating

When you purchase a home with an in-place landscape, part of the charm is always old trees. Examine them carefully before you buy. Use binoculars to examine them all the way to the top. Then have them examined by an arborist to determine what, if anything, needs to be done to get them into good vigor.

* *See Glossary*

Continuing the Scaffold

As your newly-planted tree grows, you will choose more scaffold branches to bear the weight of a snow load, a high wind, or perhaps a backyard swing or hammock. Just as you chose the southwest-facing branch for the first scaffold, the second should point northeast and rise from a point on the trunk slightly above the first scaffold branch. In this manner, the branches are chosen each year to march in a spiral upward around the trunk, with none directly above the one below.

Training a Narrow Crotch To Become Wide

"As the twig is bent, so grows the tree" - the saying goes. Many tree species have a tendency to form narrow crotches. You can be the instrument of direction by placing a spreader or a weight to pull the branch down so that a wider crotch is formed.

Spreading a tree with a mechanical spreader.

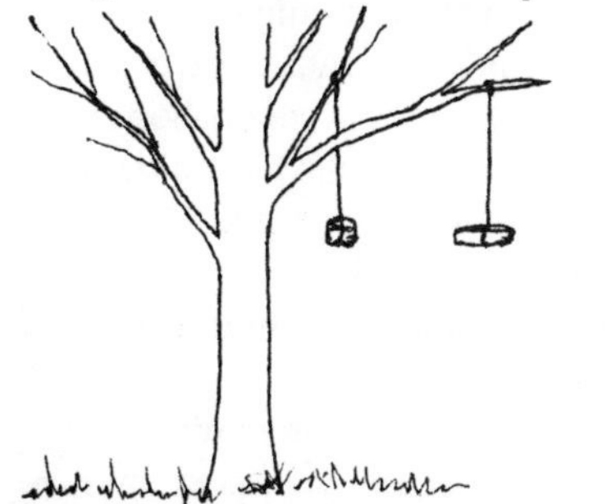

Spreading a tree with a weight tied to the branch.

* *See Glossary*

It is an easy matter to tap a nail into a 2"x2" piece of lumber at the point of the offending crotch. The gentle persuasion of the 2"x2" keeps the crotch wide until it is set by tougher, woody tissue formation. Remove the 2"x2" after one year. The nail will not harm the tree.

Weights are sometimes seen dangling from tree limbs. If this does not insult your aesthetic sense, it works equally well in preventing a narrow crotch.

Thinning a Crown

As a tree grows, it passes through three stages - the juvenile, the prime, and the decline. For each species and each individual tree within the species, the time period for each stage is different. Give your tree a long life by checking on its health at least annually. Use binoculars to examine every inch. Winter storms can sometimes crack a branch, and it will go unnoticed to become a site for infestation by insects and disease.

A tree can withstand more pruning in its youth than in its decline. The time to prune for structure is in the tree's youth because it has a greater ratio of leaves to wood volume at that time. As a tree declines, it has less leaf surface to the volume of wood and cannot afford the loss of leaves. [2]

In no way does pruning mean topping. Topping is the worst of tree pruning sins. It weakens a tree for the remainder of its life. It shortens its life. It destroys its God-given natural grace.

[2] *R. Stefan Ringgenberg, Boulder Tree and Landscape, Boulder, CO.*

Topped tree and resulting twiggy growth. The natural grace of the tree is destroyed forever.

When a crown is pruned properly, it is almost impossible to tell that it has been pruned.

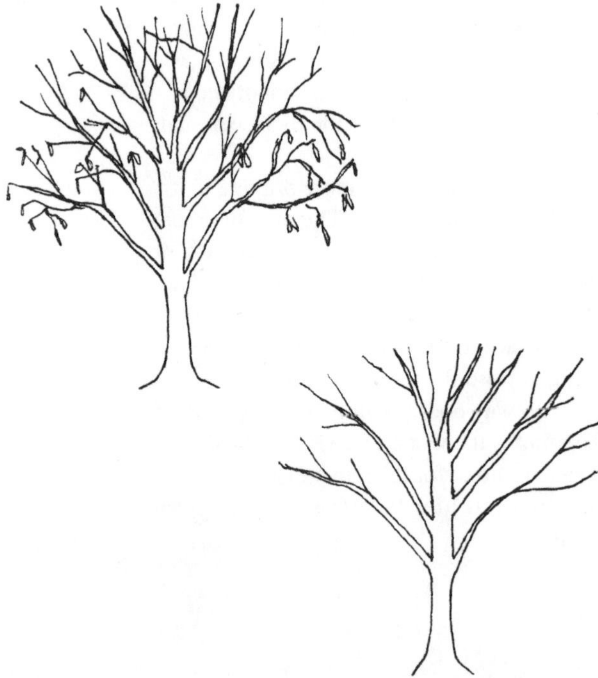

A young tree is pruned to remove the weaker of two branches that unhealthily compete for the same space. Remove the branch that inhibits the development of a more important branch.

Timing of Pruning a Deciduous Tree

Winter is the least desirable time to prune, but it is a practice that will die hard in the United States. The professional landscape manager wants to keep his employees busy in the slack season. This theory, and one he expounds in his advertising as the word of an expert, is "Prune when the saw is sharp." Though a better view is possible through bare limbs in winter, the cuts made will dry out in the arid Mountain West where winter sun is the reason we love living here. But imagine the tree in winter with all its branches. The roots contain stored nutrients produced last summer by all the leaves on those branches. Now you come along and cut off some of the branches. When spring comes, the tree has to redistribute all that stored food, so there is a tremendous growth spurt. The buds below the cuts grow with astonishing speed, leaving a weak, twiggy growth that must be pruned out. Pruning in summer has the opposite effect. The cuts close quickly because the tree is in full growth, not dormant.

The tar compound on pruning cuts that was once thought indispensable in pruning is obsolete. The tree can make a far better wound-healing compound than can be devised in a chemists laboratory. But when a tree is dormant, it is unable to make this wound-healing compound and the wound remains open to the drying sunlight. Summer pruning wounds close quickly. Do not harbor the misconception, however, that wounds heal. Unlike the human body, the wound will always be visible if you were to cut the tree down, and it is these "wounds" that give furniture a beautiful and distinctive quality.

If the thought of summer pruning is absolutely against all your principles, at least leave the shears and saws in their sheaths until March at the very earliest.

The growing season is then close at hand and the tree will soon be able to quickly close the wounds your tools have made. The best time to prune would be after the leaves have unfolded and growth has slowed. The most dangerous time to prune is when leaves are unfolding or when leaves are falling. A tree is most susceptible to shock and attack by insects and disease at this time.

How do you know when growth has slowed? You will note that leaves have lost their shine and there is no more elongation of twigs.

Summer pruning is easy. You aren't fighting wind and cold weather. Your fingers grip the shears or saw easily. There is no icy wind to make your eyes water, no cold rain trickling down inside your sleeve. You can see where branches are interfering with others and remove them quickly.

Trees That Bleed

Certain trees ooze profusely when pruned in the spring. The most likely are maple, birch, redbud, yellowwood and walnut. The oozing causes a great deal of consternation, but it is relatively harmless. It is caused by turgor or pressure of the tree tissue in spring. It does not damage the tree. Nevertheless, when trees are pruned in summer, there is no oozing and the wounds close quickly.

The Cuts

Removing a large branch is not just one saw kerf through the branch - it's three. We make a partial cut from underneath the branch to be cut to prevent it from skinning the bark when the branch falls. See illustration.

We make the second cut beyond the first, but from the top of the branch. Lastly, we make the cut just beyond the bark ridge and branch collar. See illustration. Flush cuts result in the destruction of the area where the tree manufactures its own natural healing compound. The bark ridge holds the magical elixir that will allow the cut to close quickly. True, the cut you make will leave the trunk with a slight swelling, but the tree's girth will enlarge to incorporate the swelling and it will never be seen again. On the other hand, leaving a stub is equally damaging. Any cut branch long enough to hang your hat on is dubbed "a stub!" As the bark falls away from a stub, heartrot can set in to gradually destroy the tree. You have seen these unsightly stubs on trees along city streets and country lanes.

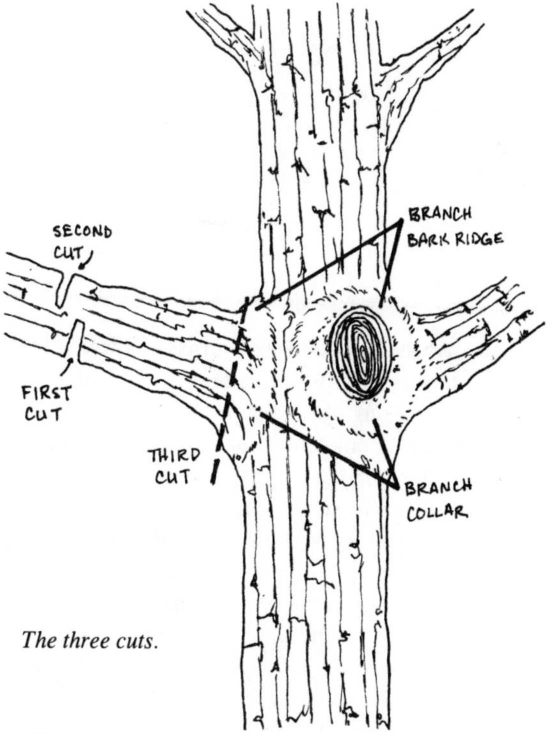

The three cuts.

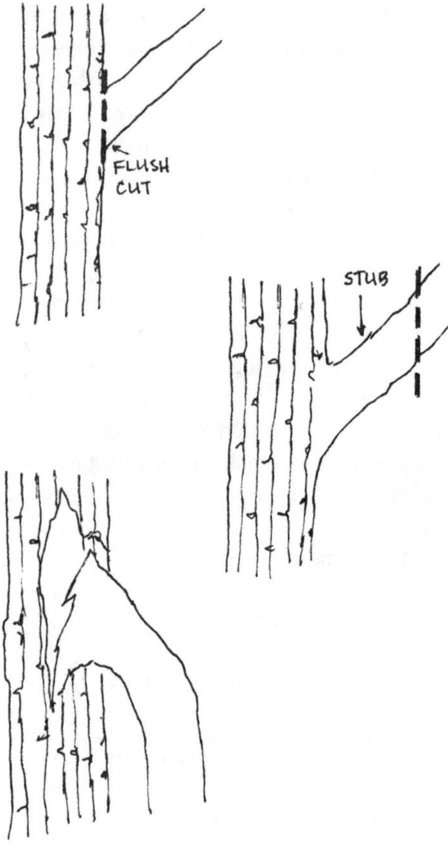

The wrong way to cut.

As the wound closes, it makes a weal of callus tissue at the edge of the cut, gradually growing toward the center until the wound is completely closed. If you cut this tree down in later years, you will find that a tree keeps its scars within. You can hasten the closing process. Each spring use a sharp new razor blade to make three or four shallow slits in the soft callous. Growth of this tissue is stimulated and the wound will close faster. Professional tree-care persons would not have the time to do this for every tree they treat, but with a single tree to mother, you have the time.

The Compartment

What happens when a tree wound is made incorrectly or a disease attacks a woody plant? It has the ability just like the human body to compartmentalize the affected area. You may have suffered or known someone who has suffered a boil. A boil is a compartment of the human body to wall off infection, to keep it concentrated in a single area so that it does not spread to the rest of the body. A tree compartment is the same. It doesn't always happen, however. A tree in poor vigor, just like a human body in poor health, cannot fend off the ailment and it spreads throughout. You, as the caretaker of a tree or shrub, have responsibilities.

Bracing

The natural growth of some tree species defies all your efforts. Elms, for example, are determined to grow with narrow crotches. Some cultivars of Linden and Maple are equally independent. Go along with their whim, but install cables to prevent high winds from damaging them.

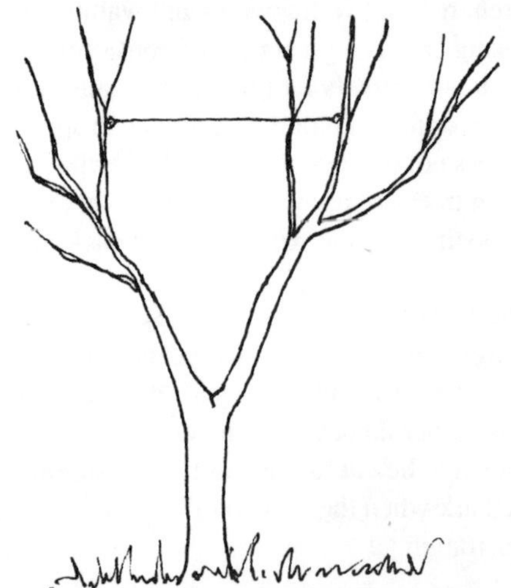

Two-way cables installed with eye-bolts will allow tree to sway, but not break with the wind.

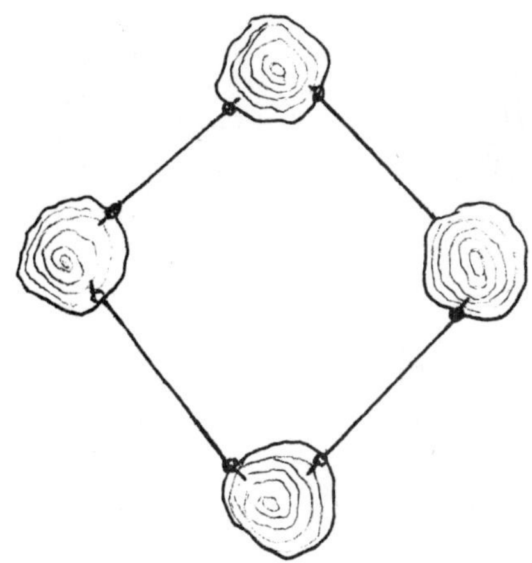

Four-way cables allow opposing branches to support each other. It is important that the cables line up in a straight line between branches to avoid an uneven pull on a branch during a windstorm.

Your electric drill, some eye-bolts, and a length of multi-strand wire will be needed. Remember to leave the wire slightly loose to allow the tree to sway a little with the wind.

Bolting

Heavy snow load and winter frost are often the cause of a lengthy split in a trunk. Frost cracks will often close when warmer temperatures arrive, but continued cracking in the same area will often leave the lip of the crack open and oozing when summer comes.

If you get to it soon enough, it is possible to draw the two sides of the split together, and they will heal quickly so that you will have a stronger tree that is unlikely to split again.

Measure the diameter of the tree at the split and purchase lag-threaded screw rod at a dealer in tree-surgery supplies. Rods having a diameter of from 5/8 inch to one inch should be used, depending upon the size of the tree. Purchase nuts that fit the rod at the same time. Use your electric drill to begin the hole through the area of the split, using a drill bit l/16" smaller than the diameter of the rod. If the split is long, figure on spacing several rods every twelve inches, alternating from one side to the other for the insertion point. If the holes are slightly staggered, rather than one directly above another, the screw rod will have greater holding power. All holes should be reamed, that is made slightly larger at the entry point, to avoid damage to the cambium when the rod is inserted. Round off one corner of the threading of the rod end that is to be inserted, and smear the end with a small amount of asphaltum putty. Insert the rod and screw it in with a vice-grip or a stilson wrench. Be sure to grip the rod at a point that will be beyond the entry point or you may damage the thread. After the rod is in place, use a hacksaw to saw off the protruding end. You may wish to saw almost through the rod before the rod is completely inserted, then break it off flush with the sapwood after it has been screwed home. A counter-sunk washer and nut will complete the work.

Installation of a screw rod, nut and washer to repair a split.

If all this is confusing to you, it is intended. It is placed in this volume for the direction of those who may live far from the services of a tree-care expert. There are many landowners in the Mountain West who will be able to teach themselves the basics of tree care. Trees, after all, are the winners when storm damage, winter frost cracks or heavy snow load cracks are repaired correctly. For those in urban areas where tree-care experts are available, it is wise to avail yourself of their services, for you can see that it is not a simple procedure.

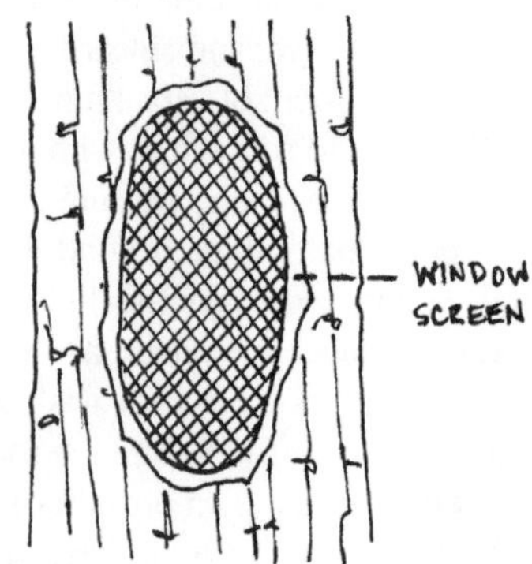

Cavity repair.

Wound Tracing and Cavity Repair

Accidents and trees seem to go together, especially if your trees are near the street. When your tree has been struck by a car, usually a nasty flap of bark is peeled back or destroyed. If a flap of bark remains, use small tacks to attach it back in place quickly, for the chances are strong that it will grow.

Wound tracing is controversial. One school of thought is that if the wound is ragged and open, use a sharp knife to smooth it, but to leave the irregular shape of the wound. The other school of thought is to trace around the wound to give it a rounded shape. You may be making the wound slightly larger, but you are giving it the ability to close.

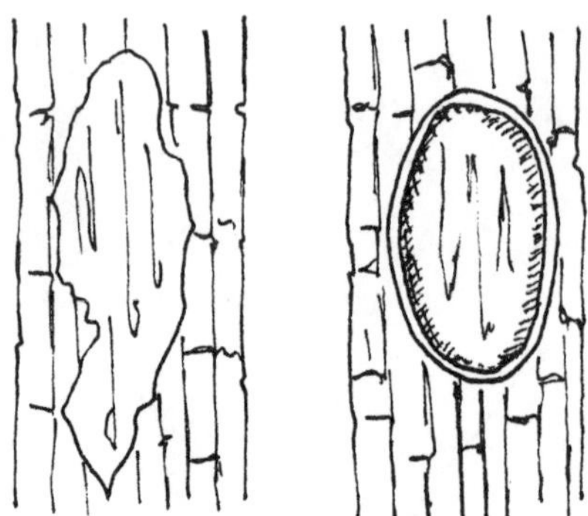
A ragged wound is smoothed with a sharp knife; or a wound is traced smooth to give it a rounded shape.

When a cavity develops in a tree, there is a nurturing urge to fill it up with something. Cavities occur in the forest all the time. There is no one running around the forest to fill them and the trees are not unduly harmed. Clean out leaves and other debris from time to time. If you are a nature lover, you will soon notice some activity. A friendly owl or woodpecker will claim the cavity as a home. Watching them will soon have you hooked on another absorbing hobby. If what you don't need is one more hobby, cut a piece of wire or plastic window screen to fit inside the outline of the cavity. Tap it in place with tacks or staples. The cavity will not close, but the tree will live many more years.

Suckers

A secondary shoot arising from a limb, the lower part of a trunk or from the ground is growing at the expense of the plant producing it, and is deemed a "sucker." Some plants sucker very freely, such as some Crabapples (*Malus spp.*), most Lindens (*Tilia spp*), Chokecherry (*Prunus virginiana*), and European Mountain Ash (*Sorbus aucuparia*). Use lopping shears to reach beneath the soil surface to cut these out as soon as they appear. This is especially important in fireblight-prone trees, such as crabapples or mountain ash, for suckers are a direct pipeline to the root. If the suckers become blighted, the tree will often succumb quickly because the root is affected. Suckers, also called water sprouts, growing from limbs can often be yanked off because they have no strong point of connection.

Root Pruning

There are various reasons for root pruning, such as to restrict the vigor of a fruit tree; to stimulate a vigorous recalcitrant wisteria to encourage flowering; or to force formation of roots within a zone so as to facilitate transplanting the following year. An example of the latter would be the digging of *Populus tremuloides* (Quaking Aspen) in the wild to move it successfully to another location.

In spring dig a trench that is wide enough to place your feet into in order to dig at the perimeter of the drip line. Roots encountered are severed cleanly; then the trench is filled again with the soil that came from the trench. If you anticipate digging the tree while the soil is still frozen, fill the trench with an inert material, such as peat-moss, vermiculite, or sand. It will be easier than frozen soil to dig (but not much!).

How To Choose A Tree Care Expert

Real estate people tell us that trees contribute up to 20 percent of your property value. Your trees are valuable and deserve professional care. There will be fly-by-night tree service people who will knock on your door, claiming to be "fully insured" (against what?), and others who will announce they are there to save your life because your trees are going to fall on you. Reputable tree services do not cruise the streets looking for work. They stay too busy with repeat business or recommendations from satisfied clients.

Look in the Yellow Pages of your telephone book under Tree Services for those who belong to the National Arborists Association. The International Society of Arboriculture coordinates a network of state chapters which sponsor training sessions for professionals in tree care. As with members of any profession, there may be disagreements about what procedure is best to follow. If there is a lot of money involved, get a second opinion. There are also members of the American Society of Consulting Arborists who do not sell or perform any actual tree service work, but for a nominal fee, will advise you about a problem. A few city foresters do consulting work in their spare time. They can provide you with an unbiased opinion.

Tree work is dangerous. Before allowing a company to begin work on your trees, check to be sure the company has a valid certificate of insurance and state workman's compensation. The insurance proves there will be coverage in the event of damage to your property. Phone the company to make sure the insurance has not been cancelled. Workman's compensation pays medical and disability costs of a person injured on the job. If an injured employee of a non-covered company cannot get enough money from his employer to pay medical bills, the worker can turn to the property owner for compensation. Your homeowners insurance may not cover it. Do not rely on a "fully insured" business card or a line in the Yellow Page advertisement.

Itinerent tree trimmers will be cheap in comparison to qualified people. Insurance and training are expensive. Do not expect qualified people to bid against an itinerant.

When you have decided upon a firm, get all of the work in writing:

• When the work will begin.
• What is to be done.
• The extent of clean-up.
• Date the work will be finished
• Total dollar amount you will be charged.

Never pay in advance. All good companies will bill you.

To economize on tree work after a storm or just for routine care, get together with neighbors to have several reputable firms bid on doing all the neighborhood work at the same time. Travel-time expense can be saved for the tree service, saving you as much as ten to fifteen percent.

Pruning Deciduous Shrubs

Refer to Chapter 6 "Planting Procedures" and 'Protection of Plants" for directions on choosing, planting, and protecting shrubs. The majority of deciduous shrubs form multiple stems. Shrubs may reach maturity much earlier than trees. In fact, many are mature within three years. Lilacs, some of the dogwoods, and some viburnums will lag along for several more years.

Pruning of shrubs is a simple process of eliminating two to four of the oldest stems each year almost to the soil line, leaving a stub of only two or three inches. There will be buds on the stubs that will be activated to become new stems. Therefore, the process is one of continual renewal, keeping the shrub forever young. Good pruning is never obvious. If you have to prune to limit size, it means you chose the wrong shrub to fit the planting site.

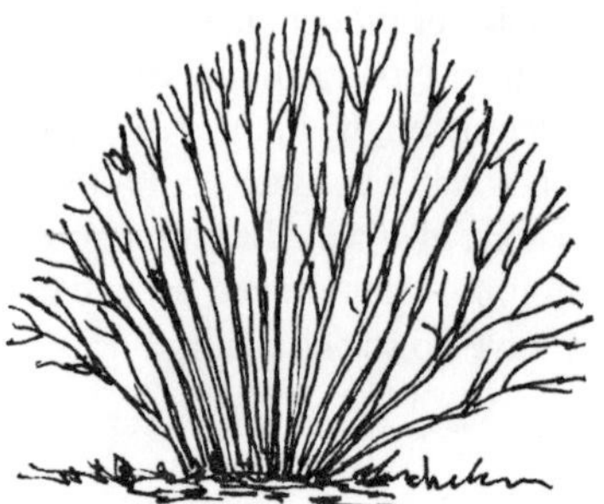

The wrong way haircut.

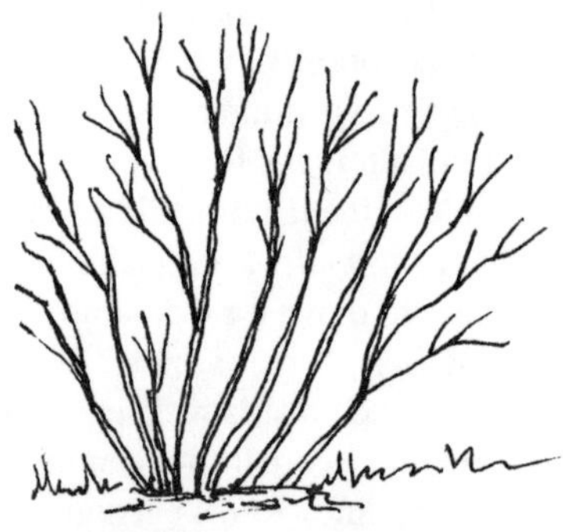

The right way - renewal pruning.

Pruning the single-stem shrub is exactly like pruning a tree, which also has a single stem. Some single stem shrub examples are: *Euonymous alatus* (Winged Euonymous), and *Prunus triloba* (Flowering Almond).

Timing of Shrub Pruning

Flowering shrubs begin to initiate blooms for next year within about three weeks of the fading of this year's blooms. The pruner who gives spring hair-cuts to each of his shrubs cuts off the potential blooms. Since the pruning urge is strong with some gardeners, urge them to prune while the shrub is in bloom. Forsythia and Bridal Wreath Spirea, for example, will furnish long, graceful stems for decorating the church or hospital lobby. Lilacs should always be shared. Cut armfuls for friends and neighbors.

Use sharp shears to cut each stem with a slanting cut; then cut again in half for an inch or two so that the stem will absorb water more readily in a bouquet.

Cutting flowering shrub branches for a bouquet is a good way to prune.

Summer-flowering shrubs are pruned in the same way - at the time they are in bloom or just after, but you may wish to wait until early spring. There are a few that perform best if they are cut to the ground in fall or winter. These include:

Buddleia spp., Butterfly Bush
Caryopteris spp., Blue Mist
Spirea x bumalda, Summer Spirea

Potentilla spp., Cinquefoil, is one that performs best when cut to the ground in February every third year.

Many shrubs are grown for their attractive fruit, and they should be pruned after fruits have formed in summer so that new shoots will become next year's blooming and fruiting wood.

Evergreen Trees

For the most part, the advise of experts is that evergreens are seldom in need of pruning, especially from the bottom. In the forest we see evergreens with their natural skirt of limbs and foliage all the way to the ground. The exception is *Pinus ponderosa*, (Ponderosa Pine) and *Pinus edulis*, (Pinyon Pine.) Both are pines of the montane savannas of the Mountain West and drop their lower branches as they age.

The skirt of limbs and foliage gives excellent wind protection. When it is removed - "limbed up" - so that you can walk under the tree, there is a definite danger for wind-throw. Because the foliage is dense, it forms a green wall against the wind. The roots of spruce, fir, and pine are likened to a giant plate that extends only a short distance beyond the dripline. When the skirt is removed, the wind hits the green wall and tips the plate of roots neatly out of the ground. A tree that has suffered this catastrophe can be saved if you act quickly. Call a tree expert, or winch the tree back into the ground yourself if you have the equipment.

If you wish to limit the growth of a pine or to make the foliage more dense, snap off the candles of new growth when they have reached their full growth, but before the needles begin to elongate. Use your fingers rather than shears, for the shears could carry disease organisms. The breakage point will be the site of several more shorter twigs.

For *Picea pungens*, (Colorado Spruce), *Abies concolor* (White Fir), or *Pseudotsuga menzesii*, (Douglas Fir), cut back the tip growth in late winter or early spring when buds are dormant. The recommended place for cuts is just beyond a side bud or side branch.

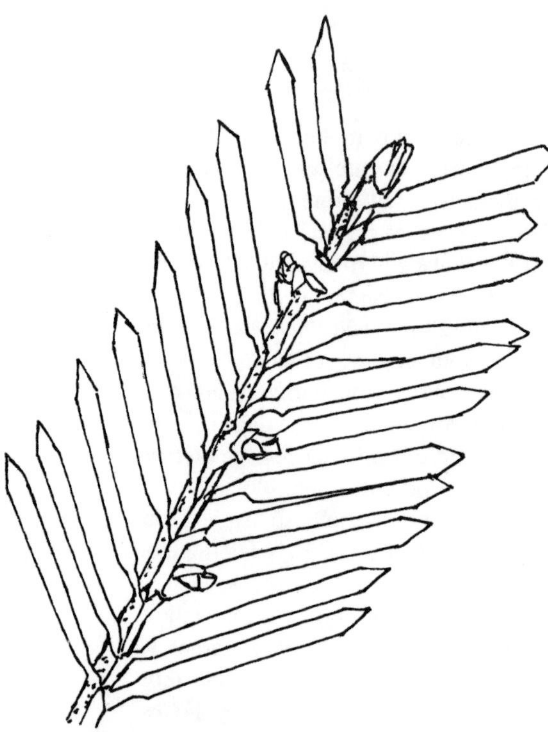

Spruce, fir, and Douglas-fir are pruned just beyond a lateral bud.

Evergreen trees with scale-like leaves and no definite buds, such as junipers and arborvitae, are pruned when the new growth is one inch long. Make the cut so that the foliage behind the cut will lap over it to mask it.

Shearing a juniper or arborvitae is long out-of-date and gives your home a look of obsolescence. It is also an admittance from YOU that you made a mistake and planted a tree where there was not enough room for it to expand to its natural habit. A *Juniperus scopulorum* (Rocky Mountain Juniper) will grow into a natural upright form that looks sheared. A *Juniperus virginiana* (Red Cedar) will form long pendulous branches that are strong and graceful. Give them both the room they need and shearing will not be needed.

Junipers are a poor risk for transplanting. If you have planted one where there is no alternative but to shear to keep it in bounds, consider removing it and starting over with the right plant for the right place. Shearing limits the life-span to about twenty-five years, whereas, a normal lifespan for a juniper in its native habitat is one hundred fifty years.

The *Pinus mugo mughus*, (Mugho Pine) is often sold as a one-gallon container plant in nurseries. It looks cute, and the unsuspecting homeowner brings home several, always planting one on either side of the front entry. Some of these are true dwarfs and propagated from dwarf stock, but it is the natural habit of Mugho Pine to reach twenty-five feet in height and twenty-five feet across with multiple trunks. Don't despair when your Mughos grow so large that you can't fight your way out of the front door. Pines transplant easily. Ask a professional to move them to the perimeter of your property where you can enjoy their picturesque silhouette at all seasons of the year.

The Character Pine

If your home is the right style of architecture, a pine shaped in a picturesque manner is an asset. Carefully observe stressed pines when you are hiking in the mountains. Their shapes are not grotesque, but strangely twisted, with balance and grace. Pruning to achieve this picture of great age is a matter of thinning to reveal the branch structure and limiting growth by removing new candles of growth or snapping them in half.

Purchase a pine (Ponderosa or Pinyon are good choices) that has an interesting branch structure, not one with symmetrical habit. The crooked speciman is usually less expensive. Look for a diagonally leaning trunk or one with a twist to a branch. You can prune off as much as one-third of the branches to give the pattern you are seeking.

In limiting the growth in spring, after the candles are fully formed but before needles have lengthened, use thumb and forefinger to remove some candles from each branch, leaving a ratio of three pointing outward to two inward. Always remove the largest candle in the bundle, for this will encourage a curving branch pattern.

Hose down your character pine with a strong stream of water from the hose often in summer and especially late fall when dead needles will fall anyway. Keep it well-watered in winter, but eliminate any hint of fertilizer, for your objective is to limit growth.

Removing candles to leave three pointing outward and two inward.
Snapping candles in half.

Broadleaf Evergreens

The usual word on pruning broadleaf evergreens is "don't." Because there are very few species of broadleaf evergreens that grow well in the Mountain West, it is not unusual to approach a broadleaf evergreen with puzzlement. The rules are the same with broadleafs as with deciduous or needled evergreens as to weak or crossing wood - remove it. Other cuts are usually not necessary, except with *Pyracantha spp.* (Firethorn). It blooms on one-year-old wood. Cut back by half last year's growth when the plant is in bloom. New blooming twigs will be initiated for next year.

Damaged broadleaf evergreens are common after a hard winter. Unprotected *Buxus spp.* (Boxwood) will be burned by winter sun; evergreen *Euonymus* species will have tan leaves that will be pushed off by new growth; *Mahonia spp.*, (Oregon Holly-grape) will also have burnished leaves that are tired and tan. No help is needed by the plant to push these off.

Pruning Herbaceous Plants

A pinch here, a snip there, a basketful of deadheads as you stroll through your garden in summer - all of these are pruning procedures. Timely trimming of our perennials promotes compact growth, prolonged bloom, larger flowers and more luxuriant foliage. Knowing which to pinch, when to cut back all comes with experience, but a little study before the crush of work comes with the growing season is in order to get ready for the best of blooming seasons.

Deadheading

A rather ominous word for simply pinching or snipping off a spent flower. The plant's objective in life is to recreate itself. When a flower has pollinated itself if it is a perfect* flower, or if it has been pollinated by wind, insect, bird, or animal, its mission has been accomplished and the petals wilt or dry. It then begins the lengthy process of making seed. Your objective is to keep that flower *trying* to recreate itself by forming new blooms; so you deadhead as you stroll through your domain each day, taking time to appreciate the beauty you have created.

With perennials that form leafy branches, deadhead by snipping back to the next branch, which will then lengthen and bloom. If you don't mind your perennials *seeding around**, allow one or two seed heads to form; then watch for seedlings at the base of the plants so that you can scoop them up for transplant to a new area. For perennials that bloom on leafless stocks, cut the spent flower all the way to the soil line.

For spring, summer, or fall blooming bulbs, cut the flowering stem all the way back to the soil level - again to prevent the bulb from using energy to make seed. Never remove the foliage. It will fall away naturally as a bulb begins its dormant period. The flower for next year is formed by the nutrients manufactured by the foliage. If you are the neatnik who can't stand the untidiness of bulb foliage in the process of maturing, study carefully the plants that will grow over the offending plant, thus masking its natural behavior. Daylilies and *Gypsophila* (Baby's Breath) come to mind.

Spring-flowering rock-alpines will make the desired compact "buns" if flower heads are sheared back on some, using the string trimmer. For example, *Achillea ageratifolia* will form tight new pearl-gray foliage; *Draba spp.* and *Aubrieta spp.* will spread into welcome buns and mats. *Campanula spp.*, however, must have each individual spent flower removed so that the new buds forming down in the foliage bun will continue to grow. The dwarf forms of columbine will seed themselves profusely, if you fail to deadhead.

Lavandula spp. (Lavender) is often grown as an ornamental in the rock garden. The urge is to cut it back sharply in early spring because it is unsightly and dead-looking at that time. As spring days become warmer, it will perk up. Old foliage becomes turgid once again, and pruning often is not needed. Cutting the flower stems all summer will keep it in production.

Daylily flowers, as implied by their name, last only one day, but there are many in each scape. As you take your daily stroll, flick off yesterdays' blooms into your basket and a single scape will last almost the whole month of July. When the scape is spent, cut it off at the soil level.

Gypsophila (Baby's Breath) erupts into a billow of bloom in early summer. Cutting back each stem will produce more flower stems all summer, but take care not to let it go to seed or no more flower stems will appear.

Cutting back summer-flowering extra-vigorous perennials is a common practice. *Achillea spp.*, *Salvia spp.*, and *Coreopsis spp.* are commonly whacked back by half, foliage as well as stems, when their first flush of bloom is over. After fertilization, new growth comes quickly, followed by new flowers. *Phlox carolina* 'Miss Lingard' will bloom again in early September if cut back after its inital flowering in

* *See Glossary*

July. *Phlox paniculata* will bloom from lateral branches after the terminal flower head is removed. Pansies, Sweet William, and Foxgloves will push themselves into longer life with more blooms if cut back sharply after the first flush of bloom is over.

The late-summer perennials, especially the *Aster spp*, Michaelmas Daisies and chrysanthemums are given a soft pinch at intervals to make them bloom on shorter stems. The normal height of a standard Michaelmas is five feet, which means they require extensive staking. You can force them into neat mounds of bloom by using thumb and forefinger to pinch out the soft whorl of topgrowth when they are but four inches tall. When they are sixteen inches tall, cut them back to eight inches, and give them a mounded shape with shorter stems toward the outside of the clump. They will still need staking, however. See Chapter 6 "Planting Procedures" for staking directions.

Chrysanthemums are also candidates for pinching. Pinch when the topgrowth is four inches tall, and keep on pinching every two weeks until Fourth of July. If your chrysanthemums persist in blooming in summer instead of fall, it means they are in need of fertilization. Fertilize with a liquid fertilizer every two weeks until August 15.

Delphinium will present you with a fall crop of flowers if well-watered and fertilized in summer. Cut the June bloom-stalks back to the first foliage; then cut these stalks again to the ground when a new ruff of foliage begins at the base of the plant.

Annuals are pinched when they are set out as bedding plants to force more compact growth. Constant pinching is necessary to prevent blooms on the annuals and perennials grown for their foliage. Examples are Coleus and Lamb's Ears (*Stachys byzantina*). However, if both of these receive high nitrogen, rather than high phosphorous, fertilizer, they make leaves instead of blooms.

Groundcovers such as *Lamium spp*., *Aegopodium* (Bishop's Weed) and *Cerastium tomentosum*, (Snow-in-Summer) will benefit from the string trimmer treatment after foliage is old and tatty or after bloom.

Ornamental grasses are too new in backyard culture to be sure of treatment, but the general concensus seems to be to leave the tall varieties to grace the winter scene, cutting down in spring to allow sunlight to activiate the crowns into growth. With the shorter, groundcover varieties, such as the sedges often grown at waterside, it is best to cut back sharply after the first frost.

Cut back any plant that becomes ratty with powdery mildew or black spot. Be sure to remove the foliage carefully to a waiting tarp or basket, for the spores of disease are easily spread.

After frost has blackened topgrowth, it's time for serious pruning of stems and foliage of perennials before winter mulch is applied. Leave about four inches of woody stems protruding, however, for these will serve as an anchor for evergreen bough protective cover for winter, especially if you live in a windy area and must use nylon netting to keep the boughs in place. Winter mulch is not applied until the soil is lightly frozen, about the end of November.

Fruit Tree Pruning

You will learn in Chapter 6 "Planting Procedures" that spring is the recommended planting time for woody plants, with bare root stock being a good choice for fruit trees.

The orchardist plants one-year-old "lining out" stock fruit trees, which are nothing more than whips, three or four feet in height. The gardener most often purchases container-grown, three-year-old trees, which are often a tangle of branches, and a puzzlement to prune.

The whip is not touched with the pruning shears, or if it has branched, it is pruned as illustrated, cutting always to an outward-facing bud.

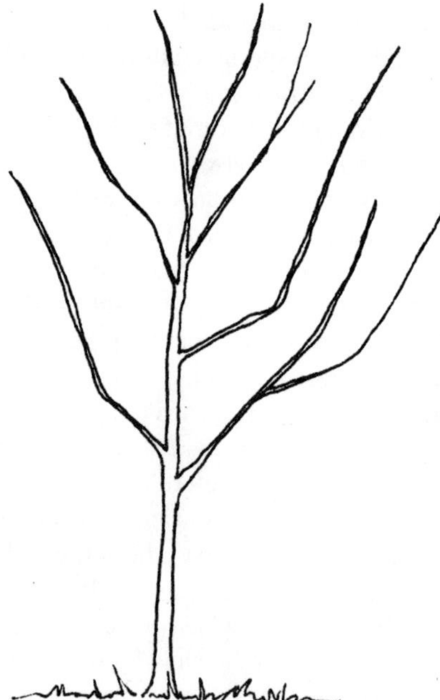

The one-year-old whip is pruned so that the lowest branch faces southwest to provide shade of the trunk and prevent winter sunscald. The second branch faces northeast. The tip is left untouched.

The three-year-old tangle is thinned to remove only weak and crossing wood. Two scaffold branches are chosen, but the remainder is left untouched to establish a good leaf crop and root system.

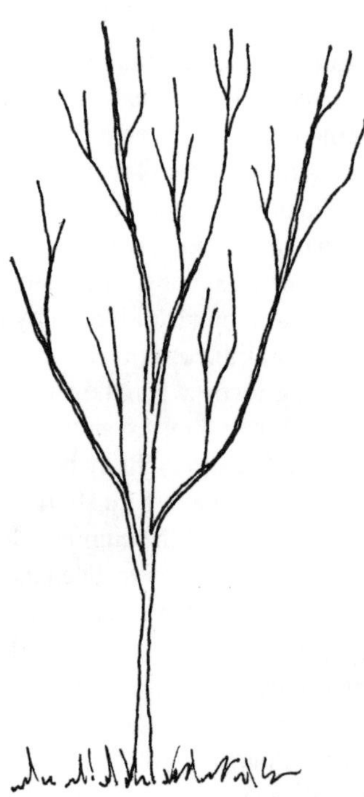

The three-year-old tangle is thinned so that the lowest branch faces southwest, the second northeast as above. Weak and crossing branches are removed. The tip is untouched.

The second year of the tree grown from a whip is similar in pruning chores to the first. Even if dwarf fruit trees have been chosen, there is little pruning to be done.

In the third year, remove branches to retain the more important so that each is receiving sunlight. Spread the branches to eliminate narrow crotches with "spreaders" made of 2x2" lumber with small, clean, sharp nails at the tip of each end. The nails are inserted into the branch to be spread to a wider angle. The spreaders are left in place only for one year. They will increase the tree's ability to hold a heavy crop of fruit without breaking, allow sunlight to enter the crown to ripen the fruit, and, lastly, allow the owner to work among the branches without damage to himself or the tree.

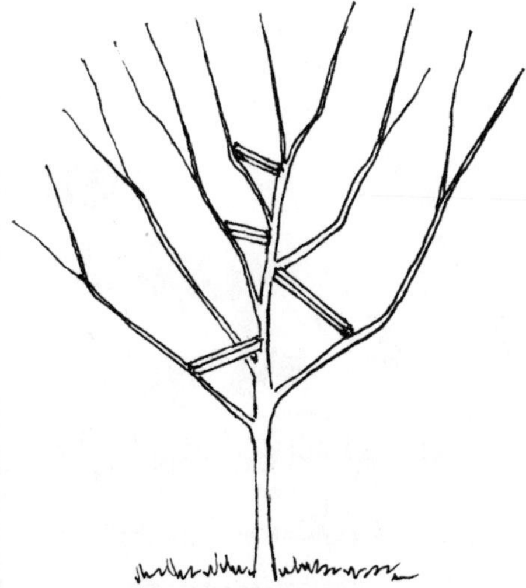

A tree thinned in the third spring, with leader (tip) headed back, and branches spread to create strong crotches for heavy load fruit bearing.

This is the last spring for pruning of apples, plums, pears, cherries and apricots. Pruning from now on will be in summer when the leaves have lost their shine and when the spring growth spurt has stopped. Peaches and nectarines will continue to be pruned in late winter, for they produce fruit on second-year wood.

Peaches and Nectarines

Plant one-year-old whips of peaches or nectarines in early spring, cutting back to 18".

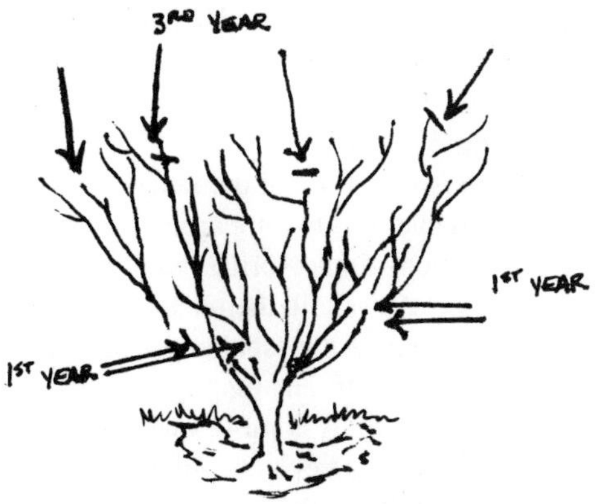

Pruning a peach at the beginning of the third growing season.

Four scaffold branches are selected at the end of the growing season. These are headed back as indicated at *a*. In the second year some of the lateral shoots are thinned, and tips of the scaffold branches are headed back lightly.

In the third spring, maintain the scaffold branches you selected last spring, but head back the tips of the scaffold branches to the nearest lateral. This will promote spreading to allow sunlight into the crown to ripen the fruit. Remove any waek or crossing branches. This is *open-center pruning*.

For successive seasons, prune in late winter to remove weak, injured, or crossing wood. There will be long whips of new growth from last year. Cut back each of these to leave six to ten flower buds. Flower buds are fat and not as tightly adpressed against the stem as leaf buds.

Peaches respond very well to being espaliered in the areas where growing them in the open is a risk because of early spring frosts on the fruit buds or where winter temperatures are often below minus 15°F degrees, the point at which trees are killed. The trees can also be grown espaliered on rows of wires. When frost threatens, a protective cover can be drawn over the trees, much as one draws drapes across windows.

Pruning Apricots

There is very little of the range of this book suitable for growing apricots. They tend to bloom about April 1, with little a grower can do to hold them back. They are very amenable to the espalier method of growing, however, and more gardeners should try them. A home-grown, tree-ripened apricot is beyond compare.

Pruning follows the same pattern as for peaches and nectarines. Flowers are produced on spurs on older wood as well as on the previous seasons' shoots. Encourage spurs during the summer by pinching back lateral shoots when they are about three inches long.

Espalier Pruning

The Espalier method of pruning goes back to the courtyards of Roman villas as well as to the Middle Ages when castles were often under seige and food-producing crops were produced within the defensible walls. Fruits trees trained flat against a south-facing wall where heat collected were ideal. Later, as monasteries were constructed the same methods were employed.

In modern times the trellis or espalier method is used as a space-saving method and as a way to grow and protect a frost-tender plant. Harvesting and care are less labor-intensive, and the espaliered trees are beautiful.

Consider using espaliered fruit trees as a perimeter fence on your property where a poor view or un-neighborly neighbors are a problem. Think of the sight of the trees in bloom in spring, and then loaded with colorful fruits in late summer. See Chapter 7, "Plant Protection," for insight as to the ease of protecting an espaliered fruit tree of doubtful hardiness during winter and again at bloom time when spring frosts make impossible the growing of many fruits in the Mountain West, such as apricot, Japanese plum, peach, or fig.

The posts and wire are not unsightly. When Williamsburg, Virginia, was the site of the ruling British governor, espaliered fruit trees were grown on wire. The posts and wire were later removed when the trees were old enough to stand alone. The same holds true for the cordon method.

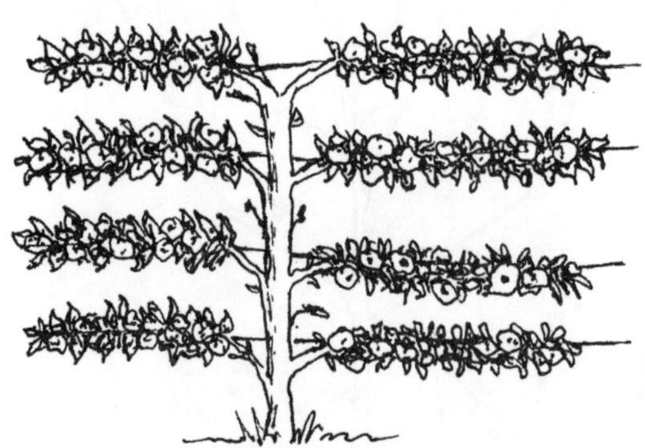

Mature fruit trees trellised on wires.

Cordoned fruit trees make an unusual fence.

One-year-old dwarf species whips are planted at the base of a wire fence, usually three-to-five wires high, with each about fifteen inches apart. The tree is allowed to grow to the top wire, and branch at will during the first season. At the beginning of the second season, the leader is clipped at the top wire and other branches selected at the locations of the other wires. A spring-type clothespin is ideal for gently forcing these branches into a 45° right angle. You may choose various patterns of trellising. Some are centuries old, such as The Tree of Life. This pattern, in addition to being very attractive, is sound in fruit culture, for the horizontal-growing branch will have the most fruit.

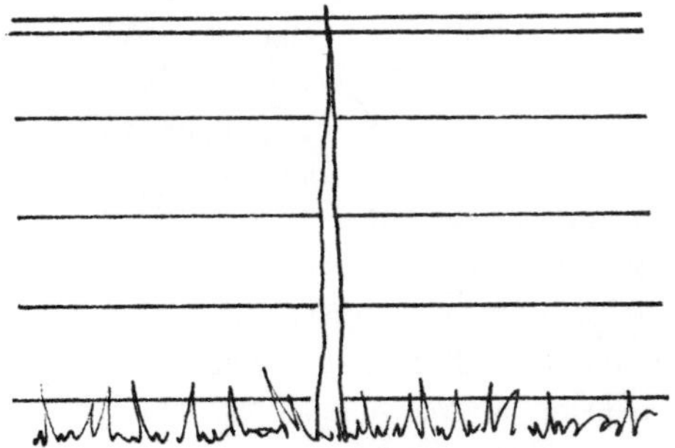

One-year-old whip is planted at base of five-wire fence. First clip is the leader at the height of the top wire. Adventitious buds will be activated. Those chosen to remain and grow will be those at the height of each wire.

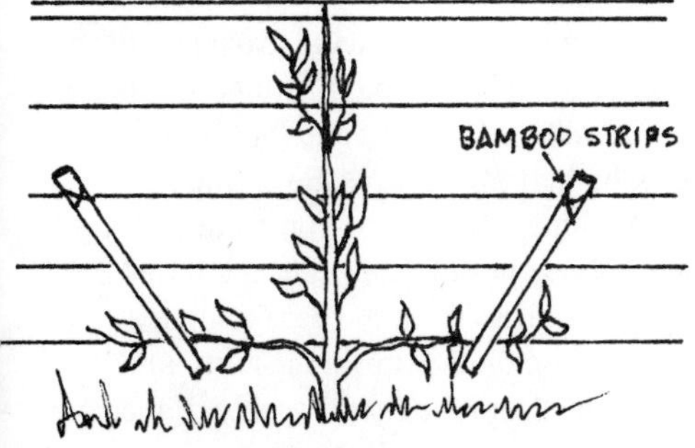

First, second, and third year training will achieve the correct pattern.

Styles of Espalier Are Centuries Old

The end of the third year of pruning doesn't mean you never prune again. In fact, owners of espalierd trees have laughingly referred to their charges as "pet trees" because they require as much attention as a pet. "One never goes out the door without pruners in the pocket," is the admonition, for there are wayward sprouts that must be eliminated as they form. Shoot elongation may be seen after the tree blooms, and these must be eliminated, saving only one replacement shoot from the many terminal shoots at the ends of each branch. Apples bloom and fruit on spurs, which are three or four inch shoots from a main branch. The spurs last about three years, and will be replaced by new spurs as the old spurs drop.

Fruiting depends on the species. For example, a mature espaliered apple will produce about one-half bushel. A pear will produce about one-fourth bushel. Cherries and plums are prolific with production of nearly a bushel. If you are growing some species of doubtful hardiness - for example, a Santa Rosa plum, on the Front Range of Colorado, you will want to follow winter protection procedures as seen in Chapter 7 "Plant Protection."

Small Fruits

Currants

Red currant bushes are pruned when set out to leave three wide-spread canes pointing outward. After the bush is mature in about three years, it is pruned on the renewal method of removing one or two of the oldest canes to the ground each year. Old canes have light-colored bark. Remove weak and crossing wood, but never head back a branch, for fruit is borne on last year's wood and on short lateral spurs of older wood. Examine all canes each spring for borers and remove any infested canes.

Black currants are pruned ruthlessly because they often carry a disease-carrying mite in the fruiting buds, causing a condition known as Big Bud. The same framework is developed as above for red currants, but more old canes are removed after the crop is harvested. Heading back each cane is encouraged because fruit buds will form on new growth before winter.

White currants are pruned to preserve a vase-shaped structure of about eight branches. Shorten all side shoots in summer and again in winter, and tip-prune leaders in winter. Allow for the occasional replacement of an original branch by a suitably placed younger one.

Gooseberries

Firm control is needed for a gooseberry, and gloves are essential in pruning them. At planting time limit the number of canes springing from the base to three. Allow two more to form each year till the third year, and no more after that, renewing each by cutting two to the ground each year, and allowing new ones to form. Unlike other shrubs, cut to the inward and upward-point bud. Large, dessert quality fruits will be formed on the bush that is heavily pruned. Gooseberry tends to layer itself, as well; so be watchful for branches that touch the ground. They will be rooted and travelling in no time to become a thicket.

In England gooseberry bushes become artful decorations as miniature topiary. Train a bush to a single stem, allowing only twigs to form at the top. Gradually remove the lowest twig until the "tree" has reached the height you desire. Four feet is a good height and allows picking of the fruit without bending.

Gooseberry bushes become artful topiary and allow picking without bending.

Raspberries

This fruit should be the universal fruit of the Mountain West because it is so easily grown here and so universally envied by the rest of the world. Because of our high-quality sunlight, raspberries can be grown successfully with only four hours of summer sunlight daily.

Pruning at planting time consists of using the single cane that comes with the purchase as a hand-hold; then removing it to four inches above ground after planting. Sprouting will occur from the root as well as from the cane stub.

Managing a raspberry patch is easiest when the canes are coralled with a post and wire arrangement. The wires unhook to make picking easy.

The canes are allowed to grow at will the first season after spring planting. In the fall of the first season, the canes are headed back by half after leaves have fallen.

The June crop will be complete on the lateral branches of those canes, but new canes will arise from the base to give a second crop on the tips in the early fall. The canes from the first season will then die and can be pruned out. As before, prune the canes back by half after leaf-fall, and you are ready for a new season. In early spring as new growth is beginning, thin to leave only the strongest canes so that about eight inches is left between canes.

Almost any variety can also be mowed off with the lawnmower in the early fall, and new canes will grow the following spring to produce berries on the tips.

Raspberries are easily controlled by a post-and-wire arrangement.

Blackberries

Only the areas with long, hot summers within the range of this book can accomodate blackberries. Other areas may try but the berries never attain the sweetness of those grown where there is a long hot growing season. New varieties will come on the market, however; so watch for them and experiment.

Blackberries are best grown as against a wall or fence as a cordon. Tie a fan of canes securely to the fence or wall in three or four intervals per cane, for they can escape more quickly than any other vine. If a cane touches the ground, it quickly forms a ratoon by rooting at the tip to become a new plant. Blackberries bear fruit on the same wood for several years, but the best fruit forms on new canes; so cut out canes that have fruited and new ones will form.

If you have a south-facing wall, try a boysenberry. They are handled in the same manner as blackberry, but are much less vigorous. You may wish to attach a roll of clear plastic above them that you can roll down over the vine so that heat is trapped around the forming berries when fall days are too cool for ripening.

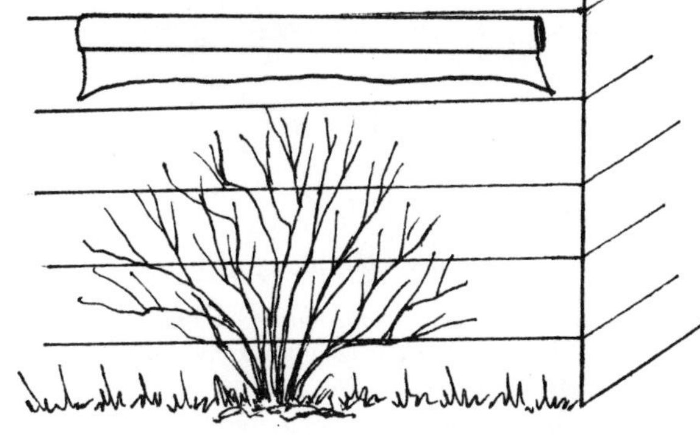

An old window blind or a roll of clear plastic attached to the wall above a tender boysenberry can be rolled down as protection on a frosty spring or fall night.

Grapes

Grape pruning is accomplished in late winter - February or March. The purpose of pruning table grapes is to limit the number of buds on wood formed the previous summer. Leaving too many buds would result in later ripening, poor quality fruit, and would weaken the vine for next years's growth and fruiting.

Training the newly planted grape vine is begun the second year. The first year let the vine sprawl all over, making as many leaves as possible and establishing its root system. At this time, it also needs copious amounts of water.

In winter after the summer of growth, the fence is erected and wires strung. The first wire is strung at about five feet high, with a second one at 2 1/2 feet above the soil level.

The vine is then given the first training cuts with the selection of a stem to become the trunk and with four canes as illustrated, and two renewal spurs for next year.

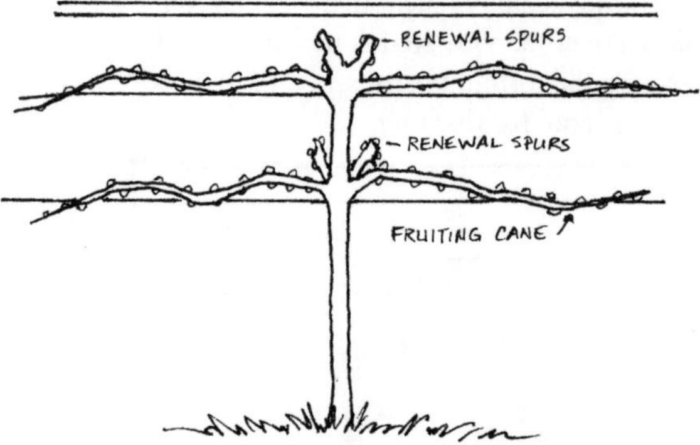

Training cuts are made during the first winter with selection of a central trunk, four arms, and four renewal spurs. The canes you save should be at least the diameter of a pencil.

Count the buds on the canes. The total should be forty. You may wish to allow as many as sixty in years to come, but no more, for you would jeopardize the vigor of the vine. The spurs that you leave should have only two buds each.

Conclusion

Pruning is an art gained as much by experience as by book learning. Keep the shears sharp, but avoid opening a wound unnecessarily because the shears are in your hand at the moment.

CHAPTER 10

Windbreak Care

Do you need a windbreak? If you live in the country in the Mountain West, you do! A windbreak gives your crops and stock animals a boost that is easily measured. If you live in a town or city, don't overlook the planting of tall evergreens on the windy sides of your property as an energy saving measure. Both country and city dweller may not be aware that wind is dictating the success or failure of crop-growing or gardening efforts. Almost everyone in the Mountain West has, at one time, experienced winter-killed perennials, late-ripening vegetables, damage to trees and shrubs, or the devastating loss of a crop of many acres. If daily wind speeds are at ten miles per hour, and if frequent storms stir up wind at fifty miles per hour or above, you would be wise to plan for a windbreak.

A windbreak benefits a property by moderating windspeed up to 10 times its height to its windward side and within 30 times its height to the leeward side. The "lee" is the windless, protected side. An added benefit of the leeward is an increase in temperature of five degrees on a windy day, a decrease in water consumption, improved germination rates, and increased yield of fruit and flowers. There will also be an increase in the selection of plants you are able to grow where a windbreak is present.

The area safest for your home and its landscaping is within two to four times the windbreak's height to leeward where wind speeds can be reduced by as much as fifty percent.

A windbreak is a grouping of deciduous and evergreen trees and shrubs planted to

There may be microclimates that are not immediately apparent.

abate the force of wind. Storms arrive from different directions at different seasons. The Cooperative Extension Service in your county will give you the general direction of weather fronts. Study the wind patterns for a year on your own land before you decide where the windbreak will be planted. There may be microclimates that are not immediately apparent. If the site is sloping, go to the Soil Conservation Service in your area for assistance in terracing the land to prevent wind and water erosion. They will also lay out direction of diversion ditches that will direct run-off water from storms or snow-melt toward the windbreak. Keeping a windbreak watered is not easy in our arid land, and conserving water will be part of your plan.

Site Preparation for the Country Home

The area needed for a windbreak is about sixty feet wide and the length of your property on the windward side(s). This may seem like a lot to give up from the production of crops, but the benefits are greater than the loss. This amount of land will be planted in five staggered rows - three of trees and two of shrubs.

Subsoiling is an agricultural term that means breaking or fracturing the soil to a depth of two to three feet. If you have only a few acres, you probably don't want to purchase equipment to do this, as it is a one-time operation. Hire a nearby farmer who has the equipment to penetrate the soil this deep. After subsoiling is complete, disc the soil to break up the clods so that a cover crop can be planted.

The next procedure is to install snow fence along the length of your property on the windward side. This will break the force of wind and wind-driven snow to collect snow for its mulching benefits and to store meltwater deep in the soil when the trees are young.

Planting a cover crop is the next procedure. The seeds of legumes, grains, and grasses in a mixture will be a good choice. The seeds are large and using a Brillion drill to plant will push them to the correct depth for good germination. Late fall seeding will take advantage of fall rains, but prevent germination, which will take place in early spring. Plow the crop under just as it begins to bloom in early summer. If you can irrigate the cover crop, plant a single legume, such as cisor milkvetch or buckwheat, and plow it under just after the flowers have faded. The decaying cover crop will add the soil nutrients needed by the windbreak trees. Cultivate lightly to control weeds throughout the summer.

In December get in touch once again with the Soil Conservation Service. They will have young seedling trees available for sale at a very nominal price for persons owning over 2 1/2 acres of rural land. The trees will arrive in early April, but you must get your order in early.

Choosing Windbreak Species

From the list available, choose three upright evergreens and one shrub evergreen. Pines and junipers are the best choice, for they are native and can withstand drought. *Pinus ponderosa* (Ponderosa Pine) is tall at maturity, and with a broad crown to baffle wind. *Pinus flexilis* (Limber Pine), on the other hand, is another native accustomed to wind as its name implies. The latter are seldom offered for sale, however. *Pinus nigra* and *Pinus sylvestris* (Scots Pine and Austrian Pine) are possibilities at lower than 7,500 feet in altitude. Both the native Juniper, (*Juniperus scopulorum*) and Red Cedar (*J. virginiana*) are excellent choices.

For the shrub evergreen that you will need, Pfitzer Juniper (*J. chinensis*) will grow eight feet high and eight feet across at maturity if irrigation can be supplied and the area kept weed-free for two years.

For the deciduous species, you will be looking for a tall tree. The native cottonwood of your area is a good candidate if water is available in abundance. If not, the Siberian elm, regarded as a nuisance tree in town, is able to withstand hardship. You may also want to choose a decduous shrub species for planting in between the tall deciduous tree species to protect it during its youth. Choose one that can provide some food for birds, such as honeysuckle or a native currant or serviceberry.

Arrangement of Species

A windbreak with an abrupt or nearly vertical tree form on the windward side is more effective than one with an incline toward the wind. Thus, the fast-growing cottonwood or Siberian Elm is planted on the outside, which will also favor its easy removal after its lifespan of about thirty years.

Plant the tallest-growing evergreen in the center, with the other two evergreens flanking. The evergreen shrub is planted on the leeward edge for catching blowing snow and providing cover for quail and other ground-feeding birds.

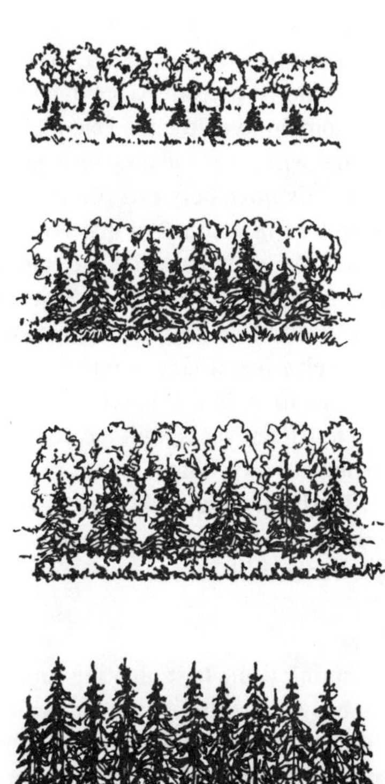

As the trees grow, the structure of the windbreak develops. The density of the profile, which is the wind-slowing aspect of the barrier, will remain for 40 years or more.

■ . . . *cottonwood or Siberian Elm is planted on the outside, which will also favor its easy removal after its lifespan of about thirty years.*

Spacing Between Rows

Distance between rows can vary without seriously affecting the effectiveness of the windbreak. The density of the profile is what matters. The advantage of wide spacing, such as twenty feet, is ease of culture and space for root development. It is hard to imagine at planting time that those little trees can possibly grow to touch together, or that the soil between rows will fill with roots. **Within rows, trees should**

be planted no less than ten feet apart and no more than twenty feet apart. The wide spacing should be used for large mechanized equipment to cultivate. Use the spacing that will accomodate your equipment. **The distance between the trees is measured by the amount of growth in ten years when the crowns will close together to form the barrier. Therefore, Siberian Elms and Cottonwoods should be spaced eight to twelve feet apart**. Conifers should be spaced six to eight feet apart in the row. After ten to fifteen years, thin the conifer rows to prevent crowding and loss of lower limbs. **Shrubs are planted three to five feet apart to prevent snow blowing through beneath the trees.**

Planting

Early spring is the best planting time. You can busy yourself digging holes during late fall and early spring after the frost has gone out of the ground. The Soil Conservation Service sometimes provides polymer gel* at a nominal price to mix with the soil. This is a very good practice, but the backfill must be absolutely dry before mixing the powder. See Chapter 4 "Soils" for the benefits of the polymer. The fertilizer cubes often sold at the same time the windbreak trees are delivered are of dubious value. More little tree's demise have been diagnosed as resulting from overfertilization than for any other cause. The cubes may be a good practice after three or more years when the trees are established.

The rows of trees in a windbreak are usually planted in straight rows. There is no law preventing you from planting some of them in groups of three or five in a more natural way. The cultivation will not be as easy between them, but if the pathway between has gentle curves, there should be no problem. The only stipulation to make an effective windbreak is that the windward row must be straight to form the vertical barrier that is most effectual in breaking the force of the storms.

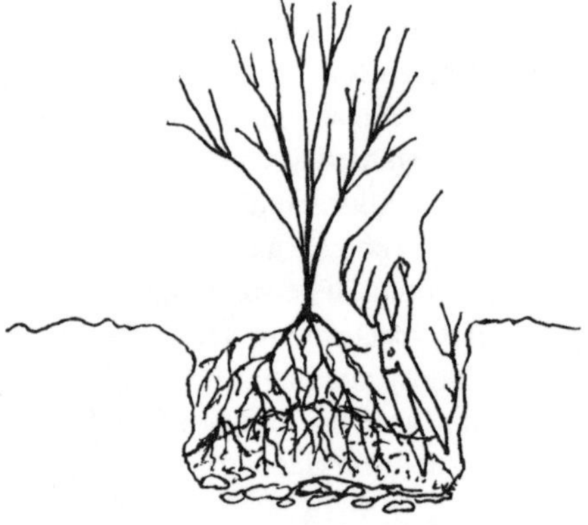

Planting holes have vertical sides. Roots too long to fit in the hole are clipped rather than pushed up the sides of the hole.

Planting depth should be the same as the plants grew in the nursery. A common mistake is setting trees too deep, thinking the deep hole will protect them. Instead, the small trees are difficult to spot during cultivation. Moreover, if the cultivator is inexperienced, the trees will be covered even more. Conifers are especially sensitive to deep planting, and may die as a result of it.

Planting too shallow is also a mistake, since parts of the root systems will dry out if above ground, and trees will also be damaged by wind whipping the tops.

Mulch the new planting with pole peelings - a product of pruning and tree removal that is often free from your county government.

* *See Glossary*

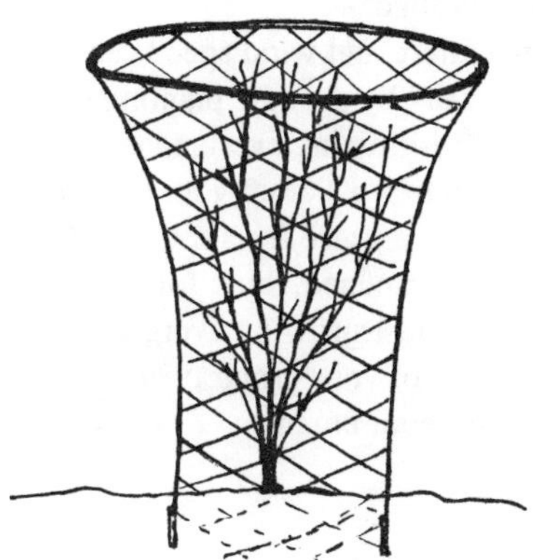

A newly planted tree protected by a wire enclosure covered with clear plastic.

Care After Planting

It has been said, "A good windbreak makes a poor pasture. If pastured, it soon becomes a poor windbreak." Windbreaks used as shade and feed lots by livestock will be damaged irretrievably.

Leaf litter is important in holding moisture and maintaining soil permeability. When the trees are young, haul bags of leaves for distribution on the soil in late fall. Disc them in to leave a rough surface for catching winter's moisture.

Irrigation

Furrow or flood irrigation supplied monthly during the growing season will give the young trees a good start. See Chapter 8 "Learning To Apply Water." In many areas of the Mountain West two years of "establishment water" is enough, and the planting can sustain itself after that. Winter watering will be necessary the first two years as well as when the ground is bare.

Weeding is imperative when the trees are young. The shade of the trees will gradually eliminate weeds later on. Discing frequently and lightly will be of greatest benefit. If you prefer to use chemical weed retardants, consult the Soil Conservaton Service. As time passes, lay down a mulch of pole peelings four inches thick. This will be effective in holding moisture and preventing weeds. As this organic mulch breaks down it will add nutrients needed for growth by the trees.

■ *Leaf litter is important in holding moisture.*

Insect and disease damage may occur. If you suspect either of these, collect some specimens of the insect and the damage, plus any suspected diseased foliage for a trip to the Cooperative Extension Office. A word of caution - don't expect the Extension Agent to be able to identify the problem if the specimens have been sitting on the dashboard of the pickup for a day or so!

Damage from Animals

Rabbits, mice, ground squirrels, gophers, voles are all suspect in the damage possibility. The Tubex-Tube* will protect from the smaller animals, but you can fashion tree protection yourself from poultry wire and clear plastic. "Thiram" is a fungicide that is, strangely, effective against rabbits. It must be sprayed on the trees about every six weeks, however.

Deer will find the windbreak attractive for browse and for rubbing the velvet from their antlers. Fencing must be eight feet high in the Mountain West to prevent the mule deer from bounding over it. This is considerably taller than necessary where the smaller deer are native. There are many chemical deterrents coming on the market that are effective in repelling animals. The wildlife division of the National Forest Service has many tips in dealing with animals. Your own dogs will remain a very effective foe of deer.

* *See Glossary*

How To Measure the Height of a Tree

There are times when it is useful to know the exact height of a tree. With a windbreak, it is useful to know the height of the windward row of trees for your records each year.

On a sunny, sunny day drive a good-sized stake into the ground. Measure its height from ground level to tip. When the length of the shadow of the stake is the same length as the stake, measure the shadow of the tree.

The City Windbreak

Air temperature and wind speed can be diminished easily by a single planting of two or three tall-growing evergreens toward the windward side of your property. You may not have space for a true windbreak, but low-branched, thick foliaged, and moderately fast-growing evergreens add to the value of your property and reduce energy requirements.

Part III

Choosing Plants to Fit Your Plan

CHAPTER 11

Trees, Deciduous and Evergreen

The diversity of trees in cities and towns of the Mountain West is owed to pioneers who lovingly cared for cuttings and nursery stock during the long trek westward. It is probable this task was initiated by or delegated to women. Journals kept by pioneer women exist today tell of caring for cuttings inserted into the moisture of potatoes so that the cutting would remain viable until it could be rooted in the new surroundings at the end of the journey. Homesickness was a reality for each family moving West. Having trees and shrubs that grew near former homes would help them grow accustomed to new territory. Fruit trees were essential for food. Word traveled quickly that very few native fruits were available in the West; thus fruit tree seeds were part of every load of goods that traveled West. Later on, nurserymen in the Midwest traveled West with sapling fruit trees packed in moist sawdust each spring. Sales were brisk among the settlers.

The native cottonwoods, aspen, willows, and poplars were planted around homesteads as quick shade, while the native Hackberry (*Celtis occidentalis*), being the closest to a hardwood, was used in making furniture, wagon wheels, and handles for tools.

Today the climate is modified with irrigation and vegetation so that almost as many genera and species of trees and shrubs that grow in the Northeast are seen growing

Choose the tree shape as carefully as you would a piece of fine furniture: columnar, round, vase, weeping, pyramidal, oval, multi-trunked.

in the Mountain West. Visitors are quickly told, however, it takes a heap more "doing" to grow some of the Northeastern species.

After World War II, thousands of low-profile, ranch-style homes were built as suburban populations soared. These were often landscaped with trees of sixty feet or more in height. Now that these are dying out, they are being replaced with trees more in keeping with the scale of the one-story home. The new homes of today are often two or more stories in height, and the sixty-foot oaks, maples, and American linden are in perfect scale.

In studying Part I, you will note that trees for shade are planted to the south or southwest of the area to be shaded. Further study will aid you in placing the framing trees, the patio shade trees, the shelter trees or windbreak on a farm or country home. Chapter 6, "Planting Procedures" and Chapter 7 "Plant Protection" will give you direction for planting and culture. In the legend below you will see the letter "P" denoting those trees that need protection. Don't be put off in choosing these, for there are degrees of protection. Planting a tree in an established neighborhood where old trees are growing, or in the protection of a building as opposed to the "out on the lone prairee" is the general meaning of the letter "P." Extensive construction of protective winter covers will be needed by a tender species, and direction will be given.

Tree shapes are an important adjunct to the style of architecture of your home. Use them wisely. Don't try to include one plant of each shape. Limit your selection to several plant types that will serve as the dominant forms in the design. You may wish to invest in one of the kits available today to make a model of your home so that you can also make models of tree shapes. Try each of them at different locations around the model of your home. Then use the lists below to choose the trees that best fit the site.

■ *. . . it takes a heap more "doing" to grow some of the Northeastern species.*

Symbols:

Percent number indicates comparison rating with 100%.

D - Can survive on natural precipitation after two-year period with establishment water*.

I - Irrigation as needed.

H - Suitable also for above 6,000 feet in altitude.

P - Needs varying degrees of protection, such as a location near buildings, other trees, or as described.

Deciduous Trees for the Mountain West

■ *Acer campestre*,
HEDGE MAPLE, IP, 60%, 15-25'. A rounded crown, small tree often used as a hedge, but serves equally well as a small tree to frame a doorway. Slow-growing.

■ *A. ginnala*,
AMUR MAPLE, IP, 60%, 15-20'. Large, multistemmed shrub to small tree with trilobed, dark, glossy, green foliage. Brilliant red fall color; winged seeds often brightly colored in summer to become a nuisance if they fall and germinate.

CULTIVAR:

'Flame' - Extremely hardy; brilliant red fall foliage; introduced by Soil Conservation Service; not tolerant of alkaline soils.

■ *A. grandidentatum*,
WASATCH MAPLE, IP, 60% 15-25'. Native of alkaline soils of Wyoming, Utah, and New Mexico; strong, orange-red fall color. Slow; difficult to locate in nurseries.

■ *A. griseum*,
PAPERBARK MAPLE, IP, 50%, to 30'. Rounded crown; deeply lobed leaves; vivid scarlet fall color. Interesting papery sheets of old bark peel off and new cinnamon-brown bark is exposed. Very slow grower. Watch for aphids.

■ *A. negundo*, BOX ELDER, ID, 50%, 25'. Familiar tree of canyons and dry and seasonal water courses in the Mountain West. Not native, but has naturalized. Knarled in old age, weak limbs, oval crown, bright yellow fall color. Subject to box elder bug, leaf rollers, aphids, spider mites, borers.

CULTIVAR:

'Flamingo' - Pink, white, and green foliage very showy in spring; handsome green and white foliage in summer; fall color is bright yellow.

■ *A. palmatum*,
JAPANESE MAPLE, IP, 50%, to 25'. Artistically branched with delicate, deeply lobed leaves that are often blood-red. Brilliant orange fall foliage. Much sought after for the Japanese garden. Unexplained die-back probably due to lack of hardiness. Needs shelter constructed over entire plant for winter, or can be grown in a tub on wheels to be wheeled to a winter shelter. Look for new, hardier selections to appear on the market in the near future.

■ *A. platanoides*,
NORWAY MAPLE,70%, IP,30-45', rounded except as noted; dense shade. All cultivars have yellow-green flowers, winged fruits, yellow fall color. Roots close to surface. Frost-cracking may be a problem. Hardening-off in fall and winter watering important.

CULTIVARS:

'Columnare' - A columnar shape that may replace poplars. The upright limbs have short branches, wide crotches.

'Deborah' - Straight stem and upright growth habit. New leaf color is reddish-purple and later turns green; heavy shade.

'Crimson King' - Maroon leaf color remains all season; the oldest red-leafed cultivar. Flowers are maroon with yellow.

'Emerald Lustre' - Vigorous grower with best branching habit of all cultivars. Leaves are thick in texture.

'Globosum' - A globose form that is low growing and with broad spreading crown, which may fill a design need.

'Parkway' - Still another shape, that of a pyramid to oval growth habit with strong central leader; good green leaf color.

'Royal Red' - Slower growing than 'Crimson King' but with dark red, thick-textured, glossy leaves exhibited throughout the season.

'Schwedler' - The cultivar under test the longest time period; reddish flowers and leaves early in the season; leaves later turn green with red veins. Fall foliage is purple.

'Superform' - Straight trunk, rapid growth, heavy shade, slightly upright habit.

■ *A. rubrum,*
RED MAPLE, IP, 70%, 30-50'.The tree most often remembered by transplanted Easterners. Spectacular red fall foliage. Spring planting only. Prefers moist, slightly acid soil. Not tolerant of urban pollution.

CULTIVARS:

'Northwood' - A vigorous oval grower with red, orange, and yellow fall color. Will withstand the occasional winter when temperatures fall below minus twenty degrees below zero F. Tested at University of Minnesota.

'October Glory' - Voted by nurserymen as the best.

'Red Sunset' - Outstanding fall red color; not as hardy as 'Northwood'.

■ *A. saccharinum,*
SOFT MAPLE, IMP, 60%, 70-80'. Attractive, shaggy bark; large limbs easily trained to wide crotch angles; yellow fall color sometimes shading to apricot. Sensitive to alkaline clay soils, resulting in chlorosis. Weak limbs cannot withstand heavy snow loads.

■ *A. saccharum,*
SUGAR MAPLE, IP, 70%, 50'. This is the maple of maple syrup fame. Smooth gray bark becoming deeply furrowed with age. Medium green foliage in summer turning to yellow, then brilliant orange-red. Slow of growth, but puts on about one foot of height per year.

CULTIVAR:

'Bonfire' - Fast growing; best color of all maples.

■ *Aesculus glabra,*
OHIO BUCKEYE, IP, 60%, 30-40'. Pyramidal shape. Pale yellow cockade flowers in spring, followed by smooth, brown, poisonous seeds. Brilliant orange fall color long-lasting.

■ *A. hippocastanum,*
HORSE CHESTNUT, IP, 60%, 70'. Blooms are held like giant candelabrum. Can withstand dry soil if spring irrigation is adequate. Orange fall color.

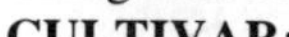

CULTIVAR:

'O'Neill Red' - 30'; Dark green palmate leaves; deep red, cockade blooms in early summer; good for small dooryard or patio shade.

■ *Ailanthus altissima,*
TREE OF HEAVEN, IP, 40%, 40-50'. This is the tree "that grew in Brooklyn," meaning that it will grow in a crack in the sidewalk, under extremely adverse conditions. Slender smooth trunk, furrowed with age; narrow crotches; compound foliage; greenish panicles of flowers followed by seeds sometimes brightly colored rose or red. Foliage said to smell "like a wet dog." Brittle, easily damaged by heavy snow loads; sucker shoots and germination of seeds a nuisance.

■ *Alnus tenuifolia*,
ALDER, IMP, 60%, 25-30'. A native that withstands wet soils. Cherry bark, deeply marked with lenticels; often multi-trunked; serrated foliage, orange in fall. Small, cone-like fruits. Good tree for townhouse patio.

■ *Amelanchier alnifolia*,
SERVICEBERRY, IMD, 60%, 15-20'. Native of much of the Mountain West. Serrated foliage; racemes of fragrant white flowers followed by sweet blue fruit used by the Indians as an ingredient of pemmican. Many sucker shoots, but can be formed into a multi-trunk tree; drought tolerant, but can withstand irrigation as well. The common name comes from use as shade for outdoor church services by the circuit-rider preachers in pioneer times. Pronunciation of the name was "Sarvisberry" at that time.

■ *A. laevis*,
SHADBLOW, IP, 70%, 25'. A dainty door-framing tree covered with white flowers in spring followed by red fruit loved by birds. Yellow-orange fall color.
CULTIVARS:
'Robin Hill' - Somewhat fastigiate; will reach 20 feet and 12 feet wide; pink flowers followed by red fruits. Fall color is yellow to red. Thin barked trunk should be wrapped in winter.

'Cumulus' - Larger flowers than other cultivars and best fall color. Recommended for street tree because it is small enough to reach maturity under overhead wires without pruning.

■ *Betula nigra*,
RIVER BIRCH, IP, 70%, 35'. Tan bark peeling in papery flakes. A native of stream banks in the foothills zone.

CULITVAR:
'Heritage' - A new introduction bred to have smooth tan persistant bark. Resistence to birch borer and leaf miner.

■ *B. pendula*,
EUROPEAN WEEPING BIRCH, IP, 60%, 60'. A white-barked tree seldom seen now because it is extremely susceptible to the bronze birch borer.

■ *B. platyphylla*,
var. japonica , IP, 60%, 60'. A white-barked, graceful tree, native of northern Japan.
CULTIVAR:
'Whitespire' - The best birch tested thus far to take the place of Betula pendula, 'European Weeping Birch', which is seldom seen in commerce because of its susceptibility to environmental problems and borer. 'Whitespire' has the same white bark and lacy foliage, but assumes a symmetrical shape with central leader. Resistant to drought and bronze birch borer.

■ *Carpinus betulus*,
EUROPEAN HORNBEAM, IP, 70%, 30-40'. Dense shade; small fruits sometimes troublesome; very slow; drought tolerant, but also tolerates wet soils; sun or partial shade. Fall color is yellow-orange.

■ *Catalpa bignonoides*,
UMBRELLA CATALPA, IP, 40%, 20'. Grafted to upright boles, forming a standard with dense head of ill-smelling large, light-green leaves; long panicles of white flowers in spring, followed by long bean-like pods that persist into winter. An ethnic tree beloved by immigrants from northern Italy.

■ *C. speciosa,*

WESTERN CATALPA, IP, 80%, 70'. Tall, straight, narrow silhouette with short, wide-angled, heavy limbs. Carries a snow load well. Large, light green leaves; white flowers sweetly scented, followed by long seed pods which drop in winter. No insects or diseases. Useful when a framing tree is needed in a narrow area. Other species now under test. Subject to winter sunscald in its youth.

■ *Celtis occidentalis,*

HACKBERRY, I, 80%, 50-60'. Native of most of the Mountain West. Strong, straight growth pattern; wide-angled crotches. Light green compound leaves; berries loved by birds, yellow fall color. Leaves attacked by psyllid which galls the leaves but does little harm to the tree. Warblers attracted to the psyllid.

■ *Cercidiphyllum japonicum,*

KATSURA TREE, IP, 60%, 40-60'. A rounded crown; often multi-trunked tree with blue-green foliage, shaggy bark with age; burnt orange then golden yellow in fall; slow to establish; not easily found in nurseries.

■ *Cercis canadensis,*

REDBUD TREE, IP, 80%, 25-30'. A sheltered spot will suit this graceful tree with heart-shaped leaves, lavender blooms before foliage. No insects or diseases, but sometimes hard to establish. Sun or dappled shade; good drainage but moist soil suit it best.

■ *Cladrastis lutea,*

YELLOWWOOD TREE, IP, 70%. Named for the yellow heart wood. Very hardy, deep-rooted and somewhat drought tolerant; compound leaves yellow in fall. Racemes of fragrant white flowers after maturity; always forms a double trunk low to soil line. Smallest trunk should be removed at early age. Difficult to locate in nurseries.

■ *Cornus florida x kousa,*

HYBRID DOGWOOD, IP, 60%, 15-20'. Worth finding the right location. Prefers light shade, cool root zone in loamy soil; pink flowers in August followed by red fruits loved by birds. Red fall foliage. Protect with constructed shelter in upper zones of this book. Turfgrass should not grow under this dogwood. It has an allelopathic reaction that will kill the dogwood. In the East a disease is killing C. florida but C. kousa is immune. The following are hybrids of the two and are resistant to disease.

CULITVARS:

'Aurora' - the pink flowers are a break-through in breeding.

'Constellation' - White flowers.

' Ruth Ellen' - Sterile white flowers.

■ *C. mas,*

CORNELIAN CHERRY, IP, 70%, 10-15'. Small tree branching near the ground. Brought by pioneers to the Mountain West; very long-lived and drought tolerant; yellow flowers beflore leaves and more reliable than forsythia. Slow to establish. Red fall fruit. Difficult to locate in nurseries.

■ *C. racemosa*,
GRAY DOGWOOD, IP, 70%, 15-20'. Small tree tolerant of alkaline soils; white flowers in May followed by white fruit on red stems. Good red fall color. Difficult to locate in nurseries.

■ *Crataegus crus-galli*,
COCKSPUR HAWTHORN, IP, 60%, 15-20'. Round crown low to ground. Small glossy bluish leaves; red-purple in fall. White flowers, red haws hang on late into winter.

■ *C. laevigata*,
ENGLISH HAWTHORN, IP, 60%, 25'. Smooth shiny leaves, sharp thorns, smooth gray bark.
CULTIVAR:
'Crimson Cloud' - Brilliant small red berries after leaves fall make it appear as a red cloud. Bred to withstand compacted soil with poor aeration.

■ *C. mollis*,
DOWNY HAWTHORN, IP, 60%, 15-20'. Another round crown low to ground. Serrated leaves pubescent beneath. White flowers, red fruits. orange fall color.

■ *C. phaenopyrum*,
WASHINGTON HAWTHORN, IP, 60%, 30-40'. Round crown; Lobed leaves; red flowers a stunning sight in spring; long-lasting red fruits; orange fall color.

■ *C. rivularis*,
RIVER HAWTHORN, IP, 70%, 15-20'. A native to be planted more often in the foundation planting of homes at the base of the inevitable downspout. It can withstand the wet soil from occasional downpours. White flowers in spring followed by red fruits loved by birds. Scarlet fall color. If grown from collected seed, it puts down a root the first year, then puts up a shoot in the second spring.

■ *C. viridis*,
no common name, IP, 70%, 25-30'.
CULTIVAR:
'Winter King' - Silver bark, glossy-green leaves; clouds of white flowers in May, followed by persistent orange-red fruits that are showy throughout the winter.

■ *Elaeagnus angustifolia*,
RUSSIAN OLIVE, D, 50%, 25-25'. An escapee from cultivation. Shaggy bark, curving trunk and limbs; gray foliage; fragrant blooms in early summer followed by gray pubescent fruits loved by birds. Will naturalize. Disease resistant when grown slowly in a dry soil. Not suitable for the home landscape; best in a windbreak.

■ *Fagus sylvatica*,
EUROPEAN BEECH, Ip, 40%, 20-35'. Heavy shade; edible nuts; requires loamy soil; very slow to establish; many cultivars available with variegated or colored foliage.

■ *Fraxinus americana*,
WHITE ASH, IP, 60'. Glossy, compound foliage; dioecious; cultivars outstanding; subject to ash/lilac borer, dieback, sawfly, fall webworm.
CULTIVARS:
'Autumn Purple' - pyramidal-rounded outline with deep green leaves; pale lavender to deep red fall foliage.

'Elk Grove' - Large dark green compound foliage casts heavy shade in summer; purple fall foliage.

■ *F. nigra*,
BLACK ASH, IMP, 70%, 40-50'.
CULTIVAR:
'Fallgold' - an upright growing cultivar that can replace the troublesome poplars. Withstands wet soils; brilliant yellow fall color.

■ *F. pennsylvanica lanceolata*,
GREEN ASH, IMP, 70%, 60'. Rapid growing; dark green compound foliage brilliant yellow in September; pyramidal to rounded crown; subject to lilac/ash borer.
CULTIVARS :
'Cardan' - cultivar developed by USDA for reclamation of strip-mined soils; round-topped; fast-growing with pale yellow fall color. It's main advantage is increased resistance to ash borer; use in windbreaks; clean cultivation needed to attain best growth.

'Cimmaron' - upright oval shape; no flowers or fruit; spectacular fall folliage is first deep burgundy, then brick-red; good storm damage resistence; tolerant of alkaline soil.
'Newport' - An improved 'Marshall's Seedless' tough and vigorous.

'Patmore' - Tolerant of city condition; oval habit; vigorous.

■ *Gleditsia triacanthos inermis*, HONEYLOCUST, I, 80%, 50'. Wide-spreading crown; small,light green compound foliage turns yellow in fall; very drought tolerant; inconspicuous flowers and essentially no fruit. subject to borers and canker when stressed.
CULTIVARS:
'Halka' - widely oval with horizontal branches able to bear a snow load; vigorous.

'Skyline' - dense, symmetrical branches; graceful, spreading.

'Suncole' - maturing at 35' with similar spread; rounded crown; yellow-green foliage striking in spring and remains a standout in the landscape all summer.

■ *Gymnocladus dioica*,
KENTUCKY COFFEE TREE, IP, 50%, 50-60'. A strong, very hardy tree with deeply furrowed bark, rounded crown. Female trees bear racemes of white flowers followed by long bean-like pods that drop all winter. A tree that evokes mixed emotions - those who love it sing its praises loudly; those who hate it, go out of their way to bad-mouth it.

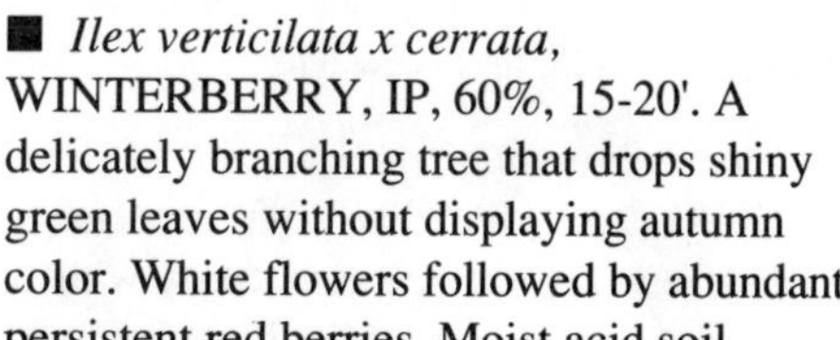

■ *Ilex verticilata x cerrata,*
WINTERBERRY, IP, 60%, 15-20'. A delicately branching tree that drops shiny green leaves without displaying autumn color. White flowers followed by abundant persistent red berries. Moist acid soil.

■ *Juglans mandshurica*,
MANCHURIAN WALNUT, IP, 50%, height unknown. This tree, under test at Colorado State Univ. has proved to be adaptable and hardy. It may become the only walnut available to Mountain Westerners.

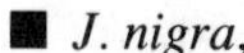

■ *J. nigra*,
BLACK WALNUT, I, 50% 50'. Strong, heavy limbs with age; weak when young; inconspicuous flowers followed by nuts; difficult to transplant. Fox squirrels plant the nuts in the lawn; resulting seedlings difficult to remove.

■ *Koelreuteria paniculata*,
GOLDEN RAIN TREE, IP, 60%, 30-40'. An outstanding tree within its range of hardiness. Does well at altitudes below 5,000 feet and in the southern range of this book - western Colorado, southern Utah,

southern Nevada, New Mexico. Light green compound foliage; sparingly branched, thus not a dense silhouette; large yellow flower panicles in July when few other trees and shrubs are blooming. Can withstand some alkalinity. Brown seed pods drop in fall, but easily removed with a blower.

■ *Laburnum x waterei*,
GOLDEN CHAIN TREE, IP, 50%, 10-15'. A small ornamental tree with yellow flowers in early summer on long pendulous racemes. Not for altitudes of over 5,000 feet; use only in the southern range of this book - western Colorado, southern Utah, southern Nevada, and New Mexico.

■ *Liriodendron tulipifera*,
TULIP POPLAR, IP, 70%, 70-80' and as wide. A magnificent tree at maturity with wide-spreading, strong, heavy branches; open silhouette; lyre-shaped leaves; yellow fall color; green, tulip-shaped flowers with orange stamens in spring; large, old specimens found in older parts of cities. Needs plenty of space. Difficult to find locally. Needs professional training in its youth.

■ *Maackia amurensis*,
AMUR MAACKIA, IP, 50%, 15-20'. A very hardy, small tree that bears attractive racemes of white flowers in July when few trees bloom. Dark green compound foliage not subject to insects or disease. Shiny, copper-colored bark in winter; transplants easily; grows readily from seed. Difficult to locate in nurseries.

■ *Maclura pomifera*,
OSAGE ORANGE, 50%, IP, 30-40'. The hedgerow and windbreak tree planted by early settlers has largely disappeared. Tough, spiny orange wood used for fence posts by settlers, bows by Indians. Short trunk, low to ground. Large green warty fruits not edible. This tree is not suitable for the home landscape, but should once again be a consideration for a windbreak or hedgerow on the country estate or farm property.

■ *Magnolia kobus*,
KOBUS MAGNOLIA, 40%, IP, 25-30'. Multi-stem trunk with pyramidal crown of dark green leaves; no fall color. Fragrant white flowers early spring in frost-free years. Likes heat; avoid southern aspect.

■ *M. soulangeana*,
SAUCER MAGNOLIA, 40%, IP, 25-30'. Rounded crown, coarse leaves, large pink and white flowers before leaves early spring in frost-free years. Likes heat; avoid southern aspect.

■ *M. stellata*,
STAR MAGNOLIA, 40%, IP, 10-15'. Pyramidal small crown; strappy, fluttery fragrant white flowers before leaves early spring in frost-free years. Likes heat; avoid southern aspect.

■ *Malus baccata mandschurica*,
MANCHURIAN CRABAPPLE, 60%, IP, 25-30'. An old species from which today's selections are made; also used as rootstock for grafted trees.

CULTIVARS:

'Adams' - rounded form, new foliage is bronze; carmine buds opening to pink; persistent fruit is burgundy; disease resistant.

'American Beauty'- excellent foliage; large double-red flowers; very light fruiting habit; an ideal street tree.

'Anne E' - a small weeping form only ten feet at maturity. Red buds open to white flowers; Oxblood fruits persist through January.

'Candied Apple' - a weeping form with red buds and single pink flowers; cherry-red fruits in July and persistent until Christmas; disease resistant.

'Centurion' - red flowers and glossy red persistant fruit. Fireblight resistant.

'David' - open, vigorous habit with pink to white flowers, abundant red fruit. Fireblight resistant. Withstands highly alkaline soil with good vigor.

'Donald Wyman' - rounded form, disease-resistant; red buds opening to white flowers. Small fruits turn from cardinal red in September to oxblood by November. A good substitute for the disease-prone 'Bechtel'.

'Dolgo' - an old favorite for jelly and pie; large pink blooms later than most; fruits drop quickly if not picked.

'Henry Kohankie' - a rounded crown; pale pink flower buds that develop into single white flowers; glossy red fruit held throughout the winter.

'Indian Summer' - wide-spreading to weeping growth habit; yellowish bark color adds winter interest; very little basal suckering; good fall color.

'Midwest' - introduced by the Soil Conservation Service for windbreaks; branches very low; flowers white; small red fruit persistent all winter; not suitable for highly alkaline soils.

'Molten Lava' - wide-spreading to weeping habit; deep red flowers in bud opening to white; fruit is red-orange and persistant. Some fireblight.

'Profusion' - purple new foliage; deep red flower buds opening to pink; red persistent fruit. Good resistence to fireblight.

'Ralph Shay' - dense growth habit; abundant fruit; some fireblight; some basal suckering.

'Robinson' - upright, spreading growth habit with single crimson flower buds that open to pink. Fruit is dark red, very abundant. Fireblight resistant.

■ *Moras alba*,
RUSSIAN MULBERRY, IP, 50%, 40-50'. Deep green foliage, inconspicuous flowers followed by purple edible fruits loved by birds, especially orioles. Fruit drops quickly after ripening, but can be swished into piles with strong stream of water from the hose; then scooped up and dried for winter bird feeding. Often dies back in a hard winter. Yellow fall foliage drops all at once when morning sun warms it after a hard freeze.

■ *Phellodendron amurense*,
AMUR CORKTREE, IP, 60%, 30-45'. A broad, round-crowned, dioecious tree with horizontal branching habit; deeply furrowed bark forms a cork-like pattern, adding winter interest. Can withstand partial shade; prefers slightly acid soil, good drainage. Panicles of greenish flowers in late May; not showy; black fruits on female trees; yellow fall foliage persisting briefly.

■ *Populus alba*,
WHITE POPLAR, 30%, I, 70'. Young trunks white or greenish. Dark green leaves, silvery beneath. Prefers moist, deep loam; roots clog sewers; nuisance germination of seeds; suckers freely; subject to many insects and disease.

CULTIVAR:

'Bolleana' - an upright-growing, but more wide-spreading cultivar of negligible value. Seldom lives twenty years. Often seen in poor quality windbreaks.

'Lombardy' - an upright-growing, weedy, fast-growing cultivar that seldom lives twenty years. White trunk, green leaves with silvery reverse. Costly to remove.

■ *P. sargentii*,
PLAINS COTTONWOOD. 40%, I, 100'. A pioneer native species that appears after flooding. Fast-growing, large, wide-spreading limbs deceptively weak. Yellow fall foliage; subject to many insects and disease. Female produces cottony mass of seeds.

■ *P. tremuloides*,
QUAKING ASPEN, IMP, 80'. An enigmatic native species, grand and beautiful in groves at altitudes over 7,000', but short-lived, troublesome at lower altitudes. White, slender trunk; dark green leaves on long petiole that causes constant motion with the slightest breeze. Yellow fall foliage. Subject to many insects and disease. Easily broken if heavy snow falls while in leaf.

■ *Prunus americana*,
AMERICAN PLUM, IM, 70%, 15-20'. A native that can be trained to a single trunk, otherwise, it is the roadside thicket loved by all. Mass of white flowers before leaves in spring; small, blue fruits for jelly, pie, or wine. Resistant to crown borer.

■ *P. x cerasifera*,
FLOWERING PLUM, IP, 60%, 12-15'. A cloud of white flowers before leaves; foliage deep purple throughout the season.

CULTIVAR:

'Newport' - very early flowering; pink flowers before leaves; seldom fruiting; dark purple foliage all summer.Subject to crown borer.

'Thundercloud' - deeper purple foliage than above; fragrant flowers. Subject to crown borer.

■ *P. maackii*,
AMUR CHOKECHERRY, IMP, 60%, 30-45'. A mop-headed tree with outstanding bright copper, shiny exfoliating bark. White flowers in May in finger-long racemes; small black fruits in August. Loved by birds. Subject to crown borer at low altitudes.

■ *P. padus*,
BIRD CHERRY, IP, 60%, 30-40'. Low, ascending branches; glossy green leaves; racemes of white flowers in late April are often frozen; thus it seldom produces fruit. First to leaf out in early April, but foliage does not freeze. Orange fall color. Subject to crown borer.

■ *P. serotina*,
BLACK CHERRY, IP, 50%, 30-40'. This is the floor-of-the-forest tree in the deciduous forests of the Northeast. Racemes of white flowers, black fruits, which are often troublesome in germinating in the lawn. Subject to crown borer.

■ *P. subhirtella*,
HIGAN CHERRY, IP, 50%, 25-30'. Seldom cultivated in the species.

■ *P. s. var. pendula*,
WEEPING HIGAN CHERRY fills the need for flowering trees with a weeping form. This tree especially beautiful when planted near still

water where the weeping form, pink blooms and orange fall color can be reflected. Subject to crown borer.

■ *P. virginiana*,
WESTERN CHOKECHERRY, IMP, 40%, 25-30'. A native of streams and river canyons. Glossy maroon bark; racemes of white flowers followed by red fruits loved by birds. Suckers freely from the base. Subject to tent caterpiller and crown borer.
CULTIVAR:
'Shubert' - leaves emerge green, but quickly turn to a dull maroon. Racemes of white flowers followed by red fruits; subject to tent caterpillar and crown borer.

■ *Ptela trifoliata*,
HOP TREE. IP, 70%, 15-20'. A little known tree with ability to withstand dry soils. Should be used more in xeriscapes; dark glossy foliage; red cherry bark; winged fruits that resemble blooms. Resistant to crown borer. Slow; hard to locate in nurseries.

■ *Pyrus calleryana*,
CALLERY PEAR, - IP, 70%. 30-40'. White flowers in May; glossy leathery foliage with bronze-red to deep purple in fall.
CULTIVARS:
'Bradford' - pyramidal form, rounding with age. Non-fruiting. A good street tree. Subject to breakage at graft point if located in high wind areas.

'Cleveland Select' - an upright form with evenly spaced branches; blooms heavily at early age; glossy green summer foliage. Non-fruiting.

'Red Spire' - Can withstand poorly aerated soils, does not break in summer storms. Brilliant red fall color.

■ *Quercus bicolor*,
SWAMP WHITE OAK, IP 90%, 40-50'. Broad, rounded crown; stout limbs; native to swampy situation in the Northeast, which makes it able to withstand lack of oxygen in heavy clay soils of the Mountain West. Severely chlorotic with lack of drainage. No insects or diseases. Yellow fall color.

■ *Q. coccinea*,
SCARLET OAK, IP 90%, 50-60'. Large, deeply lobed green leaves; deeply furrowed bark. No insects or diseases; keeps its leaves until late October, which then turn deep purple. Tolerant of city conditions.

■ *Q. gambeli*,
GAMBEL OAK, I or D, 80%, 15-25'. The only native oak of the Mountain West. Grows in thickets on dry, exposed hillsides, but can be trained to a handsome tree for the dry landscape. Very slow; difficult to establish; fall color is orange-brown.

■ *Q. macrocarpa*,
BUR OAK, IP 90%, 60-70' with equal spread. Large, flatly lobed green leaves, yellow in fall. Tolerant of drought and city conditions. No insects or diseases.

■ *Q. palustris*,
PIN OAK, IP 70%, 40-50'. Medium, deeply lobed green leaves; pyramidal shape in youth; brilliant red fall color; intolerant of alkaline soils; subject to oak galls, which seem to do it little harm.

■ *Q. robur*,
ENGLISH OAK, IP, 80%, 60-70'. Massive trunks, limbs, rounded crown; dark green indented lobed leaves persist throughout the winter as shrivelled and brown rags. No insects or diseases.

■ *Q.r. fastigiata,*
ENGLISH OAK, IP, 80%, 60-80'. May become the substitute for Lombardy Popular. Puts on 1-2' of growth annually. Very narrow silhoutte.

■ *Q. rubra,*
RED OAK, IP, 80%, 50-60'. Rounded in youth as well as age; nearly black trunk, deeply ridged; pink to red leaves in spring, turning to lustrous green in summer; russet-red in fall. Transplants readily because of negligible taproot; prefers sandy loam soil; chlorotic in heavy clay. No insects or diseases.

■ *Robinia pseudoacacia,*
BLACK LOCUST, IDP,40% 25-30'. An escapee from cultivation that is often found in thickets, ravines and canyons where water is available. Slender, straight trunk and narrow oblong crown of compound leaves. Racemes of fragrant white flowers in June, followed by long, smooth seed pods that persist into winter. Seedlings transplant easily Extremely susceptible to borers; drought tolerant. Seldom seen in commerce. *R. neomexicana* is a native of New Mexico and is often used as fence posts.

■ *Salix matsudana umbraculifera,*
GLOBE WILLOW, IP, 40%, 30-45'. Extremely fast grower if moisture needs are met. Slender, pointed foliage; silver on reverse; globe crown; yellow fall foliage; bears cottony seed masses after about twenty years; drops water sprouts; afflicted with all the same insects as poplars and cottonwoods.

CULTIVARS:

'Tristis' - a hardy weeping form that will reach 50' in height and 50' in spread. Foliage is bright green; yellow fall foliage; golden bark. See above for negative aspects.

'Golden Curls' - a hardy, golden barked, weeping form with corkscrew branches and leaves. Ultimate height is fifteen feet with a spread of six feet. The leaves are a golden green. See above for negative aspects.

■ *Sophora japonica,*
JAPANESE PAGODA TREE, SCHOLAR TREE, IP, 50%, 45-60'. A feathery light green compound foliage; yellow blooms in August when little else is blooming; yellow, then brown seed pod hangs on into winter. Prefers loamy, well-drained soil; tender to cold when young; needs firm staking until crown is established.

■ *Sorbus aucuparia,*
EUROPEAN MOUNTAIN ASH, IMP, 50%, 25-30'. Compound green leaves; flat clusters of white blooms in spring, followed by orange/red berries loved by birds. Subject to fireblight, walnut scale.

CULTIVARS:

'Cardinal Royal' - a cultivar developed by Univ.of Michigan. Vigorous grower, upright, oval shape; fruit clusters very large and take on color early in season.

'Meinichii' - an upright, pyramidal form from Europe that is a very strong grower with unusual lobed foliage.

■ *Syringa reticulata,*
JAPANESE TREE LILAC, IP, 50%, 40-50'. A stunning tree for the landscape that has a view of the top of this tree because the white fragrant bloom clusters are held at the top. Subject to lilac/ash borer. Resistant to oystershell scale.

CULTIVAR:

'Ivory Silk' - Best to date with giant trusses of bloom. Resistant to both borer and scale.

■ *Tilia americana,*
AMERICAN LINDEN (Basswood),IP, 70%, 60-80'. Heart-shaped leaves; yellow fragrant flowers in June; a good bee tree from which the finest honey is made; smooth bark subject to sunscald in winter; strong; early leaf drop of yellow autumn foliage; subject to scale in August; suckers at the base in its youth.

■ *Tilia cordata,*
LITTLELEAF LINDEN, IP, 70%, 40-50'. Dense broad pyramidal form; good street tree.

CULTIVARS:

'Chancellor'- upright, narrow pyramidal form; resistant to storm damage and drought. Golden fall foliage.

'Corzam' - a formal pyramid of shining foliage in summer; golden in fall.

'Glenleven' - very rapid growing cultivar originating in Canada.

'Greenspire' - an old cultivar still very satisfactory; pyramidal, branching low to ground; very resistant to insects and disease.

■ *T. tomentosa,*
SILVER LINDEN, IP, 80%. Broadly pyramidal; due for rise in popularity due to new cultivars that are resistant to aphids because of tomentose underside of leaves.

CULTIVAR:

"Green Mountain' - Also resistant to scale, thus no black mold is attracted to limbs.

■ *Ulmus x hollandica,*
HOLLAND ELM, IP, 50%, 80'. A still unproven species that may replace *Ulmus americana* AMERICAN ELM. Because of susceptibility to Dutch Elm Disease, it is virtually impossible find an American Elm in commerce today.

CULTIVARS:

'Urban' - a profuse upright branching habit; pyramidal; developed at USDA Research Center in Delare, Ohio, for resistence to Dutch Elm disease and phloem necrosis.

'Liberty' - an introduction of the Elm Research Institute at Harrisville, New Hampshire, also resistant to Dutch Elm Disease. Trees are available at reduced price for cemeteries, golf courses, and municipalities. For information call 1-800-FOR-ELMS.

'Princeton' - An introduction of Princeton Nurseries touted as DED resistant. Now being planted in Washington D.C.

■ *U. pumila,*
SIBERIAN ELM, ID, 40%, 45-50'. Often the only tree that will survive the hardship situation of the plains. Weak wood; subject to disease and insects, narrow crotches, troublesome seeds, very little fall color; holds foliage very late in season.

■ *Xanthoceras sorbifolium,*
YELLOWHORN, IP, 50%, 15-20'. A striking, strong, wide-spreading small tree with curious white and maroon flowers in spring. Resistant to insects, disease, drought. There are old specimens of this tree on the Western Slope of Colorado.

EVERGREEN TREES

Most newcomers to the Mountain West soon discover the evergreens are as beautiful as those in the East, South, or Far West. Trips to the mountains soon reveal that the habitat of each has a definite pattern that predisposes the same tree growing in the home landscape. For example, the junipers and pines grow on the south or west-facing slopes, while the spruce and fir grow on the north where the snow lies deep in winter and moisture is abundant during the growing season. These same trees in the home landscape will thrive under similar conditions. The juniper planted in the lawn next to the sprinkler head will decline gradually. A Pinyon Pine planted in the lawn will develop weak, wand-like limbs that cannot take a snow load. Similarly, the spruce or fir will struggle for years when planted at the top of a berm where snow seldom stays more than a day or two and water drains away quickly.

Always note the ultimate height of an evergreen before you plant. Views of our mountains are important to most people in the Mountain West. For some, a long look at them is the first thing they do upon arising in the morning. An evergreen can quickly grow to obscure the view. The native Rocky Mountain Juniper (*Juniperus scopulorum*) as well as the Pinon Pine (*Pinus edulis*), are useful in the home landscape for the one-story home because their ultimate height seldom exceeds twenty five feet. Spruce and firs can quickly grow to monstrous size, blocking entrances, air-flow, views, overhead power lines and cables. They can give unwanted shade in winter, crowd other plants into extinction - even push porches off their foundations! Be aware of the spread of an evergreen that you plant as well as the height. Known as the "skirt", the spread of a Colorado Spruce, for example, can be twenty-five feet. Limbing it up* to open up a view or a walkway is a risk because it destroys the fulcrum of balance of the tree, making it an easy target for wind throw. Limbing up a tree to grow a shade-loving plant, such as rhododendron is a risk also; for the spruce roots are close to the surface and high competitors. Piling a new soil mixture over the roots is an additional risk, as the tree roots can be quickly smothered from lack of oxygen.

A limbed up evergreen is an easy target for windthrow when wind strikes the solid green wall of foliage of the limbs above the now-bare trunk.

Our native evergreens will be found at varying altitudes. Keep these in mind as you to try to simulate the growing conditions for natives in your landscape.

Plains	-	below 6,000 feet
Foothills	-	6,000 to 8,000 feet
Montane	-	8,000 to 10,000 feet
Subalpine	-	10,000 to 11,500 feet
Alpine	-	11,500 and above

* *See Glossary*

In reading Chapter 7 "Plant Protection", you will find many methods to protect a new planting. The most applicable to a newly planted evergreen is the three-legged burlap screen. It will never win a prize for beauty, but it gives the young evergreen that was a costly addition to your landscape a chance for establishment. You (and the neighbors) will forget the unattractive device that shielded the tree when it emerges from protection as a vigorous healthy tree.

The three-legged burlap screen protects a newly planted evergreen for one or more years.

EVERGREEN TREES FOR THE MOUNTAIN WEST

■ *Abies concolor* ,
WHITE FIR, IMP, 90%, 60-80'. This native is the queen of needled evergreens in the Mountain West. Soft, short needles; interesting cones with age, somewhat drought tolerant. Almost insect and disease free. Often gangly in its youth, like any teenager.

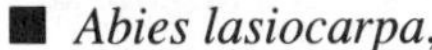

■ *Abies lasiocarpa*,
ALPINE FIR, IP, 50%, 20-40'. A slender tree with shelves of gray-green foliage, tiered upward. This native is often the "banner" tree just at timberline. Banner trees are those with a line of foliage only on the lee side, the wind having scoured away all traces of foliage on the windward side. Requires a moist, shaded site in its youth, but will thrive if its head is in the sun. Seldom available at nurseries.

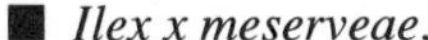

■ *Ilex x meserveae*,
MESERVE HOLLY, IP, 50%, ultimate height in the Mountain West unknown at this time. Mrs. F. Leighton Meserve selected evergreen hollies from interspecific crosses of I. rugosa, and I. aquifolium. The results have produced many named cultivars, the best of which may be yet to come.
CULTIVARS:
'Blue Prince' - a male that forms compact, broad pyramid with lustrous green foliage; produces abundant pollen to pollinate a whole grove of female trees. Seems to prosper best when grown on north side of structure, such as your home, where winter sun never reaches it, but summer sun is abundant in the morning. Both 'Blue Prince' and 'Blue Princess' will put on the most growth if a structure covers them in winter.

'Blue Princess' - one of the best to be introduced so far; tested hardy to minus-twenty degrees F. Broad, shrubby, bluish green foliage; abundant dark red fruits. See above for precautions.

■ *Juniperus scopulorum,* ROCKY MOUNTAIN JUNIPER, ID, 70%, 25-35'. The native "cedar" of the Mountain West, with many cultivars selected from the wild that are now patented. Shaggy bark, natural pyramidal form without shearing; often forms several trunks; blue berries, and resistence to drought and insect attack make it a favorite. Shearing to force it to conform to height demands will shorten its life. It often lives one hundred fifty years in its native habitat, but only twenty years in a sheared form in a home landscape. Susceptible to breakage by heavy snow load.

CULTIVARS:

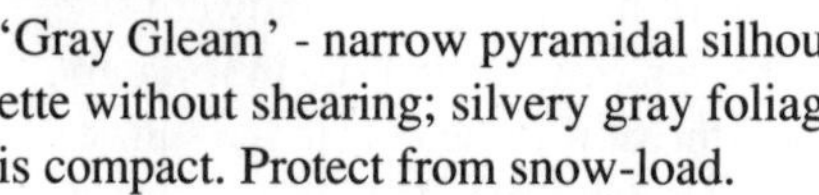

'Gray Gleam' - narrow pyramidal silhouette without shearing; silvery gray foliage is compact. Protect from snow-load.

'Moonglow' - broad pyramidal form; dense, compact silvery-blue foliage.

'Wichita Blue' - pyramidal bright blue foliage, inconspicuous berries.

■ *Juniperus virginiana,* RED CEDAR, IHD, 80%, 25-35'. This native of the Northeast is surprisingly more adaptable to the home landscape than the native species. Its strong, wide-spreading, graceful branches are more resiliant and able to withstand heavy snow loads. Dark green foliage, blue berries.

CULTIVARS:

'Canaertii' - conical shape, blue berries in great abundance.

'Idyllwild' - pyramidal shape, dark green foliage; effective screen or hedge.

'Skyrocket'- very narrow columnar form, blue -green foliage and inconspicuous berries; sometimes listed as a *J. scopulorum* selection.

■ *Larix kaempferi,* JAPANESE LARCH, IP, 60%, 50-60'. A deciduous conifer characterized by an interesting open habit; short horizontal branches and tufted, soft green needles. Golden yellow fall foliage. Needs good drainage and an acid soil of 5.5 to 6.5 pH.

■ *Picea densata,* BLACK HILLS SPRUCE, IHP, 70%, 20-35'. An easily managed tree that can become a Bonsai or "character" tree in your landscape. Short needles, dense habit. Snap the new growth in half to limit growth.

■ *Picea englemanni,* ENGELMANN SPRUCE, IHP, 50%, 60-80'. A native pine found on west-facing slopes. It has deep green, short needles, small cones and is difficult to establish; seldom seen in nurseries.

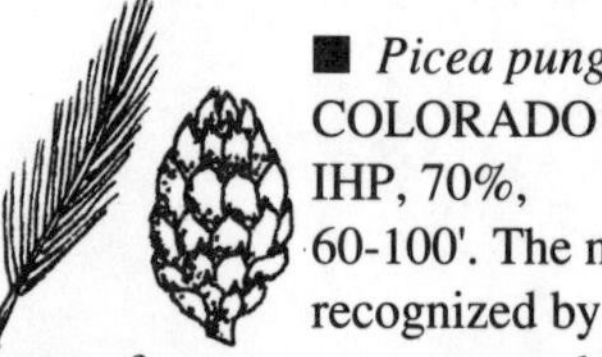

■ *Picea pungens,* COLORADO SPRUCE, IHP, 70%, 60-100'. The native spruce recognized by all. Seedlings vary from green to gray to blue. The blues are known as "shiners" in the nursery trade; may be patented, and will command a higher price. Short, stiff needles; subject to an insect that causes new growth to form purple galls that turn brown by August. This tree is effective in the home landscape located at the perimeter of the large property where you can enjoy its magnificence from your windows.

> The needles of pines are held in bundles known as fascicles. The list below will aid you in identifying pines by the number of needles held in a fascicle.

■ *Pinus albicaulis*,
WHITEBARK PINE, IH, 60%, 50-60'. Five needles to the fascicle. Similar to Limber Pine, but cones are short and round; disintegrate to release seeds. Native of northern reaches of this book; seldom available at nurseries.

■ *Pinus aristata*,
BRISTLECONE PINE, IHP, 70% 15-25'. The oldest living trees on earth - 4,900 years. Five needles in the fascicle. The native pine of timberline where it hangs on as a twisted, tortured shape of great age. Resin-dotted short needles. At lower altitudes the heavily needled branches are wand-like and resemble the brush of a fox, hence it is often sold as "Foxtail Pine". Drought resistant; insect resistant.

■ *Pinus contorta latifolia*,
LODGEPOLE PINE, IHP, 60%, 35-50'. Two needles in the fascicle. This native is seldom seen at Foothills or Plains altitudes, yet it makes a full, symmetrical tree when grown alone and without competition. Native stands are very close with slender trunks and few lower branches. Very tolerant of dry, clay soils.

■ *Pinus edulis*,
PINYON PINE, ID, 80%, 10-25'. Two needles in the fascicle. The native pine of the Southwest. The northern-most stand is located in Owl Canyon, just north of Fort Collins, Colorado. The picturesque form is often twisted from hardship. In cultivation and with too much water it forms soft, wand-like branches that are easily damaged under a heavy snow load. It should be grown with establishment water; then allowed to survive on natural precipitation. It has two sets of roots - one wide-spreading to catch every drop of water, and the other deep to protect itself during drought. This tree is a survivor. The cones produce highly prized edible seeds.

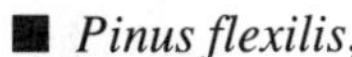

■ *Pinus flexilis*,
LIMBER PINE, IHP, 60%, 25-40'. Five needles in the fascicle. The native pine of the Krumholz, meaning the subalpine zone. Though there are relic populations located in pockets all through the Mountain West, this tree, more than any other, is the symbol of rocky, wind-swept ridges of the subalpine region. It's common name is the clue to its survival. Limber, resiliant limbs withstand the forceful winds and heavy snow loads. A taproot anchors it firmly. When grown at lower altitudes, this tree is full and abundant with needles of medium length and small, tough cones. Like all pines, it is drought tolerant, but must have well-drained, loose soil.

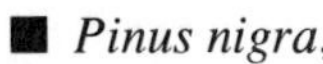

■ *Pinus nigra*,
AUSTRIAN PINE, IHP, 60%, 30-40'. Two needles in the fascicle. This non-native has dark, dense foliage; rounded crown with age, drought tolerant and disease resistant.

■ *Pinus ponderosa*,
PONDEROSA PINE, IHD, 80%, 40-50'. Two or three needles in the fascicle. This is the native pine of the savanah of the Montane zone. Long, glossy needles, rounded open crown; an excellent tree in the dry landscape. Subject to insect attacks when epidemics sweep crowded forests.

■ *Pinus reflexa*,
SOUTHWESTERN WHITE PINE, IHP, 70%, 45-60'. Five needles in the fascicle. This pine is a native of New Mexico, but does well in cultivation in Colorado and northward. It resembles Eastern White Pine with five needles in the fascicle; long decorative cones; difficult to locate in nurseries.

■ *Pinus strobus*,
WHITE PINE, IHP, 50%, 60-70'. Five needles in the fascicle. This non-native has long, soft feathery foliage. It is not tolerant of clay or alkaline soils, developing chlorosis. Where its conditions can be met, it is a very beautiful tree.

■ *Pinus sylvestris*,
SCOTS PINE, IHP, 60%, 30-40'. Two needles in the fascicle. This non-native is the most rapid growing of pines, putting on eighteen inches to two feet each year. It has deep green foliage and the crown is open, not dense.

■ *Pseudotsuga taxifolia*,
DOUGLAS FIR, IHP, 50%, 30-40'. A native that is uninteresting in the home landscape. Short, medium green needles, conical shape. Interesting winged cones are a redeeming feature; winter host to the gall-making insect that infests Colorado Spruce.

■ *Taxodium distichum*,
SWAMP CYPRESS, IP, 40%, 30-50'. A non-native tree for clay soil where its ability to survive without oxygen to the roots simulates its native habitat in swamps. It obtains oxygen by means of surface roots. Soft green needles turn bright orange in late October before they drop. Not easily located at nurseries.

■ *Taxus cuspidata*,
PYRAMIDAL JAPANESE YEW, IP, 50%, 15-20'. A pyramidal tree with dense, deep green foliage; inconspicuous flowers; red fruit. Can be sheared. Sunscalds in winter sun. An eastern exposure in moist soil suits it best.

CULTIVAR:

'Capitata' - a broad pyramid useful for hedging or as a specimen or accent plant.

■ *Thuja occidentalis*,
GOLDEN GLOBE ARBORVITAE, IP, 50%, 15-20'. Fans of foliage held vertically giving a feathery appearance. In areas of heavy snow fall the tree is literally pulled apart by the weight. Use bird netting bands to wrap, spiral fashion, around the tree, to hold foliage together in winter.

CULTIVARS:

'Compact American' - good deep-green foliage.

'Emerald' - narrow, pyramidal, bright emerald green that remains well in winter.

'Woodwardii' - a more globose clone under test at Colorado State Univ.; very dark green foliage; very promising.

■ *T. orientalis* , ORIENTAL ARBORVITAE, IP, 50%, 10-12'. Similar to other forms, but foliage more coarse.

CULTIVAR:

'Elegantissima' - yellow tips on foliage which turns bronze in winter.

Dwarf Conifers

Dwarf conifers are mutations that occur in nature as slow-growing seedlings of normal trees or as mysteriously slow-growing shoots called witches' brooms, which are dense tufts of growth in an otherwise normal tree.

Collectors of dwarf evergreens are a fast-growing group who are finding that the diminutive forms available today are ideal in every way. They enliven the winter scene when planted in a mixed border of perennials; yet they never crowd a neighbor or need dividing. They give the foundation planting the important scale and proportion without ever overgrowing their bounds. The rock garden offers many sites for the dwarf conifer, but should not be planted in polka-dot fashion. Plant them in groups of three or five as they would grow in nature. Groups are also effective as a background for a sloping rock garden. In form dwarf conifers are available in columns, globes, pyramids, and as crawlers to drape over banks and walls. In colors they are available in all those of their full-sized parents - blue, gray, silver, gold, and every shade of green.

Trees stunted by hardship growing conditions are not dwarfs, nor are Bonsai trees which have been kept small by regular pruning of branches and roots. Both of these types of trees would grow to normal height given normal growing conditions.

Before going overboard on dwarf conifers, be aware that their growth rate is extremely slow. It is not unusual for a miniature to grow less than three feet in twenty years. Others may attain six feet in twenty years, but seldom is that growth rate exceeded. Pruning is not needed to keep dwarf conifers small. Prune only to remove a misplaced or unhealthy branch.

Sources for dwarf conifers are not easy to locate. Too often unsuspecting buyers are taken in by the label "compact" thinking it means dwarf. "Compact" means only dense, thick growth habit, but the plant labeled thus will usually attain a normal height and width. Nurserymen are often willing to order a collection of dwarfs for their good customers. Their wholesale discount may be passed on with considerable saving. Otherwise, the Ma-and-Pa type specialty mail-order nurseries are the best bet. These dedicated people will most often sell correctly named, well-grown specimens. Their drawback is that, though inexpensive, the specimens are usually very small. A teacup-sized plant may not make a showing in your lifetime.

Western Mail Order Sources for Dwarf Conifers

Coenosium Gardens,
6642 S. Lone Elder Road, Aurora, OR 97002 catalog $3, refundable.

Colorado Alpines, Inc.,
P.O. Box 2708, Avon, CO 81620 catalog $2, minimum order $25.

Forest Farm, 990 Tetherow Rd., Williams, OR 97544 catalog $3.

Siskiyou Rare Plant Nursery,
2825 Cummings Rd.,
Medford, OR catalog $2.

CHAPTER 12

Shrubs, Deciduous and Evergreen

The gardening world may be standing on the threshold of a surge in the planting of ornamental shrubs. The flowering perennials have been at the peak of popularity for about five years, and, for gardeners, it's time to move on, while keeping the old, to a new allegiance. As with the zealots of climbing or cooking, this seeming fickleness is typical and not at all alarming. The "been-there-done-that" alignment of those with years of experience in gardening is only a desire to learn everything there is to know about every plant, a consuming passion that afflicts all gardeners. As the culture of each is acquired and perfected, the gardener is ready to take on another plant or another group of plants. Shrubs may be the next peak to conquer.

Shrubs are woody plants, as are trees, but they are usually lower in height, and may be many stemmed. They are useful in foundation plantings, screens, borders, hedges, and informal groups in an island in the turf.

For the new homeowner, shrubs save the day by filling in quickly and giving the home a lived-in look while the trees are growing. Shrubs can be expected to reach maturity within five years, though those that are slower will be noted in the text.

For soils, planting, pruning, and protection, see Chapters 6, 7, and 9. Use shrubs that lose their leaves (deciduous) for approximately two-thirds of the foundation planting, with the remainder being evergreen. Season of bloom and fall foliage colors are important, while silhouette, texture of foliage add a more subtle influence in your appreciation of the scene. Branch pattern and twigs are dominant in the winter scene.

There are only a few cultural differences in growing shrubs that vary from the culture of trees. Hardening of wood in late summer is important for both trees and shrubs. Summer and winter watering is the same in importance. Gathering of fallen leaves in the shrub border in fall may be against your neatness ethic, but leaving the leaves to rot and enrich the soil under shrubs is a better practice. After all leaves have fallen, use a spading fork to fork them just under the soil surface so that they will not blow away during the winter. You will have a rich compost by spring and your shrubs will not need chemical fertilizers.

In Chapter 9 "Pruning" you learned shrub pruning usually involves no more than pruning during or just after bloom, and then removing two or three stems or trunks each year all the way to the soil surface. New stems will sprout from buds on the old trunks and will soon take their place as blooming or fruiting trunks. This is known as "renewal pruning." New blooms begin forming for next year's display within three weeks of this year's bloom.

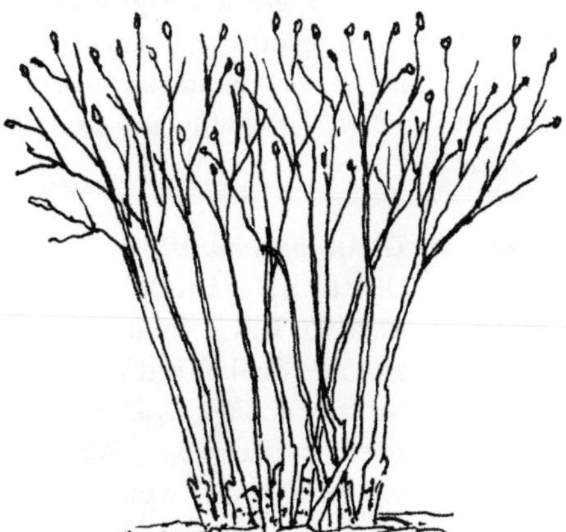

Replacement of new trunks after old trunks have been removed on deciduous shrub.

Symbols

Percent number indicates comparison rating with 100%.

D - Can survive on natural precipitation after two-year period with establishment water*.

I - Irrigation as needed.

H - Suitable also for above 6,000 feet in altitude.

L - Low - under four feet.

M - Medium height - four to six feet.

P - Needs varying degrees of protection, such as a location need buildings, trees, other shrubs, or as described.

T - Tall - over six feet.

■ *You will have a rich compost by spring and your shrubs will not need chemical fertilizers.*

* *See Glossary*

Deciduous Shrubs

When more than one species of the same genus is listed, only the first listing is complete. All those following are abreviated with the first letter of the genus.

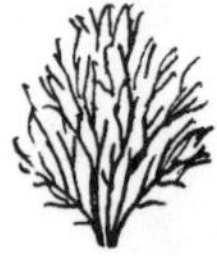

■ *Acanthopanax sieboldianus*,
HARDY ARALIA, IP, 60%, T. A graceful shrub with unusual five-leaf arrangement. Inconspicuous blooms. Withstands root competition and deep shade.

■ *Acer ginnala*,
AMUR MAPLE, I, 50%, T. Can be trained to a single trunk. Inconspicuous flowers followed by key-shaped seeds which are sometimes colorful. Brilliant red fall color.

■ *A. glabrum*,
ROCKY MOUNTAIN MAPLE, IH, 50%, T. A desirable native for a moist site. Wand-like branches will stiffen up if stressed a little with drought. Petioles and winter buds are bright red. Yellow fall foliage.

■ *A. tataricum*,
TATARIAN MAPLE, I, 70%, T. Leaves not as deeply lobed as *A. ginnala*, Yellow fall color.

■ *Aesculus parviflora*,
BOTTLEBRUSH BUCKEYE, IP, 70%, M. White cockade blooms in June; thrives in heavy shade and withstands root competition. Leaves are palmate. Build a shelter over these each winter for five years; then they should be able to remain unprotected throughout the winter.

■ *Alnus tenuifolia*,
THINLEAF ALDER, IH, 60%, T. A multi-trunked shrub for condominium patio or tall background. Requires copious moisture. Cherry brown, lenticel-marked bark. Dioecious*. Dripping with male catkins in spring. Female seeds resemble tiny cones.

■ *Amelanchier alnifolia*,
SERVICEBERRY, IH, 60%, T. Slow, but worthwhile. Horizontal branching, white flowers in early spring, followed by purple fruits; loved by birds.
CULTIVARS:
'Smokey' - large fruit good for pie or jelly.
'Strata' - strong, horizontal branching.

■ *Amorpha canescens*,
LEAD PLANT, D, 60%, L. Slender, green foliage with silver reverse. Fingers of purple blooms stand above foliage in August. Very hardy and drought resistant.

■ *Aralia spinosa*,
DEVIL'S WALKING STICK, IP, 40%, T. Useful in background of tall mixed shrub border. Thorny, club-like branches, large compound leaves. May freeze to the ground in severe winters.

■ *Azaleas* - See Chapter 18, Azaleas and Rhodoendrons

* *See Glossary*

■ *Berberis koreana*, KOREAN BARBERRY, IP, 60%, M. With evergreen bough protection, this spiny shrub will produce flowers and red berries. Without protection it seldom blooms or fruits, but has bright green, lustrous foliage that turns orange-red in fall.

■ *Berberis mentorensis*, MENTOR BARBERRY, IP, 60%, M. Tolerant of city conditions; orange-red fall color held all winter until new leaves push off old.

■ *B. thunbergii*, RED-LEAVED BARBERRY, IP, 70%, L. The shrub that no dog will raise its leg to. Small leaves, prickles, good red fall color.

CULTIVARS:

'Atropurpureum' - reddish-purple foliage, yellow flowers and red fruits.

'Aurea' - bright yellow leaves; good for accent.

'Crimson Pygmy' - very dwarf; excellent small hedge.

'Gold Ring' - compact red foliage that develops a curious gold ring around the edge in midsummer

'Rose Glow' - deep red foliage; new foliage is mottled with silvery pink. Bright scarlet foliage in fall.

■ *Betula fontinalis*, ROCKY MOUNTAIN BIRCH, IPH, 50%, T. A native that prefers a moist site; good combined with *Alnus tenuifolia*. Slender, gracful branches; multi-trunks. yellow autumn foliage.

■ *Buddleia alternifolia*, FOUNTAIN BUTTERFLY BUSH, IP, 60%, T. Long arching stems of lavender flowers in early summer. Needs to be thinned by cutting half of stems to the soil level after flowering. Does not kill back to ground in winter.

■ *B. davidii*, BUTTERFLY BUSH, IP, 60%, T. Kills to the ground each winter. Long, trusses of flowers in summer attractive to butterflies.

CULTIVARS:

'Black Knight' - deepest purple; fragran.t

'Empire Blue' - violet-blue with orange eye.

'Pink Charming' - china-pink.

'White Bouquet' - white clusters with yellow eye; fragrant.

■ *Buxus microphylla*, DWARF BOXWOOD, IP, 60%, L. Broad-leaved evergreen. Needs evergreen bough protection in winter. Bright glossy miniature leaves. Easy to increase by cuttings for use as a mini-hedge in front of annuals at your entry.

■ *B. sempervirens*, BOXWOOD, IP, 60%, L. Broadleaved evergreen. Needs protection from winter sun with evergreen boughs or boxes. Needs organic soil and organic mulch. Never allow to dry out.

■ *Callicarpa bodinieri*, BEAUTYBERRY, IP, 70%, M. Of winter value for its tiny bead-like lavender berries in abundance on arching branches; stunning with the *C. americana alba*, which produces white berries. Needs protection of shade cloth or plastic bag around and over the top in winter; fill with leaves that do not break down quickly, such as Green Ash. Winter watering imperative.

■ *Calluna vulgaris*,
HEATH OR HEATHER, IP, 50%, L. Evergreen slender leaves; pink bells in spring; needs acid organic soil; moist site in full sun; evergreen bough protection in winter.

■ *Calycanthus floridus purpureus*,
CAROLINA ALLSPICE, IP, 70%, M. Summer blooms of brown that emit fragrance likened to strawberries, pine-apple, or spice; purple foliage; attractive planted with a yellow-leafed shrub.

■ *Caragana arborescens*,
SIBERIAN PEA SHRUB, D, 70%, T. Can withstand extreme hardship. Legume like yellow flowers in spring. Leggy branching habit; useful in windbreak, tall background on a farm or for a country estate.

■ *C. pygmaea*,
PYGMY PEA SHRUB, D, 70%, L. A miniature version of the above, but more shapely. Useful for the xeric landscape.

■ *Caryopteris incana*,
BLUEBEARD, IP, 70%, L. Slender leaves, clusters of blue flowers in August when few other shrubs in bloom. Good underplanted with *Lycoris squimigera*. Should be cut to ground in winter.

■ *Cercis canadensis*,
REDBUD, IP, 80%, T. A sheltered spot will suit this graceful, ofen multi-trunked shrub or small tree. Heart-shaped leaves, lavender blooms before foliage. No insects or disease, but sometimes hard to establish. Sun or dappled shade; good drainage.

■ *Cercocarpos montanus*,
MOUNTAIN MAHOGANY, D, 50%, M. A native shrub of dry hills. Twisted, fuzzy-tailed seeds will drive themselves into the soil if moisture is present; Plant it where rising or setting sun will silhouette the seeds.

■ *Chaenomeles japonica*,
JAPANESE FLOWERING QUINCE, IP, 50%, M. Build a plastic covered frame around it (not over) in fall and fill with green ash leaves to protect its spring bloom buds. Rosy red blooms followed by large green warty fruits sometimes used for jelly. Needs plenty of water.

■ *Chionanthus virginicus*,
FRINGE TREE, IP, 40%, T. A tall shrub or small tree that needs a frame protection in winter until it becomes acclimatized. White tassel-like flowers in early summer. Light green leaves.

■ *Clethra alnifolia*,
SUMMERSWEET, IP, 60%, M. Scented white flowers in August; glossy leaves; golden fall color.

■ *Cornus alba*,
TARTARIAN DOGWOOD, IP, 70%, M. Opposite leaves on red stems that are brighter in winter. Sparse flowers are white followed by white berries.

CULTIVAR:
'Argenteo-Marginata' - VARIGATED SHRUB DOGWOOD, IP, 60%, M. Familiar red stems of a native dogwood, but with cool green and white leaves in summer. Subject to scale.

■ *C. mas,*

CORNELIAN CHERRY, IP, 70%, T. Small tree or shrub, Brought by pioneers to the Mountain West; very long-lived and drought tolerant. Yellow flowers before leaves and more reliable than forsythia. Slow to establish. Red fall fruit. Difficult to find in nurseries.

■ *C. racemosa,*

GRAY DOGWOOD, IP, 70%, T. Early summer clusters of creamy-white flowers followed by white berries; red fall color and red stemmed in winter.

■ *C. sericea,*

REDTWIG DOGWOOD, IP, 70%, T. A desirable native with red stems in winter; green leaves, prominently veined; sparse white flowers; white berries.

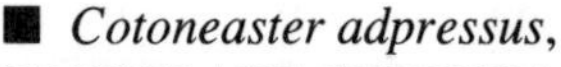

CULTIVARS:
'Isanti' - a compact version.

'Lutea' - a yellow-stemmed version - a good contrast when planted with the red-stemmed cultivar.

'Siberica' - able to withstand severe low temperatures; very bright stems; white flowers and berries; attractive planted with Colorado Blue Spruce.

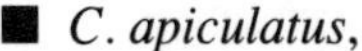

'Silver and Gold' - variegated green and white leaves, yellow stems in winter.

■ *Corylus cornuta,*

BEAKED FILBERT OR HAZELNUT, IP, 50%, T. A very slow-growing native for a moist site in dappled shade with no root competition. Smooth bark; long pointed leaves; nuts are snapped up by squirrels before they ripen.

■ *C. avellana,*
EUROPEAN FILBERT, IP, 50%, T. Seldom available in nurseries in the species. See cultivar below.
CULTIVAR:
'Cortorta' - Curiously twisted branches; pendulous catkins in spring; a good display against a dark brick wall; very slow growing.

■ *Cotinus coggygria,*

SMOKETREE, IP, 50%, T. An undistinguished shrub until the fluff of cottony "smoke" of seed masses appears. The "smoke" disguises the seeds. Very attractive in the purple cultivar.
CULTIVAR:
'Velvet Cloak' - purple leaves, purple 'smoke'; brilliant red foliage in fall.

■ *Cotoneaster adpressus,*

PROSTRATE COTONEASTER, IP, 70%, L. A slow miniature version of taller species.
CULTIVAR:
'Little Gem' - dense twiggy mass of stems covered with red berries; Foliage is lustrous and dark green. Effective displayed as a tracery over a large boulder.

■ *C. apiculatus,*

CRANBERRY COTONEASTER, IP, 70%, L. Arching branches; small pink flowers following by long-lasting, cranberry-sized red berries.

■ *C. integerrima*,
EUROPEAN COTONEASTER, IP, 70%, M. Rounded habit, good for hedging; nodding pink flower clusters; red fruits.

■ *Crataegus douglasii*,
BLACK HAWTHORN, I, 50%, T. A thicket-forming shrub useful on the farm or country property for songbird habitat and barrier against intruders. Very thorny; white flowers; red fruits; orange-red fall color.

■ *C. crus-galli*,
COCKSPUR HAWTHORN, IP, 50%, T. Rounded crown, wide spreading; white flowers, red fruits persisting all winter. Very long thorns.

■ *Daphne x burkwoodii*,
BURKWOOD DAPHNE, IP, 70%, L. A shapely rounded shrub with uniform foliage; fragrant flower clusters in May. No fruits; very little fall color.
CULTIVAR:
'Carol Mackie' - Fragrant white flowers, variegated green and white edged with pink foliage. Height dependent on amount of water; with only moderate water, it will mature at three feet.

■ *Deutzia x Lemoinei*,
LEMOINE DEUTZIA, IP, 40%, M. A fountain of arching branches; very dainty foliage. No fruits; very little fall color.
CULTIVAR:
'Compacta' - arching branches covered with very small white flowers in spring. Cover in winter with evergreen boughs, box or basket filled with leaves.

■ *Diervilla lonicera*,
DWARF BUSH HONEYSUCKLE, IP, 50%, M. A native that spreads by stolons. Useful only on ranch, farm, or country estates for hill-holding. Yellow flowers, red fruits.

■ *Elaeagnus commutata*,
SILVERBERRY, IP, 70%, M. Small silver leaves on arching branches makes this shrub useful in cooling a south-facing red brick wall in the foundation planting; dry silver berries relished by birds. Some suckering at the base.

■ *E. umbellata*,
AUTUMN OLIVE, DP, 50%, T. Wide-spreading shrub with silvery leaves covered with brown scales; inconspicuous fragrant flowers followed by silvery pink berries.
CULTIVAR:
'Cardinal' - spiny, with fragrant flowers in early summer; followed by edible red fruits. Adaptable to any site, but prefers uncrowded space.

■ *Euonymus alata*,
WINGED EUONYMUS, IP, 80%, T. Glossy green summer foliage, inconspicuous flowers, spectacular rose-red foliage in September; corky wings on stems; tiny persisting red fruits. Prefers some shade, consistent moisture; winter watering.
CULTIVAR:
'Compacta' - same as above, but matures at five feet.

■ *E. Fortunei*,
WINTERCREEPER, IP, 70%, L. Broadleaf evergreen that can be clipped into any form Withstands shade; reddish purple in winter.

CULTIVARS:

'Ivory and Jade' - pronounced white margin on round green leaves.

'Sparkle and Gold' - large bright gold leaves have green centers.

■ *Forsythia intermedia*,
FORSYTHIA, IP, 50%, M. Traditional greeting of spring. Yellow blooms cascading from arching branches before leaves. Difficult to keep shapely.

CULTIVARS:

'Goldleaf' - lime green foliage in spring, gold in summer; best in light shade.

'Lynwood Gold' - masses of gold blooms early spring.

'Northern Sun' - assures blooms even after the hardest of winter.

■ *Fothergilla gardenii*,
BOTTLEBRUSH, IP, 60%, M. A choice shrub preferring acid soil. Creamy cockade blooms in spring before leaves; yellow-orange fall color. Non-suckering; little pruning needed.

■ *F. major*,
BOTTLEBRUSH, IP, 60%, T. A ten-foot version of the above.

■ *Genista tinctoria*,
DYER'S BROOM, IP, 40%, T. A shrub often grown by flower arrangers for its early fragrant golden blooms. Prefers acid soil. Give it a plastic bag of leaves over the top in winter; winter watering imperative.

■ *Hamamelis vernalis*,
VERNAL WITCH HAZEL, IP, 50%, T. A shrub for the large mixed border. February flowers give excellent winter effect. Prefers early fall planting.

■ *Hibiscus syriacus*,
ROSE OF SHARON, IP, 50%, T. Holly-hock-like flowers in August when few others shrubs are in bloom. Spent flowers drop daily.

CULTIVARS:

'Bluebird' - sky-blue single flowers.

'Diana' - pure white very large flowers.

■ *Hippophae rhamnoides*,
SEABUCKTHORN, D, 50%, T. A shrub for barrier and songbird habitat; can withstand wind and dry sandy soil. Gray foliage, red berries on female plants.

■ *Holodiscus dumosa*,
ROCK SPIREA, D, 70%, M. A native of rocky hillsides and canyons. Creamy trusses of bloom on arching branches lasting all summer. Flame orange in fall.

■ *Hydrangea arborescens*,
HILLS OF SNOW HYDRANGEA, IP, 60%, M. Extra large white flower heads in summer. Erect growing, prefers part shade, moist site. No fall color.

■ *H. macrophylla coerulea*, LACECAP HYDRANGEA, IP, 50%, M. Blue sterile flowers in acid soil; pink sterile flowers in alkaline; blooms on new wood, and can be cut to ground in fall to keep it at three or four feet.

■ H. quercifolia, OAKLEAF HYDRANGEA, IP, 70%, T. Deeply lobed oak-like foliage; white platters of bloom; prefers rich loamy soil; deep maroon fall foliage.

■ *Hypericum frondosum*, SHRUBBY HYPERICUM, IP, 60%, L. Blue-green leaves with clusters of large orange-yellow flowers in summer.

■ *H. kouytchense*, KOUYTCHENSE HYPERICUM, IP, 60%. L. A dainty mound for rockery or border, blooming in early summer with yellow flowers that have prominent stamens.

CULTIVAR:

'Sungold' - profuse 2" yellow flowers all summer; rounded, compact habit.

■ *Ilex verticillata*, WINTERBERRY, IHP, 50%, M. A deciduous holly grown with one male and five females. Vivid scarlet berries in winter; inconspicuous flowers. Native of Canadian swamps but tolerant of good garden soil if never allowed to go dry.

CULTIVARS:

'After Glow' - an early-blooming compact female with large orange-scarlet fruit and small glossy leaves.

'Nana' - a small version of the above, maturing at about three feet.

■ *Jamesia americana*, CLIFF JAMESIA, IPH, 80%, M. A native named for Dr. Edwin James, the physician-botanist who accompanied Major Stephen Long in the 1820 expedition that mapped the eastern slope of Colorado. Dr. James and two others made the first recorded ascent of Pike's Peak. This shrub has velvety, veined leaves that turn rose, then red in fall. Cream and pink flower clusters are followed by black fruits. Found growing in crevices of cliffs. Prefers moist, gritty soil.

■ *Kalmia latifolia*, MOUNTAIN LAUREL, IPH, 40%, L. A tempermental shrub that prefers acid soil, partial shade, and constant moisture to produce its exquisite clusters of bell-like flowers. Needs evergreen bough protection in winter.

CULTIVARS:

'Heart of Fire' - a proven heavy bloomer with deep red blooms.

'Snowdrift' - dense, compact shrub with showy white flowers.

■ *Kolkwitzia amabilis*, BEAUTY BUSH, IP, 70%, M. Arching branches bear pink tubular flowers in masses in early June. Can be pruned severely after flowering. Suckers from the base.

■ *Ledum groenlandicum*, LABRADOR TEA, IH, 40%, L. A small shrub for high altitude cold, wet, acid soil, boggy places, such as near a small waterfall. Slender rust-powdered leaves with wooly white powder on reverse. Produces clusters of white flowers;

■ *Ligustrum amurense*, PRIVET, IP, 40%, M. A half-hardy hedge plant that is unpredictable as a hedge, but not unworthy as a single specimen. Small leaves; withstands severe clipping. White, inconspiuous flowers; no fruits.

CULTIVAR:

'Lodense nanum'- a dwarf that can substituted for Boxwood.

■ *Lonicera sp.* HONEYSUCKLE, IP, 60%, T. At this writing the genus Lonicera is under attack by the Honeysuckle Aphid, *Hyadaphis tartaricae*. Some species are more susceptible than others. Geographical areas vary as to susceptibility. There is every reason to expect that the problem will be overcome and that this valuable genus once again will take its place in our landscapes.

■ *L. syringantha*, LILAC HONEYSUCKLE, IPH, 60%, M. A shrub for mountain homes where the honeysuckle aphid is not likely to abide. Lilac flowers highlight arching branches in spring, followed by red berries. From Tibet, it is very hardy.

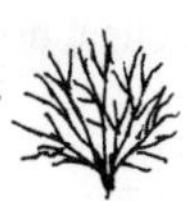

■ *L. maackii*, AMUR HONEYSUCKLE, IP, 60%, M. A nearly evergreen shrub, with leaves remaining till December.

CULTIVAR:

'Rem Red'- a tall upright shrub with rounded top; white and yellow flowers in early summer, followed by red berries that persist into winter. It is resistant to the honeysuckle aphid.

■ *Lysium halimifolium*, MATRIMONY VINE, D, 40%, M. Not a thing of beauty, but something that will grow where nothing else will. More a shrub than a vine. Small purple flowers, red berries. Good for disguising unsightly outbuildings.

■ *Magnolia soulangeana*, SAUCER MAGNOLIA, IP, 40%, T. Large pink and white saucer flowers before leaves. Leaves are coarse and limbs weak. A stunning plant when spring frost and snow allow it to bloom. Give it a sheltered location on the east.

■ *M. stellata*, STAR MAGNOLIA, IP, 40%, M. White ribbonlike blooms before leaves. More reliable than above species.

■ *Nandina domestica*, DWARF HEAVENLY BAMBOO, IP, 40%, L. Worthy of trial despite its tenderness. Stiff, slender leaves turn fiery red in autumn and remain all winter. Give it good drainage, winter watering, partial shade.

■ *Paeonia suffruticosa*, TREE PEONY, IP, 50%, L. A woody-stem version of beloved herbceous peonies. Extensively hyrbidized; many colors available. Give eastern exposure and protect in winter with constructed covers in northern areas of the range of this book.

■ *Philadelphus coronarius*,
SWEET MOCKORANGE, IP, 60%, T. The fragrance of orange blossoms is wafted from single white cuplike blooms in early summer.

CULTIVAR:

'Aureus' - bright lime green foliage and white blooms. Attractive faced down with Berberis "Rosy Glow".

'Dwarf Snowflake' - a small version of the species.

■ *Physocarpus monogynus*,
MOUNTAIN NINEBARK, IPH, 60%, L. A native useful as a low spreader for a north-facing slope of a mountain home. Masses of white flowers in spring.

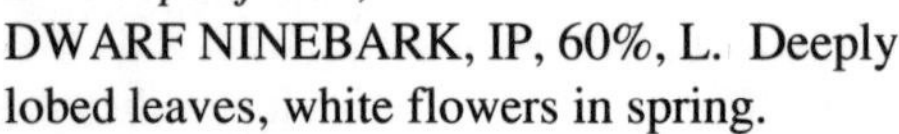

■ *P. opulifolius*,
DWARF NINEBARK, IP, 60%, L. Deeply lobed leaves, white flowers in spring.

CULTIVAR:

'Dart's Gold' - lime green foliage looks cool all summer. Attractive planted against dark evergreens.

■ *Potentilla fruticosa*,
CINQUEFOIL, IPH, 60%, L. A standard in the foundation and tree-and-shrub border as a low fountain of yellow flowers in the foreground. Subject to spider mites. Should be cut to the ground every three years in February.

CULTIVARS:

'Abbotswood' - white blooms in early June.

'Day Dawn' - soft yellow flowers.

'Red Ace' - yellow flowers in summer, changing to red in fall.

'Tangerine' - coppery flowers in cool weather or part shade.

■ *Prunus americana*,
AMERICAN PLUM, IPH, 80%, T. A native that forms the roadside thicket at Plains altitude. Useful as background or single-trunked specimen. White flowers before leaves. Resistant to crown borer.

■ *P. besseyi*,
WESTERN SANDCHERRY, IP, 40%, M. A native of the Plains. Small white flowers in spring, followed by small black edible plums that have large stones, very little flesh.

CULTIVAR:

'Hansen's' - better quality fruit, more uniform growth.

■ *P. x cistena*,
PURPLE-LEAVED SANDCHERRY, IP, 50%, T. Good background tall shrub for mixed border. Purple leaves effective with shrubs of lime-green foliage adjacent; white blooms before leaves. Subject to crown borer.

■ *P. tomentosa*,
NANKING CHERRY, IP, 40%, T. Pink blooms before leaves; red edible fruit. Subject to crown borer.

■ *P. triloba*,
FLOWERING ALMOND, IP, 50%, M. A vision of pink flowers in spring before leaves. Arching branches; no fruit. Subject to fireblight.

■ *Purshia tridentata*, ANTELOPE BRUSH, D, 40%, M. A native of dry, rocky hillsides. Fragrant yellow flowers in spring. Good for xeric landscape.

■ *Rhamnus cathartica*, COMMON BUCKTHORN, D, 40%, T. An escapee from cultivation, but not invasive in the Mountain West. Good for tall thorny background shrub borders. Glossy foliage, clusters of white flowers followed by black berries. Bark is used medicinally as a cathartic.

■ *R. frangula*, ALDER BUCKTHORN, IP, 60%, T. A tall hedge or barrier with white flower clusters and red berries that turn to black. Needs an organic soil and lots of water to establish. Sometimes listed as TALLHEDGE.

■ *Rhododendron* - See Chapter 18, AZALEAS AND RHODODENDRONS

■ *Rhodotypos scandens*, JETBEAD, IP, 50%, M. A neat, well-behaved shrub with light green leaves, white flower cups in spring followed by persistent shiny bead-like seed clusters. Prefers a rich, moisture retentive soil.

■ *Rhus glabra*, SMOOTH SUMAC, I, 50%, T. A native with fern-like foliage and a habit of moving in all directions. If you can keep it in bounds, it has stunning scarlet fall foliage. Seed heads held high on branches are loved by returning bluebirds.

■ *R. glabra lacinata*, CUTLEAF SUMAC, IP, 50%, M. Does not sucker as much as above species; withstands some shade.

■ *R. trilobata*, LEMONADE SUMAC, THREE-LEAF SUMAC, D, M. An arching-branched native with lobed leaves, inconspicuous flowers followed by sticky red berries loved by birds. Indians and settlers made a summer drink from the leaves that tasted lemony. When pruned, the fresh cuts smell like skunk.

■ *R. typhina*, STAGHORN SUMAC, I, 50%, T. Another version of R. glabra but with fuzzy branches like a deer with horns in velvet. Very picturesque in winter.

■ *R. typhina lacinata*, CUTLEAF STAGHORN SUMAC, I, 50%, T. A cutleaf version of above. Very tropical looking when planted near a waterfall.

■ *Ribes alpinum*, ALPINE CURRANT, IP, 60%, L. A well-behaved small shrub that tolerates some shade. Inconspicuous flowers followed by red berries. Can be clipped into a low hedge.

■ *R. aureum*, GOLDEN CURRANT, IP, 70%, M. Mounded, arching habit covered with spicy-fragrant yellow flowers in spring; yellow or red berries loved by birds. Thicket type growth also makes good nesting habitat.

■ *R. cereum*,
SQUAW CURRANT, D, 50%, L. Rocky hillsides suit this native. Dry, red berries follow small pink flowers.

■ *Robinia hispida*,
ROSE ACACIA, I, 50%, T. Spreading habit by suckers. Heads of rose pea-like flowers in early summer. Often used as shade for cows.

■ *Salix caprea*,
GOAT WILLOW, FRENCH PUSSYWILLOW, I, 40%, T. Suckering and often aphid and scale infested, this is, nevertheless, beloved in spring for the fuzzy gray catkins. Try to get someone else to grow it for you.

■ *S. gracilistyla*,
JAPANESE PUSSY WILLOW, IP, 50%, M. Noted for red and gray catkins dusted with yellow pollen.

■ *S. irrorata*,
BLUESTEM WILLOW, IH, 40%, T. A native of swamps and lake banks. Small gray fuzzy catkins break from a jet-black calyx in spring.

■ *S. matsudana*,
GOLDEN CORKSCREW WILLOW, IP, 60%, M. Yellow bark in winter; corkscrew weeping branches; curled foliage; yellow fall color.

■ *S. melanostachys*,
BLACK PUSSYWILLOW. IP, 50%, T. Noted for striking black catkins.

■ *S. purpurea nana*,
DWARF ARCTIC BLUE WILLOW, IP, 60%, M. Non-native, but useful mound of slender gray-green leaves always in motion. Plant it at the base of the downspout in the foundation planting. Cut it to the base every three years. Subject to oystershell scale.

CULTIVAR:
'Gracilis' - brilliant red and yellow branches in winter and a soft, gray-green fountain of foliage in summer.

Note: All willows are fast to grow and quick to die. They should be cut to the ground every three to five years or replaced when they begin to wane.

■ *Sambucus canadensis*,
AMERICAN ELDER, IP, 40% T. Fast-growing shade for the new home. Giant plates of white flowers followed by edible black berries. Often wilts quickly in summer from lack of water and inability to pump water into its stems. Mist it in afternoon during hot weather.

CULTIVAR:
'Aurea' - lime-green foliage.

■ *Shepherdia argentea*,
BUFFALOBERRY, I or DH, 60%,M. Leathery green leaves, silver beneath. Inconspicuous flowers; bitter red berries on female plants. Indians used this berry as an ingredient of pemmican.

■ *Shepherdia canadensis*, RUSSET BUFFALOBERRY, I or D, 60%, M. A native of shaded rocky hillsides with dark green leathery leaves that are russet beneath. Bitter red berries.

■ *Spirea x bumalda*, FROBEL SPIREA, IP, 70%, L. Rose-pink flower clusters in early summer. Orange fall color.

CULTIVARS:

'Crispa' - deeply incised foliage; deep pink flowers.

'Gold Flame' - bronze foliage in spring, turning to yellow-green in summer; red flowers.

'Limemound' - dense, yellow-green leaves; pink flowers.

■ *S. vanhouttei*, BRIDALWREATH SPIREA, IP, 80% M. An old favorite for bridal bouquets. Covered with white flower clusters on arching branches. Small blue-green leaves; orange fall color. Winter watering. Renewal pruning will make it last a century.

■ *Symphoricarpos albus*, SNOWBERRY, IP, 70%, L. Arching branches, inconspicuous flowers followed by clusters of large white berries loved by birds. Withstands shade.

■ *S. orbiculatus*, CORALBERRY, IP, 50%, L. Arching branches, clusters of red berries NOT loved by birds.

■ *Syringa x chinensis alba*, CHINESE LILAC, IP, 70%, T. Trusses of white blooms from every twig in late May. Matures at 10-15'.

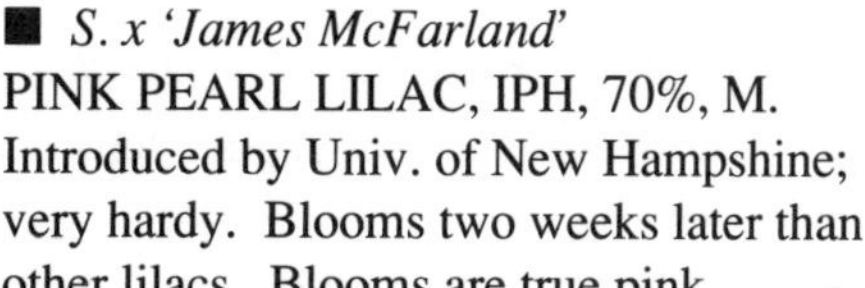

■ *S. x 'James McFarland'* PINK PEARL LILAC, IPH, 70%, M. Introduced by Univ. of New Hampshine; very hardy. Blooms two weeks later than other lilacs. Blooms are true pink.

■ *S. josikaea*, HUNGARIAN LILAC, IP, 70%, M. These have become available once again.

CULTIVARS:

'Eximia' - rose-red blooms.

'Palida' - pale violet.

'Rosea' - deep rose.

■ *S. meyeri*, DWARF LILAC, IP, 70%, M. Very fragrant small lavender trusses borne heavily on a globe-shaped form seldom over five feet. Blooms two weeks later than S. vulgaris. Makes an excellent untrimmed, dense hedge.

■ *S. persica*, PERSIAN LILAC, IP, 70%, M. Rounded form without "bare legs'. Fragrant, feathery lavender blooms. Does not sucker at the base.

■ *S. vulgaris*, COMMON LILAC, IPH, 60%, T. Long clusters of fragrant flowers. The plant most likely to be brought from "home" when covered wagons came to the Mountain West. Subject to oystershell scale, borers. Suckers at the base.

CULTIVARS: (There are many others.)
'Adelaide Dunbar' - intense deep-purple flowers

'Charles Joly' - double flowers of reddish-purple.

'Congo' - deep ruby red, heavy substance.

'Miss Ellen Wilmott' - very fragrant long white trusses.

'President Grevy' - double blue.

■ *Tamarix hispida*,
KASHGAR TAMARIX, I or D, 20%, T. Feathery foliage and large pink plumes of minute flowers. Naturalized along the Colorado River and regarded as a waterhog pest. Nevertheless, it is valuable in a home or commercial landscape where there is poor drainage or high pH, for it can withstand a pH of 11.0. Plants should be selected for deep pink blooms and dug from the wild, with permission of the landowner.

■ *Viburnum acerifolium*,
OAKLEAF VIBURNUM, IP, 60%, T. Lacy white flowers, red fall foliage; withstands shade. Will require constructed cover in northern areas.

■ *V. burkwoodii*,
BURKWOOD VIBURNUM, IP, 60%, M. Glossy leaves, fragrant lacy blooms followed by large clusters of black berries. Claret wine fall color.

■ *V. carlessii*,
KOREAN SPICE VIBURNUM, IP, 60%, M. The most popular of all Viburnums. Balls of white blooms, tinged with pink; strong fragrance; brilliant crimson in fall.
CULTIVAR:
'Diana' - blooms later and seldom frost nipped.

■ *V. opulus*,
CRANBERRY BUSH, ARROWWOOD, IP,70%, T. A shrub brought to America by very early settlers. Oak-like leaves, lacy white blooms, followed by red berries that are seldom taken by birds.
CULTIVARS:
'Compactum' - a very dense branch and foliage pattern; ultimate height is about eight feet.

'Nanum'- a small, dense shrub; non-fruiting, but a mass of red twigs in winter. Seldom over two feet.

■ *V. plicatum tomentosum*,
DOUBLEFILE VIBURNUM, IP, 70%, M. A good choice where tall trees cast dappled shade. Heavy flowering of flat flower clusters that resemble lace caps, followed by red berries turning to black.
CULTIVARS:
'Mariesii' - a medium size with large white flowers in spring. Branch pattern is horizontal, giving an effect of espalier.

'Shasta' - a superior introduction from the National Arboretum.

■ *V. prunifolium*,
BLACK HAW, IP, 70%, T. A standard in shrub borders where it serves well with insect-free leathery foliage, small white flower clusters in late spring, followed by black berries (haws). Fall color is brilliant red.

■ *Vitex agnus-castus*, CHASTE TREE, IP, 50%, T. A shrub that can be trained to a single trunk. Small blue flowers in late summer. Needs covered winter protection, or it can be allowed to freeze to the ground and it will come up again in spring, similar to Butterfly Bush.

■ *Weigela florida*, CARDINAL FLOWER, IP, 70%, M. Arching graceful form, each branch covered with rose-red fading flowers in early summer.

CULTIVARS:

'Minuet' - a dwarf variety developed in Canada.

'Red Prince' - same red flowers, but they retain color better than species.

'Variegata' - cool green and white foliage provide excellent contrast for red blooms. A slow grower.

■ *Yucca glauca*, SOAPWEED, D, 60%, L. Linear leaves, each bearing a sharp tip, arranged in sphere. A native that is effective as an accent in the dry landscape. Flowers are tall scapes of creamy bells pollinated by a moth.

Shrubs for a Tall Border - Over Six Feet

Acanthopanax sieboldianus	HARDY ARALIA
Acer ginnala	AMUR MAPLE
A. glabrum	ROCKY MOUNTAIN MAPLE
A. tataricum	TATARIAN MAPLE
Alnus tenuifolia	THINLEAF ALDER
Aralia spinosa	DEVIL'S WALKING STICK
Betula fontinalis	ROCKY MOUNTAIN BIRCH
Buddleia alternifolia	FOUNTAIN BUTTERFLY BUSH
B. davidii	BUTTERFLY BUSH
Caragana arborescens	SIBERIAN PEA SHRUB
Cercis canadensis	REDBUD
Chionanthus virginicus	FRINGE TREE
Cornus mas	CORNELIAN CHERRY
C. racemosa	GRAY DOGWOOD
Corylus cornuta	BEAKED FILBERT OR HAZELNUT
Cotinus coggygria	SMOKETREE
Crataegus douglasii	BLACK HAWTHORN
Crataegus crusgalli	COCKSPUR HAWTHORN
Elaeagnus umbellata	AUTUMN OLIVE
Euonymus alata	WINGED EUONYMUS
Fothergilla major	BOTTLEBRUSH
Genista tinctoria	DYER'S BROOM
Hamamelis vernalis	VERNAL WITCH HAZEL
Hibiscus syriacus	ROSE OF SHARON
Hippophae rhamnoides	SEABUCKTHORN
Hydrangea quercifolia	OAKLEAF HYDRANGEA
Magnolia soulangeana	SAUCER MAGNOLIA
Philadelphus coronarius	SWEET MOCKORANGE
Prunus americana	AMERICAN PLUM
P. x cistena	PURPLE LEAF SAND CHERRY
P. tomentosa	NANKING CHERRY
Rhamnus cathartica	COMMON BUCKTHORN
Rhamnus frangula	ALDER BUCKTHORN
Rhus glabra	SMOOTH SUMAC
R. typhina lacinata	CUTLEAF STAGHORN SUMAC
Robinia hispida	ROSE ACACIA
Salix caprea	GOAT WILLOW, FRENCH PUSSYWILLOW
S. irrorata	BLUESTEM WILLOW
S. melanostachys	BLACK PUSSYWILLOW
Sambucus canadensis	AMERICAN ELDER
Syringa x chinensis alba	CHINESE LILAC
S. vulgaris	COMMON LILAC
Tamarix hispida	KASHGAR TAMARIX
Viburnum acerifolium	OAKLEAF VIBURNUM
V. opulus	CRANBERRY BUSH
V. prunifolium	BLACK HAW
Vitex agnus-castus	CHASTE TREE

Shrubs of Medium Height - Four to Six Feet

Aesculus parviflora	BOTTLEBRUSH BUCKEYE
Berberis koreana	KOREAN BARBERRY
B. mentorensis	MENTOR BARBERRY
Callicarpa bodinieri	BEAUTYBERRY
Calycanthus floridus purpureus	CAROLINA ALLSPICE
Cercocarpos montanus	MOUNTAIN MAHOGANY
Chaenomeles japonica	JAPANESE FLOWERING QUINCE
Clethra alnifolia	SUMMERSWEET
Cornus alba sibirica	SIBERIAN REDTWIG
Corylus cornuta	BEAKED FILBERT
Cotoneaster integerrima	EUROPEAN COTONEASTER
Deutzia x Lemoinei	LEMOINE DEUTZIA
Diervilla lonicera	DWARF BUSH HONEYSUCKLE
Elaeagnus commutata	SILVERBERRY
Euonymus alata compacta	WINGED EUONYMUS
Forsythia intermedia	FORSYTHIA
Fothergilla gardenii	BOTTLEBRUSH
Holodiscus dumosa	ROCK SPIREA
Hydrangea arborescens	HILLS OF SNOW HYDRANGEA
H. macrophylla coeulea	LACECAP HYDRANGEA
Ilex verticillata	WINTERBERRY
Jamesia americana	CLIFF JAMESIA
Kolkwitzia amabilis	BEAUTYBUSH
Ligustrum amurense	PRIVET
Lonicera syringantha	LILAC HONEYSUCKLE
Lysium halmifolium	MATRIMONY VINE
Prunus besseyi	WESTERN SANDCHERRY
P. triloba	FLOWERING ALMOND
Rhodotypos scandens	JETBEAD
Rhus glabra lacinata	CUTLEAF SUMAC
R. trilobata	THREE-LEAF SUMAC
Ribes aureum	GOLDEN CURRANT
Salix gracilistyla	JAPANESE PUSSYWILLOW
S. matsudana	GOLDEN CORKSCREW WILLOW
S. purpurea nana	DWARF ARCTIC BLUE WILLOW
Shepherdia argentea	BUFFALOBERRY
Spirea vanhouttei	BRIDALWREATH SPIREA
Syringa x 'James McFarland'	PINK PEARL LILAC
Syringa meyeri	DWARF LILAC
S. persica	PERSIAN LILAC
Viburnum burkwoodii	BURKWOOD VIBURNUM
V. carlesii	KOREAN SPICE VIBURNUM
V. plicatum tomentosum	DOUBLEFILE VIBURNUM
Weigela florida	CARDINAL FLOWER

Low Shrubs - Under Four Feet

Amorpha canescens	LEAD PLANT
Buxus microphylla	DWARF BOX-WOOD
B. sempervirens	BOXWOOD
Calluna vulgaris	HEATH OR HEATHER
Caragana pygmaea	PYGMY PEA SHRUB
Caryopteris incana	BLUEBEARD
Cotoneaster adpressus	PROSTRATE COTONEASTER
C. apiculatus	CRANBERRY COTONEASTER
Daphne arbuscula	DAPHNE
Ilex verticillata 'Nana'	WINTERBERRY
Kalmia latifolia	MOUNTAIN LAUREL
Ledum groenlandicum	LABRADOR TEA
Ligustrum amurense 'Lodense nanum'	PRIVET
Nandina domestica	DWARF HEAV-ENLY BAMBOO
Paeonia suffruticosa	TREE PEONY
Physocarpus monogynus	MOUNTAIN NINEBARK
Potentilla fruticosa	CINQUEFOIL
Ribes alpinum	ALPINE CURRANT
R. cereum	SQUAW CURRANT
Spirea x bumalda	FROBEL SPIREA
Symphoricarpos albus	SNOWBERRY
S. orbiculatus	CORALBERRY

Shrubs for Dappled Shade

Cornus sp.	DOGWOOD
Corylus cornuta	BEAKED FILBERT
Euonymus alata	WINGED EUONYMUS
E. Fortunei	WINTERCREEPER
Forsythia suspensa	FORSYTHIA
Hydrangea sp.	HYDRANGEA
Ligustrum amurense	PRIVET
Lonicera sp.	HONEYSUCKLE
Nandina domestica	DWARF HEAV-ENLY BAMBOO
Philadelphus sp.	MOCKORANGE
Rhodotypos scandens	JETBEAD
Ribes aureum	GOLDEN CURRANT
Sambucus canadensis	ELDERBERRY
Symphoricarpos albus	SNOWBERRY
S. orbiculatus	CORALBERRY
Viburnum carlessii	KOREAN SPICE VIBURNUM

Shrubs for Hot, Dry or Alkaline Places

Chaenomeles sp.	FLOWERING QUINCE
Cotoneaster integerrima	EUROPEAN COTONEASTER
Holodiscus dumosa	ROCK SPIREA
Lycium halimifolium	MATRIMONY VINE
Potentilla fruticosa	CINQUEFOIL
Prunus americana	AMERICAN PLUM
Prunus virginiana	CHOKECHERRY
Rhamnus cathartica	COMMON BUCK-THORN
Rhus trilobata	THREE-LEAF SUMAC
Sambucus canadensis	ELDERBERRY
Shepherdia argentea	BUFFALOBERRY
Symphoricarpos alba	SNOWBERRY
S. orbiculatus	CORALBERRY
Syringa vulgaris	COMMON LILAC
Tamarix hispida	KASHGAR TAMARIX
Yucca glauca	SOAPWEED

Shrubs for Color of Bloom

Yellow

Caragana arborescens	PEA SHRUB
C. pygmaea	PYGMY PEA SHRUB
Cornus mas	CORNELIAN CHERRY
Diervilla lonicera	DWARF BUSH HONEYSUCKLE
Forsythia suspensa and cvs	FORSYTHIA
Genista tinctoria	DYER'S BROOM
Hamamelis vernalis	VERNAL WITCH HAZEL
Hypericum frondosum	SHRUBBY HYPERICUM
H. kouytchense	SUNGOLD HYPERICUM
Lonicera maackii 'Rem Red'	AMUR HONEYSUCKLE
Paeonia suffruticosa cvs.	TREE PEONY
Potentilla fruticosa and cvs.	CINQUEFOIL
Purshia tridentata	ANTELOPE BRUSH
Ribes aureum	GOLDEN CURRANT
Rosa	ROSE

Pink and Red

Buddleia alternifolia	BUTTERFLY BUSH
Chaenomeles cvs	FLOWERING QUINCE
Daphne x burkwoodii	BURKWOOD DAPHNE
Hibiscus syriacus cvs.	ROSE OF SHARON
Kalmia latifolia	MOUNTAIN LAUREL
Kolkwitzia amabilis	BEAUTY BUSH
Magnolia soulangeana	SAUCER MAGNOLIA
Paeonia suffruticosa cvs.	TREE PEONY
Prunus beseyi	WESTERN SANDCHERRY
P. tomentosa	NANKING CHERRY
P. triloba	FLOWERING ALMOND
Ribes cereum	SQUAW CURRANT
Robinia hispida	ROSE ACACIA
Spirea x bumalda cvs.	FROBEL SPIREA
S. josikaea 'Eximia', 'Rosea'	HUNGARIAN LILAC cvs.
Syringa sp. and cvs.	LILAC species and cultivars
S. vulgaris	COMMON LILAC
Syringa x 'James McFarland'	PINK PEARL LILAC
Tamarix hispida	KASHGAR TAMARIX
Weigela florida	CARDINAL FLOWER

Shrubs for Color of Bloom

White or Cream

Acanthopanax sieboldianus	HARDY ARALIA
Aesculus parviflora	BOTTLEBRUSH
Amelanchier alnifolia cvs.	SERVICEBERRY
Buddleia alternifolia cvs.	BUTTERFLY BUSH
Chionanthus virginicus	FRINGE-TREE
Cornus alba cvs.	DOGWOOD
C. racemosa	GRAY DOGWOOD
Cotoneaster adpressus cvs.	PROSTRATE COTONEASTER
Crataegus sp.	HAWTHORN
Deutzia x Lemoinei	LEMOINE DEUTZIA
Fothergilla gardenii	BOTTLEBRUSH
F. major	BOTTLEBRUSH
Holodiscus dumosa	ROCK SPIREA
Hydrangea sp.	HYDRANGEA
Kalmia latifolia cvs.	MOUNTAIN LAUREL
Paeonia suffruticosa	TREE PEONY
Philadelphus coronarius	MOCK ORANGE
Physocarpus monogynus	NINEBARK
Prunus americana	AMERICAN PLUM
Prunus besseyi	WESTERN SANDCHERRY
Prunus x cistena	CISTENA PLUM
Rhamnus cathartica	COMMON BUCK-THORN
R. frangula	ALDER BUCK-THORN
Rhodotypos scandens	JETBEAD
Spirea vanhouttei	BRIDALWREATH SPIREA
Syringa vulgaris cvs.	COMMON LILAC
S. x chinensis alba	CHINESE LILAC
Viburnum sp. and cvs.	ARROWWOOD

Blue, Lavendar or Purple

Amorpha canescens	LEAD PLANT
Buddleia alternifolia	BUTTERFLY BUSH
B. davidii cvs.	BUTTERFLY BUSH
Callicarpa bodinieri	BEAUTYBERRY
Caryopteris incana	BLUEBEARD
Cercis canadensis	REDBUD
Cotinus coggygria cvs.	SMOKETREE
Hydrangea macrophylla coerulea	LACECAP HYDRANGEA
Lonicera syringantha	LILAC HONEY-SUCKLE
Lycium halimifolium	MATRIMONY VINE
Syringa josikaea cvs.	HUNGARIAN LILAC
S. meyeri	DWARF LILAC
S. vulgaris cvs.	COMMON LILAC
Vitex agnus-castus	CHASTE TREE

Evergreen Shrubs

Evergreen shrubs give the color, texture, and interest for the gardener to survive the drab, brown, often snow-less winters in the Mountain West. There are not as many evergreen shrubs available to us as there are deciduous shrubs, but their importance is not diminished. The evergreen shrub's greatest asset is not its shape, texture, or color, however; it is its ability to protect other plants from wind-driven snow, rain, and hail. It can take the brunt of wind, ameliorating the hot, dry wind, or the cold, dry wind - both a multi-annual event in the Mountain West.

In placing an evergreen shrub, remember that its visual weight is greater than that of a deciduous shrub. It dominates because of the density of foliage and intensity of color. A few, such as the dwarf white pine, present a fluffy, fuzzy appearence. Its color, nevertheless, is deep green, and the visual weight is heavier than a deciduous shrub of comparable density, such as a *Viburnum.*

As you choose an evergreen shrub, keep in mind that you won't need as many in number as you will of deciduous shrubs. Place them with care and thought for the background against which they will be seen. A deep green *Juniperus sabina tamariscifolia* will be lost against a dark brick structure, but a gray or yellow-green cultivar will make the structure seem less somber and weighty.

■ *Juniperus chinensis*, SPREADER JUNIPER, ID, 80%, T. This is the standard "spreader" of the 40's when thousands of ranch-style homes were built in look-alike subdivisions in America. The cultivar of that time, 'Pfitzer', has an ultimate height of six-to-eight feet, which soon overwhelmed the picture window, and the spread of the same dimension soon crowded the entry. This shrub is, nevertheless, invaluable in the country landscape or at the perimeter of a property where its graceful arching branches screen, shield, and provide a background for other plants. With establishment water for two years, it can usually survive with natural precipitation for twenty five to thirty years.

CULTIVARS:

'Fruitland' - height 3', spread 4-6';bright green foliage, compact, dense growth.

'Gold Coast' - height 3', spread 4-5'; brilliant gold color deepens with cold weather.

'Hetzii Glauca' - height 5'7', spread 8-10'; blue-green foliage, fast-growing.

'Pfitzeriana Aurea' - height 3', spread 4-6'; bright green foliage with yellow tips; fast-growing.

'Pfitzeriana Compacta' - height 3', spread 4-6'; gray-green foliage; very dense.

■ *Juniperus horizontalis*, CREEPING JUNIPER, IP, 80%, average of 12". This useful "hill-holder" is finally taking its place in erosion control while adding four-season beauty. In areas of 20-24" annual precipitation, it can hold its own after two years of establishment water.

CULTIVARS:

'Blue Chip' - height 8-10", spread 6-8'; silver-blue feathery foliage.

'Prince of Wales' - height 6", spread 5-6'; a very hardy cultivar, worthy of high altitude or latitude; bright green foliage.

'Wiltonii' - height 6", spread 6-8'; an old stand-by with outstanding blue foliage; female plants have very large blue fruits loved by Townsend's Solitaire.

■ *Juniperus sabina*,
IP, 80%, height average 12", spread 8'. A very tough, resiliant species long in cultivation.

CULTIVARS:

'Broadmoor' - height 12", spread 4-5'. Semi-upright, spreading, with blue-green foliage.

'Buffalo' - height 12", spread 5-6'. A very hardy, cultivar able to withstand high altitude and northern winters; bright green foliage.

■ *J. sabina tamariscifolia*,
TAM JUNIPER, IP, 80%, height 1-2', spread 8-10'; dark green foliage. An old stand-by.

CULTIVAR:

'New Blue' - height 1-2', spread 8-10'. A blue-green foliage variation for the old favorite Tam Juniper.

■ *J. squamata*,
MOUND JUNIPER, IP, 70%, height 2', spread 2'. A native of Tibet, but it sun-scalds in Mountain West winter sun. Royal blue foliage makes it a stand-out in the rock garden.

■ *Mahonia aquifolium*,
OREGON HOLLY-GRAPE, IP, 70%, height 5', spread, 4'. A non-native broadleaf evergreen with glossy, spiny leaves that resemble holly. Sunburns if planted in winter sun, but grows quickly if given an eastern exposure and a burlap screen in winter.Yellow flowers in early summer followed by blue berries loved by birds. Watch for a larva that skeletonizes leaves, but is easily picked off.

■ *Picea abies*,
NORWAY SPRUCE, IHP, 50%, height 2', spread 3'; a very hardy shrub form of this tree of the North;, flat-topped mound of dark green needles.

CULTIVARS:

'Nidiformis' - height 2', spread 3'; Hardy to Zone 2, this little flat-topped mound is useful in an entry garden or rock garden.

'Repens' - height 2', spread 2-3'; a globe of dense dark green foliage with arching branches in layers.

■ *P. glauca*,
ALBERTA SPRUCE, IP, 60%, height 5-10', spread 4-5'. A miniature tree form useful in the foundation planting.

CULTIVARS:

'Conica' - height 5-10', spread 4-5'; conical shape for a vertical accent in the rock garden or entry garden; bright green foliage.

■ *P. mariana*,
BLACK SPRUCE, IP, 70%, height 3', spread 3'. A dwarf form of a very hardy, pest-free tree is available.

CULTIVAR:

'Nana' - height 3', spread 3'; a perfect globe of dense, blue-green foliage.

■ *P. pungens glauca*,
COLORADO SPRUCE, IP 70%, height 3', spread 4-5'; A dwarf shrub form of Colorado's state tree is available.

CULTIVAR:
'Globosa' - height 3', spread 4-5'; round silhouette, flat-topped globe of silvery-blue foliage. May become pyramidal with age.

■ *Pinus densiflora*,
TANYOSHO OR TABLE TOP PINE, IP, 50%, hieght 9-10', spread 12-15'. This tall, many stemmed shrub is best viewed from below where you can look up into its multi-trunks, or from above where you can observe its table-top flatness of long needled branchlets.
CULTIVAR:
'Umbraculifera' - height 9-10', spread 12-15'; very slow growth, but a unique habit for the hillside or bermed garden where it can be appreciated; two needles to the fascicle*.

■ *P. Mugo*,
MUGHO PINE, IP, 80%, height 6-25', spread 6-20 '. Often purchased at discount garden centers in one-gallon containers and planted by the front entry. This multi-stemmed spreader is very effective planted at the perimeter of the property where its beauty can be enjoyed, but only guaranteed dwarf stock, propagated from known dwarfs, can be relied upon. Two needles to the fascicle
CULTIVAR:
'Mops' - height 3', spread 3'; A true dwarf from Holland that will be on the market in this country soon. Would be an excellent addition to the foundation planting.

■ *P. strobus*,
WHITE PINE, IP, 50%, height 6', spread, 6'. A shrub form of the white pine of the East is available.
CULTIVAR:
'Glauca Nana' - height 3', spread 2-3'; blue-green feathery soft foliage; very slow growing.

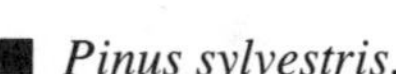

■ *Pinus sylvestris*,
SCOTS PINE, IP, 60%, height 5'6', spread 5-6'. A shrub form of the tough non-native Scots Pine. Two needles to the fascicle.
CULTIVAR:
'Glauca Nana' - height 5-6', spread 5-6'; blue-green foliage on a rounded mound of dense horizontal branches with ascending branchlets.

■ *Pyracantha angustifolia cv.*, 'Gnozam', GNOZAM PYRACANTHA, IP, 60%, height 6', spread 6-8'. A broadleaf evergreen of variable hardiness in all but the southern part of the Mountain West. Glossy leaves, masses of white flowers in late spring, followed by orange berries that are colorful all winter if the birds don't discover them. It will thrive in one landscape, but succumb to winter next door. It can withstand winter sun; cannot withstand drought; needs hardening off in late summer. Blooms on second year wood. Careful pruning will keep it shapely. Pyracantha is easy to espalier and is especially attractive on a dark brick wall. Subject to fireblight.
CULTIVARS:
'Gnozam' - height 6', spread 6-8'. A hardier selection from the earlier "Gnome" introduction. Give it an organic soil and organic mulch.

* *See Glossary*

■ *P. coccinea*,
FIRETHORN, IP 60%, height 5-6'. The standard species that became popular after WWII.

CULITVAR:

'Mohave' - height 9-12', spread 9-12'. A giant introduction that has proven resistance to fireblight.

Rhododendron - See Chapter 18 "Azaleas and Rhododendrons."

■ *Taxus x media*,
YEW, IP, 50%, height 6', spread 4-5'. If your soil has been prepared according to recommendations in Chapter 4, Soils, you can grow yews with no difficulty. The flat, needle-like foliage is dark green and can be tightly trimmed for a formal hedge. Inconspicuous flowers followed by red fruits, but not profuse.

CULTIVARS:

'L.C. Bobbink' - height 6', spread 6-8'. Fine textured, glossy foliage needs little trimming to achieve a globe form.

'Brownii' - height 6', spread 9'. A compact form that shears well.

'Everlow' - height 1 1/2', spread 4-5'. A very low-growing spreader , highly resistant to sunscald in winter.

'Sebian' - height 3-4', spread 4-5'. Very dark green, very winter hardy and shade tolerant.

■ *Thuja occidentalis*,
ARBORVITAE, IP, 50%, height 2-3', spread 2-3'. Flat fans of foliage radiate upward from a cen-tral trunk. Not easily grown in the northern range of this book. Use a constructed cover in winter. Heavy snow load causes spreading. Wrap it with bands of bird netting to avoid damage.

CULTIVARS:

'Aurea' - height 3', spread 3'. A golden globe of feathery foliage without trimming. A good subject for sunny, protected courtyard.

'Hetz Midget' - height 24", spread 24". An extremely dwarf and slow growing form for trough or rock garden.

'Rheingold' - height 4', spread 3-4'. A slow-growing compact mound of striking golden-orange year round.

'Woodwardii' - height 3-4', spread 3-4'. The arborvitae for the north or for high altitude. Extremely hardy, but can still be damaged by snow load or wind.

CHAPTER 13

Hedges

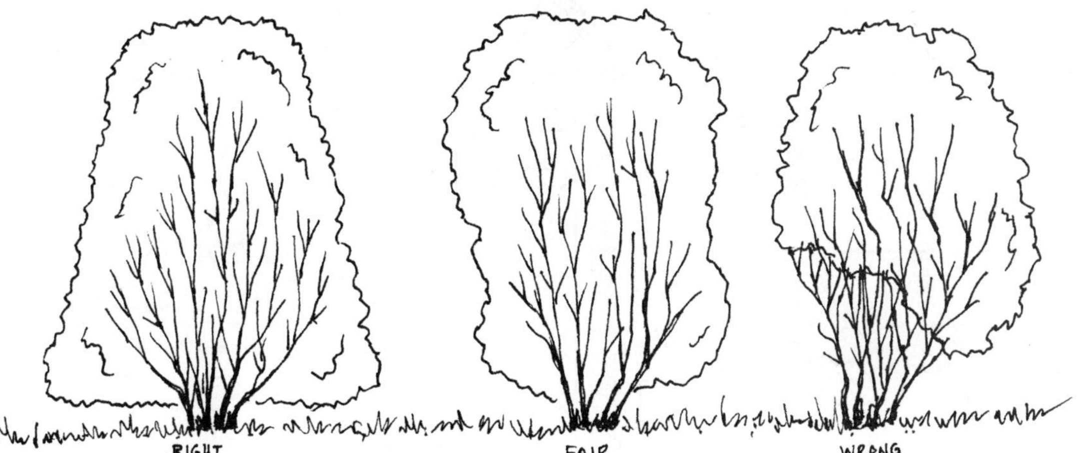

Today the hedge is back in the running as a garden feature. Traditionally, hedges enclosed and separated. They were the walls of the garden and the inside partitions. In the Victorian period clipped hedges were popular, with the privet or boxwood hedge used as a maze for the amusement of children and adults. Today the maze is maintained on the grounds of many of the stately homes of Great Britain as a curiosity, rather than as a useful landscape feature.

Privacy is highly valued in our lives today. At the same time, the soft and billowy look is popular; so it follows that the informal (meaning unclipped) hedge has appeared on the landscape scene. And despite modern power hedge-clipping equipment, not many gardeners have the time to clip a hedge.

There are few landscapes that cannot use a hedge, if not to mark a boundary, then as a small architectural feature to highlight an entry, or to serve as a background for garden sculpture, or a flower border. The thorny hedge is useful in confining children, pets, and livestock. The burglar, whose most valuable asset is his hands, will hesitate a long time before risking damage to them by attempting to get to the window that is underplanted with a thorny hedge. Hedges are often used in adjunct with stone or masonry walls. Hedges can lower the visual height of a high fence that may be needed to block a view or traffic noise. The twigginess of a hedge is far more effective in baffling noise and odors than an inanimate fence or wall.

A hedge can lower the visual height of a fence or wall.

■ *The clipped hedge highlights the entry, yet, because it is of short length, it is easy to maintain.*

■ *If the soil varies, so will the plant growth.*

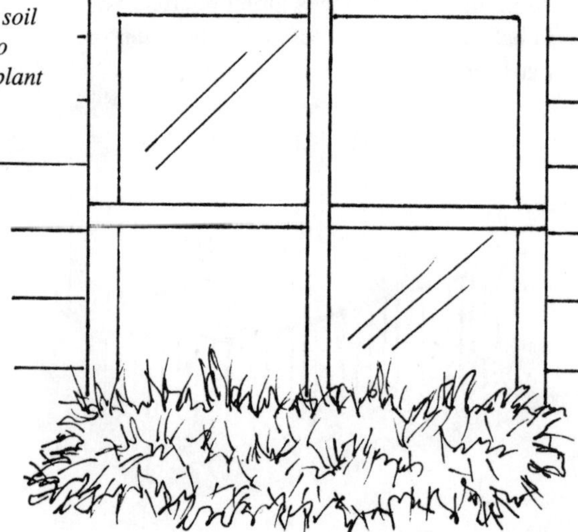

A short length of a thorny hedge under a window will thwart a burglar.

Preparing Soil for a Hedge

Hedges grow at a disadvantage because their roots overlap laterally, resulting in intense competition for available nutrients and water. Therefore, it pays to invest time and funds into soil preparation.

If the soil over your entire property was not prepared as outlined in Chapter 4, strip the soil of existing vegetation for the distance of the hedge. Make a trench three feet wide and six inches deep. Use a rotary tiller to loosen the soil another eight inches deep, mixing compost or sphagnum peatmoss plus one pound per one hundred square feet of triple superphosphate as you till. It is important that the soil be consistently good throughout the planting area. If the soil varies, so will the plant growth, with leaf color and rate of growth differing to produce an uneven effect.

Planting a Hedge

Deciduous hedge plants are usually set in place bare root in very early spring. The additional cost of container-grown plants is unnecessary. Evergreen hedge plants are usually purchased as tube-grown seedlings, which are inexpensive and fast-growing. Evergreen hedges also are best set out in early spring -late March or early April.

Spacing

6-12 inches for miniature species
12-18 inches for low-growing species
18 inches to 3 feet for larger species

Double-file Spacing

Hedges of tall species are often planted in a staggered row. The double-file hedge will be wider and is seldom clipped.

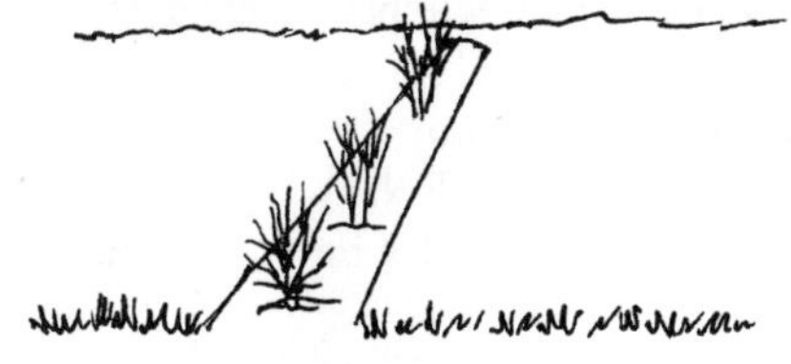

Planting a single-file hedge.

Planting a double-file hedge.

To mark an area for planting, measure off the distance between plants and make a nick in the soil with your shovel. Do not space plants by measuring as you go, because some plants are wider than others, and the result will be uneven spacing. Dig the holes with uniformity of size in mind. They should measure the same, edge to edge.

Deciduous plants are set slightly lower than they grew in the nursery, leaving a depression to hold water. Evergreens are planted at the same depth they grew previously. Spread the roots of deciduous hedge plants widely and pull pulverized soil around them until the trench is half full, then water well to settle before filling the trench and watering once more. With tube-grown evergreens, dig individual holes at each interval; then peel away the tar paper tube as you slip the plant into the hole, covering immediately. Air reaching roots of evergreens will damage them irretrievably.

Pruning at Planting Time

Hedge plants are cut back sharply at planting time to force new growth low on the stems so as to give quick, dense growth. For example, barberries are cut back by two-thirds; privets should be cut back by three-quarters. It may seem like the stubs that are left will never take hold, but they will branch quickly and evenly as the season advances. Pruning the evergreen hedge plant at planting time is only a matter of clipping back the leader if this is to be a trimmed hedge. No pruning is required for the unclipped evergreen hedge.

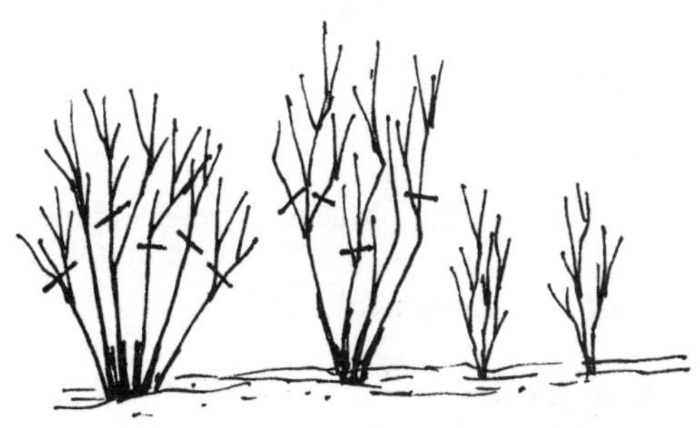

Pruning the deciduous hedge at planting time.

At about midsummer, give your hedge its first trimming if this is to be a clipped hedge. Stretch a line (preferably a colored cord) down the center of the hedge, and two more - one at each side. Shear the sides to meet in the center, pyramid fashion. This is to permit the lower portion of the hedge to fill out, for the sun must reach it. In the second season, give it a flat top, but continue to prune frequently and lightly for two years. After that, the hedge will need trimming in early June and probably again in September, but a clip here and there of a wayward shoot will keep it neat. Never use power hedge-clipping tools until the hedge is mature - about five years.

Plants for Hedges

Legend

D - useful for hot, dry conditions.
H - suitable for altitudes of 7-9,000 feet.
S - will withstand shade.
W - will withstand poorly drained conditions.

Note
When more than one listing of the same genus occurs, the second and all others following are abbreviated with the first letter of the genus.

TALL, 12-30 FEET

■ *Acer campestre*,
HEDGE MAPLE. Makes an impenetrable hedge 12-15 feet high. Good yellow fall color. Not drought tolerant.

■ *A. ginnala*,
GINNALA MAPLE. 15-25 feet high. Good red fall color.

■ *A. negundo*,
BOXELDER. DH. 20-30 feet high. Grows where nothing else will. Subject to many insects. Loved by warblers because of the insect food supply.

■ *A. tatarica*,
TARTARIAN MAPLE. 15-20 feet high. Stronger than *A. ginnala*. Good red fall color.

■ *Caragana arborescens*,
SIBERIAN PEA SHRUB. DH. 15-30 feet high. Yellow flowers in spring. Coarse.

■ *Cornus mas*,
CORNELIAN CHERRY. 12-15 feet high. A feast for the eyes in early March when covered with yellow blooms. Easy to maintain as a full, unclipped hedge.

■ *Crataegus laevigata*,
ENGLISH HAWTHORN. W. Thorny barrier, good red fruits for birds. Subject to fireblight.

■ *Elaeagnus angustifolia*,
RUSSIAN OLIVE. DH. 20-30 feet high. Gray foliage, fragrant blooms, fruits loved by birds. Thorny, difficult to maintain as a clipped hedge.

■ *E. umbellata*,
AUTUMN OLIVE. 15-20 feet high. Male and female required for attractive red fruits loved by birds. Gray foliage.

■ *Juniperus scopulorum*,
ROCKY MOUNTAIN JUNIPER. DH. 12-25 feet high. Evergreen native available in named cultivars. Does not need shearing. Will grow in natural pyramidal form.

■ *Malus pumila*,
CENTURION. Crabapple. 20x8 feet high. Branches close to ground with columnar habit; red flowers; persistent red fruits. Good nesting site for birds. Fireblight resistent

■ *Moras alba*,
WHITE MULBERRY. DH. 20-30 feet high. Good yellow fall color. Fruits loved by birds, useful in pies, jellies, and wine.

■ *Quercus imbricaria*,
SHINGLE OAK. 15-20 feet. If conditions are not too hot or dry, this should be used in place of Russian Olive. Good color, dense, pest-free.

■ *Picea pungens*,
COLORADO SPRUCE. H. 20-30 feet high. Evergreen. Extremely hardy, and somewhat drought tolerant. Shallow-rooted, but impenetrable as a very tall hedge. Plant eight feet apart.

■ *Rhamnus cathartica*,
COMMON BUCKTHORN. 15-20 feet high. Thorny; seeds of fruits are cathartic. Pest-free.

■ *R. frangula*,
TALLHEDGE BUCKTHORN. 12-20 feet high. Thornless, chlorotic in highly alkaline soils. Good glossy foliage.

■ *Sambucus canadensis 'Aurea'*.
GOLDEN ELDER. 12-15 feet high. Popular yellow-green leafed large shrub with white flowers followed by blue black fruits good for pies, jams, jellies, and wine. Often wilts suddenly in midsummer when roots cannot pump water fast enough to replace water. Not for the dry landscape.

■ *Syringa meyeri*,
LATE LILAC. 12-15 feet high. Rounded natural form that never needs shearing. Blooms fragrant, held high at maturity. No suckering.

■ *S. persica*,
PERSIAN LILAC. 12-15 feet high. Good dark lavender blooms, feathery. Very little suckering.

■ *Syringa vulgaris*,
COMMON LILAC. 12-15 feet high. Good substance of bloom available in many cultivars that are often called "French." Suckers freely.

■ *Ulmus pumila*,
SIBERIAN ELM. DH. 12-30 feet high. Grows where nothing else will. Weak wood, subject to many pests. Thousands killed by early, deep freeze in October, 1991.

■ *Viburnum prunifolium*,
BLACKHAW VIBURNUM. 12-15x8 feet high. Good leathery green foliage, red in fall. White blooms followed by black fruits loved by birds.

■ *V. trilobum*,
CRANBERRY BUSH VIBURNUM. 12-15 feet high and nearly as wide. Tri-lobed foliage, red berries seldom eaten by birds, thus hang on decoratively all winter. Red fall foliage. Dormant oil spray in early spring before foliage will eliminate threat of aphids.

MEDIUM, 4-12 FEET

■ *Berberis thunbergi*,
JAPANESE BARBERRY. 4-6 feet high. Thorny, green foliage. Good orange fall color.

■ *B. thunbergi atropurpurea*,
RED-LEAVED BARBERRY. 4-6 feet high. Red foliage all season; orange in fall. Thorny.

■ *Cercocarpos montanus*,
MOUNTAIN MAHOGANY. DH. 6-12 feet high. Native of dry, rocky soil in the foothills. Plumed seeds attractive in autumn.

■ *Chaenomeles japonica*,
FLOWERING QUINCE. 4-6 feet high. Rose-red flowers very early spring; good green with red tipped foliage in summer. Orange fall color.

■ *Cornus sericea 'Isanti'*,
COMPACT REDTWIG DOGWOOD. S. 4-8 feet high. Compact red stems in winter, green in summer. Good green foliage, white flower clusters, white berries.

■ *Cotoneaster integerrimus*,
EUROPEAN, COTONEASTER, 4-6 feet high. Shiny, disease and insect-free foliage. Nodding clusters of pink flowers in spring, red berries in fall.

■ *Elaeagnus commutata*,
SILVERBERRY. 3-6 feet high. Shiny silver foliage, no thorns. Good accent against dark background or to cool hot colors nearby.

■ *Euonymus alata 'Compacta'*,
COMPACT BURNING BUSH. S, 4-6 feet high. Early show-stopping red fall color, corky twigs, small red berries held throughout winter. White flowers.

■ *E. alata 'Monstrosa'*,
CORKY BURNING BUSH. S 8-12 feet high. Twigs have pronounced corky ridges, attractive in winter. Same flowers, berries, and fall color as above.

■ *Juniperus Sabina 'Tamariscifolia'*,
TAMY JUNIPER. 4-6 feet high. An easily managed evergreen hedge. Good drought tolerance.

■ *Ligustrum amurense*,
PRIVET. 4-8 feet high. Shears well. Not reliably hardy. Often one or two plants within a hedge will die during a hard winter.

■ *L. vulgare 'Lodense'*,
'LODENSE PRIVET'. 4-8 feet high. Slightly more hardy.

■ *Lonicera tatarica*,
TARTARIAN HONEYSUCKLE. 4-8 feet high. Subject to 'honeysuckle aphid', though infestation throughout the region is waning. Deep rose blooms, followed by red berries. First to leaf out in spring.

■ *Mahonia aquifolium*,
OREGON HOLLYGRAPE. S. 4-8 feet high. A broadleaf evergreen. Sunscalds in winter sun. Shiny foliage; yellow flowers followed by blue fruits.

■ *Philadelphus coronarius*,
MOCKORANGE. 8-12 FEET. Many named varieties (see Chapter 12, Shrubs). Early foliage followed by fragrant white flowers.

■ *Rhus trilobata*,
THREE-LEAF SUMAC. DH. 6-12 feet high. Native of dry rocky hillsides. Attractive rounded shape if left unclipped. Tough, leathery lobed foliage, inconspicuous flowers followed by red fruits loved by birds.

■ *Rubus deliciosus,*
BOULDER RASPBERRY. 4-6 feet high. Rounded form, native of rocky slopes, brown, shreddy bark; raspberry-like, insipid red fruit loved by birds, good orange fall color.

■ *Salix atropurpurea nana,*
DWARF ARCTIC BLUE WILLOW. 5-6 feet high, five feet in width. Rounded form of thin, dark branches; tiny velvety catkins in spring; green leaves with silvery reverse. Even a slight breeze keeps it always in motion. Subject to oystershell scale.

■ *Spirea Vanhouttei,*
BRIDALWREATH SPIREA. 5 feet high, five feet in width. The traditional unclipped hedge; a cascade of white flower clusters for two weeks in spring; delicate small leaves; good orange fall color.

LOW, 1-4 FEET

■ *Buxus microphylla,*
DWARF BOXWOOD. 1-2 feet high. Broadleaf evergreen; shiny green foliage traditionally clipped. Sunscalds in winter, but easily covered with burlap or baskets.

■ *Berberis thunbergi nana,*
DWARF BARBERRY. 3-4 feet high. Small tough foliage, thorny. yellow inconspicuous flowers followed by small red berries. Red-leafed forms available. All forms of this plant repugnant to dogs, therefore, a good plant for in front of a plant that is often damaged by dogs, such as *Arborvitae.*

■ *Caragana pygmaea,*
PYGMY PEA SHRUB. DH. 3-4 feet high. Good foliage, yellow pea flowers. Not attractive in winter.

■ *Potentilla fruticosa,*
BUSH CINQUEFOIL. 3-4 feet high. Good native for windy areas. Yellow flowers all summer. Not attractive in winter. Entire planting should be cut to ground every three years. Many named varieties available.

■ Ribes alpinum,
ALPINE CURRANT. 3-4 feet high. Rounded form, small-scale foliage; very little fall color; fruits are intermittent. Not attractive in winter.

■ *Symphoricarpos albus,*
SNOWBERRY. 3-4 feet high. Rounded, arching sprays of delicate foliage, inconspicuous flowers followed by big white berries in early fall.

■ *S. orbiculatus,*
CORALBERRY. 3-4 feet high. Rounded arching spray of delicate foliage, inconspicuous flowers followed by red berries seldom eaten by birds.

CHAPTER 14

The Perennials - Island or Border

The perennial border or the newer island have enjoyed extravagant popularity of late. You aren't "anybody" unless you have a perennial border and an island or two. There is more psychological motive behind this need than to keep up with the neighbors or to increase the value of the property. It is a satisfying goal to find the right plant for the right place; to fit the plants together in a perfect pattern of bloom succession; to blend the colors of bloom and textures of foliage - height and width notwithstanding. An impossible dream? Isn't the perfect golf swing, the perfectly played hand of bridge, the perfect performance of any endeavor the equivalent?

In gardening, the acquisition of a perennial garden is a demonstration of the ongoing acumen of a gardener - conquering one more aspect of the fascinating realm of horticulture.

Site

There are shady borders and sunny borders, and a mix of the two is often a charming likelihood when you have mature trees and shrubs in the area. The island planting can be viewed from both sides. A tree or shrub is often a reason for the island planting and acts as an anchor.

A site with a built-in background, such as a picket or rail fence will give the perennials an immediate look of belonging. Beware of the solid board fence or a high masonry wall to back them up. Lack of air circulation and radiated heat will always be their nemesis. Root competition from a background of flowering or evergreen shrubs is also a difficult situation for perennials, but if the background shrubs are planted in moderation, the perennials will thrive.

The sun in its arc in the sky at different months during the growing season will influence which way your composite blooms will face. For example, if your border is on the western perimeter of your property with trees or your home blocking morning sun, the composite (daisy-type) blooms of your perennial border will face your neighbors on the west, and you will see only the calyx and back side of the petals of the blooms. A perennial border is still a possibility in this area, but you will choose plants with spike flowers, such as delphinium or those with clusters of bloom, such as summer phlox.

The length and depth to make a perennial garden is bewildering for a neophyte. You aren't inclined to let this thing take over your life, yet you are eager and curious to learn to grow the many beauties you've seen at the botanic garden.

An old saying - "The depth of a perennial border should be the length of your arm plus your hoe-handle" - is still a good admonition. Make no mistake, a perennial border or island is not a low-maintenance item. If you decide to make it deeper, install stepping stones so that you won't crush seedlings as you are weeding. The length of the border is your choice. Don't be deterred by a small space. There are myriads of choices of perennials for every garden.

The depth of a border should be the length of your arm plus your hoe handle.

The island planting can be viewed from both sides. A tree or shrub often acts as an anchor.

Soil Preparation

If you have prepared the soil over all of your property according to the directions in Chapter 4, no preparation is necessary. If you are starting with a subsoil, heavy clay, or a sandy silt, you would be wise to remove one third of the existing soil to be used in compost-making or as "fill" in another area. Replace the volume you removed with compost, sphagnum peatmoss or weathered manure. Using sand in the mixture or placing assorted rocks in bottom of the excavation is an obsolete practice that creates concrete if sand is used, or an artifical water table if rocks are used.

Design

It is a common practice to plant "anchor" shrubs at each end of a perennial border as well as a group of shrubs near the center of a very long border to give added height and winter interest. Small flowering trees of graceful form will also add appeal.

Long ago there were rigid rules for the perennial border. The tall spike-flowered plants stood in the rear, with medium-sized, round-flowered plants in the center. Creepers, always the same species, lined the edge of the foreground. Thankfully, this era has passed, and we group plants for blocks of color, uncaring for their height and shape so long as they don't block the view of another in the rear.

Companionable colors will be the most difficult to achieve, with contrasting textures of foliage a close second. If it all eludes you, try studying a color wheel in an art book from the library. The colors opposite one another are contrasting; those shading into each other are companions. Read the work of Gertrude Jekyll, a famous designer of perennial borders in the late nineteenth and early twentieth century. She worked out companion colors of flowering plants for each week of the growing season, beginning at one end with the cool colors, blue, lavender, and purple and ending with the hot oranges and reds, using, always, a white, silver, or gray plant as a "sanitizer" between warring colors. This may not seem a monumental task to the uninitiated gardener, but coordination of the bloom times for each plant is not easy.

Repetition of plants or plant forms is important in the border, lest it resemble a "one of everything" garden. Draw the viewer's eye forward by the repetition of the same plant at a reliable interval. Draw up a plan that will assure some bloom every week of the growing season, then repeat the plan further on down the border. A good interval length is twelve feet.

Bulbs Under

The addition of spring, summer, or fall-flowering bulbs among perennials is a sensible way to lengthen the season and increase the display possibilities. The tough part is to remember where they are. Nothing will dismay you more than to slice through a fat tulip bulb when digging a hole to plant a perennial. The plastic lid from a coffee can, pierced with a u-shaped piece of wire will keep you aware of the bulbs' parking spot and signal "Bulbs Under" Write the name of the bulb on the plastic lid.

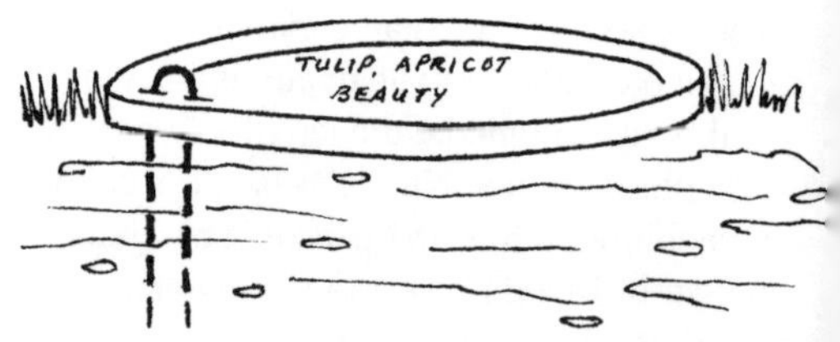

Use a plastic coffee can lid to mark the spot where bulbs are planted in the perennial border. A u-shaped wire will hold it in place.

Adding Annuals

For the purist, a perennial garden does not contain any annuals; but for the artist, annuals are the binding of the border. The biggest show will be in June, but annuals are too small at that time to make much of a show. However, in July, when there are only a few perennials blooming, annuals come into their full display, lasting through frost. Thus, with the second fall-blooming of many perennials plus the annuals, the early autumn perennial border is a glorious sight. If your objective is a bright display throughout the entire growing season, by all means add bedding-plant annuals as soon as the last frost date is past. To make their addition simple, add those that seed themselves at random year after year.

Annuals That Seed Themselves

Botanic Name	Common Name	Size	Color
Anchusa capensis	Forget-Me-Not	med	blue
Antirrhinum majus	Snapdragon	med	all
Centaurea cyanus	Bachelor Button	med	many
Cleome spinosa	Spiderflower	tall	pink/white
Delphinium ajacis	Larkspur	tall	blue
Dianthus chinensis	Heddewigii China Pink	low	pink
Eschscholzia californica	Calif. Poppy	low	orange
Helianthus annuus	Sunflower	tall	yellow
Ibiris coronaria	Candytuft	low	white
Linum grandiflorum	Flax	med	blue
Lunaria annua	Honesty	med	white
Mirabilis jalapa	Four O'Clock	tall	many
Moluccella laevis	Bells of Ireland	tall	green
Nemophila menziesii	Baby Blue Eyes	low	blue
Nigella damascena	Love-in-a-Mist	med	blue
Papaver rhoeas	Shirley Poppy	med	many
Petúnia x hybrida	Petunia	low	many
Phlox drummondii	Phlox	low	many
Tagetes patula	French marigold	low	yellow/orange

Selection of Plants

You will select many well-known plants for your border, but don't always be satisfied with the tried-and-true. Pioneering is in the Mountain Westerners blood. You will find many new and unusual perennials suited only to the Mountain West. Perennial nurseries have sprouted everywhere as popularity increased. With tiresome certainty they offer the same plants. Let your favorite nursery know the plants you are seeking very early so that they have time to order them. Using mail-order nurseries is acceptable also, but you run the risk of plants being damaged during shipment. If you buy by mail, specify the date they must be delivered with a statement that will wake up the order-taker, such as "Shipment will not be accepted after (date)_____". For some reason, many mail-order nurseries equate the climate of the Mountain West with the Arctic or Sub-Arctic, and tend to ship plants to you in the heat of summer instead of early spring.

Planting

If only small sizes are offered, buy three of each and plant them in a triangle about four inches apart. They will grow together before season's end to give a good showing next year. Some species will take off into good growth immediately, but an old garden saying, "the first year it sleeps, the second year it creeps, and the third year it leaps" is still worthy of note. Leave enough room between plants for the "leaping" phase.

Transplanting

Perennials that resent disturbance will be noted in the lists, but most are amenable to being transplanted at any time. Generally, however, plants that bloom in spring will adjust to new surroundings and be ready to bloom if they are transplanted the previous fall. Plants that bloom in fall are best transplanted just as they emerge in spring. Divide clumps every three years to keep them young and healthy. Discard the center of the clump, dividing only the outer, younger portion. Many perennials are rejuvenated when transplanted and will bloom with renewed vigor and strength.

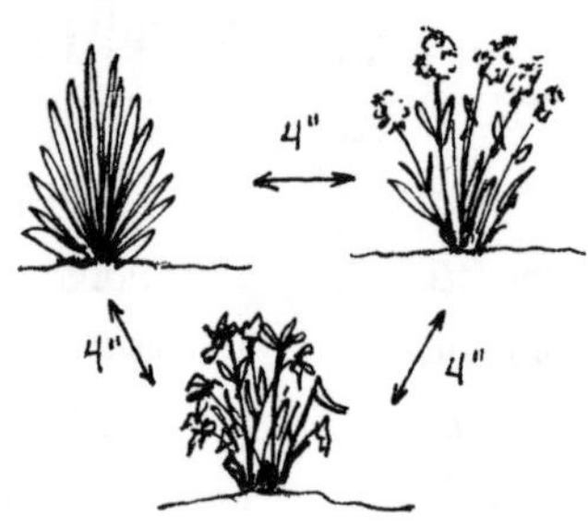

Plant small-sized plants in a triangle for a good showing next year.

Water

A drip system is an ideal way to water the perennial border, for it keeps foliage dry - a good precaution against disease - and it allows for much longer lasting blooms when they are not blasted with strong streams of water from a sprinkling system.

Fertilization

As the plants are emerging in spring, scatter a vegetable/flower fertilizer over the entire border, watering it in well. As the season progresses, use soluble granular fertilizer at two-week intervals. At mid-summer, scatter your half-finished compost between and around plants, for it will finish decomposing while acting at the same time as a mulch to cool the soil, conserve water, and prevent weeds.

Weeds

Weeding will still be a hand or sharp hoe operation, but if the soil is mulched and moist, a weekly half-hour session will suffice. Planting through crosses cut in a cloth weed-barrier will be necessary if you are dealing with very weedy ground. Mulch the weed-barrier to keep it from being punctured or blown away.

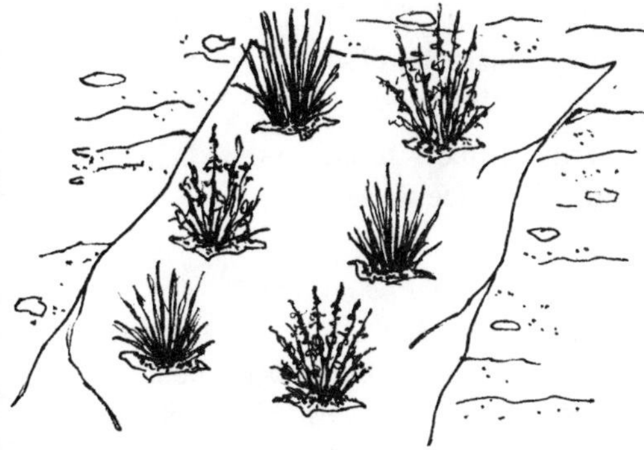

If the site is extremely weedy, lay down a fabric weed barrier and drip irrigation system. Plant through crosses cut in the fabric.

Deadheading

Gardeners sally forth each day, light-weight shears and small bucket in hand, to cut off the daily harvest of spent flowers, called "deadheads" or sometimes "sleepy heads". This is an excuse to view the fruit of your labors and to examine each plant closely, as well as to keep plants blooming. Cut each spent flower back to the nearest node so that it will re-grow and produce another flower. The objective in the life of every plant is to re-create itself (make seed); and it's your objective to prevent it and keep the plant blooming. Be a good garden-keeper - don't stuff the deadheads under a bush for the same reason that you didn't shove dust under your mother's carpet! (SHE will know it's there!) Empty your bucket into the compost or into the trash if there are any diseased or distorted leaves that would contaminate the compost.

■ *Be a good garden-keeper - don't stuff the deadheads under a bush.*

Staking

Nothing will dismay you more than floppy perennials. There is an easy solution, but you have to remember to do it as leaves are emerging in spring. Lay a circle or rectangle of poultry wire over the top of the leafy stems, and they will grow through the interstices of the wire. As they grow, pull up gently on the wire to pull the stems together. They will sway but not break in the wind. For very heavy and tall stems, such as delphinium, lay a second circle when they reach four feet in height. In windy areas, drive a stake at the back of the plant out of view; thread the wire circlet over the stake to hold the foliage even more steady and upright.

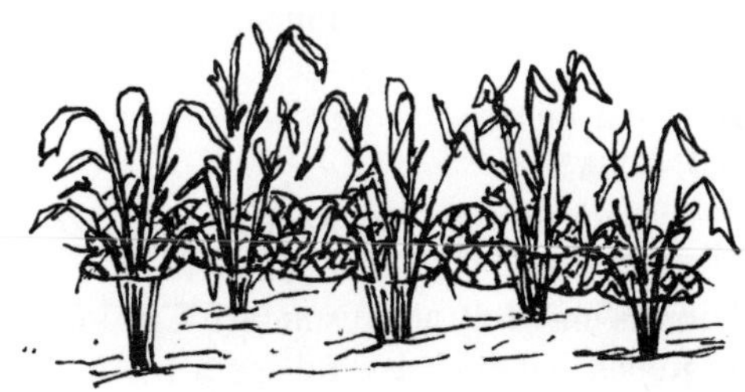

Staking with circles of chicken wire will keep your plants upright without unsightly rope and string contraptions.

Enjoy your perennials, but don't be a slave to them. Most of them will survive with very little care, provided the soil preparation was thorough. Be generous in dividing them with friends and new gardeners.

(listings show height x spread)

■ *Achillea filipendulina*,
YARROW. Ferny foliage; corymbs of bloom useful as cut flowers, fresh or dried.
CULTIVARS:
'Coronation Gold' - 3'x 2'; 3-inch corymbs of bright gold mid-summer and fall.

'Gold Plate' - midsummer 6" corymbs; good companion in front of *Miscanthus sinensis* 'Varigatus'.

■ *A. millefolium*,
COMMON YARROW. Ferny foliage, weedy, but many fine cultivars available.
CULTIVARS:
'Cerise Queen' - bright rose-pink.

'Debutante' - a series of all colors except blue.

'Fire King' - crimson

'Lilac Queen' - lavender

'Salmon Beauty' - coral salmon

■ *A. x taygetea*,
CULTIVAR:
'Moonshine'- ferny gray foliage, pale yellow 4" corymbs in early summer. Becomes unsightly at midsummer. Cut it to the ground and fresh new foliage will appear. Combine with *Salvia x superba* and English lavender.

■ *A. ptarmica*,
SNEEZEWEED. Only the double form of this invasive, floppy species should be planted.
CULTIVAR:
'The Pearl' double, white, drys well; invasive but easy to pull.

■ *Aconitum napellus*,
MONKSHOOD. 4'x 1.5'. For part shade; June flowering; each flower in this spike resembles a helmet or hood. Mulch in spring; resents disturbance; seeds around*. All parts poisonous.
CULTIVARS:
'Bicolor' - white flowers edged with blue in midsummer.

'Bressingham Spire' - long-blooming, violet blue, compact.

'Newry's Blue' - strong, upright habit; early, dark blue flowers.

■ *Aegopodium Podagraria*,
BISHOP'S WEED. 2'x 2'. A variegated foliage that cools the dry shade, poor soil locale where it will grow. Bloom should be prevented. Use this plant only as a last resort. It is very invasive.

■ *Alcea rosea*,
HOLLYHOCK. 5-10' x 3'. An old-fashioned background plant bearing tall stalks of familiar cup-shaped flowers in early summer.
CULTIVAR:
'Powder Puff' - pouf of petals makes the bloom resemble a tuberous begonia bloom. Available in all colors except blue.

■ *Alchemilla mollis*,
LADY'S MANTLE. 2'x3'. Mounds of rounded foliage; foam of chartreuse flowers in May. Dries well. Prefers afternoon shade.

* *See Glossary*

■ *Anaphalis margaritacea*,
PEARLY EVERLASTING. 3'x3'. Native with gray foliage; clusters of white flowers in August. Dries well.

■ *A. triplinervis*,
slow, larger flowers.

■ Anchusa officinalis,
BUGLOSS, ALKANET. 2'x 4'. A vigorous plant with brilliant blue flower clusters in midsummer. Seeds around*.
CULTIVAR:
'Blue Angel' - a dwarf variety that substitutes for the alpine forget-me-not in the rock garden.

■ *Anemone spp*,
LILY-OF-THE-FIELD. Many species of showy flowers with yellow stamens. Spreads by underground stolons. All like a rich moist soil.

■ *A. huphensis*,
JAPANESE ANEMONE. 1'x 3'. Basal foliage gives rise to tall branching stems of delicate pink or white single flowers in early September.

■ *A. nemerosa*,
EUROPEAN WOOD ANEMONE.
6" x 6". Delicate lacinated foliage appears in spring; nodding single white, blue or pink flowers. Prefers dappled shade.

■ *A. pulsatilla*,
PASQUE FLOWER. 6" x 12". A native that blooms in very early spring with fuzzy-stemmed, nodding blue, purple, or white flowers.

■ *A. robustissima vitifolia*,
GRAPE-LEAF ANEMONE. 3' x 3'. Leaves shaped like those of grape. Single, pink flowers rise above foliage in early September. Difficult to establish, but spreads quickly when it finally takes hold.

■ *Anthemis tinctoria*,
GOLDEN MARGUERITE. 2' x 2'. Yellow daisies that are constant throughout the summer. Will grow in hot dry soils.

■ *Aquilegia sp.*,
COLUMBINE. 2'x3'. A familiar wildflower of the Mountain West; ferny compound leaves; flowers with long spurs. Part shade preferred. Many species and cultivars available. Some are:

■ *A.x hybrida*,
BIEDERMEIER, a strain developed in Holland with short spurs, bicolors in every combination. Seeds around*.

■ *A. caerulea*,
Colorado's state flower of blue and white.
CULTIVARS:
'McKanna's Giant' - red, pink, blue, and white

'Nora Barlow' - double, red, white, and pink.

A. buergeriana, pale yellow.

A. canadensis, pink.

■ *Arabis caucasica*,
ROCKCRESS. 2"x2'. Mats of hairy, ever-gray leaves with sprays of pink or white flowers in spring. Shear after flowering. Makes a good edging for the perennial border. Withstands suns or shade.

* *See Glossary*

■ *Artemisia sp.*,
SOUTHERNWOOD, SAGE. 2'x2'. A sanitizer for warring colors; feathery, silver foliage. Flowers insignificant in all species, and should be prevented.

■ *A. absinthum,*
CULTIVARS:
'Lambrook Silver' - tall, upright, well-branched.

'Powis Castle' - named for a Welsh castle; Bushy mound of feathery silver foliage. Seldom flowers.

■ *A. ludoviciana,*
a taller species.
CULTIVARS:
'Silver King' - tall, stiff foliage, almost pure white.

'Silver Queen' - long silver, white leaves.

■ *A. schmidtiana*
CULTIVAR:
'Silver Mound' - a dwarf mound of feathery, silver foliage for the foreground or as an accent.

■ *Aruncus dioicus,*
GOATSBEARD. 3'x6'. A tall background plant for part shade and moist spot. Branching stems bear panicles of long-lasting creamy flowers. Male and female plants - male is the showier.

■ *Asclepias tuberosa,*
BUTTERFLY WEED. 2'x2'. A native that insists upon infrequent watering and clay soil. It is late to emerge in spring. Orange flowers attractive to butterflies.

■ *Aster x frickartii,*
FALL ASTER. 3'x2'. The flowers that signal the beginning of autumn. Lavender blue daisies on neat mounds. Pinch back when plants reach eight inches to promote branching.
CULTIVAR:
'Wonder of Staffa' - large yellow disks, lavender blue rays; good as a cut flower.

■ *Aster nova-angliae,*
MMICHAELMAS DAISY. 4'x2'. The roadside daisy of New England. Drought-resistant; difficult to stake. It is the backbone of the border in September.
CULTIVARS:
'Alma Potschke' - With a name like this, it has to be beautiful, and it is. Brilliant rose clusters so numerous as to conceal foliage.

'Harrington's Pink' - delicate pink cascades of bloom.

'September Ruby' - bright purple; earlier than two above.

'Treasurer' - deep lilac.

■ *A. nova-belgi,*
NEW YORK ASTER. Cultivars vary in size. Fertilize sparingly to keep them hard-stemmed and less floppy.
CULTIVARS:
'Alert' - 10"-15"; deep crimson.

'Marie Ballard' - 4'x2'; double powder blue.

'Sailor Boy' - 3'x2'; navy blue

'Winston Churchill' - 1'x1'; early red.

■ *Astilbe x arendsii,*
MEADOWSWEET. 3'x2'. Lacinated basal foliage; plumy panicles in early summer of white, peach, pink, and rose-red. Prefers rich acid soil; part shade.

■ *Aurinia saxatilis,*
BASKET OF GOLD. 1'x3'. Gray persistent foliage; dense panicles of brilliant yellow flowers in early spring. Cut back immediately after flowering.

■ *Baptisia australis,*
FALSE INDIGO. 4'x3'. Spires of deep blue pea-like flowers in early summer. Prefers dappled shade and rich, moist, acid soil. Oak-leaf compost dressing every fall; then cover with evergreen boughs.

■ *Bergenia cordifolia,*
HEART-LEAVED BERGENIA. 2'x2'. Thick, cabbagelike evergreen leaves; deep pink flower clusters on tall stems above foliage in early spring. Tolerates shade; foliage burns in full sun.

■ *Boltonia asteroides,*
BOLTONIA. 4'x2'. Late summer white ray flowers with prominent yellow disks on strong, upright foliage that does not need staking.
CULTIVAR:
'Snowbank' - flowers are more brilliant white than species.

■ *Brunnera macrophylla,*
SIBERIAN BUGLOSS. 2'x2'. Early spring heart-shaped leaves and blue blooms similar to forget-me-nots. Will withstand dry shade if soil is rich with organic matter and some clay.
CULTIVAR:
'Hadspen Cream' - variegated foliage will add light to a shade planting.

■ *Campanula spp.*
BELLFLOWER. Almost as many species and varieties available as roses. Predominently blue, pink, white, and rose-red flowers in summer.

■ *C. carpatica,*
CARPATHIAN BELLFLOWER. 8"x18". One of the most charming of bluebells.
CULTIVAR:
'Blue Clips' - medium blue flowers smother the plant in June. If cut back, it will flower again in September.

'White Clips' - white flowered form of above.

■ *C. glomerata,*
CLUSTERED BELLFLOWER. 1'x3'. Clasping clusters of flowers along the stem. Very invasive in rich soil. Keep it starving to keep it checked. White form available.

■ *C. medium,*
CANTERBURY BELLS, 3'x2'. The biennial cup-and-saucer of every cottage garden in June. Pink, blue, white.

■ *C. persicifolia,*
PEACH-LEAVED BELLFLOWER. 3'x2'. Tall stems bear loose racemes of bells in June. Prefers part shade. A must for an English garden.
CULTIVARS:
'Telham Beauty' - large light blue flowers.

'White Pearl' - double white flowers.

■ *C. rapunculoides,*
CANCER OF THE GARDEN, CREEPING BELLFLOWER. 3'x2'. The most vicious of weeds, creeping by underground rootstocks. Deceiving pretty blue bells line the stems. Cloth weed barrier topped with 4" of gravel may smother it.

■ *C. rotundifolia,*
BLUEBELL OF SCOTLAND. 1'x2'. This native of the montane zone of the Mountain West is the same bonny bluebell beloved by Scottish Highlanders for centuries. It prefers

part shade, rich, moist soil, but can withstand the opposite. A tiny dwarf is available for the rock garden.

■ *Catananche caerulea*,
CUPID'S DART. 3'x2'. Blue ray flowers with black center disks; papery calyx. Blooms all summer. Drys well, but closes at night. Place in silica gel for drying.

■ *Centaurea macrocephela*,
YELLOW CORNFLOWER. 2'x2'. Large clumps of rough foliage give rise to bright lemon yellow thistles, good for cutting, in June. Somewhat invasive.

■ *C. montana*,
MOUNTAIN BLUET. 2'x2' Linear foliage; lacy blue flowers in June. Invasive.

■ *C. uniflora*,
ROCK GARDEN CORNFLOWER. 6"x5". Gray foliage, bright lavender lacinated flowers in May. Choice.

■ *Centranthus ruber*,
VALERIAN. 3'x3'. Rosy-red flower clusters all summer. Very large root can crack concrete. Seeds around*.

■ *Ceratostigma plumbaginoides*,
PLUMBAGO. 1'x1'. Deep, gentian-blue flowers appear from shiny green foliage in August and September. Foliage then turns brilliant red after frost. Late to appear in spring. Plant *Colchicum* and *Sternbergia* bulbs under it and they will bloom with it. Spreads slowly.

■ *Chrysanthemum spp.*,
CHRYSANTHEMUM. A large and diverse genus that boasts the most popular ornamental for perennial borders.

■ *C. coccineum*,
PAINTED DAISY. 2'x1'. Early summer brings on the multi-colored flowers in every shade except blue or yellow.

■ *C. frutescens*,
MARGUERITE. 3'x2'. White ray flowers with yellow disk bloom all summer if kept deadheaded. Not always hardy. Winter-over in cold frame.

■ *C. leucanthemum*,
OX-EYE DAISY. The wilding of open spaces throughout the Mountain West.

■ *C. x morifolium*,
GARDEN CHRYSANTHEMUM, CUSHION MUM. Widely cultivated in every garden for September/October flowers. Named varieties vary with each dealer. Divide every spring; fertilize generously to prevent midsummer bloom. Pinch every two weeks until July 1 to keep them bushy and low. Can be transplanted in full bloom, and are thus passed around neighborhoods.

■ *C. parthenium*,
FEVERFEW. 3'x3'. Highly invasive, lovely white daisy with dainty cut foliage that will succeed in any situation.

■ *C. x superbum*,
SHASTA DAISY. 3'x3'. Strong-stemmed white ray flowers with golden disk that appears in every garden.

CULTIVARS:

'Aglaya' - blooms without fail all summer.

'Alaska' - an old stand-by.

'Esther Read' - double white.

'Little Miss Muffet' - dwarf.

* *See Glossary*

■ *Cimicifuga racemosa*,
BUGBANE, BLACK SNAKEROOT. 6'x2'. Very tall spires of white flowers in mid-summer into fall. Part shade; moist rich soil.

■ *Clematis x hybrida*,
SHRUB CLEMATIS. 2'x2'. Attractive foliage of an upright form of a familiar vine. Flowers are urn-shaped with flared petals. Needs staking.

CULTIVAR:

'Betty Corning' - small bells are silver on outside; lavender blue inside. Blooms from June thru September; shade tolerant, but needs moisture.

■ *Coreopsis verticillata*,
TICKSEED. 2'x2'. Another yellow daisy few gardens would be without.

CULTIVARS:

'Moonbeam' - needled foliage topped by pale yellow ray flowers all summer if deadheaded.

'Zagreb' - darker, more golden version of the above.

■ *Corydalis lutea*,
YELLOW BLEEDINGHEART. 2'x2'. Fine foliage similar to columbine; yellow flowers with prominent lips all summer. Prefers part shade; moist, rich soil. Self sows.

■ *Delphinium grandiflorum*,
LARKSPUR. 6'x2'. And grand it is, for the Mountain West excels in growing this stately perennial with crowded stalks of blue, maroon, purple, white, lavender, and even yellow. Many strains available. Grow from chilled, fresh seed.

■ *Dianthus spp.*,
GARDEN PINK. A variable, interbred genus centuries old. Most are sweetly scented. Grassy leaves, flowers rising above.

■ *D. alwoodii*,
COTTAGE PINK. 1'x1'. Vigorous tufts of gray foliage.

CULTIVARS:

'Essex Witch' - deep rose.

'Her Majesty' - double white.

■ *D. barbatus*,
SWEET WILLIAM. 1'x2'. A biennial with showy flower heads in every color except blue or yellow.

■ *D. deltoides*,
MAIDEN PINK. 1'x2'. Loose, bright green foliage.

CULTIVARS:

'Albus' - white.

'Brilliant' - crimson.

■ *D. grantianopolitanus*,
CHEDDAR PINK. 1'x2'. Neat, dense mounds of blue-green foliage. Pink, white, or rose flowers.

CULTIVAR:

'Tiny Rubies' - deep ruby-wine, single flowers.

■ *D. knappii*,
YELLOW DIANTHUS. 1'x2'. From Yugoslavia, this is the only yellow-flowered "pink". Keep it on the dry side; full sun.

■ *Dicentra eximia*,
WILD BLEEDING HEART. 3'x3'. For morning sun or part shade, this lover of deep, moist soil bears drooping flowers of

pantaloon shape in rose and white. Sits out July, but will begin to bloom again in the fall.

■ *D. spectabilis*,
BLEEDING HEART. 2'x2'. Rosy-red flowers will continue all summer if deadheading is diligent.

■ *Dictamnus albus*,
GAS PLANT. 2'x2'. Strong vertical stems with pink or white flowers that emit a flamable gas on a hot summer night. Resents disturbance.

■ *Digitalis purpurea*,
COMMON FOXGLOVE. 4'x2'. Short-lived, poisonous perennials for part shade. Purple, pink, and white flowers.

■ *Doronicum cordatum*,
LEOPARD'S BANE. 1'x1'. A shy little plant with heart-shaped foliage with "pinked" edge. Yellow ray flowers in very early spring. Foliage often dies down in summer. Prefers part shade.

■ *Echinacea purpurea*,
PURPLE CONEFLOWER. 3'x2'. Coarse, hairy foliage with long-lasting pink daisies with erect orange disk.
CULTIVARS:
'Bright Star' - pink.
'White Lustre' - white.

■ *Echinops ritro*,
SMALL GLOBE THISTLE. 3'x2'. Thorny green foliage, gray on reverse, topped by blue globe-shaped flowers

■ *Epimedium*,
see Chapter 17 Rock Gardens.

■ *Erigeron x hybridus*,
FLEABANE. 3'x2'. Finely cut daisies in June. Subject to powdery mildew, but will produce new, clean foliage if cut to the ground.
CULTIVARS:
'Pink Jewel' - not pink, but lavender.

'Forster's Darling' - bright pink.

'Darkest of All' - deep violet.

■ *Eryngium coeruleum*,
SEA HOLLY. 3'x2'. Spiny-toothed foliage. Blue or white flower heads, each with a curious basal bract. Will withstand drought and heat.

■ *Erysimum allionii*,
WALLFLOWER. 2'x2'. Fragrant orange, peach, or yellow flower clusters in May and June. Blooms between May tulips and June perennials.

■ *Euphorbia polychroma*,
CUSHION SPURGE. 18"x2'. As mound of closely set leaves topped by chartreuse cymes. Red foliage in fall. Does not become invasive.

■ *Filipendula ulmaria*,
QUEEN-OF-THE-MEADOW. 6'x2'. Continuous swaying spires of white all summer. Moist, rich soil.

■ *Gaillardia x grandiflora*,
BLANKET FLOWER. A native that is welcome for its all-summer ray flowers of burgundy, orange, brown, and yellow.
CULTIVARS:
'Baby Cole' - dwarf red with yellow petal tips.

'Burgundy' - deep red.

'Yellow Queen' - yellow throughout.

■ *Gentiana spp.*,
GENTIAN. 2'x2'. Most species will be treated in Chapter 17 Rock Gardens.

■ *G. dahurica*,
DAHUR GENTIAN. 1'x1'. A low mound of linear leaves with blue and white cup flowers all summer. Good for the front of the border.

■ *Geranium spp.*
CRANESBILL. 3'x3'. Not to be confused with the common pot plant which is a *Pelargonium*. Palmate, shiny leaves with wispy stems of five-petalled flowers that form a projection like a crane's beak when in seed.

■ *G. endressii*,
Does especially well in a wet summer.
CULTIVAR:
'Wargrave Pink' - salmon-pink flowers.

■ *G. incanum.*
CULTIVAR:
'Johnson's Blue' - true blue flowers all summer.

■ *Geum borisii*,
AVENS. 6"X6". Low, hairy, round leaves with bright flowers in May.
CULTIVARS:
'Lady Stratheden'- semidouble, clear yellow.

'Mrs. Bradshaw' - bright orange.

'Red Wings' - bright red.

■ *Gypsophila paniculata*,
BABY'S BREATH. 4'x3'. A foam of white or pink flowers obscures the foliage. Easily dried. Best grown in place from seed because it resents transplanting.
CULTIVARS:
'Bristol Fairy' - double white.

'Perfecta' - larger flowers than above.

'Pink Fairy' - double, light pink flowers.

■ *Helenium autumnale*,
SNEEZEWEED. 4'x2'. Tall, stiff stems of ray flowers in late August and early September.
CULTIVARS:
'Bruno' - deep red-brown.

'Moorheim Beauty' - red with yellow petal tips.

■ *Helianthemum nummularium*,
SUNROSE. 1'x3'. Many cultivars of this creeper that covers itself with terminal flowers, each with a tuft of stamens.
CULTIVARS:
'Buttercup' - yellow.

'Fire Dragon' - gray foliage, orange red flowers.

'Raspberry Ripple' - pink and white striped flowers.

■ *Helianthus multiflorus*,
SUNFLOWER. 4'x2'. A selection of the Kansas flower. Very hardy, drought resistant, and invasive.

■ *Heliopsis helianthoides*,
FALSE SUNFLOWER. 4'x3'. A background plant in the late summer border. Double ray flowers in sunny colors.
CULTIVARS:
'Golden Greenheart' - green center disks.

'Incomparabilis' - rated highest.

'Summer Sun' - long-lasting, golden.

■ *Helleborus niger*,
CHRISTMAS ROSE. 2'x3'. A late-winter blooming plant in the Mountain West. Thrives on winter sun and summer shade. Needs deep, rich, moist soil. Resents disturbance.

■ *Hemerocallis x hybrida*,
DAYLILY. 3'x3'. A vast complex of plants highly hybridized. See them in bloom at a public display, such as a botanic garden, in order to choose cultivars for you own garden. The mainstay for the July garden, this plant is indispensible.

SOME POPULAR CULTIVARS:

'Chicago Thistle' - fragrant lavender.

'Fairy Tale Pink' - pink, repeat bloom.

'Hyperion' - an old standard yellow.

'Stella d'Oro' - dwarf yellow; repeat bloom

■ *Heuchera x brizoides*,
CORAL BELLS. 3'x1'. A durable, long-lived plant for the foreground of the border. Handsome evergreen foliage; spires of delicate flowers in shades of pink, red, white, and rose.

CULTIVARS:

'Bressingham Hybrids' - mixed colors.

'Chatterbox' - large pink flowers.

'Palace Purple' - brown/purple foliage; white flowers.

'Spitfire' - red flowers.

■ *Hibiscus moscheutos*,
ROSE MALLOW. 5'x3'. A background plant similar to old fashioned hollyhock. Rose, pink, white, and red available.

■ *Hosta x hybrida*,
PLANTAIN LILY. 2'x3'. The ideal shade garden plant grown for its large attractive leaves; withstanding root competition (even of shallow-rooted maples) and drought, but responding with extra vigor to a cool, rich, moist soil. Those with strong upright stems withstand fewer attacks by slugs.

SOME POPULAR CULTIVARS:

'Albo-picta' - young growth pale yellow; solid green by summer.

'Honey Bells' - green and white foliage; strong stems.

'Frances Williams' - puckered blue-green foliage.

■ *Hyssopus officinalis*,
HYSSOP. 4'x3'. An herb of aromatic blue-green foliage; spikes of white, blue, or rose. Self-sows everywhere. Easily grown from seed.

■ *Ibiris sempervirens*,
CANDYTUFT. 1'x1'. A white-flowered, low border plant also used in shady beds in combination with blue forget-me-nots and underplanted with red Emporer tulips for a red, white, and blue spring garden. *Armeria maritima* is also a good companion.

CULTIVARS:

'Little Gem' - compact white form, 6" in height.

'Purity' - large flowers 8" tall.

'Snowflake' - brilliant white on 8" stems.

■ *Iris x germanica*,
BEARDED IRIS. 3'x3'. Countless hybrids in every rainbow color. Three upward petals are the "standards"; three downward petals are the "falls". Easily hybridized. Choose plants in bloom for immediate digging and transplanting to your garden. Iris are very drought tolerant, often rotting

when grown in the border. To prevent rot, plant very shallowly, covering only the roots and leaving the rhizome exposed. The exposed rhizome will become bronzy in color, but will not rot from the amount of water needed for neighboring perennials in the border.

■ *I. orientalis*,
ORIENTAL IRIS. 4'x2'. Very old species passed down through generations in the Mountain West. Flowers are like giant butterflies resting on tall sturdy foliage. There is a pale lavender, but the white with yellow throat is most effective in the border. No pests or diseases.

■ *I. sibirica*,
SIBERIAN IRIS. 4'X2'. Tall, linear foliage is more attractive in the border than that of I.x germanica. Blooms are reflexed and heavily veined. Very free of pests and diseases. Divide in the fall.

CULTIVARS:

'Caesar's Brother' - velvety, deep purple.

'Flight of the Butterflies' - violet blue.

'Little White' - a dwarf white at 15"

■ *Kniphofia uvaria*,
RED HOT POKER. 3''x2'. A drought-tolerant plant with spikes of orange tinged with blue in June.

■ *Lavatera cachemiriana*,
MALLOW. 3'x2'. A long-blooming perennial that should be planted in groups of six or more, sowing seeds in place. Bright pink hollyhock-like flowers borne on spikes all summer.

■ *Liatris spicata*,
BLAZING STAR. 4'x2'. Spikes of purple or white with linear foliage. Grows from a fat tuber. Selections from these natives of plains and foothills are:

CULTIVARS:

'Kobold' - bright purple.

'Alba' - white.

■ *Ligularia stenocephala*,
GOLDEN GROUNDSEL. 5'x2'. A noble spire of golden flowers in July. Sharp-toothed foliage is decorative all season. Needs a moist, partly shaded site.

■ *Limonium latifolium*,
SEA LAVENDER. 2'x1'. An airy mass of tiny lavender flowers that dry well. Basal leaves are late to emerge in spring. Resents transplanting.

■ *Linum perrene*,
BLUE FLAX. 2'x2'. A short-lived perennial dear to the gardener for its sky-blue flowers opening new each morning. Seed heads dry for attractive winter bouquets. Prefers moderately dry soil.

■ *Lobelia cardinalis*,
CARDINAL FLOWER. 2'x2'. Tall stems support leafy racemes of deep red flowers. Prefers a rich, moist soil along a stream with some shade. Not easy.

■ *L. siphilitica*,
GREAT BLUE LOBELIA. 2'x2'. A blue version of the above, but much more amenable to arid soils of the Mountain West. Will withstand a half day of sun.

■ *Lunaria rediva*,
PERENNIAL HONESTY. 4'x2'. Rough, hairy stems with terminal racemes of fragrant white or lavender flowers. Each will form a flat seed pod, useful in dried arrangements.
CULTIVARS:
'Alba' - white flowered.

'Variegata' - foliage splashed with cream. Easy from seed.

■ *Lupinus x hybrida*,
LUPINE. 3'x3'. Invaluable spikes of closely set flowers of the pea family. Short-lived; easily replaced by planting fresh seed. Russell hybrids available from nursery-grown stock. Deep colors do not fade in western sun.

■ *Lychnis chalcedonica*,
CAMPION. 3'x3'. Clusters of scarlet flowers on long stems. Lower foliage often browns in midsummer. Plant behind orange daylilies and *Alchemilla mollis*.

■ *L. coronaria*,
CORN COCKLE. 2'x2'. Fuzzy gray foliage with deep maroon flowers over long blooming period. Does well in poor dry soil. Self-sows. White form availabe.

■ *L. viscaria*,
CATCHFLY.6"x6". Basal foliage, sticky stems with bright pink flower clusters. Plant with a gray foliage plant, such as *Stachys lanata*, for good contrast.

■ *Lysimachia punctata*,
YELLOW LOOSESTRIFE. 4'x2'. Stiff, erect stems form large colonies with spike flowers of yellow in midsummer. Tolerant of dry shade.

■ *Lythrum salicaria*,
LOOSESTRIFE. 4'x3'. Upright branching stems of spike flowers in shades of rose. A pest plant in the upper Midwest and East. Cultivars are still being grown in the Mountain West.
CULTIVARS:
'Dropmore Purple' - rich violet.

'Morden's Gleam' - carmine rose.

'Robert' - bright fuchsia.

■ *Macleaya cordata*,
PLUME POPPY. 8'x3'. Formerly *Bocconia*. Lobed leaves and feathery spikes of soft beige. Very invasive. Make sure you have room for this giant.

■ *Malva alcea*,
HOLLYHOCK MALLOW. 4'x2'. Tall, stiff, spikes of open cups in profusion in June. Drought tolerant.
CULTIVAR:
'Fastigiata' - superior to the species; deep rose flowers.

■ *Meconopsis spp*.,
ASIATIC POPPY. These much-prized poppies demand cool, moist summers and relatively mild winters - conditions seldom found in the Mountain West. Some species will try the patience and skill of the most ardent and expert gardener.

■ *M. betonicifolia*,
HIMALAYAN BLUE POPPY. 4'x2'. Andrew Pierce of Denver Botanic Garden grows this rare blue beauty in rich, moist soil in the east-facing foundation planting of his mountain home at Evergreen, Colorado.

■ *M. cambrica*,
WELSH POPPY. 2'x1'. The least demanding of the genus. Yellow flowers; neat clumps of bright green, hairy foliage not atractive to slugs.

■ *Mertensia lanceolata*,
FOOTHILLS BLUEBELL. 2'x2'. Pink flower buds open to nodding clusters of intensely blue bells. Dies back in a hot, dry summer.

□ *Mimulus guttatus*,
MONKEY FLOWER. 6"x6". These yellow flowers with red speckles will appear all summer for the gardener fortunate to have a stream or bog garden.

□ *Mirabilis multiflora*,
DESERT FOUR O'CLOCK. 4'x6'. Very drought-tolerant suitable for wild or xeriscape. Heart-shaped leaves. Magenta or pink flowers close in late morning.

■ *Monarda didyma*,
BEEBALM. 3'x3'. Selected from our native plants, the cultivated species range in color from pink to purple. Protect from powdery mildew. Keep moist.

CULTIVARS:

'Adam' - clear red.

'Croftway Pink' - soft rose pink.

'Prairie Night' - rich purple.

□ *Myosotis alpestris*,
FORGET-ME-NOT. 6"x6". Indispensible self-sower among spring bulbs, the intense blue flowers announce the season.

□ *Nepeta mussinii*,
LAVENDER CATMINT. 3'x3'. Misty blooms of pale lavender cover the gray mound of foliage in June. Cut back to about eight inches, it will re-bloom in August and September. Not particularly attractive to cats.

■ *Oenothera tetragona*,
SUNDROPS. 3'x2'. A cheery yellow cup that is effective with annual larkspur in early summer. Roots spread widely, but easily pulled.

■ *Paeonia lactiflora*,
COMMON GARDEN PEONY. 4'x3'. Regarded as Queen of the Perennial Border. Shoots emerge from woody roots in early spring. Enormous flowers appear from early to late May and early June, depending upon variety. Foliage remains handsome all season. See Chapter 6 for planting directions.

CULTIVARS:

'Festiva Maxima' - early white with red blotch.

'Gay Paree' - Japanese type single with cherry outer petals and shell pink center at midseason.

'Sarah Bernhardt' - apple blossom pink late season double.

'Seashell' - clear light pink single for midseason.

■ *P. tenuifolia*,
FERNLEAF PEONY. 3'x3'. A rare form with ferny dense foliage; blood-red flowers atop a ruff of leaves.

■ *Papaver orientale*,
ORIENTAL POPPY. 3'x2'. Flamboyant poppies for the late spring border. Weather often ruins them, but if you can enjoy them for an hour, they are worth it. See Chapter 6 for planting direction.

CULTIVARS:
'Bonfire' - flame red flowers with a black center.

'China Boy' - soft orange flowers with ruffled white base.

'Victoria Louise' - clear pink.

'Raspberry Queen' - raspberry pink with black center.

■ *Patrinia gibbosa*,
PATRINIA. 2'x1'. A seldom-grown plant that should gain wider popularity. Rounded clumps of foliage bearing loose clusters of acid yellow flowers over a very long period. Rich, moist soil a necessity.

■ *Penstemon spp.*,
BEARD TONGUE. To give you an idea of the size of this genus, they are classified as small, large, mat, scarlet, and clustered. Every garden should have at least five species.

■ *P. barbatus*,
Basal foliage and tall spires of one-inch flowers, each with a yellow-bearded lower lip.
CULTIVARS:
'Rose Elf' - long-blooming rose pink flower.

'Prairie Fire' - vermillion flowers.

P. pinifolius - shrubby with finely cut foliage; orange-red flowers. Resents transplanting.

P. secundiflorus - a native of dry, gravelly slopes; pale lavender flowers in early spring.

P. stricta - the most commonly seen penstemon of the Mountain West. Royal blue flowers over a long period. Seeds around.

P. virens - the roadside penstemon of exquisite light blue flowers. Grows well in clay and gravel mixture. Not long lived if fertilized or heavily watered.
■ *Perovskia atriplicifolia*,

RUSSIAN SAGE. 4'x3'. A newcomer to the perennial scene with tall, silvery-gray foliage and misty lavender blooms in July and August. Dries well.

■ *Phlox carolina*,
CAROLINA PHLOX. 3'x3'. Early-flowering, mildew and red spider mite resistant. Tolerant of light shade.
CULTIVAR:
'Miss Lingard' - A cloud of white flower clusters in early June. Can be cut back for re-bloom.

■ *P. divaricata*,
WILD BLUE PHLOX. 1'x1'. A mainstay of the early spring garden in part shade. Pale blue clusters on creeping mats of foliage. Charming with early yellow tulips.

■ *P. paniculata*,
GARDEN PHLOX. 4'x2'. Clusters of fragrant florets. Subject to powdery mildew if drought occurs. Support stems with circlets of chicken wire.
CULTIVARS:
'Dodo Hanbury Forbes' - clear light pink.

'Mt. Fuji' - large white flower clusters.

'Prime Minister' - pink with a deep rose eye.

■ *P. subulata*,
CREEPING PHLOX. 2"x3'. Fast-spreading mats of prickly foliage that becomes a sheet of color in spring; yet can withstand drought and remain looking good all season.

CULTIVARS:
'Early Blue' - delicate blue.

'Betty Blake' - pure white.

'Laura' - pale pink.

'Red Fox' - deep rose.

■ *Physostegia virginiana,*
OBEDIENT PLANT. 3'x2'. Fast-spreading clumps of sharp-toothed foliage; spires of curious bracted flowers in July; long-lasting.
CULTIVARS:
'Rosy Spire' - crimson flowers.

'Summer Snow' - a standout with Canterbury Bells.

'Variegata' - variegated cream and green foliage; lilac flowers.

■ *Platycodon grandiflorus,*
BALLOON FLOWER. 2'x2'. Late-appearing foliage with erect stems of bulbous buds that resemble hot-air balloons; opening to pointed petals over a long period. White and pink forms available.

■ *Polemonium caeruleum,*
JACOB'S LADDER. 2'x2'. A native for part shade. Early appearing foliage is arranged like rungs on a ladder. Blue or pink flowers, loosely clustered, in June. Resents transplanting.

■ *Primula spp.,*
PRIMROSE. A large genus that includes some very demanding species. The easiest to grow are P. polyantha, but once you've tried your hand at some of the others, primroses can become an addiction. Most require dappled shade.

■ *P. auricula,*
SECTION AURICULA. 6"x1'. Almost evergreen rosettes of foliage topped by an umbel of fragrant flowers. Usually yellow.

■ *P. beesiana,*
SECTION CANDELABRA. 2'x2'. For those fortunate to have a stream running through their property, this tall swaying beauty is available in rainbow colors. Must have cool, moist, organic soil.

■ *P. denticulata,*
SECTION DENTICULATA. 1'x1'. Formerly known as the cashmere primroses, these balls of flowers atop bare stems appear in early May. Many colors available.

■ *P. polyantha,*
ENGLISH PRIMROSE. 6"x1'. Funnelform flowers for early spring combinations with forget-me-nots, the new fiddles of ferns, and tulips.

■ *Pulmonaria saccarata,*
LUNGWORT. 1'x2'. A rising genus that will see many ornamentals in a few years. For areas with spring sun and summer shade.
CULTIVARS:
'Mrs. Moon' - green foliage splashed with silver blotches. Pink flowers fading to blue.

'Roy Davidson' - foliage blotched with silver, light blue flowers.

■ *Ranunculus aconitifolius,*
BUTTERCUP. 2'x3'. Very dark foliage and glistening double white cups. Prefers moist, rich soil. Mulch well in winter.

■ *R. lingua*,
GREATER SPEARWORT. 3'x2'. Creeping by stolons, this charming invader is in every spring garden. Blooms are shiny yellow. Easy to pull. Useful for eroding streambanks.

■ *Rodgersia pinnata*,
5'x 3'. An unusual plant from China with no common name. Bold clumps of bronze-flushed leaves; panicles of bright pink in late summer; for streambanks or bog gardens.
CULTIVAR:
'Superba' - pink.

■ *Rudbeckia spp.*,
CONEFLOWER. 4'x3'. Natives of this continent, this broad spectrum of ray and disk flowers is the supporting color of the August garden.

■ *R. fulgida*,
ORANGE CONEFLOWER. 3'x3'. A long succession of flowers; self-sows.
CULTIVAR:
'Goldsturm' - the best yellow with brown/ black center.

■ *R. hirta*,
BLACK-EYED SUSAN. 4'x2'. This familiar roadside flower still has a place in every garden. Self-sows.
CULTIVAR:
'Gloriosa Daisy' - a tetraploid that has larger flowers than the parent.

■ *Ruta, graveolens*,
RUE. 2"x2'. Grown for its delicate blue-green foliage, this herb can cool the hot colored blooms of the perennial border.
CULTIVAR:
'Blue Mound' - does not always overwinter well. Mulch well or lift it for overwintering in the coldframe.

■ *Salvia spp.*,
SAGE. Many species from which to choose for combinations of bloom at every month of the growing season.

■ *S. grandiflora*,
BLUE SAGE. 6'x2'. Formerly *S. pitcheri*, this tall, floppy plant bears clear forget-me-not blue spikes in late August. Not reliably hardy. Mulch heavily in winter.

■ *S. farinacea*,
MEALY-CUP SAGE. 3'x3'. Not reliably throughout the range of this book, the spikes of blue flowers are easily dried; stems are also blue.
CULTIVAR:
'Blue Bedder' - seen in every municipal garden combined with yellow marigolds. Ideal in the foreground with white alyssum and "Moonbeam" *Coreopsis.*

■ *S. x superba*,
PURPLE SAGE. 3'x3'. Spikes of deep purple. Plant with *Achillea* MOONSHINE, a lavender chrysanthemum, and a white form of *Dictamnus* GAS PLANT.
CULTIVARS:
'East Friesland' - deep purple; resents disturbance, but seeds around.

'May Night' - deep purple; earlier blooming than above; good with pink and white tulips. Continues blooming all summer.

■ *Sanguisorba canadensis*,
BURNET. 4'x2'. A favorite in bog gardens or along streambanks. Tall erect spikes of white flowers in late summer. Difficult to locate, Full sun at 5,000+ altitude and; part shade at lower altitude.

■ *S. obtusa,*
2'x2', A Japanese species with gray green foliage and rose purple flowers which mature to pale pink.

■ Scabiosa caucasica,
PINCUSHION, 2'x1'. Domed heads of many tiny flowers, each with a protruding stamen like a pin.
CULTIVARS:
'Clive Greaves' - lavender blue flowers.

'Miss Willmott' - white flowers.

■ *Sedum purpureum,*
STONECROP. 3'x3'. One of many species that have yielded superior perennials for the border. Fleshy foliage, drought tolerant; prefer full sun.
CULTIVAR:
'Autumn Joy' - maroon bloom clusters in September turn to chocolate brown for a winter color interest.

■ *S. spectabile,*
SHOWY STONECROP. 18"x18". Domed heads of tightly packed flowers in September and October.
CULTIVARS:
'Brilliant' - an electric pink.

'Stardust' - white fading to pink.

'Variegatum' - variegated cream, pink, and green foliage

■ *Senecio cineraria,*
DUSTY MILLER. 2'x1'. A "sanitizer" of gray, finely dissected folage for the front of the border. Lives over the winter and for several seasons, but is of poor appearence until about June 1.

■ *Sidalcea malviflora,*
MINIATURE HOLLYHOCK. 4'x2'. Long-stemmed spikes of pink-to-rose flowers. Long-lasting if kept deadheaded.

■ *Solidago x hybrida,*
GOLDENROD. 3'x3'. Blamed unjustly for hayfever, this pasture pest bears plumes of gold in late summer. Though invasive, it can be controlled, and adds a much needed spike form to the late summer scene.
CULTIVAR:
'Cloth of Gold' - deep yellow on 1.5' stems.

'Goldenmosa' - bright yellow on 1' stems.

■ *Stachys byzantina,*
LAMB'S EARS. 6"x3'. A felty, gray-leafed plant for the foreground of the border. Spikes of lavender flowers are clipped before they form if you prefer the foliage as a foil for other flowers, such as *Heuchera* 'Palace Purple'.

■ *Stokesia laevis,*
STOKE'S ASTER. 2'x2'. Flower heads of lacinated petals available in white, pink, blue, lilac, and yellow.

■ *Thalictrum aquilegifolium,*
MEADOW RUE. 4'x2'. Blue-green foliage like columbine; broad panicles of nodding lavender flowers in early June. Seeds around. Prefers dappled shade.

■ *Thermopsis montana,*
GOLDEN BANNER. 3'x3'. This native will set off every planting of iris in early summer. A good yellow spike flower; long-lived, attractive palmate foliage all season.

■ *Tiarella wherryi*,
FOAMFLOWER. 1'x2'. A foam of delicate white flowers from lobed, toothed foliage in spring. Moist, shady situation; only moderately rich soil preferred; mulch heavily in winter.

■ *Tricyrtis hirta*,
HAIRY TOAD LILY. 1'x1'. With a name like that, it better be beautiful! A status symbol plant at the moment. Fuzzy foliage; unbranched flower stems with variously spotted and speckled flower clusters; each long-lasting. Provide moist soil, rich with oak-leaf compost, for acidity is needed.

■ *Trollius europeus*,
GLOBEFLOWER. 1'x2'. Clumps of dark green foliage appear in very early spring. Flowers are solitary globes of delicate yellow with incurving petals. Prefers part shade.

■ *Valeriana*,
see *Centranthus ruber*.

■ *Verbascum x hybridum*,
MULLEIN. 6'x2'. A cultivated form of a familiar roadside weed. Wooly basal foliage and rising spires of deep rose or yellow or white.
CULTIVARS:
'Cotswold Gem' - terracotta.

'Cotswold Queen' - yellow.

'Mont Blanc' - white.

■ *Verbena bonariensis*,
VERVAIN. 4'x2'. A heat and drought tolerant perennial to match the popular annual form. Tiny lilac-to-purple flowers rise above basal foliage. Plant with *Stachys byzantina*.

■ *Veronica spp.*,
SPEEDWELL. 2'x3'. A genus growing in popularity. Spike flowers closely set in every color but yellow.

■ *V. incana*,
silvery gray foliage.
CULTIVAR:
'Minuet' - pink flowers all season if deadheaded.

■ *V. latifolia*,
sprawling stems need chicken wire circlet to hold them together.
CULTIVAR:
'Crater Lake Blue' - only blooms once in June, but the spikes of incredible blue make it worth growing.

■ *V. spicata*, very dark green folige.
CULTIVARS:
'Blue Charm' - shiny green foliage, lavender blue spikes.

'Blue Peter'- good medium blue.

'Icicle' - intensely white.

'Red Fox' - not red, but a deep rose.

■ *V. subsessilis*,
3'x2'. compact clumps of dark green foliage.
CULTIVAR:
'Sunny Border Blue' - voted by perennial growers to be in the top ten. Navy blue flowers on two foot stems.

■ *Viola spp.*,
VIOLET. 6"x1'. Loved by most, cursed by some, these low tufts of heart-shaped foliage are recognized for their fragrant flower of familiar shape.

■ *V. canadensis*,
CANADA VIOLET. Neat clumps of foliage support a white flower with yellow throat, flushed with purple on the underside.

■ *V. cornuta*,
HORNED VIOLET. Enjoying poplarity at the moment, this lively lavender flower will appear all summer if deadheaded. Can withstand heat.

■ *V. odorata*,
GARDEN VIOLET. The familiar purple florists violet sold in bunches in cities in winter. Nostalgic scent.

■ *Yucca glauca*, SOAPWEED. 6'x3'. A native plant useful as a sculpture; sharply pointed strap leaves; June bloom of creamy trusses.

Perennials for Full Sun

BOTANIC NAME	COMMON NAME
Achillea	YARROW
Alcea	YARROW
Anaphilis	HOLLYHOCK
Aegopodium	PEARLY EVERLASTING
Anchusa	BISHOP'S WEED BUGLOSS
Anemone	LILY-OF-THE-` FIELD
Anthemis	GOLDEN MARGUERITE
Arabis	ROCKCRESS
Artemisia	SAGE
Asclepias	BUTTERFLY WEED
Aster	FALL ASTER
Aurinia	BASKET-OF-GOLD
Boltonia	BOLTONIA
Brunnera	SIBERIAN BUGLOSS
Campanula	BELLFLOWER
Catananche	CUPID'S DART
Centaurea	CORNFLOWER
Centranthus	VALERIAN
Ceratostigma	PLUMBAGO
Chrysanthemum	CHRYSANTHEMUM
Clematis	SHRUB CLEMATIS
Coreopsis	TICKSEED
Delphinium	LARKSPUR
Dianthus	PINK
Dictamnus	GAS PLANT
Doronicum	LEOPARD'S BANE
Echinacea	PURPLE CONE FLOWER
Echinops	GLOBE THISTLE
Erigeron	FLEABANE
Eryngium	SEA HOLLY
Erysimum	WALLFLOWER
Euphorbia	CUSHION SPURGE
Filipendula	QUEEN-OF-THE-MEADOW
Gaillardia	BLANKET FLOWER
Gentiana	GENTIAN
Geranium	CRANESBILL
Geum	AVENS

BOTANIC NAME	COMMON NAME
Gypsophila	BABY'S BREATH
Helenium	SNEEZEWEED
Helianthemum	SUN ROSE
Helianthus	SUN FLOWER
Heliopsis	FALSE SUNFLOWER
Hemerocallis	DAY LILY
Heuchera	CORAL BELLS
Hibiscus	ROSE MALLOW
Hyssopus	HYSSOP
Ibiris	CANDYTUFT
Iris	IRIS
Kniphofia	RED HOT POKER
Lavatera	MALLOW
Liatris	BLAZING STAR
Ligularia	GOLDEN GROUNDSEL
Limonium	SEA LAVENDER
Linum	BLUE FLAX
Lunaria	PERENNIAL HONESTY
Lupinus	LUPINE
Lychnis	CAMPION
Lysimachia	YELLOW LOOSESTRIFE
Lythrum	LOOSESTRIFE
Maclaeya	PLUME POPPY
Malva	HOLLYHOCK MALLOW
Mirabilis	DESERT FOUR O'CLOCK
Monarda	BEE BALM
Nepeta	LAVENDER CATMINT
Oenothera	SUNDROPS
Paeonia	PEONY
Papaver	POPPY
Patrinia	PATRINIA
Penstemon	BEARD TONGUE
Perovskia	RUSSIAN SAGE
Phlox	PHLOX
Physostegia	OBEDIENT PLANT
Platycodon	BALLOON FLOWER
Ranunculus	BUTTERCUP

BOTANIC NAME	COMMON NAME
Rodgersia	RODGERSIA
Rudbeckia	CONE FLOWER
Salvia	SAGE
Sanguisorba	BURNET
Scabiosa	PINCUSHION
Sedum	STONECROP
Senecio	DUSTY MILLER
Sidalcea	MINIATURE HOLLYHOCK
Solidago	GOLDENROD
Stachys	LAMB'S EARS
Stokesia	STOKE'S ASTER
Thalictrum	MEADOWRUE
Thermopsis	GOLDEN BANNER
Trollius	GLOBE FLOWER
Verbascum	MULLEIN
Verbena	VERVAIN
Veronica	SPEEDWELL
Yucca	SOAPWEED

Perennials for Dappled Shade

BOTANIC NAME	COMMON NAME
Aconitum	MONKSHOOD
Alchemilla	LADY'S MANTLE
Anemone	ANEMONE
Aquilegia	COLUMBINE
Aruncus	GOAT'S BEARD
Baptisia	FALSE INDIGO
Bergenia	HEART-LEAF BERGENIA
Brunnera	SIBERIAN BUGLOSS
Campanula	BELLFLOWER
Cimicifuga	SNAKEROOT
Corydalis	YELLOW BLEED-ING HEART
Dicentra	BLEEDING HEART
Digitalis	FOXGLOVE
Helleborus	CHRISTMAS ROSE
Hemerocallis	DAYLILY
Ligularia	GOLDEN GROUNDSEL
Lupinus	LUPINE
Mertensia	BLUEBELL
Monarda	BEE BALM
Myosotis	FORGET-ME-NOT
Polemonium	JACOB'S LADDER
Primula	PRIMROSE
Ruta	RUE
Sanguisorba	BURNET
Tiarella	FOAM FLOWER
Trollius	GLOBE FLOWER
Viola	VIOLET

Bloom Calendar

Opening in April

Aurinia
Anemone
Helleborus
Ranunculus
Trollius

Opening in May

Alchemilla
Anchusa
Aquilegia
Arabis
Bergenia
Brunnera
Dicentra
Doronicum
Geum
Ibiris
Iris
Linum
Myosotis
Paeonia
Papaver
Primula
Ruta
Thalictrum
Tiarella
Viola

Opening in June
Achillea
Aconitum
Astilbe
Campanula
Centaurea
Centranthus
Chrysanthemum
Clematis
Coreopsis
Delphinium
Dianthus
Digitalis
Erigeron
Filipendula
Gaillardia
Geranium
Geum
Heuchera
Hosta
Iris
Lavatera
Linum
Limonium
Lychnis
Malva
Mirabilis
Nepeta
Oenothera
Papaver
Penstemon
Platycodon
Rodgersia
Rudbeckia
Sanguisorba
Scabiosa
Senecio
Sidalcea
Stachys
Thalictrum
Thermopsis
Tiarella
Verbascum
Verbena
Veronica
Yucca

Opening in July
Echinacea
Euphorbia
Gentiana
Heliopsis
Hemerocallis
Hosta
Kniphofia
Ligularia
Lythrum
Monarda
Phlox
Physostegia
Rudbeckia
Scabiosa
Sidalcea
Solidago
Verbena
Veronica

Opening in August
Artemisia
Boltonia
Ceratostigma
Chrysanthemum
Gentiana
Helenium
Helianthus
Hibiscus
Hosta
Liatris
Lobelia
Physostegia
Rudbeckia
Salvia
Sedum
Solidago
Stokesia
Veronica

Opening in September
Anemone
Aster
Chrysanthemum
Cimicifuga
Clematis
Delphinium
Heliopsis
Helenium
Tricyrtis

Suggested Reading

"Color Schemes for the Flower Garden", by Gertrude Jekyll, The Ayer Company, Salem, New Hampsire, 1983.

"Color In My Garden", by Louise Beebe Wilder, Atlantic Monthly Press, New York, reprinted 1990.

"Pests of the West", 1992 by Whitney Cranshaw, PhD, Entomology, Colorado State University, Fort Collins, CO, Fulcrum Publishing, Golden, CO.

Perennial Border for Late Spring, Summer & Fall

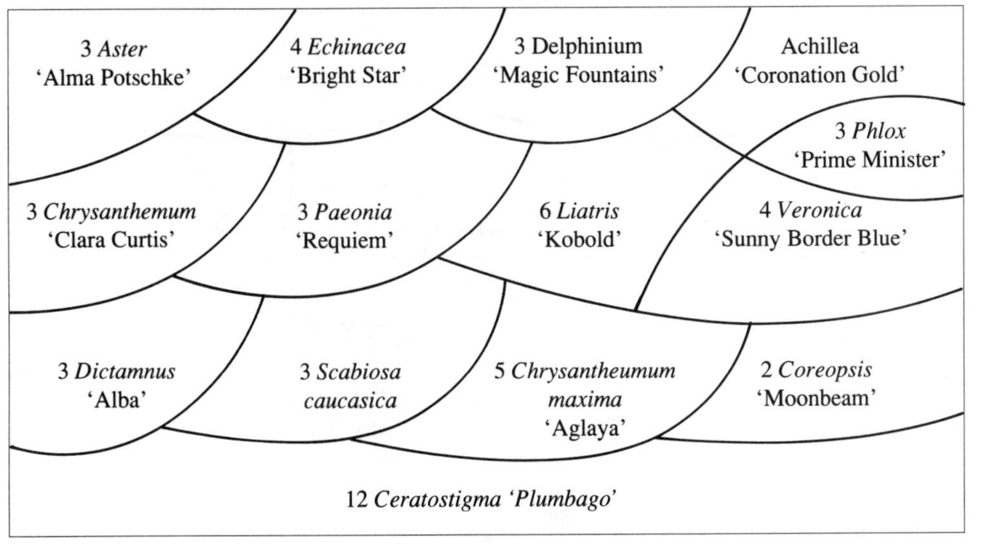

Perennials for a Hot, Dry Area

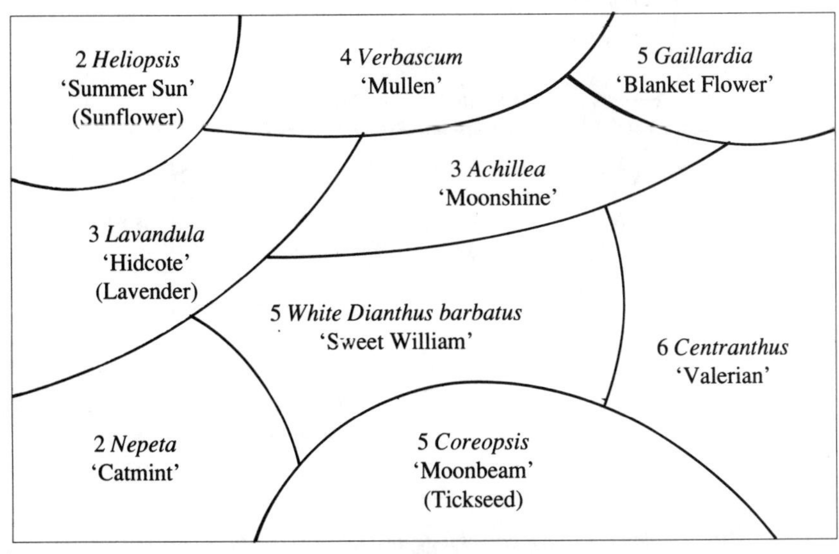

Dappled Shade Border

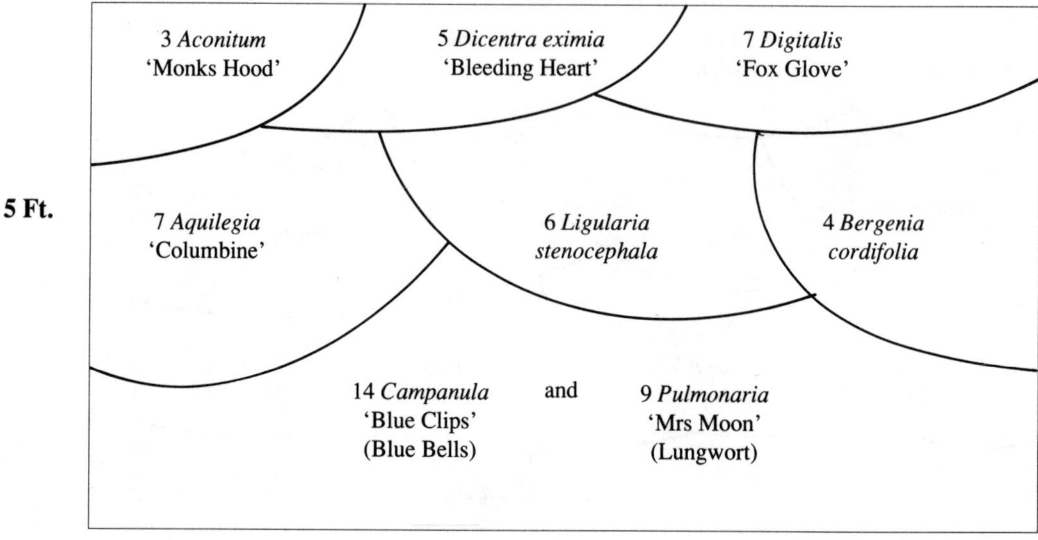

A white garden for those who are away from home.

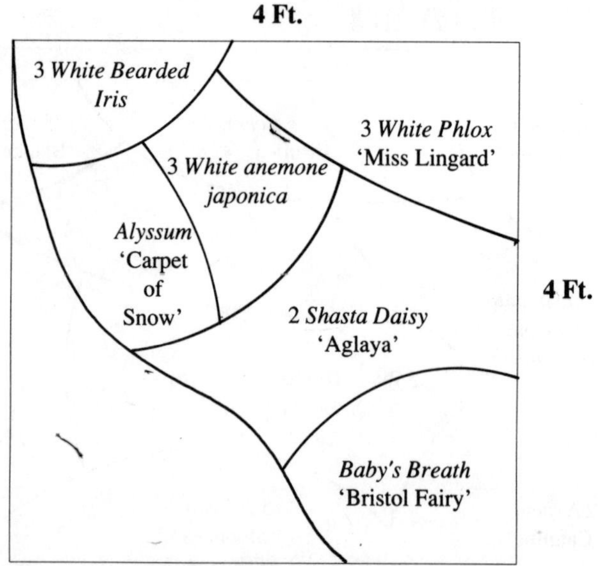

After sundown brilliant colors fade away, but white starts out clear and bright. This is a plot to delight the eye at day's end.

Annuals as Fillers or Focus of Color

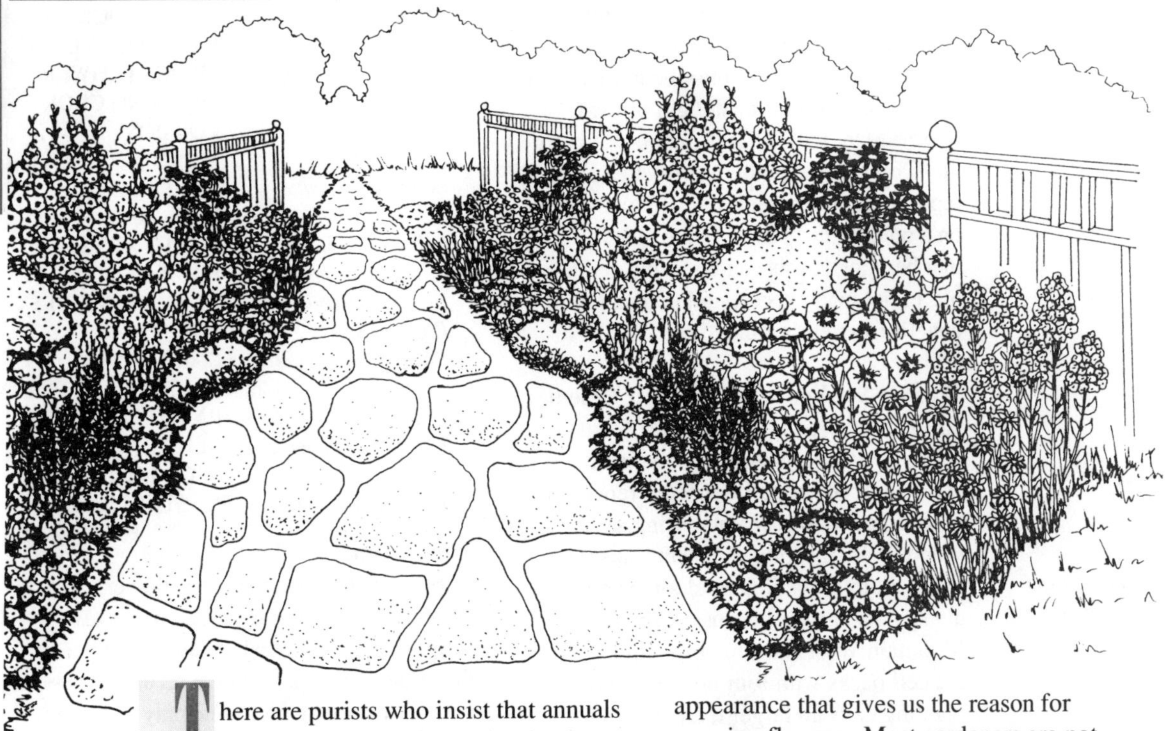

There are purists who insist that annuals have no place in a flower border, but they are being replaced by those who recognize the value of color in the border at the seasons when perennials are out of bloom. There are perennials that are touted to be in bloom from April to October, but the quality of bloom in these plants is overstated. The greatest number of perennials burst forth for about three weeks and lapse into sporadic bloom for the remainder of the season. For example, delphinium is a June-bloomer in most states, and it will put on a show again in September. Daylilies are the mainstay of the July garden, with a few varieties performing with a bloom or two in June and again in August.

■ *Most gardeners are not satisfied with a here-and-there- bloom.*

Annuals, however, are counted upon to give the border the *stuffed-with-color* appearance that gives us the reason for growing flowers. Most gardeners are not satisfied with a here-and-there bloom. They want a riot of color to resemble the pictures in the magazines.

Annuals will hit their stride from late June till frost, filling in when perennials have finished their big show. Annuals are also the flowers we count on for window boxes, hanging baskets, and containers on the patio, for they can be crowded more successfully than perennials. If you are mindful of regular care and added nutrients, annuals will give you all-summer color in containers.

The term *bedding plants* is familiar to everyone who has wandered into a nursery in spring. Thousands upon thousands are grown in a high-tech industry that flourishes throughout the Mountain West.

Despite the fact that annuals are easy to grow as window-sill seedlings, many gardeners prefer to buy them as started plants ready to set out into the garden. The gamblers, much to the delight of the nurseryman, will set their plants out before the average date of the last frost and replace them at once if they are cut down on a cold night. June 1 is the usual date that bedding plants can be safely set into place, but many species tolerate and will benefit from earlier planting.

Tips for Seeding Annuals That Resent Transplanting

If you plan to grow your own annuals from seed, consult a library reference for procedures to follow for starting seed indoors. Many annuals resent transplanting, yet direct seeding outdoors is not always the answer because spring in the Mountain West is a sometime thing. Use the cell packs with four dozen or more planting cells no larger than one's thumb. Pack the cells with a soil-less mix, such as Pro-mix; sow one or two seeds in each cell and proceed according to directions on the seed packet as to temperature requirements. After germination, place the cell packs in sunlight or under florescent lights until true leaves unfold. Then it is a quick transplant to four-inch pots for each plant if it is still too cold for outdoor planting. Your seedlings will prosper also if grown on in a cold frame. Skip the potting on* to the four-inch pot if you germinate the seed just before the date of the last average killing frost and transplant the cells directly to the place they are to grow and bloom out-of-doors.

■ *The snip here and snip there. . . wrecks havoc.*

** See Glossary*

Annuals That Resent Transplanting

Alcea rosea	HOLLYHOCK
Clarkia spp.	SATIN FLOWER
Cleome Hasslerana	SPIDER FLOWER
Convolvulus spp.	MORNING GLORY
Cosmos spp.	COSMOS
Ipoemea spp.	MORNING GLORY
Lathyrus odoratus	SWEET PEA
Layia elegans	TIDY TIPS
Lobularia maritima	SWEET ALYSSUM
Mirabilis jalapa	FOUR O'CLOCK
Nemophila spp.	BABY BLUE EYES
Papaver spp.	POPPY
Phacelia campanularia	CALIFORNIA BLUEBELL
Salpiglossis sinuata	PAINTED TONGUE
Trachymene coerulea	BLUE LACE FLOWER
Tropaeolum spp.	NASTURTIUM

The Cutting Garden

Every gardener addicted to flower arranging has a cutting garden tucked away somewhere. The snip here and snip there of the arranger wrecks havoc with the fullness of bloom in the border. The only solution is to grow rows of flowers for cutting in another area, such as next to the vegetable garden, where ease of culture, not aesthetic excellence, is your aim. Favorites for the cutting garden are those species that are long-lasting indoors, such as asters, marigolds, petunias, zinnias, and everlastings.

Alternate Methods

The cutting garden is an area where another method of culture can be tried for placing annuals in full bloom in the flower border. Growing annuals in pots until they are in full bloom, then transplanting to the border is risky. Transplant shock usually sets them back and bloom often stops. At our higher altitude the sun drills its heat into the sides of pots, whether plastic or clay, to heat the soil. The roots then transpire too quickly and the pot dries out.

A continuous drip system is one solution. Lacking that, it's YOU, the gardener, who waters those pots two or three times per day.

Sinking the pots, rim deep, into rows in the vegetable garden is another solution. Use a small tiller to work up a row before lifting six inches of soil out of the row and setting it aside. Set the pots of growing annuals into the trench, shoulder to shoulder, packing soil around each pot to a point just above the rim. Use a drip system hose with an emitter for the top of each pot. Cover the dripper hose with fabric weed barrier for true low maintenance.

You can also grow annuals in rows in the cutting garden with the intention of transplanting them to the border. Water copiously the plants to be dug on the day before digging each plant carefully and transplanting immediately and in full bloom to the border; watering in and covering with a box or basket for twenty-four hours to reduce shock. Physiologically, an annual plant that resents transplanting in its 'youth' is better able to withstand transplant at full bloom. Try this method and let others know if you are successful. That is how we learn in horticulture!

A Different Cultural Method for the Slow Pokes

The altitude of the Mountain West is a disadvantage for annuals that require a long growing season. Our soils are cold in spring. At the other end of the growing season, temperatures in the fifties in August cool the soil rapidly and some plants make buds that never have time to open before frost.

If you have a cold frame (and if not, why not?), transplant the lazy late-comers into four or five-inch pots before frost cuts them down and pack them away into the cold frame. Be faithful in lowering the cover of your coldframe at night in early fall, and opening it to full sun in daytime. As soon as real winter is predicted, cover the entire contents of the frame with an insulating material, such as straw, plastic bubble-wrap, or several layers of floating row cover. Insulating material should be under the pots as well as on top. When you open the frame in early March, you will find plants already green and ready to grow and bloom. Keep them in the frame until danger of the last frost has passed before transplanting them as you would any bedding plant. You will find they bloom the entire season and you will get your money's worth. Good candidates for this treatment are: Heliotrope (*Heliotropium arborescens*), Blue Lace Flower (*Trachymene coerulea*), Fountain Grass (*Pennisetum setaceum*).

Another ploy with the coldframe involves planting seed of slow-poke annuals in pots in September, nine months in advance of when the flowers can be expected. Seedlings will have true leaves and maybe even four sets of leaves before you put the coldframe to bed for the winter. Be sure to open it on a warm January day to water the seedlings if they seem dry. When you open the frame in March, you will have strong, leafy seedlings, and by May 15th when it's time to set them out, chances are strong they will be in bloom. Good candidates for this cultural method are: annual carnations (*Dianthus indicum*), the F1 hybrid *Dianthus* such as *D. chinensis* 'Fire Carpet', or the annual dahlias.

■ *The altitude of the Mountain West is a disadvantage for annuals.*

The Soft Pinch

Long ago it was necessary to pinch out the tip growth of each annual plant at the time it was set out into open ground in the garden. The high-tech hybridization processes have given reason to eliminate this cultural procedure; for in the Mountain

■ *. . .in the Mountain West, the growing season is short at best.*

West, the growing season is short at best. Pinching is a pruning that is not necessary for the hybrid plant. For others, however, you can use your own judgment. If the plant seems leggy with a lengthy distance between nodes where leaves are located, then it is wise to pinch out the soft tip growth so that branching will occur and the plant will stand up strongly.

In midsummer most annuals slow down in growth and in new blooms. It is at this period that the soft pinch is given again or for the first time to hybrids. Fertilization and a copious watering follows. The plants will respond with new branches and more blooms.

Deadheading

The entire objective in the life of a plant is to re-create itself. A flowering annual germinates, grows, blooms, sets seeds, and dies in the same growing season. Your role as the spoiler is to prevent seed from forming and to keep the plant blooming. It will continue to bloom as long as the wilted, spent flowers are removed. This is called *deadheading*. It is a pleasant task to sally forth every morning or in the cool of the summer evening with your scissors or shears and a bag to deadhead yesterdays' spent blooms. In deadheading flowers with long stems, cut back to the nearest branch so that it will make a new branch that will bloom. Take care not to drop the dead flower heads, for the clutter is unattractive, and it is kin to sweeping dust under the rug! The debris will break down quickly in the compost heap.

List of Annuals for the Mountain West

■ *Abelmoschus moschatus*,
MUSK MALLOW. 12". Well-branched plants bear huge crops of single pink or red hibiscus-like flowers each day. Not a plant for a cool-night area. A native of the hot, dry season of India.

■ *Adonis aestivalis*,
PHEASANT'S EYE. 18". Prolific blood-red cups with black centers; feathery foliage; spring-flowering, not for beginners.

■ *Ageratum houstonianum*,
FLOSSFLOWER Traditional low bedder with blue or white stemless panicles. 'Blue Mink' and 'Summer Snow' perform well in the low category; 'Blue Horizon' and 'Blue Bavaria' are 14". Deadheading is essential for continued bloom; or shear in midsummer when bloom begins to wane; fertilize and expect late August and September bloom.

■ *Agrostemma githago*,
CORN COCKLE. 3'. Slender branched stems bearing five-petal flowers in shade of cerise and plum-pink with white center. Sow seeds where they are to grow two weeks before average date of last frost.

■ *Amaranthus caudatus*,
JOSEPH'S COAT. 30" Grown as a background plant for its exotic ropes of flowers of yellow and scarlet.

■ *Ammi majus*,
BISHOP'S FLOWER. 30". The annual form of Queen Anne's Lace, and much more manageable. Use the airy white umbels in masses at the back of the border between warring colors, such as red and purple. Dries well. Seeds around but not an annoying amount.

■ *Anagallis linifolia*,
PIMPERNEL. 2-6". An intense gentian blue creeper for the rock garden or a hanging basket. Closes by 3 P.M. each day, opens at 8 A.M. Start seed indoors in March. Self-sows easily.

■ *Anchusa capensis*,
BUGLOSS, ALKANET. 8" *A. capensis* 'Blue Angel' is a good substitute for the unforgettable blue cushion plant - alpine forget-me-not (*Eritrichium elongatum*)- in the rock garden. A. officinalis 'Blue Bird or 'Dawn' are tall (20") and vigorous plants for borders or containers.

■ *Antirrhinum majus*,
SNAPDRAGON. 12". Tall, medium, and dwarf varieties of this familiar spike, trumpet flower available in all colors except blue. Plant in groups of three or five.

■ *Arctotis stoechadifolia*,
AFRICAN DAISY. 3-4'. Full sun suits this daisy available in yellow, cream, peach, orange, red, lilac, and plum. Closes at night. Pinch back in midsummer for fuller plants and more blooms.

■ *Begonia semperflorens*,
WAX BEGONIA. 1'. Important in every border and in containers for its ability to bloom continuously in sun or shade. The varieties 'Whiskey', 'Gin', and 'Vodka' have a metallic sheen on the foliage, with white, pink, and red blooms.

■ *Brachycome iberidifolia*,
SWAN RIVER DAISY. A trailer for border or basket of finely divided, gray-green foliage with masses of scented blue

daisies. Pinch to encourage compact growth. May cease blooming in hot weather; cut back and fertilize, and bloom will resume in cooler weather.

■ *Brassica oleracea*,
ORNAMENTAL CABBAGE. 1'. A magnificent orb of color in fall; coloring best after first frost. Heads differ in color from green and white, pink and rose, to deepest purple. Subject to cabbage insects. Do not use as indoor decoration because they emit a cabbage odor in a warm room.

■ *Calendula officinalis*,
ENGLISH DAISY. 1'. Excellent daisy for cool night areas. Available in shades of apricot and yellow.

■ *Calliopsis tinctoria*,
COREOPSIS. 18". The annual version of the perennial *Coreopsis*. 'Early Sunrise' will live over a year or two in some areas. Bright yellow, semidouble flowers top tall, straight stems. Deadheading a necessity to keep it blooming.

■ *Callistephus chinensis*,
CHINA ASTER. 12-18". One of the top cut flowers for the home in long-growing-season areas. Tall, medium, and dwarf available. Every color except yellow.

■ *Catharanthus x hybrida*,
6" VINCA OR PERIWINKLE. Shiny, round leaves on this 15" plant give way to five-petaled flowers in cool colors. White with a red eye is 'Peppermint Cooler', while 'Pretty In Pink' has pink flowers with a white eye. Ideal for hanging baskets at high altitude where hummingbirds will buzz incessantly.

■ *Celosia cristata*,
CRESTED COCKSCOMB. 9-15". Big crests of color in blood red, gold, yellow, pink, and salmon.

■ *C. plumosa*,
PLUMED COCKSCOMB has the same colors available. Needs full sun, heat and will tolerate dry soil. Start seeds in warm soil.

■ *Centaurea cyanus*,
CORNFLOWER, BACHELOR BUTTON. 9-24". Feathery flowers in shades of blue, pink, rose, and white. Shear after first bloom, fertilize, and will rebloom until frost. Self sows.

■ *C. cineraria,*
DUSTY MILLER. 12". A silver foliage plant that often lives several years.

■ *Chrysanthemum parthenium*,
FEVERFEW. 1-3'. Found in every abandoned farm yard of the West. Light green, lacinated foliage. White ray flowers with yellow center. Seeds around, but easy to pull. Tolerates full sun to deep, dry shade.

■ *C. ptarmiciflorum*,
SILVER LACE DUSTY MILLER. 12". A good sanitizer between warring colors as well as a show-off in an area of part shade. Bloom should not be allowed. Grown for its lacinated silver leaves.

■ *Cleome Hasslerana*,
SPIDER FLOWER. 3-4'. Tall, bush plant with spiraling, scented sprays of white, rose, lilac, or white blooms. Start early indoors at cool temperature.

■ *Coleus x hybrida*,
FLAME NETTLE. 12-15". Astonishing range of brilliant colored foliage. Shades of chartreuse, brown, yellow, pink, scarlet, bright red, maroon, some with crinkled edges. Ideal for containers in light shade. Remove flower spikes as they form. Can be carried over the winter and cuttings taken in spring to perpetuate valued colors.

■ *Convolvulus tricolor*,
MORNING GLORY. A bush (15") or vine in brilliant blue, maroon, pink, or white. 'Blue Ensign' is an award-winning bush type with blue flowers with a white and yellow center. Needs full sun, heat. Nick the seed, soak overnight before planting.

■ *Cosmos bipinnatus*,
COSMOS. 3-4'. Tall, feathery foliage with ray flowers of every color except blue. Often self-sows copiously. 'Sea Shells' has a cornucopian petal and is more difficult to grow. Must have good drainage. Nitrogen fertilizer promotes leaves instead of flowers.

■ *Cynoglossum amabile*,
CHINESE FORGET-ME-NOT. 15". Coarse foliage, true-blue spikes of flowers. Often self-sows. Short period of bloom.

■ *Dahlia x hybrida*,
DAHLIA. 15". Old-fashioned flowers now revived. Unwin hybrids in every shade except true blue; easily grown from seed. Plants form clumps of underground tubers that can be lifted and stored and replanted the following spring, but best treated as an annual.

■ *Delphinium orientale*,
24". DELPHINIUM or *Consolida ambigua*, LARKSPUR. Name depends on which catalog you have. Not to be confused with perennial Delphinium, this annual of 15-24" has a spike flower in shades of blue, lilac, plum, pink, and white. Sow seed in fall or late winter. Good with annual poppies and *Calendula*. Pull when bloom is finished. Self-sows easily.

■ *Dianthus x alwoodii or D. chinensis, or D. heddewigii, or D. deltoides*.
PINKS. 2-20". A large choice of scented border plants with fringed or picotee petal edges. 'Snowfire' is a reliable red with a white edge that often lives several years.

■ *Digitalis purpurea*,
FOXGLOVE. 36" Foot-long basal leaves; spikes of finger-shaped flowers in shades of pink, rose, lavender and purple. This annual version of the perennial is easier. Grow in light shade in a place sheltered from wind.

■ *Dimorpotheca x sinuata*,
AFRICAN DAISY OR CAPE MARIGOLD. 12" An upfacing daisy with a dark center in shades of apricot, yellow, pink, and rose. Flowers close at night.

■ *Dyssodia tenulobia*,
DAHLBERG DAISY. 6". A tiny yellow daisy from South Africa with finely cut foliage. Useful in hot, dry places or containers. Self-sows. Fetid odor when disturbed. Effective when combined with *Phacelia campanularia*.

■ *Eschscholzia californica*,
CALIFORNIA POPPY. 8". A useful poppy in shades of orange, cream, and yellow. For hot, dry places. Combine with blue larkspur or 'Blue Ensign' morning glory. Scatter seed on cool soil in very early spring. Self-sows.

■ *Euphorbia marginata*,
SNOW-ON-THE-MOUNTAIN. 12-24". A cool green-and-white foliage plant for middle or back of the border. May become a weed because its explosive seeds spread widely. 'Summer Icicle' is dwarf.

■ *Felicia Bergerana or F. dubia*,
KINGFISHER DAISY. 6". A yellow centered blue daisy with needled foliage. Useful in window boxes, impervious to wind. Heavy feeder. Prefers sandy loam and perfect drainage.

■ *Gazania rigens*,
PARKING LOT FLOWER. 18". The daisy in every color except blue. Has a dark blotch at the center and withstands the conditions of radiated heat and pollution in a parking lot planting. Bottom heat required for germination.

■ *Gilia capitata*,
BIRD'S EYES OR BLUE THIMBLE FLOWER. 2'. Blue or lavender globes atop leafless stems. Yellow-green foliage intricately divided. Needs staking. Direct seed only. Cannot withstand transplanting.

■ *Godetia spp*.,
CLARKIA. 8". Single and double papery cups on 10" plants that will bloom all summer if deadheaded. Prefers the cool nights and moist conditions of high altitude planting.

■ *Gomphrena globosa*,
GLOBE AMARANTH. 24". An everlasting with heads of flowers that resemble clover blooms. Available in red, rose, pink, and white.

■ *Gypsophila, elegans*,
BABY'S BREATH. 36". Quite different from the perennial version. Clusters of white, pink, and rose. Self-sows nicely. 'Covent Garden' is used widely in the cut-flower trade.

■ *Helichrysum spp*.,
STRAWFLOWER. 3-5'. Many species of daisy-type flowers that bloom at the end of summer. Because many heads open at different times, take a needle and long thread to the garden to cut each head while it is still a bud, using the needle to pierce the calyx; move it on down to the end of the thread; repeat the process daily. Buds will open as they dry so that unattractive yellow center does not show. Use wire to form a stem for each flower head.

■ *Heliotrope x hybrida*,
CHERRY PIE. 24". Fragrant royal-purple flower clusters from mid to late summer. Combine with pale pink phlox. Cut back severely to bring in as a houseplant in fall.

■ *Hesperis matronalis*,
SWEET ROCKET. 18". Spikes of lilac, purple, and white flowers from midsummer till frost. Fragrant in the evening. Can become very invasive.

■ *Hunnemannia fumariafolia*,
MEXICAN TULIP POPPY. 1-3'. Bright yellow, textured flowers on bushy plants. Prefers direct seeding into warm soil.

■ *Hypoestes phyllostachya*,
PINK POLKA DOT. 8" A foliage plant welcome in containers for a partly shady patio. Pale pink leaves dotted with green. Prefers moist soil, morning sun.

■ *Ibiris odorata*,
CANDYTUFT. 8". Resembles alyssum; slender spires of pink, carmine, maroon, rose, white, and lavender. Fragrant. Self-sows. Sow direct in early June or indoors ten weeks before last frost.

■ *Impatiens balsamina*,
LADY SLIPPER. 15-24". Camellia-like flowers between leaves up and down the stems. May be transplanted in full bloom to fill in the border elsewhere. Heavy feeder. Soak seeds twenty-four hours before planting where they are to grow. White, apricot, rose, purple, lavender.

■ *Impatiens Wallerana*,
BUSY LIZZIE. 9". The standard bedding plant for a shady situation, but it easily withstands full sun at mile-high or above altitude. Every color available except true blue and yellow. One species with variegated foliage. Double varieties also available. Will have more sustained bloom if it has two hours of morning sun. Prefers rich, moist soil. For solid color, bed these four inches apart.

■ *Impatiens linearifolia*,
NEW GUINEA IMPATIENS. 12-15". Seldom available from seed. Prefers full sun. Slender, spurred flowers, all colors. Good indoor plant for winter bloom.

■ *Kochia scoparia f.trichophylla*,
BURNING BUSH, SUMMER CYPRESS. 3'. Farmers get nervous when they see this plant grown as an ornamental because seeds can scatter to become a noxious weed. This rounded bush of light green foliage turns brilliant red in fall. Use as an annual hedge or accent plant and destroy before seeds drops.

■ *Lathyrus odoratus*,
SWEET PEA. An annual vine also available in bush form. Fragile, frilled pea flowers of unparalleled fragrance. High country dwellers excel with this plant, but everyone should grow them. Keep them picked to keep them coming.

■ *Lavatera x hybrida*,
MALLOW. 2'. Branched plants covered in mid-summer with hollyhock-like flowers. 'Mont Blanc' is a white award-winner. Available also in rose and pink. Inevitably succumbs to a root-rot disease but worth growing for the two-month show.

■ *Leptosiphon x hybrida*,
STARDUST. A charming creeper for the rock garden or in a container for up-close viewing. 'French Hybrids Mixed' sown a pinch at a time every two weeks on gravelly soil will give you a succession of blooms in orange, yellow, pink, cream, and carmine. Sadly, it does not self-sow.

■ *Limnanthes douglasii*,
FRIED EGGS. 6". Yellow daisy with white petal tips. Good as a path edging for early summer at high altitude, or as a dense carpet close to the entry. Good with Lobelia 'Cambridge Blue'. Roots must be kept cool, moist. If ground is not disturbed in fall, will reseed easily.

■ *Limonium sinuatum, L. Bonduellii, L. Suworowii,*
STATICE. 2-3'. Clusters of tiny flowers surrounded by papery bracts in soft shades of blue, pink, yellow, white. The standard dried material for winter bouquets. Needs full sun, well-drained, very warm soil. Forms a taproot. Sow direct or in cells that are transplanted as soon as true leaves form. Fertilize at planting time; sidedress with 14-14-14 in early June. Begin picking when florets are 3/4 open and stems snap; hang to dry in cool, dry place.

■ *Linaria bipartita,*
TOADFLAX. 9". A warning against this one. It is too invasive to be included in the garden scene of the Mountain West. Though it is a pretty little snapdragon-like yellow and white spike flower, it is almost as noxious as *Linaria dalmatica* or *Linaria vulgaris* the perennial species. Be kind to your friends who are farmers or stockmen and eliminate this plant from your flower bed plan.

■ *Linum grandiflorum,*
FLAX. 2'. The annual form of the favorite perennial Blue Flax. 'Rubrum' is a deep red with an orange-red center. Closes at night, but remains open all day. Make successive sowings three weeks apart.

■ *Lobelia erinus,*
No common name. 3-12". A summer annual "must" in every garden. Deep blue to sky blue to white or pink flowers on erect or trailing stems. Shear lightly in mid-summer for continued bloom. 'Blue Moon' and'Blue Butterfly' are highly rated. 'Cambridge Blue' is a tireless light blue trailer.

■ *Lobularia maritima,*
SWEET ALYSSUM. 2-12". The darling of every garden. Loved for its fortitude, fragrance, and friendliness. White, pink, rose, or purple blooms appear early. Shear when bloom wanes in July to stimulate new blooms. Hardy till winter cuts it down. Self-sows. Start seeds in cool soil, transplant quickly to where they are to grow.

■ *Lunaria annua,*
HONESTY, MONEY PLANT. 3'. A biennial forming foliage the first year, which dies down in autumn. It reappears the following spring to bloom and die. Lilac flower spikes form in summer of the second year, followed by papery seed pods used in dry arrangements. 'Stella' has variegated foliage and white flowers.

■ *Machaeranthera tanacetifolia,*
TAHOKA DAISY. 2'. A pale blue daisy with yellow center for the hot, dry area. Feathery foliage.

■ *Malope trifida grandiflora,*
MALOPE. 3'x3'. Lobed, toothed leaves are topped by glistening, late-summer five-petaled flowers. Chill seed three days before sowing on peat, barely covering. Bottom heat. Does not make much growth until weather warms. Pink, rich red, and shiny white available.

■ *Matthiola, spp.*
TEN-WEEK STOCK. 18". M. 'ANNUA' is descended from an ancient perennial variety. A must for the fragrance garden. Basal foliage with spikes crowded with single or double flowers, powerfully scented. Sow in discreet patches in the border in very early spring or mid-summer for fall flowering. *M. bicornis* is night scented. All cultivars soon fade in hot weather.

■ *Mesembryanthemum spp.*
ICE PLANT. 2-4". A ground-cover creeper of starlike flowers all summer. Prefers full sun and poor soil. 'Yellow Ice' is acid yellow with red center.

■ *Mirabilis jalapa*,
FOUR O'CLOCK. 3-4'. Tall, bushy plants for hot, dry locations. Flowers open in late afternoon in red, yellow, crimson, white, or rose with stripes; showy veins. Becomes perennial if roots reach under a protected place, such as the house foundation.

■ *Moluccella laevis*,
BELLS OF IRELAND. 2-4'. Tall spires of green bracts inserted with white flowers. Used as line material in arrangements, as well as in dried arrangements. Feature groups of these as a sanitizer between warring colors in the border.

■ *Myosotis alpestris*,
FORGET-ME-NOT. 6-8". The true blue, five-petalled old-fashioned flower known for being the perfect companion for yellow tulips and white candytuft (*Ibiris*). If deadheaded, it will bloom till summer heat knocks it down; then explosive seed heads form and you will have them forever. Needs rich, soil and a constant supply of moisture.

■ *Nemesia strumosa and N. versicolor*,
No common name. 7-9". Low plants smothered with flowers in red, white, tangerine, and yellow. For cool climates in the high country or shady beds on the Plains.

■ *Nemophila maculata*,
BABY BLUE EYES. 6". An ephemeral of California slopes. Trailing, delicate plants with five-petaled blue flowers, each with a single black dot. For hanging baskets or in masses in a semi-shaded bed.

■ *Nicotiana alata*,
SHOOFLY PLANT, TOBACCO PLANT. 12". Said to be a repellent for many insects, including whitefly. Coarse foliage produces funnel-shaped flowers attractive to hummingbirds. The 'Nikki' series is pink, lime green, and deep red.
N. sylvestris is very tall with fragrant white blooms. 'Breakthrough' is very early and dwarf for the front of the border. Pronounced Nik-KO-shee-ana.

■ *Nierembergia hippomanica*,
CUP FLOWER. 12". 'Purple Robe' has feathery foliage and small, purple-blue cups all summer. Shear lightly at mid-summer for more blooms in fall.

■ *Nigella hispanica*,
LOVE-IN-A-MIST. 12". Soft, feathery foliage and delicate flowers of blue, pink, or white. Reseeds everywhere. Seed pods used in dried arrangements, wreaths.

■ *Papaver commutatum, P. paeoniflorum, P. rhoeas, P. somniferum*,
SHIRLEY POPPY. 10-18". A pallette of early single or double flowers with fringed, laced or marked petals. Blood red to palest pink, orange, yellow, white. Sow seed on cold soil early spring; taproot; pull when flowering is over in July. Self-sows.
P. somniferum is illegal, but enforcement is unlikely since gardeners are not apt to use it as a drug. Growing season is not long enough in the Mountain West to produce a drug from the plant.

■ *Papaver nudicaule*,
ICELAND POPPY, 12". The mainstay of the mountain garden; long-lasting and self-sowing. Shades of white, yellow, orange, pink. Not easy at lower altitudes unless given a little shade.

■ *Pelargonium x hortorum*,
GERANIUM. 8-24". Clustered flower heads over basal, kidney-shaped foliage, often with a dark zone. The "zonals" are most popular, with every color except blue or yellow. 'Martha Washington' geraniums are especially good in window boxes and in hanging baskets in light shade and high humidity.

■ *Penstemon x Hartwegii*,
BEARDTONGUE. 1"-3'. An enigmatic genus that delights every gardener except the person who must know the exact lineage of every plant in his garden. Most species are perennials, but the half-hardy annuals are available usually as mixed packets of seeds from various tender species, such as *P. acuminatus, P. digitalis, P. palmeri, P. venustus*. Colors are white, pink, lavender, crimson, scarlet, and every hue in between. Prepare seed for germination by lightly rubbing between two sheets of sandpaper. Sow indoors in moist media in February at cool temperatures. Pot on* seedlings when true leaves are achieved. Good display massed according to height in full sun. Water well but infrequently.

■ *Petunia x hybrida*.
PETUNIA. 8-24". Many varieties popular bedding flowers in every hue and shade, with bi-colors and doubles available. The most popular annual.

■ *Phacelia campanularia*.
CALIFORNIA BLUEBELL. 9". An intense gentian blue flower with protruded stamens that give it a starry look. Needs sandy soil. Useful in groups as an edger combined with *Dyssodia* (Dahlberg Daisy) and *Portulaca* 'Swan Lake'.

■ *Phlox drummondii*.
PHLOX. 6". Clusters of five-petaled flowers on stiff stems. Shades of pink, crimson, violet, white, salmon, and bi-colored.

■ *Portulaca grandiflorum*,
MOSS ROSE. 6". 'Cloudbeater' has been developed to stay open in cloudy weather. 'Swan Lake' is a double white. This low groundcover is ideal for the hot, dry place. Red, pink, salmon, white cactus-like flowers from midsummer till frost. Closes at night.

■ *Reseda odorata*,
MIGNONETTE. 12-15". Spikes of unassuming flowers in red and yellow emit a fragrance unparalleled. Use one plant in a window box to fill the house with fragrance or in drifts in the border. Can withstand part shade.

■ *Ricinus communis*,
CASTOR OIL PLANT. 6'. Tall, decorative foliage that is maroon at the tip. Clusters of sulphur-yellow flowers followed by clustered red spiny seeds pods. Poisonous.

* *See Glossary*

■ *Salpiglossis sinuata*,
PAINTED TONGUE. 24". Petunia-like blooms in exotic shades of red-brown, deep blue, purple, rose and yellow. It flops unless staked with a few twiggy branches as it grows. It is quite cold-tolerant and can be brought indoors in autumn to a cold sun porch for winter bloom. Sheltered half-shade. Pinch out the center when it reaches six inches.

■ *Salvia spp.*,
SAGE. 12-24". Many species are half-hardy; none as well-known as the scarlet spike flowers of public parks. Now available in lime green, salmon, deep purple, white, and porcelain blue. Likes rich soil and heat. Avoid transplant shock.

■ *Scabiosa atropurpureus*,
PINCUSHION FLOWER. 3'. A daisy with pouf of stamens in the center resembling pins in a pincushiuon. Long period of bloom. Blue, lilac, white, pink, maroon.

■ *Schizanthus hybrida*,
POOR MAN'S ORCHID. 12". A wide variety of colors for a warm, sheltered place. A dwarf, compact variety available. This plant is featured at the famous Butchart Gardens, Victoria, British Columbia.

■ *Senecio cineraria*,
DUSTY MILLER. 12-15". Rounded, incised silver foliage with good rain resistence. Use it to mute strident colors. Do not allow to bloom; foliage plant only.

■ *Tagetes spp.*
MARIGOLD. 3-24". Almost made it as America's national flower. Available in tall, medium, and low; big, heavy African blooms to tiny singles with names like 'Paprika' and 'Signet'. Investigate them all. There's a place in every sunny garden for marigolds.

■ *Tithonia rotundifolia*,
MEXICAN SUNFLOWER. 30". A good sunflower to combine with *Helianthus spp.* Vivid, orange-scarlet flowers on tall plants from midsummer until frost. Stands heat well.

■ *Torenia fournieri*,
WISHBONE FLOWER. An unusual, rich, butter-yellow bloom with red, purple, or blue markings. Profusion of blooms hides the foliage. Good in pots on the sheltered patio or in a shady bed.

■ *Tropaeolum nanum*,
NASTURTIUM. 6-12". Round leaves topped by brittle-stemmed, ruffled flowers of cream, yellow, orange, and red. Dead-heading an absolute. Grows best in poor soil but adequate water. *T. majus* is a trailing species that is attractive grown at the feet of low shrubs and trained upward to bloom in the sun amid the shrub foliage.

■ *Verbascum bombyciferum*,
MULLEIN. 3-4'. A biennial forming rosettes of fuzzy foliage the first year and tall spikes of fleecy silver studded with yellow flowers the second summer, after which it dies. *V.b.* 'Silver Lining' has silver foliage.

■ *Verbena x hybrida*,
VERBENA. 9-12". All colors except yellow. Flower heads studded with showy stamens. Very heat tolerant. Germination rate poor.

■ *Viola x wittrockiana*,
PANSY, VIOLA, JOHNNY JUMP-UP. 6". These rise in popularity as more color forms become available, some with faces and some without. Purple-black, brown, and orange are examples. Easily grown from seed. Deadheading essential.

■ *Xeranthemum annuum*,
IMMORTELLE. 2-3'. Lance-shaped, woolly leaves; lavender, rose, pink, red, and white papery flowers for use in winter bouquets. Stake plants with brush for support. Cut when fully opened. Hang upside down in cool, airy place.

■ *Zinnia x hybrida*,
ZINNIA. 3-36". A favorite for hot places; rich soil; direct seeding preferred because it resents transplanting. Avoid high humidity. Pure white and ice green through all shades of pink, red, yellow, and gold. Available as dwarf, mid-size to giant size. Plant a few zinnia seeds beneath yellowing bulb foliage to mark the spot where bulbs are growing that need lifting and dividing after frost in the fall.

Over 30 Inches

Agrostemma	CORN COCKLE
Amaranthus	JOSEPH'S COAT
Ammi	BISHOP'S WEED
Arctotis	AFRICAN DAISY
Chrysanthemum parthenium	FEVERFEW
Cleome	SPIDER FLOWER
Cosmos	COSMOS
Digitalis	FOXGLOVE
Gypsophila	BABY'S BREATH
Helichrysum	STRAWFLOWER
Hunnemannia	MEXICAN TULIP POPPY
Kochia	BURNING BUSH
Limonium	STATICE
Lunaria	MONEY PLANT
Matthiola	TEN-WEEK STOCK
Mirabilis	FOUR O'CLOCK
Moluccella	BELLS OF IRELAND
Nicotiana	FLOWERING TOBACCO
Penstemon	BEARDTONGUE
Ricinus	CASTOR OIL PLANT
Scabiosa	PINCUSHION FLOWER
Tagetes	MARIGOLD
Tithonia	MEXICAN SUNFLOWER
Verbascum	MULLEIN
Xeranthemum	IMMORTELLE
Zinnia	ZINNIA

2-12 Inches

Abelmoschus	MUSK MALLOW
Ageratum	FLOSS FLOWER
Anagallis	PIMPERNEL
Anchusa	ALKANET
Antirrhinum	SNAPDRAGON
Begonia	BEGONIA
Brachycome	SWAN RIVER DAISY
Brassica	FLOWERING KALE
Calendula	CLARKIA
Catharanthus	VINCA, PERIWINKLE
Celosia	FLAME NETTLE
Centaurea	BATCHELOR BUTTON, CORNFLOWER
Chrysanthemum ptarmiciflorum	SILVER LACE DUSTY MILLER
Dianthus	PINK
Dimorpotheca	STAR OF THE VELDT
Dyssodia	DAHLBERG DAISY
Eschscholzia	CALIFORNIA POPPY

Felicia	KINGFISHER DAISY
Geranium	GERANIUM
Gilia	BIRD'S EYES, BLUE THIMBLE
Godetia	SATIN FLOWER
Gomphrena	GLOBE AMA-RANTH
Gypsophila	BABY'S BREATH
Hypoestes	PINK POLKA DOT
Ibiris	CANDYTUFT
Leptosiphon	STARDUST
Limnanthes	FRIED EGGS
Lobelia	LOBELIA
Mesembryanthemum	ICE PLANT
Myosotis	FORGET-ME-NOT
Nemesia	NEMESIA
Nemophila	BABY BLUE EYES
Nierembergia	CUP FLOWER
Nigella	LOVE-IN-A-MIST
Papaver	POPPY
Pelargonium	GERANIUM
Penstemon	BEARD TONGUE
Petunia	PETUNIA
Phacelia	CALIFORNIA BLUEBELL
Phlox	PHLOX
Portulaca	MOSS ROSE
Salvia	SAGE
Schizanthus	POOR MAN'S ORCHID
Senecio	DUSTY MILLER
Tagetes	MARIGOLD
Torenia	WISHBONE FLOWER
Tropaeolum	NASTURTIUM
Verbena	VERBENA
Viola	PANSY, VIOLA
Zinnia	ZINNIA

12-24 Inches

Anchusa	BUGLOSS, ALKANET
Antirrhinum	SNAPDRAGON
Begonia	WAX BEGONIA
Brassica	FLOWERING KALE
Calliopsis	COREOPSIS
Callistephus	ASTER
Celosia	COCK'S COMB
Centaurea	BATCHELOR BUTTON, CORNFLOWER
Coleus	FLAME NETTLE
Convolvulus	MORNING GLORY
Consolida	LARKSPUR
Cynoglossum	CHINESE FORGET-ME-NOT
Dahlia	DAHLIA
Delphinium	LARKSPUR
Dianthus	PINK
Euphorbia	SPURGE
Gazania	PARKING LOT FLOWER
Gilia	BIRD'S EYES
Gomphrena	GLOBE AMA-RANTH
Heliotrope	CHERRY PIE
Hesperis	SWEET ROCKET
Hunnimannia	MEXICAN TULIP POPPY
Impatiens balsamina	BUSY LIZZIE
Impatiens linearifolia	NEW GUINEA IMPATIENS
Lavatera	MALLOW, ROSE MALLOW
Limonium	STATICE
Linaria	TOADFLAX
Linum	FLAX
Machaeranthera	TAHOKA DAISY
Matthiola	TEN-WEEK STOCK
Malope	MALOPE
Moluccella	BELLS OF IRELAND
Pelargonium	GERANIUM
Petunia	PETUNIA
Penstemon	BEARD TONGUE
Reseda	MIGNONETTE
Salpiglossis	PAINTED TONGUE
Salvia	SAGE
Scabiosa	PINCUSHION FLOWER
Tagetes	MARIGOLD
Zinnia	ZINNIA

Annuals That Dry Well for Winter Bouqets

Chrysanthemum
Gomphrena
Helichrysum
Limonium
Mollucella
Nigella
Scabiosa
Xeranthemum

Annuals That Require Light for Germination

Ageratum
Alyssum
Begonia
Browallia
Cleome
Coleus
Gaillardia
Godetia
Helichrysum
Impatiens
Moluccella
Nicotiana
Petunia
Portulaca

Annual Seeds That Prefer Light for Germination

Antirrhinum
Arctotis
Celosia
Cosmos
Matthiola
Mimulus
Tithonia
Torenia

Annual Seeds That Require Darkness for Germination

Nigella
Phlox
Viola

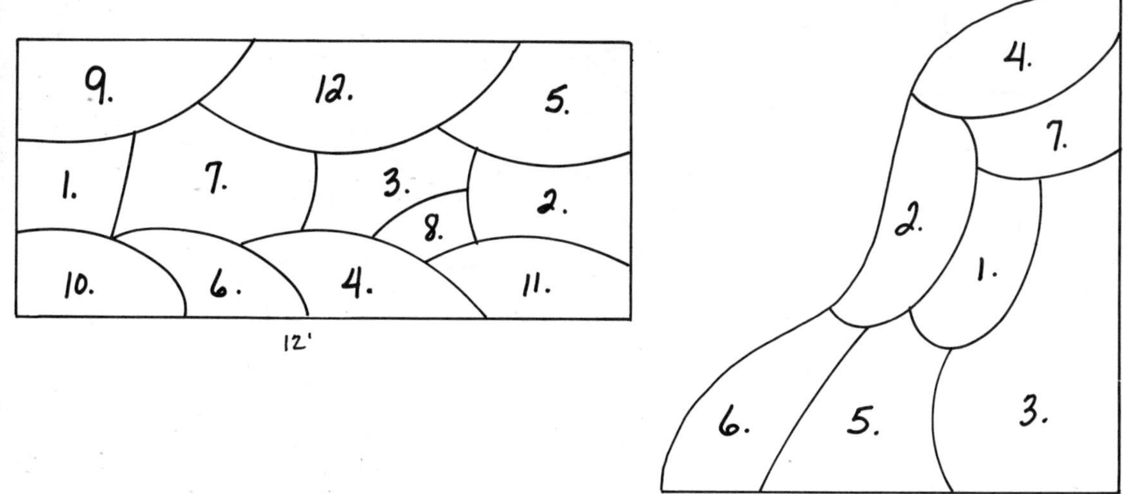

Dooryard Garden of Annuals

1. *Celosia argentea* - plumed Cocks Comb
2. *Ageratum houstonianum* - Floss Flower
3. *Tagetes* in variety - tall, Marigold
4. *Nasturtium* - dwarf, in variety
5. *Matthiola incana* - white stock
6. *Zinnia angustifolia* - dwarf, in variety
7. *Zinnia elegans* - tall, in variety

12 Vigorous, Foolproof Annuals

1. *Gypsophila elegans* - Baby's Breath
2. *Celosia argentea* - plumed Cocks Comb
3. *Dahlia x hybrida* - dwarf Dahlias
4. *Lobelia erinus* - "Blue Moon"
5. *Tagetes* - tall, in yellow varieties
6. *Phlox drummondi* - in variety
7. *Scabiosa atropurpurea* - pin cushion on flower
8. *Salvia farinacea* - 'Victory'
9. *Nicotiana 'Niki White'* - flowering tobacco
10. *Verbena hortensis* - 'Peaches 'n Cream'
11. *Lobularia, alyssum* - 'Wonderland Mixed'
12. *Zinnia elegans* - tall, Zinnias

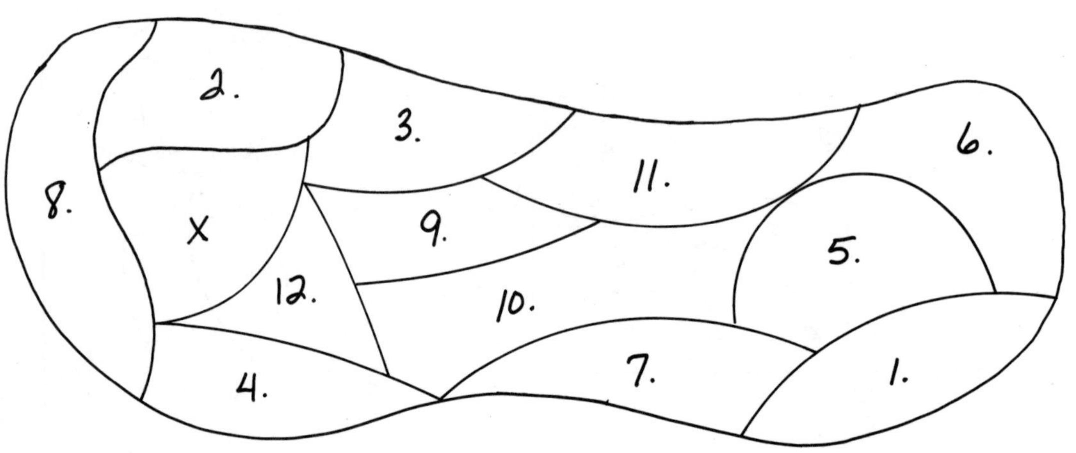

12 Unusual Annuals for an Island

1. *Arctotis stoechadifolia* - African Daisy
2. *Nemophila menziesii* - Baby Blue Eyes
3. *Phlox drummondi* - Annual Phlox
4. *Nierembergia caerulea* - Cup Flower
5. *Nemesia strumosa* - Nemesia
6. *Phacelia campanularia*- California Bluebell
7. *Callirhoe digitata* - Popy-mallow
8. *Salvia splendens* - Sage
9. *Moluccella laevis* - Bells of Ireland
10. *Malope trifida* - 'White Queen'
11. *Brachycome iberidifolia* - Swan River Daisy
12. *Salpiglossis sinuata* - Painted Tongue

X. *Amelanchier laevis* - Serviceberry Tree

CHAPTER 16

Groundcovers - Alternative to Turfgrass

Vast areas of turfgrass are outmoded. The water to keep it green, the will to mow it, and the money to purchase it are in short supply. Turf is enjoyable on playing fields and the passive areas of parks, but you need only one to two thousand square feet of quality turf to set off your foundation, your tree-and-shrub border, and to cool your summer view. It is generally accepted that not more than two thousand square feet of turf is needed to enhance even the grandest mansion.

There are often surfaces in your landscape, such as steep banks; hot, dry areas, or deep shade where groundcovers that can withstand these condtions are preferable to grass. There are a number of plants that will be suitable, but before you select a groundcover, decide upon the "look" that you want. Do you want a mat-former that knits together to become a sheet of green or a sheet of color, depending upon the season? Or would you prefer a groundcover that can withstand some foot traffic, such as one that would be planted between paving stones? Is there an immense area to be covered? Do you want to encourage or discourage foot traffic? Do you want one that spreads? Or one that is refined and dainty?

Next, assess the aspects of the areas that you want to cover. Is there sun or shade? Is it hilly or flat? If it is hilly, which direction does it face? How much water is available? Altitude and latitude, please. How much care do you wish to give? Must it be evergreen? After you have answered all of these questions, you may conclude that there is more to growing a groundcover that you thought, but don't be discouraged. There are plants for every conceivable situation.

■ . . . *don't be discouraged. There are plants for every conceivable situation.*

Groundcovers Under Six Inches

■ *Aethionema grandiflorum*,
PERSIAN STONECRESS. Full sun; steel-blue, needle-like foliage; pink flowers in May.
CULTIVAR:
'Warley Rose' - longer bloom period than species.

■ *Ajuga reptans*,
BUGLE. Sun or shade. Not agressive, but spreads quickly; blue spires of bloom in late spring.
CULTIVARS:
'Alba' - white blooms.

'Burgundy Glow' - leaves are reddish brown, green, and cream generously flushed with beet pink. If interplanted with Colchicum bulbs, will make a charming carpet in September.

'Silver Beauty' - gray-green foliage with patches of cream; needs shade.

■ *Antennaria rosea*,
PUSSYTOES. Full sun. Mat of gray rosettes; blooms are pinkish and resemble the pads on feline toes. Male and female plants; both attractive; drought tolerant.

■ *Anthemis nobilis*,
CHAMOMILE. An ancient carpeting plant from the Middle Ages. Sun or light shade; fragrant underfoot; yellow flowers intermittently.

■ *Arabis alpina*,
ROCKCRESS. Sun or dappled shade. Evergreen; thick gray-green leaves; white flowers in spring.
CULTIVARS:
'Pink' - candy-pink flowers.

'Snowcap' - vigorous; very dwarf.

. *Fernandi-Coburgi variegata*,
:n and white foliage; white flowers; spreads slowly; very dwarf.

■ *A. procurrens*, smaller scale, evergreen; part shade; drought tolerant.

■ *Arctostaphylos uva-ursi*,
KINNIKINICK. Sun or part shade; very good drainage required; acid soil preferred. True Westerners pronounce it "KINNY-kinick." Small round-leaved creeper; pink flagon-shaped blooms become red berries in fall. Very choice; slow.

■ *Arenaria verna caespitosa*,
MOSS SANDWORT. A good paving plant; prefers well-drained soil and full sun. Long-lived; tiny white flowers in spring.

■ *Calluna vulgaris*,
SCOTCH HEATHER. A fine tracery of leaves to cover acid soil under rhododendrons or azaleas; pink blooms in late summer. A covering of evergreen boughs in winter is needed.

■ *Coptis trifolia*,
GOLDTHREAD. Shiny evergreen carpet for acid soil under evergreens that have been limbed up. Waxy, white flowers in spring.

■ *Cytisus decumbens*,
BROOM. A creeping mat of nearly evergreen foliage; pale yellow or white blooms.
CULTIVAR:
'Vancouver Gold' - an introduction from the Univ. of British Columbia. Bright yellow flowers in May; no scent. Very slow.

☐ *Delosperma cooperi*,
PURPLE ICE PLANT. Succulent leaves of gray-green. Bright purple flowers in late summer. Not always hardy.

☐ *D. nubigenum*,
ICE PLANT. Bright green creeper that often becomes invasive. Never mulch it. Yellow star-like flowers in June. Foliage turns bright red in winter.

☐ *Euonymus kewensis*,
CREEPING EUONYMUS. Waxy evergreen foliage; does not climb; prefers part shade. Insignificant bloom.

☐ *Frageria vesca*,
CREEPING STRAWBERRY. Sun or shade. Lobed leaves; long runners root at the nodes; small red fruits sweet and tasty. This plant is suitable for historic sites.
CULTIVAR:
'Alpine' will grow at high altitude if there is snow cover in winter.

☐ *Galium odoratum*,
SWEET WOODRUFF. Delicate leaves; white star blooms in May; dappled shade; moist soil; somewhat invasive. Used in May wine in Europe.

☐ *Gypsophila repens*,
CREEPING BABY'S BREATH. Mound of minute leaves, slowly creeping; airy pink or white flowers in June.

☐ *Hedera helix*,
ENGLISH IVY. Evergreen creeper steeped in tradition and folklore. Sun or shade; will climb readily and must be kept under control.
CULTIVAR:
'Thorndale' is a vigorous cultivar.

■ *Houttuynia cordata variegata*,
CHAMELEON PLANT. Deep green, heart-shaped leaves edged in red, yellow, and white. Not reported to be invasive in the Mountain West, but watch it carefully. Prefers moist soil.

■ *Indigofera spp.* - a new prostrate creeper; very drought-tolerant; rose pea-like flowers.
CULTIVAR:
'Rose Carpet' - only cultivar marketed so far.

■ *Lamium maculatum*,
LAMIUM. Sprawling mats of variegated foliage with nestled blooms.
CULTIVARS:
'Silver Beacon' - foliage is silver and green; flowers bright lavender.

'Shell Pink' - very pale pink flowers.

'White Nancy' - white flowers.

■ *Lysimachia nummularia*,
CREEPING CHARLIE. A mat of round leaves that root at the node. Not always hardy. Protect with evergreen bough mulch in winter.
CULTIVAR:
'Aurea' - the only one to grow; yellow green foliage effective as a contrast plant or dripping over the edge of a container.

■ *Mentha requienii*,
CREEPING MINT. Sun or shade; prefers moist conditions; mossy effect, inconspicuous flowers.

■ *Pachysandra terminalis*,
PACHYSANDRA. Evergreen groundcover of the eastern United States and Canada where it is over-planted; prefers acid soil and shade. Sun and wind are its enemies.

■ *Paxistima myrsenites*,
OREGON BOXWOOD. Prostrate native of the montane zone; shiny, evergreen leaves; inconspicuous bloom; prefers acid soil; bronzy in winter.

■ *Phlox subulata*,
CREEPING PHLOX. Broad mats of needled foliage that is almost evergreen; sheets of color in May of every color except yellow. Sun or shade; can withstand shaded drought in summer. Plant under deciduous shrubs for bloom before the shrubs are in leaf. Investigate all the varieties.

■ *Potentilla tridentata*,
CINQUEFOIL. A creeper available with white flowers; low, glossy mat of three-lobed foliage; prefers acid soil.

■ *Saxifraga sarmentosa*,
STRAWBERRY GERANIUM. Not hardy in the northern range of this book. Lobed leaves; moist shade; pink buds and white flowers in June.

■ *Sedum acre*,
STONECROP. Sun, poor soil. Yellow flowers in June. Spreads rapidly.

■ *Sempervivum tectorum*,
HOUSE LEEK. Morning sun; very good drainage; sandy soil enriched with acid compost. Evergreen rosettes look like sculptures of soap. Many colors and named varieties available. Excellent for preventing erosion on a slight slope.

■ *Thymus spp.*,
THYME. The strewing herb of the Middle Ages. Still useful as a creeper between stepping stones. Emits strong odors when bruised. Lemon scented most effective. 'Woolly' is a fuzzy gray-green.

■ *Vinca minor*,
PERIWINKLE. Sun or shade. Strong, evergreen leaves; blue flowers in May. Somewhat invasive. Do not try to pull apart a clump to make root divisions. Plant the clump and it will spread quickly.

■ *Veronica liwanensis*,
CREEPING VERONICA. Sun. A mat of very small dark green foliage; a sheet of blue flowers in late May.

Groundcovers 6 Inches to 12 Inches

■ *Aegopodium podagraria variegatum*,
BISHIP'S WEED. For poor soil and dry shade where nothing else will grow. It is extremely invasive. Green and white foliage, white umbel flowers.

■ *Artemisia schmidtiana*,
SILVER MOUND ARTEMISIA.
A perfect globe of delicate gray foliage. Can withstand some shade, but prefers sun. Should be prevented from flowering.

■ *Asarum canadense*,
WILD GINGER. Round leaves, brown/purple flowers seldom seen. Spreads by rhizomes; can withstand deep shade; choice.

■ *Aubrieta deltoidea*,
AUBRIETA. Prefers sun; mound of green covered with lavender or deep purple flowers in May; shear after flowering.

■ *Bergenia cordifolia*,
HEART-LEAVED BERGENIA. Dappled shade; leaves shaped like paddles; evergreen; showy pink flowers in May.

■ *Brunnera macrophylla*,
DWARF ANCHUSA. Large, heart-shaped leaves and clusters of blue flowers at daffodil time. Ideal planted among them.

■ *Cerastium tomentosum*,
SNOW-IN-SUMMER. Delicate gray foliage becomes a sheet of white flowers for two weeks in June; shear after bloom; spreads rapidly. Tolerates sun, dry, poor soil.

■ *Ceratostigma plumbaginoides*,
BLUE PLUMBAGO. Shiny round foliage late to appear in spring. Brilliant blue flowers in August; bright red fall foliage. Spreads slowly.

■ *Convallaria majalis*,
LILY OF THE VALLEY. Spatulate leaves and sprigs of fragrant white bells in spring; prefers moist shade in spring, but drier soil in summer will prevent slug damage.

■ *Cornus canadensis*,
BUNCHBERRY. Native evergreen of the montane zone. Suitable for shady city gardens of manufactured acid soil. Contrasts well with ferns. White blooms in late spring. Order from eastern specialty catalogs.

■ *Coronilla varia*,
CROWN VETCH. Fast-growing, trailing mounds of small green leaves in summer; pink and white flowers; To prevent it from catching windblown trash in winter, mow or shear to six inches in November. Excellent erosion control. Set individual plants in deep planting "dishes" on a hillside and keep watered well the first year. Can then be maintained with natural precipitation if amounts are above eight inches April through October.

■ *Cotoneaster apiculatus*,
CRANBERRY COTONEASTER. Evergreen, creeping shrub; delicate tracery of foliage is attractive over the face of boulders. Big red berries last well. All cotoneasters resent transplanting.

■ *C. microphyllus* - diminutive version of above; suitable for a small rock garden.

■ *Daphne Cneorum*,
GARLAND FLOWER. A procumbent evergreen shrub for protected location away from wind. Narrow foliage; dense, fragrant heads of flowers in early summer, reblooming a little in fall.

■ *Dianthus spp.*
PINK. Needled gray-green foliage; some evergreen, but mats down under snow. Spicily fragrant flowers in pink, red, white, and yellow (*D. knapii*). Prefers gritty soil on the dry side.

■ *Epimedium x versicolor*,
BARRENWORT. Queen of groundcovers for dappled shade. Heart-shaped foliage topped in May by delicate scapes of flowers, each resembling a bishop's hat. Foliage turns red in fall and remains handsome all winter. Cut it back in March so that sunlight can reach the crown and flowers will appear. No insects or disease. Moist, acid soil preferred.

■ *Festuca ovina var glauca*,
BLUE FESCUE. An ornamental grass that forms oval mounds of ice blue; withstands heat and drought; buff colored flowers but no seed.

■ *Helianthemum nummularium*,
SUNROSE. Dwarf shrub of gray-green foliage and masses of round-petaled flowers in May and June. Yellow, apricot, white, red, lavender, and pink available.

■ *Hosta spp.*
PLANTAIN LILY. Broad, spatulate leaves in varying textures and shade of blue, green, green and white, chartreuse. Flowers in scapes of white, rose, or lavender in midsummer. Moist shade; protect from slugs.

■ *Ibiris sempervirens*,
CANDYTUFT. Evergreen narrow foliage; white flowers in May. Attractive with blue forget-me-nots and apricot tulips. Seeds around, but not invasively.

■ *Juniperus horizontalis*,
CREEPING JUNIPER. Premier evergreen groundcover for sun, wind, drought, and poor soil. Will do better, however, with good soil prepartion and a "dish" to hold water when planted on a hillside. Many colors of foliage available. Consider using several for a Persian carpet effect. It is the ideal hill-holder for prevention of erosion.

■ *Liriope spicata*,
LILY TURF. Strappy foliage; lavender spike blooms. Valuable for erosion and dust control in cities; not reliably hardy for northern reaches of this book.

■ *Myosotis alpestris*,
FORGET-ME-NOT. A charmer studded with incredible blue flowers in May and June; mounds of foliage remain for rest of season. Not long lived, but self sows.

■ *Primula spp.*,
PRIMROSE. Not a sturdy groundcover, but few can surpass it for effect in the spring garden. Prefers part shade at lower altitudes; full sun above 8,000 feet. Investigate the many species.

■ *Rosa spp.*,
TRAILING ROSES. Many species of climbers not hardy when trained on treillage are completely hardy as creepers. Plant at the top of banks to train downward. Bloom is outstanding when plants are planted thirty inches apart and sheared to promote twiginess until the plants are established. Good species to choose are:
CULTIVARS:
'Creeping rugosa'- red or pink varieties.

'Crimson Rambler' - orange-red blooms.

'Dorothy Perkins' - dainty pink blooms; very hardy.

'Max Graf' - pink blooms; often used in highway planting.

■ *R. wichuriana*,
MEMORIAL ROSE. Semi-evergreen trailer with clusters of pink flowers. Not reported to be invasive in the Mountain West. Roots at nodes, spreading slowly.

■ *Sanguinaria canadensis*,
BLOODROOT. Blue-green foliage, white flowers like miniature peonies; first to bloom in spring. Prefers acid soil; dislikes competition; spreads by rootstock.

■ *Saponaria ocymoides*,
SOAPWORT. Sun or part shade. Rapidly spreading dainty foliage; a sheet of pink flowers in early June.

■ *Stachys lanata*,
LAMB'S EARS. Thick, silver, furry foliage attractive with other colors and textures of foliage. Sun, rich soil preferred. Lavender spikes of bloom often removed to achieve uniform effect of foliage.

■ *Tiarella cordifolia*,
FOAM FLOWER. One of the best for moist soil and part shade. Light green leaves; dainty trusses of white flowers. Shows off best planted in a mass down a slight slope.
CULTIVAR:
'Wherryi' - a more prolific selection.

IF YOU KNOW ONLY THE COMMON NAME:

COMMON NAME	BOTANIC NAME
ANCHUSA, DWARF	*ANCHUSA*
ARTEMISIA	*ARTEMISIA*
AUBRIETA	*AUBRIETA*
BABY'S BREATH	*GYPSOPHILA*
BARRENWORT	*EPIMEDIUM*
BERGENIA	*BERGENIA*
BISHOPS' WEED	*AEGOPODIUM*
BLOODROOT	*SANGUINARIA*
BUNCHBERRY	*CORNUS*
CANDYTUFT	*IBIRIS*
CHAMOMILE	*ANTHEMIS*
CINQUEFOIL	*POTENTILLA*
COTONEASTER, CRANBERRY	*COTONEASTER*
CROWN VETCH	*CORONILLA*
DAPHNE	*DAPHNE*
EUONYMUS, CREEPING	*EUONYMUS*
FESCUE, BLUE	*FESTUCA*
FOAM FLOWER	*TIARELLA*
FORGET-ME-NOT	*MYOSOTIS*
GOLDTHREAD	*COPTIS*
HOUSE LEEK	*SEMPERVIVUM*
IVY	*HEDERA*
JUNIPER, CREEPING	*JUNIPERUS*
LAMB'S EARS	*STACHYS*
LAMIUM	*LAMIUM*
LILY TURF	*LIRIOPE*
MINT, CREEPING	*MENTHA*
MOSS SANDWORT	*ARENARIA*
PACHYSANDRA	*PACHYSANDRA*
PAXISTIMA	*PAXISTIMA*
PERIWINKLE	*VINCA*
PHLOX, CREEPING	*PHLOX*
PLANTAIN LILY	*HOSTA*
PLUMBAGO, BLUE	*CERATOSTIGMA*
PRIMROSE	*PRIMULA*
PUSSYTOES	*ANTENNARIA*
ROSE	*ROSA*
SNOW-IN-SUMMER	*CERASTIUM*
SOAPWORT	*SAPONARIA*
STONE CRESS	*AETHIONEMA*
STONECROP	*SEDUM*
STRAWBERRY, CREEPING	*FRAGERIA*
SUNROSE	*HELIANTHEMUM*
VERONICA, CREEPING	*VERONICA*
WOODRUFF, SWEET	*GALIUM*

CHAPTER 17

Rock Gardens

A rock garden in the Mountain West is a natural. Boulders and rocks are abundant, but by no means a given, even though volcanos, glaciers and streams have strewn rocks and boulders throughout the region. Volcanos were responsible for the greatest number of rocks and boulders, as well as for the soils of the Mountain West. U-shaped valleys signal that a glacier was present in the not-too-distant past. A "rock linc" will often be found on the valley floor or on the plain beyond where the glacier dropped or pushed boulders as it moved and melted. Roaring torrents carried a bed-load of rocks, smashing and wearing them to roundness, as they worked their way downward along the stream. Smooth cobble "river biscuits" line many rivers and creeks in the Mountain West, each resembling the sourdough biscuits of the early hard-rock miners. The river biscuits are somewhat exclusive in the Mountain West. The early miners would be amused to see them today serving a modern-day purpose as a foot-traffic barrier in parking lot medians or in curb-side danger zones. No one wants to risk a turned ankle by venturing to walk on them.

In a rock garden, boulders and stones are almost secondary to the plants; but their placement is critical to the success of the rock-alpine plants.

For the sake of aesthetics, it is recommended that boulders from only one geologic formation be used. If you study the rock-alpine plants in their native habitat, you see that, though the plant communities are varied, the rocks between and around them are of the same type in geologic time. Thus, lichen-covered rock, often known as "moss rock", would not combine with glittering, quartz-filled granite or sandstone slabs. Similarly, standing rocks, like Rover's tomb-stone, detract from the plants and appear unnatural. Stones and boulders with no distinguishing characteristics and no particular color will suit your purpose. The shape will depend upon whether there is an existing hill. Use every opportunity to study natural outcroppings to build a rock garden that is a small representation of a natural rock formation.

Site Selection

Decide first on the rock garden size that your property can accomodate. To be effective, it should be in an area by itself with background and flank plantings, such as an evergreen grouping to screen out conflicting views and give the desired effect of being a little piece of a mountain scene transplanted into your garden. The mound in the middle of the lawn stuuded with stones like almond pudding is unnatural and difficult to maintain. A slope facing north-east is the ultimate in rock garden siting, with the opposite, south-west, being the worst. The north-east selection will give you more likelihood of snow cover in winter that will protect plants from drying winds and fluctuating temperatures. Sunlight at noon in midsummer will be slanted to give plants warmth but not blistering heat, a condition approximating a natural site.

A site in full sun will give you the opportunity to grow the greatest diversity of plants, but don't overlook the possibilities of a shady site for a woodland rock garden where the rarest and most beautiful rock plants can be grown.

A hill or even a slight change of grade is not necessary (see Paving Stone Gardens) for a successful rock garden, but this lack means you will have to construct hillocks or mounds set with boulders. If the architecture of your home is compatible, stone walls can be constructed with pockets ready to receive the plants. Fortunate is the gardener who finds an old sunken stone foundation on his property, for a rock garden site has already been built for him.

A sunken garden is fitting for formal architecture.

Site Preparation

If turf is growing in the areas you have selected, rent a sod-cutter to remove it to put to composting. A gardener never discards soil. Stack it up-side-down in slabs in some out-of-the-way place. Remove any roots or tough weeds from the rock garden site, using a chemical, such as glyphosate, if necesary. Stoloniferous grass, Bishop's Weed (Aegopodium), and bindweed come to mind as the most pesky. Solarize the soil by laying clear plastic over the area and securing the edges tightly. This will bake the soil sufficiently to kill weeds as well as weed seed. This method takes three months during the heat of summer, however.

■ *. . . don't overlook the possibilities of a shady site for a woodland rock garden where the rarest and most beautiful . . . plants can be grown.*

A path through the rock garden is an essential amenity, for the plants are small and will require close viewing. A seat from which to enjoy the scene and rest the gardener's weary bones will be appreciatated. A small pool is a natural addition to the rock garden. Building the rock garden and pool at the same time can be a pleasant springtime project. See Chapter 19 "The Water Garden."

■ *It is unlikely there are many communities in the Mountain West that are far from a stone quarry.*

Boulders and Stones

Use the largest boulders to form the base. It is important they they should be placed so as to lie in the same direction, with the heaviest and broadest side downward. In addition, each boulder is placed *so that it slopes backward.* Rain and melt-water will trickle back into a slope, thus watering the roots of plants, and soil will not be washed away to unseat the boulders.

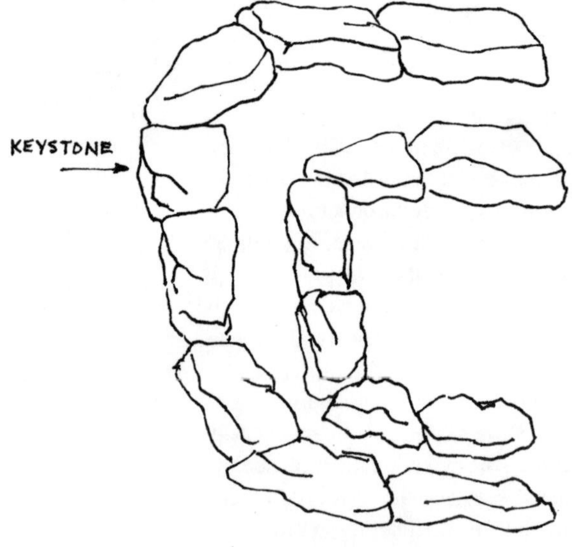

Position boulders to tip back into a slope so that water will trickle backward to water plant roots instead of washing soil away to unseat the boulder.

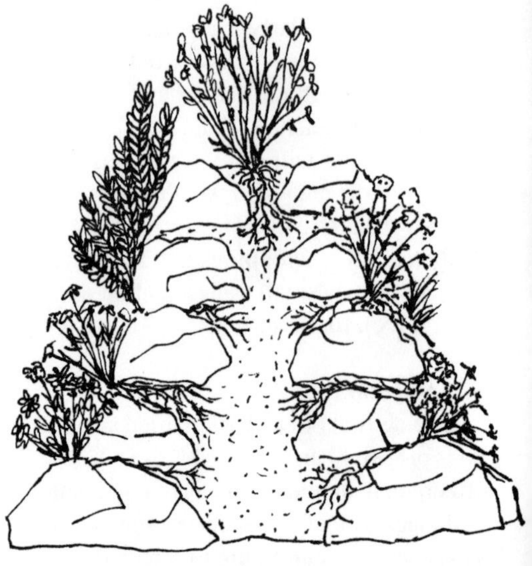

Stone walls without mortar, known as dry walls, are not difficult to construct with cut sandstone, broken concrete, or stones selected from a quarry.

It is unlikely there are many communities in the Mountain West that are far from a stone quarry. If stone is not available or if it is expensive in your community, consider using broken concrete. When concrete is broken up for hauling away, the concrete saw or jack-hammer breaks it into pieces of turkey-platter size. This material has every criteria for a rock garden. It has two flat sides and each piece is of uniform thickness. It is non-descript. It will have an alkaline reaction, which many rock plants need. It is easy to carry and form into a wall planted with rock-alpines. Free-standing walls are especially attractive of this material and can become a section of the perimeter boundary between you and your neighbors.

Moving stone and boulders is heavy work. Learn to use a steel bar as a lever to position a boulder. A piece of canvas and a

A way to move stone without strain.

scoop shovel or child's sled can become a way to drag a stone. Building a tripod for swinging a rock into place is a principle of physics that will serve you. Move the tripod after each swing of the stone.

Take the time to dig a depression to receive the boulder so that one-third of its dimension is underground. It will then look like its been there for centuries.

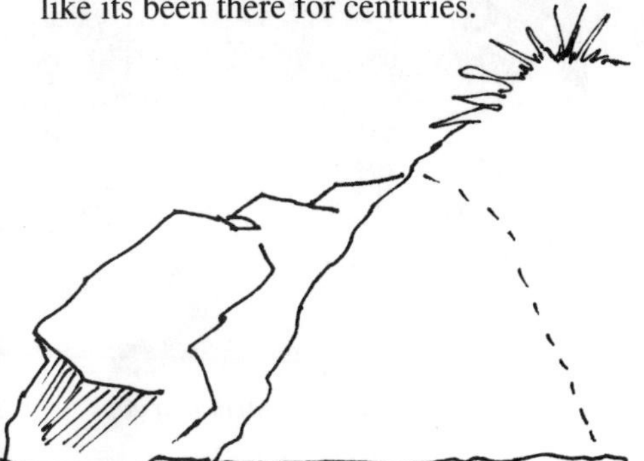

A seated boulder looks like it has been there for centuries.

Soil Preparation

As with all phases of gardening, the success depends upon the soil preparation. With rock gardening, the main element is drainage, for in nature alpine showers are sudden and brief, sometimes several times daily, but the water runs off through gravelly grit that is of low fertility. Organic matter, though seldom present in any great quantity in nature, is important in the home garden, with home-generated compost being the best. Well-weathered manure or sphagnum peatmoss is acceptable.

Rock Garden Soil Mix

- 1/4 clay soil
- 1/4 compost, weathered manure, or sphagnum peatmoss
- 1/4 sharp pea gravel
- 1/4 coarse sand or chicken grit

Tamp the soil mix in place; then water it in to eliminate air pockets. If you are planning to use a stone wall in your rock garden, plant as you build it. Positioning the roots back into the crevice is far easier than trying to stuff them into a crevice later on.

The Paving Stone Garden

Sometimes a rock garden will not fit anywhere within a home landscape; yet the gardener, if determined, will find a place. Such a site is the crevices between stones in a patio or path. Leaving a space for plants is a charming setting for rock plants. Since most stone or concrete pavers are set into sand and grit, the soil mix is ideal for many of the choice rock plants.

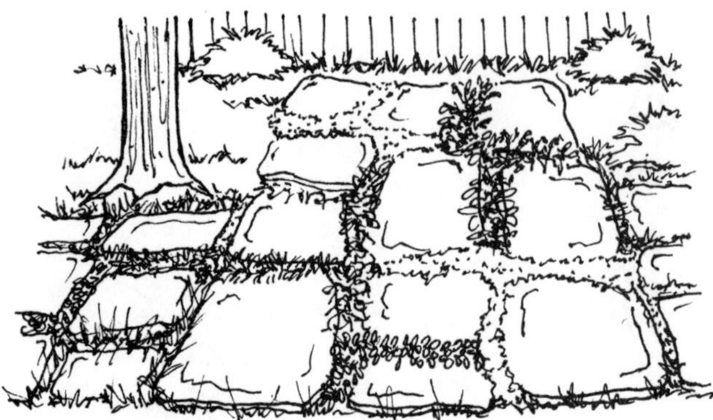

Planting among the stones of a patio or path is an ideal setting for choice rock plants.

A small area around a tree, such as a maple that has troublesome surface roots, is a practical way to show off shade-loving rock plants and the "river biscuits" of the area. The stones will protect the tree trunk from "lawnmoweritis" as an added benefit.

A multi-purpose planting for shade-loving rock plants with the smooth-textured "river biscuits." The tree is protected from "lawnmoweritis" as well.

The Trough Garden

The gardener with no garden is in a lamentable but not insurmountable situation. Movable troughs are sold at nurseries and from rock garden society plant sales. These are made of a special mix of concrete, peatmoss, and various other organic materials to resemble the ancient stone troughs used in the Middle Ages as household sinks and stock-watering vessels. The pseudo-troughs meet the qualifications for rock plants. Select a trough for planting the rarest and most difficult, the smallest and most exquisite. Wood blocks or lengths of concrete pipe will raise the trough within close viewing distance. Select different forms, such as rectangular, square, and round troughs for the best display. Troughs are also ideal for planting rock plants that may be of doubtful hardiness in your area. You can tote them to a cool basement, garage or lath house for the winter, but don't forget they will need watering at least monthly.

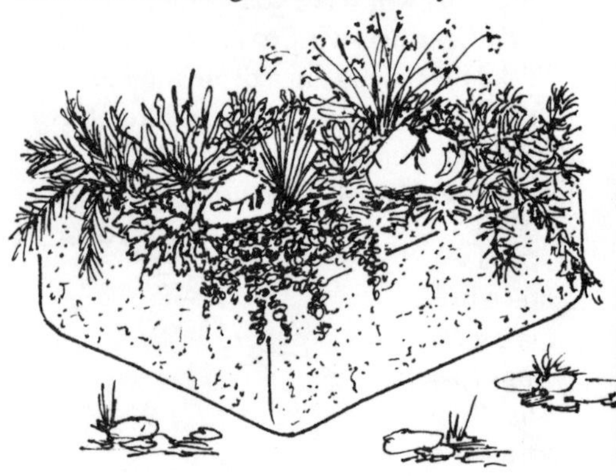

Trough gardens offer the gardener a way to have a rock garden on an apartment balcony.

Culture

Because the soil mixture is fast-draining, rock gardens require frequent watering, but not in great amounts. Drip systems are recommended, and can be installed before plantings are made. If the surface is level, the porous hose can be installed just under the soil surface, giving all plants an equal amount of water. If certain sections of the rock garden, or certain plants require less water, they should be grouped together.

Fertilization is controversial, with one faction swearing by the slow-release type fertilizer. Others prefer spring/fall applications of a high phosphorous fertilizer. Still others believe that fertilization of any kind, other than that of the organic matter added to the soil mix, will produce soft, watery growth that is unattractive as well as tender during a hard winter. Experience with your own rock garden will produce the results you want.

Transplanting is controversial also, but general agreement points toward August as the month for dividing and transplanting of plants. This gives each plant time for root establishment before cold weather. Planting of new plants is often in spring when plant societies and nurseries have more rock/alpine plants available.

Weeding will always be with us. Hand weeding on hands and knees is the usual method for rock gardens, but it may produce more interest than one might think. As you weed, you will find that your choice babies have made babies! Finding a small seedling among the weeds always brings a smile and a calculating thought, "Shall I give it away to a friend, or save it to trade for one I don't have at the Rock Garden Society plant exchange?"

Growing plants from seed will be the most satisfying way to stock your rock garden, and, of course, the cheapest. Join the American Rock Garden Society to take part in the annual seed exchange and receive a quality quarterly journal that will give you tips on growing from seed and cuttings.

Topdressing a rock garden with very fine gravel is a generally accepted practice. It not only gives uniformity to the planting, but it conserves moisture and prevents erosion.

Plant Selection

A rock garden of any size needs a few woody plants to give backbone to the planting. A collection of dwarf evergreens is appropriate also. Consider dwarf deciduous shrubs like *Nandina domestica nana* (Dwarf Heavenly Bamboo), or *Cotoneaster apiculata* 'Tom Thumb' (Cranberry Cotoneaster). The plants that will give the most satisfaction and the feel of a mountain scene will be the low, the dwarf, the creeping, and the bun-like plants that withstand the extreme hardship conditions of the tundra and upper Montane zone. Your garden will soon have plants that represent these zones from all over the world.

■ *A rock garden of any size needs a few woody plants to give backbone to the planting.*

The following lists are presented to get you started in the fascinating hobby of rock gardening. You will progress in stages, from the desire to have something pretty blooming in your rock garden at all times during the growing season to becoming the connoisseur of the exquisite plants available from the alpine regions throughout the world.

Bulbs

The minor bulbs can be accomodated in any type of rock garden. They are the tiny natives of Asia Minor, and also considered minor in significance by the bulb growers. Use them in groups of six or a dozen. Choose from the species tulips that bloom earlier than deciduous trees leaf out, as well as from the miniature daffodils, grape hyacinths, crocus, snowdrops, snowflakes, bulbous iris, and the summer-blooming lily, *Lilium tenuifolium*. Foliage of all the minor bulbs matures quickly and won't spoil the later display of your rock plants.

A Beginner's List of Rock Plants for at Least Four Hours of Sun in Spring & Summer

(Rock Gardeners pride themselves on speaking Latin only)

NAME	COLOR	HT.	FLOWERS IN
Acantholimon glumaceum	pink	6"	June/July
Achillea ageratifolia	white	3"	May/June
Aethionema 'Warley Rose'	pink	4"	May/June
Alyssum serpyllifolium	yellow	1"	April/May
Anacyclus depressus	white	3"	April/June
Androsace sempervivioides	pink	3"	April/June
Antennaria dioica 'Nyewood'	red	3"	June/July
Aquilegia saximontana	blue	7"	April/July
Arabis caucasica 'Snow Cap'	white	6"	April/June
A. ferdinandi-coburgi 'Variegata'	white	1"	April/May
Arenaria montana	white	5"	May/June
Armeria maritima	pink	4'	April/July
Aster alpinus	lav	8"	May/June
Aubrieta deltoidea	purple	3"	April/June
Aurinia saxatilis	yellow	12"	May/June
Campanula cochlearifolia	blue	3"	June/August
C. portenschlagiana	blue	3"	June/July
C. poscharskyana	blue	5"	June/August
Centaurea uniflora	lav	6"	May/June
Cerastium tomentosum 'Yoyo'	white	6"	June/July
Ceratostigma plumbaginoides	blue	10"	Aug/Sept.
Cheiranthus allionii	orange	12"	April/May
Delosperma cooperi	purple	1"	May/Oct
D. nubigenum	yellow	1"	April/June
Dianthus deltoides	pink	8"	May/June
D. erinaceus	pink	2"	June/July
D. simulans	pink	2"	May/June
Draba brunifolia	yellow	3"	March/April
D. rigida	yellow	3"	March/April
Erigeron chrysopsidis 'Grand Ridge'	yellow	3"	April/Oct
Eriogonum flavum	yellow	6"	May/June
Erisimum kotschyanum	yellow	3"	May/June
Gentiana septemfida	blue	10"	July/August
G. sino-ornata	blue	3'	July/August
Geranium dalmaticum	pink	5"	June/July
G. 'Johnson's Blue'	blue	15"	May/July
Globularia trichosantha	blue	9"	May/June
Gypsophila repens 'Rosea'	pink	7"	May/June
Helianthemum x nummullarium	many	10"	May/June

NAME	COLOR	HT.	FLOWERS IN
Ibiris sempervirens	white	10"	May/June
Iris pumila	many	3"	March/April
I. setosa v. canadensis	purple	8"	May
Lavandula angustifolia 'purpurea nana'	lav	10"	June/July
Lewisia cotyledon	pink	12"	May/June
Papaver alpinum	many	5"	May/August
Penstemon angustifolius	blue	10"	April/May
P. teucrioides	blue	1"	May/June
P. virens	blue	10"	April/May
Phlox bifida 'Betty Blake'	white	3"	May/June
P. b. 'Colvin's White'	white	3"	May
P. 'Laura'	pink	3"	May/June
Psilotrophe bakeri	yellow	12"	May/August
Rosularia aizoon	yellow	6"	MayJune
Saponaria pumilio	pink	2"	April/May
Saxifraga aizoon minutae	white	1/2"	June
S. caespitosa 'Purple Robe'	red	7"	April/June
Scabiosa graminifolia	lav	6"	June/August
Sedum kamtschaticum variegatum	orange	3"	June/July
S. spathulifolium 'Cape Blanco'	yellow	3"	May/June
Sempervivum arachnoideum	*	2"	-0-
S. jovibarba 'Chocoletto'	*	2"	-0-
S. tectorum, many varieties	*	2"	-0-
Silene acaulis	pink	1"	April/May
S. hookeri	red	3"	April
S. schafta	pink	3"	July/Sept.
Sisyrinchium montanum	blue	8"	May/June
Thymus 'Porlock'	lav	8"	June/Aug.
Townsendia grandiflora	white	4"	May/June
Veronica armena	blue	3"	May/June
V. liwanensis	blue	1"	April/June
V. pectinata	blue	3"	April/June
Viola corsica	blue	5"	March/Oct.
Zauschneria californica subsp. arizonica	red	7"	July/Oct.

** Not grown for flowers*

A Beginner's List of Rock Plants for Dappled Shade

NAME	COLOR	HT.	FLOWERS IN
Anemone nemerosa	white	5"	April/May
Aquilegia bertolonii	blue	5"	May/June
Asarum europaeum	brown	4"	June/July
Asplenium scolopendrium 'marginatum'	-0-	10"	
Bergenia cordifolia	pink	14"	April/May
Calluna vulgaris, many varieties	many	4"	Aug/Sept.
Campanula rotundifolia	blue	9"	May/Oct.
Corydalis lutea	yellow	9"	May/Oct
Dicentra eximia	pink	9"	May/July
Dodocatheon pulchellum	pink	12"	May/June
Doronicum orientale	yellow	12"	April/May
Epimedium alpinum	red	10"	May/June
E. rubrum	red-white	6"	May/June
E. sulphureum	yellow	6"	May/June
Galium odoratum	white	4"	May/June
Helleborus foetidus	green	18"	Feb/May
Hosta 'Gold Drop'	lav	8"	July
H. 'Rock Princess'	lav	6"	July
Lamium maculatum 'Silver Beacon'	lav	4"	May/Oct
L.m. 'White Nancy'	white	4"	May/Oct
Mimulus cardinalis	red	8"	July/August
Myosotis alpestris	blue	6"	April/June
Phlox stolonifera	pink/blue	8"	June/July
Polemonium reptans	blue	10"	April/June
Primula auricula	many	6'	April/May
P. denticulata	pink	8"	March/April
P. cashemeriana	maroon	8"	April
P. marginata	blue	4"	April/May
Pulmonaria angustifolia 'Mrs. Moon'	pink/blue	6"	April/May
Saxifraga x 'Mossy Variegated'	white	6"	May/June
Tiarella cordifolia	white	12"	April/May

Suggested information sources

American Rock Garden Society
P.O. Box 67, Millwood, N.Y. 10546
Annual membership $25, quarterly journal and seed exchange participation included.

Rocky Mountain Chapter of American Rock Garden Society
Treasurer, Jim Lawrence
Box 304, Jamestown, CO 80455.
Annual membership, individual $7.50, household $10.00. Meetings: every third Wednesday,
7:30 P.M. at Denver Botanic Garden
909 York, Denver, except November, December, May, June, July, August.

Suggested Reading

"Alpine Garden Plants",
by Will Ingwersen,
Blanford Press,
Dorset, England 1981

"Rock Gardens",
by William Schacht,
Universe Books,
New York, 1981

CHAPTER 18

Azaleas and Rhododendrons

Growing azaleas and rhododendrons in the Mountain West requires extra effort. Make sure you are up to this project before you begin, for plants thrown hastily into our alkaline soils will lead to sure disappointment. The reason azaleas and rhododendrons are not seen growing in many landscapes of the Mountain West is that they are found in the acid soil regions of the U.S. and Canada.

Almost all soils west of the Mississippi River are alkaline. The Mississippi River is known as the "Lime Line" because the high acid soils of the East where agricultural lime must be added to keep the soil somewhere near neutral (pH of 7.0) end at the river, and those west of the river are alkaline (above 7.0 pH). There are a few pockets of acid soil in the West, such as in the coastal areas of Oregon and Washington, and in all of the sphagnum peat bog areas of Canada . Contrary to popular belief, the peat-sedge bogs of the Mountain West in the United States are all alkaline.

Site

To choose the best site for azaleas and rhododendrons on your property, take one full year to chart the path of the sun as it strikes each area. If you have lived on your property for a long time, this may not be necessary because you are very familiar with the shady and sunny places at different seasons of the year. For the most part the azaleas we can grow in the Mountain West are deciduous, but they need spring and summer sun in the morning or late afternoon, but not at noon. Rhododendrons, on the other hand, are almost all evergreen, but need some morning sun in spring and early summer. Winter shade is essential for the same reason we wear sunglasses all winter - the winter sun in the Mountain West is relentless, and though not hot, it can scald the leaves of a broadleaf evergreen, such as the rhododendron because of its drying action.

Often the best site for rhododendrons is a north-facing foundation of your home where there is no root competition from other trees or shrubs. The best site for azaleas may be in the front of a mixed shrub border, despite the root competition. Planting either under a limbed-up spruce, pine, fir, or juniper is a dubious practice because the roots of these evergreens are extremely close to the soil surface and would be fierce competitors for water and nutrients needed by the rhododendrons.

Soil

Soil must be amended to a pH of below 6.0. The best amendment is oak-leaf compost or one made of fruit tree leaves, liquid coffee and coffee grounds. It is difficult to make an oak-leaf compost in less than two years, for the leaves are tough and leathery and slow to break down. Chopping the leaves will hasten the breakdown, but not much. Sphagnum peatmoss is also an acidifier, and easily available. Don't believe all the advertising blurbs about soil sulfur. It is very slow to change the pH of a sandy clay or a silt clay soil.

Use a two-thirds measure of sphagnum peatmoss added to soil loosened from the chosen site if there is no acid compost available. Carry off two-thirds of the soil you have removed to be used elsewhere. Mix the peat into the one-third soil you have left to create a raised bed about three inches in height. This will give the drainage needed by the rhododendrons and azaleas.

Hopefully, you are preparing the soil in mid-summer so that it will settle. The compost organisms will continue to work as long as you keep the newly-made bed moist.

A newly-made bed for rhododendrons or azaleas is raised about three inches for good drainage.

Selection of Plants

Choosing rhododendrons for the Mountain West will seem like a backward process, but it's the only way to guarantee success. First, secure a catalog from a well-known western grower. Second, with paper and pencil, jot down all those listed that are able to withstand a winter temperature of minus twenty-five degrees below zero. The list will be pitifully short. Next, jot down those able to withstand minus-fifteen. This list will cheer you somewhat.

Now, find those from your lists with bloom periods after May 15. Once again, the list is short. Lastly, choose colors that bloom at the same time that are compatible. Red and purple won't find many supporters, nor will yellow and maroon. In the mountains where snow cover can be expected to lie deep all winter, the list lengthens of those that can be planted. The miniature rhododendrons in the rock-alpine display garden at Vail, Colorado, are gaining international fame. The mail-order and local nursery sources of rhododendrons and azaleas increase each year.

Cost

Cost of the plants is often a surprise, but remember, these plants take a long time to grow from a cutting or seed. Budget deals are often found if you order five or more of the same cultivar. Small-size plants (six to eight inches) are often less than fifteen dollars.

Culture

After you have chosen the site, amended the soil, and ordered the plants, you will anxiously await the plants, which will arrive bare-root and carefully wrapped, or in one-gallon pots. Experts agree that combing out some of the roots will give the plants a better start. This means knocking the plant out of the pot and immersing the root ball in a tub of warm water and literally combing the roots away from the soil or peat media in which it is growing. Use your fingers to gently loosen the roots until at least one inch of the tender roots are free from the root ball. Make haste to cover the bare roots with a damp cloth when you carry the plant to the planting hole.

Build a hill within the hole on which to prop the plant so that two inches of the rootball is above the grade of the hole; then sift the backfill soil around the fragile roots until the hole is half full. Run water gently into the hole to drive out pockets of air before completing the backfill. Mulch with pine needles, making sure that the roots that were left above the soil level are covered; soak the area thoroughly. The plant will sink gradually and the two-inch area of roots above-ground will be covered.

The soil of the beds should never be allowed to dry completely, but soggy roots are also a danger. Let your fingers be your guide. Make a vertical hole with your trowel and test the bottom of the hole for moisture with your fingers. Increase the humidity around the plants on a hot July day with a light misting from the hose.

Fertilization is controversial. Chemical fertilizers, such as Miracid, have been successful, but some experts believe that a mulch of composted pine needles is the best. A pine needle mulch will never break down satisfactorily. You must make a separate compost pile of pine needles, soil, fresh manure (preferably rabbit), and water to make a pine needle compost. Let it break down for a year.

Timing of fertilization application is important. New growth begins immediately after flowering. If you have decided to fertilize, dissolve it in water according to directions and pour it around the root run of each plant. Buds are formed in fall.

After flowering, careful cutting of the spent bloom is needed to prevent the plant from making seed. Take care not to cut into the new growth that forms around each bloom.

Winter protection is up to you. Left unprotected, the leaves of rhododendrons curl, but many varieties take on a beautiful bronzy red color. Winter watering is essential in periods when snow cover is absent.

There is no doubt that rhododendrons will bloom best if there is a lightweight frame over them in winter to protect them from drying wind and fluctuating temperatures, but that may not be the look you want for the landscape of your home from November to April each year. They will survive and bloom without the frame.

Don't try to protect them by shoveling snow around and over them, for the weight will break branches. Placing a "fence" of evergreen boughs in front of them will protect them from windburn and help to collect snow around them.

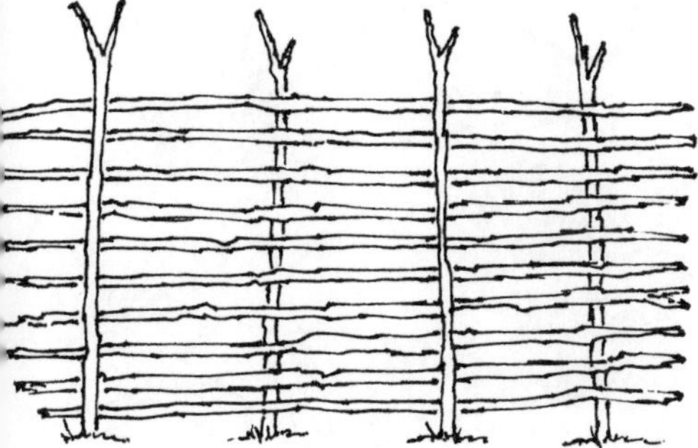

A wattle-fence woven from pliant willow branches will protect rhododendrons in winter and will last for several winters.

A protective cover is held together with screws for easy storage in summer.

Size

The ultimate size of a rhododendron in the Mountain West is a shocker. Don't expect the twenty foot giants you've seen in western Oregon or in Mississippi. The average height that can be expected at maturity is about four feet in five to seven years. Expected width is about the same. Azaleas will be somewhat smaller, but we have no knowledge of ultimate height of the new cultivars that have been bred at the University of Minnesota, and which are proving to be satisfactory in our area. These are the Northern Lights series, and reports are excellent of their bloom rate and survival. Plant your rhododendrons and azaleas close enough so that branches will touch within five years for the best display.

Insects and Disease

The climate of the Mountain West may not be the best for rhododendrons and azaleas, but we are way ahead of other areas in lack of insects and diseases that can attack them. There are NONE. Besides being a wonder to behold at bloom time, they give the gardener a sense of one-upmanship that is needed in this land of hardship and plant failure.

Suggested Gardens to Visit

Denver Botanic Garden
909 York St., Denver, CO. From I-25 take the 6th Ave. Exit east to Josephine St.; north 1/2 mile to parking.
Entrance Fee: $5.00

Rock/Alpine Garden, Vail, CO. Hwy I-70 from Denver (east) or Grand Junction (west). Exit 176 will lead to parking at the tennis club. Walk down the asphalt path to the Gerald Ford outdoor theater, the rock/alpine garden, and the Betty Ford Garden. No Fee.

Suggested Catalog Sources

Greer Gardens
1280 Goodpasture Island Road
Eugene, OR 97401-1794
Cost: $3.00

Forestfarm
990 Tetherow Road
Williams, OR 97544-9599
Cost: $3.00

CHAPTER 19

Water Garden

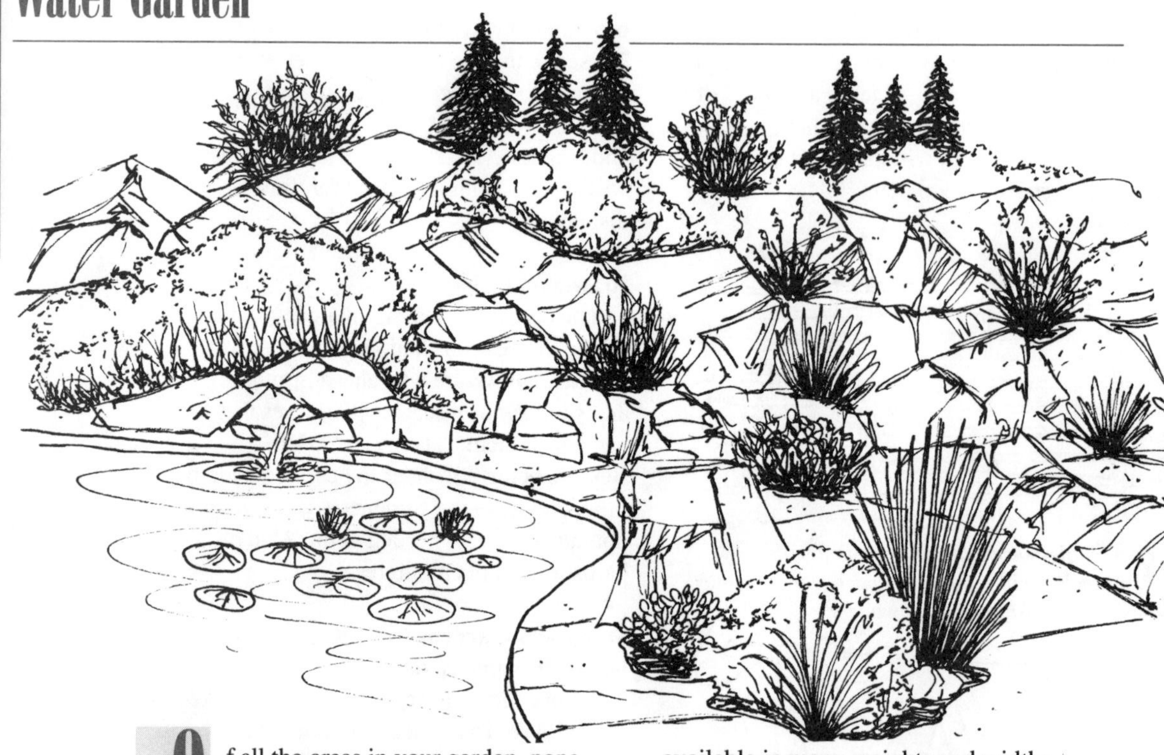

Of all the areas in your garden, none will give you more enjoyment with less work than the water garden. In this arid land the sight and sound of water is a luxury. The darting fish and dragon flies, birds taking a morning bath, the song of frogs at evening, the wonder of the unfolding lilies, the sound of water trickling into a cloud-reflecting pool - all this is a restful scene. A gardener needs a place to sit down without guilt to take in the fruits of his labors. Yet a lily pool, after initial installation and filling, takes much less work than other garden areas and uses no more water than the amount used in brushing your teeth daily.

Construction Materials

No longer is concrete used in pool construction, nor is it necessary to have a drain. Polyvinyl chloride, known as PVC, is available in many weights and widths. High-density polyethylene (HDPE) costs less than PVC but is not as flexible. Butyl rubber film is very flexible, but at a forty to fifty mil weight, can be very difficult to cope with when one is pushing the liner into corners of the pool. The thirty mil PVC comes in sizes up to thirty feet wide; the others in twenty foot widths. Make your choice and call a retail dealer in these materials. They are accustomed to dealing with municipalities who need acres of these materials with which to line reservoirs, but they are, nevertheless, very courteous to small-time gardeners. Nurseries and garden centers carry water garden kits, but the cost will be greater.

Pre-formed fiberglass pools are available in small sizes, and can be ordered in larger sizes.

Also needed in the construction of your pool will be an edging material. The Mountain West has an abundance of dealers in stone pavers, concrete block and boulders. Keep in mind that lichen-covered stone is not recommended for an area where there will be foot traffic, for the lichen will be worn away.

Site Planning

Since water tends to run downhill, the place your water garden will look most natural is at the base of a slope, provided this place receives at least six hours of full sun each summer day. But what if your lot is flatter than Kansas? You have three choices: (1) Place your pool at the edge of your deck or patio so that one edge of the pool is slightly UNDER it. No one but you will know that there is NOT a large body of water under your deck or patio, and the pool will become an integral part of your outdoor recreation area. The close proximity of this pool to your chaise lounge will give you more opportunity to watch the antics of pool life than any other site. (2) You can construct an illusion of a change in grade by placing your pool where the earth removed from the site will form a background rock garden, with, perhaps, a waterfall. Additionally, evergreens planted behind the earth and rock mound will further disguise and make it part of the landscape. (3) A third possibility as a site for a lily pool is directly adjoining an island planting. The edge of the pool that adjoins the planting will give both the planting and the pool a natural look.

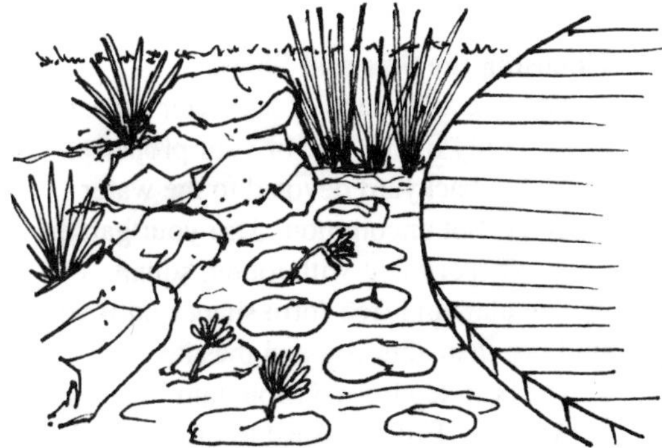

A lily pool with one edge slightly under the edge of deck or patio will give you the best view.

■ *No one but you will know that there is NOT a large body of water under your deck or patio.*

Faced with a flat lot, the lily pool with a rock garden on one edge will give the most natural effect.

A pool edge adjoining an island planting of ornamental grasses, shrubs, and small flowering trees lends informality to a large landscape.

The pool is now ready for coping with the material of your choice. Extend the coping stones or concrete pavers an inch or two over the pond edge to conceal the liner as well as to shade it from ultra-violet rays.

Wait a week after the pool is filled before installing plants, fish, or snails. This is to allow for evaporation of chemicals used in treating municipal water supplies. Use this time to finish planting the rock garden or island planting adjoining the pool. As you plant evergreens, the mound will look more natural. Deciduous trees are not encouraged, for leaf-fall is the only troublesome period in pool maintenance.

Planting the Pool

■ *The colors and kinds of water lilies are spectacular.*

Plastic buckets and dishpans are the standard containers for water lilies. Spring plant sales are the best place to buy water lilies, for their price is not cheap, and you can always find a bargain in a named variety at a neighborhood or botanic garden plant sale.

The colors and kinds of water lilies are spectacular. The majority of those you choose will be hardy, but in a year or two you may want to investigate the tropical water lilies, especially the night-bloomers if you are gone all day.

The soil used for planting water lilies is the heaviest clay you can find. The mineral nutrients in the clay are needed by the lilies, and the heaviness is needed to prevent fouling of the water. Do not use commercial potting soil. It is mixed with peatmoss and perlite, which will float to the water surface. Plant each tuber in a separate tub, slightly off-center. Push one lilytab (waterlily fertilizer) into the soil near, but not touching, the tuber. Cover with soil, and topdress with at least one inch of pea gravel. Hold the tub over the spot where you want the tub to be placed. Allow it to fill with water before lowering it gently to the bottom. Purchase enough lilies so that their pads (leaves) will cover sixty percent of the water surface. You want some area of open water to reflect clouds and sky.

Install in pots of sand bunches of an oxygenating grass (purchased at a pet store), such as Anacharis (*Elodea canadensis var. gigantea*) or Cabomba (*Cabomba caroliniana*). *Myriophyllum spp.* is also available at pet stores and is useful when fish are spawning. You will need one bunch of oxygenating grass for each square foot of water surface. Place the grass pots on the bottom of the pool where they will not be shaded by water lily pads. All of the above oxygenating grasses are hardy and will begin growing each summer in your pool as soon as the weather is settled and the water warms. High altitude pool owners can save a pot or two in a tub over the winter, or re-stock it in their pools every summer.

The purpose of the oxygenating grasses is to furnish oxygen for the fish and snails. The fish respire carbon dioxide for the benefit of the plants; thus the pool is balanced.

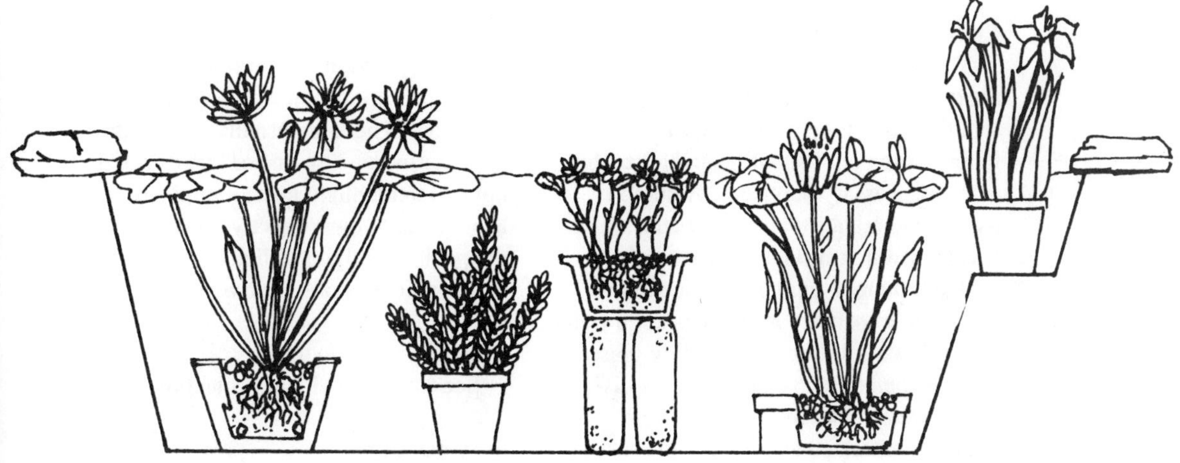

Diagram of a planted lily pool.

Fish and Other Water Creatures

Goldfish are the easiest, most undemanding pets you may ever have. They add depth and motion to the pool. If you are a beginning water-gardener, leave the exhibition Koi and fancy fantails for a year or two down the road to determine if you will want the expense and time-consuming care of them. Buy little one-inch Comet goldfish (about six cents each), and buy no more than one inch of fish for each three-to-five gallons of water. The little Comets school nicely and grow to five to six inches by the end of summer.

There are 7.5 gallons of water in a cubic foot. Therefore multiply 7.5 x number of cubic feet to find the number of gallons.

To find the number of cubic feet: For a rectangle: length x width x depth = number of cubic feet. For a circle: 3.14 x (1/2 diameter x 1/2 diameter) x depth = number of cubic feet.

The snails come in various kinds. Japanese trap-door snails are excellent and are fast breeders, but other kinds available at the pet store will serve as well. For a pool surface of twenty to thirty square feet, you will need fifteen snails. This is usually a life-time investment, as they live over from year to year.

The Creeping Crud

About three weeks after your pool is finished and lilies, fish, snails and oxygenating grasses are installed, you will awake one morning to find your pool in bloom. Sad to say, this does not mean a riot of colorful blooms. It means it is covered with green muck (algae). What to do? Nothing! It will take about three more weeks for the pool to balance itself, and you will awake again one morning to find that the water is clear. Do not drain and refill the pool; feed the fish only every third day; do not add water.

■ *. . . you will awake again one morning to find that the water is clear.*

If Algae Does Not Clear

If weather is very warm and there has been a contamination of the pool, sometimes algae refuses to clear. Use a chemical purchased at the pet store or at #1 source listed at the end of this chapter. It is called "Acurel-E." Also effective are: Algimycin PLL, Deep Water, and Anchors Away.

Pumps and Filters

The appearance of the "bloom" also spurs the purchase of a filter. This purchase will filter all of the water every two to six hours, taking out fish waste and algae, but it is an unnecessary purchase. A pump is used to recirculate water in a waterfall. A trickle of water through the rocks of your background rock garden is a nice touch. However, a roaring torrent does not a water garden make! Lilies, oxygenating grass, and fish cannot withstand violently disturbed water. The lilies and grass are gradually unseated and float to the surface. Fish die quietly. Birds and other wildlife will be frightened away. The fast-moving water also serves to cool the water so that it never warms enough in the Mountain West for plants to survive, let alone bloom and thrive. If you wish to install a small waterfall, buy a pump that will recirculate less than five gallons hourly. The sound of a trickle of water is very attractive to birds. To achieve a bigger sound from a drip of water, install a concave rock behind the point where the water drops into the pool.

■ *Leaf-fall is the biggest chore you will have with a lily pool.*

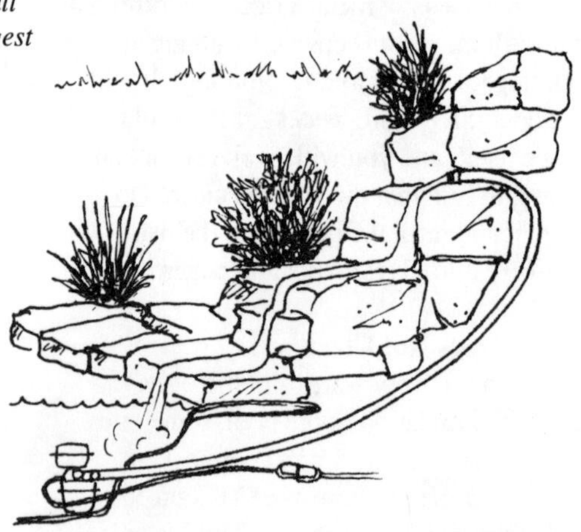

Diagram of a pool with waterfall, pump, and filter.

Night Lighting

Adding low-voltage lighting to a pool adds more enjoyment than any other accessory These are usually sold in strings of six or more. Use one or two directed upward to highlight nearby shrubs or trees. Mount one to light directly downward into the pool. The lights will attract insects, which will be appreciated by the fish.

Danger From Flood

See Chapter 7 "Plant Protection."

Summer Care

Arm yourself with a small net with a long handle (sold at pet stores) to retrieve floating debris that may get into the pool after a wind storm. Use long-handled lopping shears to sever yellowed lily pads and spent blooms at their point of emergence. This care may be needed once a week, but seldom more. Feed the fish if you wish, but they easily survive on mosquito larvae and the insects that alight.

Fall Care

Leaf-fall is the biggest chore you will have with a lily pool. It is necessary to cover the pool during leaf-fall season. Use anything at hand, such as old window screens, shade cloth purchased at a nursery, bedsheets, boards, or a plastic tarp. Make certain it is tucked under the coping stones to prevent the entry of even one leaf into the pool. You can also build an elegant pool cover from 2"x2" lumber and top it with fiberglass panels. As soon as all leaves have fallen, reach into or wade into the pool to clip off all lily pads and oxygenating grass. Clip off cattails to leave three-inch stubs above the water. The stems are hollow and they need the oxygen that will be provided to the roots. Remove foliage from any other bog plants. Any debris at the bottom of the pool should be removed as well. Every three to five years, it is a good practice to rent a pump to remove all the water from the pool. As the water level lowers, you will be able to net and save the fish. Use a soft brush or broom to get the bottom of the pool as clean as possible, but do not touch the sides. The slime that is attached to the sides is a vital part of the health of the pool. Refill the pool as before and it will quickly balance in the cool weather of fall.

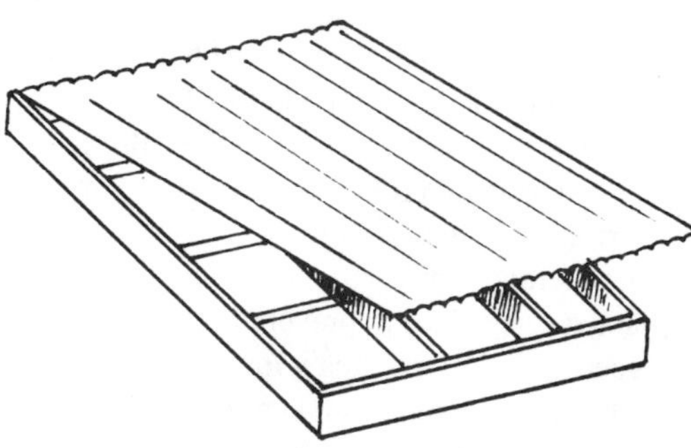

Build an elegant cover for leaf-fall season and winter from 2"x2" lumber and fiberglass panels.

Winter Care

Remove the window screens or other devices. If you do not care to install a pool heater as described above, place a length of metal pipe upright in the pool so that it rests on the bottom with at least four feet of length upright and out of the water. The pipe will attract heat and prevent the water from freezing for a time. Depending on geographic area, however, the water will eventually freeze, and your pool will be an added dimension of beauty in all its icy splendor. To keep your fish alive, you must pour a kettle of boiling water down the pipe every day or two to melt the ice and allow for the release of harmful gases. Usually this chore lasts from middle of December till the middle of March. Straight-tailed goldfish, such as the little Comets you purchased, are a species of carp that burrow into the gravel at the top of the lily tubs to spend the winter in suspended animation. Fish do not eat in winter. Adding fish food to the water will foul it. As soon as the ice melts in March, you may wish to cover the pool again till the windy season has passed. Skimming wind-blown trash from the pool is an unpleasant task.

The lilies will begin to grow in early April, with a pad or two reaching the surface. Fertilize at that time with one of the lilytabs sold at nurseries for each bucket or pan of lilies.

Dividing Lilies

Sooner than you think, the lilies will need dividing. The signal for need of division of hardy lilies is the formation of flowers on stems that stand above the water surface. Fall or spring are good seasons for this chore. After lifting the tubs or buckets (you may need help for this) to a nearby plastic tarp, turn the entire root ball out and begin cutting the tubers apart with a sharp knife. Replant three to five tubers in new (heavy, remember) soil, and pack the remaining tubers with moist peatmoss in plastic bags to be given to friends or the garden club plant sale. The bags can be kept in the bottom of the refrigerator or in a cool basement through the winter if necessary.

■ *. . . your pool will be an added dimension of beauty in all its icy splendor.*

Dividing lilies is a messy, and often cold job. Don't wait too long in fall to do it, nor try to do it too early in spring. The chill in the bones is not worth it.

Safety Measures

If there are toddlers in the family or in the neighborhood, your pool is an "attractive nuisance" in legal terms. You can construct a child-proof fence, which is very unattractive. Instead, consider a horizontal fence of galvanized wire four inches under the water surface. Secure it tightly to pipe poles, laid horizontally and concealed with stones, boulders and plants. The plants and fish will not be disturbed, and you will have peace of mind.

The Tub Water Garden

■ *Apartment and condominium dwellers are not left out of the water garden scene.*

Apartment and condominium dwellers are not left out of the water garden scene. Children will delight in having their own water garden as well. Half-barrels are a glut on the market now that the nation's consumption of hard liquor has diminished. Elegant ceramic, clay, and metal pots are also available in large sizes. Your container need not be water tight, but it should hold at least four gallons of water. You will line it with PVC cut to fit as in the directions above. Fill your lined container to the half-way mark with sandy loam. Cover with 1/4" of coarse sand or pea gravel. Thoroughly saturate the soil. Fill the container to 1" above the soil/sand level with a very gentle stream of water in order not to disturb the bottom and muddy the water. You are now ready to plant one water lily tuber at a 45° angle in the middle of the container. A bog plant, such as Pickerel Weed (*Pontederia cordata*), and a grass plant, such as Miniature Cattail (*Typha minima*) are next to be planted at the outer edges. Last to be planted is a generous bunch of oxygenating grass in the off-center. Now move your tub to a spot where it will receive at least six hours of full sun daily; then continue filling to the top. Balance will be achieved within three weeks. Three mosquito fish or guppies are recommended, but you may want to try small Comet goldfish. Three snails will be your clean-up crew!

The Country Pond

If you live in the country, it may be prudent or just an added attraction to have a pond. A place for watering stock and a breeding place for food fish is reason enough to install a large pond. PVC liners are available in very large sizes, but you may want to count upon tamped clay to hold the water. If you choose either of these materials, install a one foot layer of coarse sand over the bottom before filling. Install a headgate for filling the pond from an irrigation ditch, using a wier to filter the water before it enters the pond. Give the pond vertical sides to prevent the growth of algae, but leave one area with a sloping side so that young animals and children can climb in and out easily. A small section of sand beach is a nice amenity.

Stock your pond with food fish or ornamentals. Mosquito fish are also available, but you must assure the authorities who sell them that they cannot get into a native waterway. Plant the yellow pond lilies that are native to ponds throughout the Mountain West. These lilies are available from #1 source listed below. Pond-side plantings for the country pond are standard. There is nothing lovelier than a weeping willow (*Salix Tristis*) reflected in the water. The native yellow-flowered water iris (*Iris pseudocorus*) is much prettier than cattails - though the cattails will come unbidden, their seeds borne on the wind. Aquatic additions to a landscape add a dimension that should not be missed. Investigate all of the ways a water feature could be added to your garden.

Suggested Reading

"Ornamental Water Gardening" by The Shereth Group, P.O. Box 6492, Denver, CO 80206. 1991, $8.95.

"Water Gardens", A Harrowsmith Gardener's Guide, edited by David Archibald and Marry Patton, Camden House, Willowdale, Ontario, Canada. 1990, $9.95.

"How To Identify and Control Water Weeds and Algae", James A. Schmidt, publisher, Applied Biochemists, Inc. 5300 West County Line Road, Mequon, Wisconsin 53092, 1-800-558-5106.

Suggested Sources:

1. Lilyponds Water Gardens, P.O. Box 188, Brookshire, Texas, 77423-0188. catalog $5.
2. Van Ness Water Gardens, 2460 North Euclid Avenue, Upland, CA, 91786-1199. catalog $6.
3. Queen of the River Fish Co., 13810 N. 115th St., Longmont, CO 80501. tel. (303) 651-2514. Pond, food, and mosquito fish.

CHAPTER 20

Gardens for Mountain Homes

Newcomers sometimes have romantic illusions of living on a mountain top, which is only a small misconception. Coming from the pen of a mellowed native, the aim of this chapter is to soften the blow of reality. It is hard to come to terms with Mother Nature's vagaries of weather, unfriendly or too friendly creatures, and the cold actuality that some of the amenities of life in the city do not exist in the high country. Nevertheless, nothing can surpass the clear air, the people, and a thousand incredible sights and sounds of the high altitude Mountain West.

Landscape Planning at High Altitude

Residences and get-away cabins are landscaped differently. The get-away weekend cabin is just what it says. You wish to get away from the hum-drum of weekday life, which probably includes yard work. Plant the lot, if any planting is necessary, with native trees, shrubs, and flowers. If the ground is reasonably undisturbed, let Nature revegetate the area as she will. If the ground has been drastically disturbed during construction, grade it to slope slightly away from the dwelling, and amend the soil with six inches of compost, weathered manure or sphagnum peatmoss. Plant trees, both deciduous and evergreen, and shrubs in natural appearing groups. Let the soil revegetate with native grasses and wildflowers. Give yourself the safe, dry footing of a path to stroll around your land, especially through a section of woodland, if one exists. A path of pole peelings* mounded slightly to drain well is silent, safe, and easy to come by. If there is a change of grade near your precious trees,

* *See Glossary*

excavate to expose, but not cut, the roots; then place stones to form steps over the roots to protect them from the compaction of foot traffic.

A woodland walk must protect roots of trees.

Make Do or Replace?

For many permanent residents at altitudes over six thousand feet, the home grounds have soil that is not soil YET. It is a gritty decomposed granite that, in an eon or two, will break down to sand, silt, and eventually clay. Since you can't wait that long, it may be the better part of valor to forget trying to amend it and replace it with topsoil hauled from the flatlands or purchased locally. High country dwellers soon learn that the second family vehicle should be a pick-up truck, since hauling costs are exorbitant. Buying topsoil from a local high-country dealer is not always prudent. Mountain soils are cold and poor. Black, rich-looking soils of a mountain meadow can be highly alkaline from salts washed into them from geologic formations high in salt. Ask for pH soil test results before buying. High country dwellers in areas where there are coal mines have experimented with some success in adding coal dust (powdered coal) to soils to make them attract heat to warm more quickly in spring. Coal is organically sound and will add a minute amount of nitrogen.

■ *High country dwellers soon learn that the family vehicle should be a pick-up truck.*

If local sources of topsoil are not found to be acceptable, your best avenue is probably one of hauling topsoil of medium quality from the flatlands and amending it yourself with locally purchased weathered manure. Ranchers clean barns and corrals annually and may allow you to purchase the weathered manure.

Raised Beds and Thermal Masses

Long periods of wet weather in spring and fall are the despair of the high country gardener. Raised beds are the only solution. Even better are raised beds made of stones or boulders that attract heat on a sunny day and release it slowly at night or during wet weather. The sharp drainage of the raised bed will mean dry, warm soil more quickly after the winter has passed or after a summer deluge.

Raised beds of heat-attracting boulders can also be backed by stone walls that protect plants from the prevailing wind.

Electric heat tape can be installed at the root level of plants needing special protection.

Electric heat tape is inexpensive in short lengths. It does not last for many years but is a wise choice for the gardener who wants to protect special plants, such as those around the entry. Install it about three inches under the soil surface.

High Altitude Sunlight

■ *It is the unparalleled sunlight that gives plants greater vigor and more brilliantly colored blooms.*

At high altitude rainfall is usually adequate in summer, and there are some cloudy days and, hopefully, plentiful snow in winter. It is the unparalleled sunlight that gives plants greater vigor and more brilliantly colored blooms. The ultra-violet light, from which we protect our own eyes, along with a number of other factors, is the benefactor.

High Altitude Wind

Wind speeds at 70 miles per hour are common in the high country. Not much is said about it. Chambers of Commerce probably forbid it, but if you haven't experienced high country wind, you are in for a drying, electrifying phenomena like no other. It is no wonder that plants and people must be protected from it. A windbreak is essential. See Chapter 10, "Windbreak Care."

Sunken Garden

A sunken garden is valuable at high altitude. An excavated area of three to four feet deep and as long and wide as your need is adequate to catch reflected heat and to serve as a protection from wind. If a series of small flowering trees and shrubs is planted at the top level of the sunken garden, the wind passes over without harm. This area will be more frost prone, however. Placing boulders and heat-absorbing stones at intervals in this garden will add a little protection from frost.

A sunken garden is protected from wind but is more frost prone.

The English walled garden is also appropriate in the Mountain West. A south-facing wall soaks up heat during the day and releases it slowly at night. For both plants and people, it is a structure well worth the time and expense to construct.

Keeping Winter Damage at a Minimum

All of the plant protection methods listed in Chapter 7 will serve you in protecting your garden. Maximum effort is not always needed after plants become acclimatized and when adequate snow cover lowers the plant's temperature gradually. An occasional season will bring your plants through the winter, only to have them succumb to the SPRING! Deep temperature fluctuations after snow has gone are not uncommon, and you must be ready with coverings of every sort when this occurs.

The Micro-Climate Is Everything

There are no consistent rules in mountain horticulture. One side of the mountain is different from the other side as if it were a continent away. You are on your own in discovering where the micro-climates are in your landscape. Keep notes of your observations of weather types, which way the storms come from, and where the snow lies deep or melts early in spring. Train your eyes to see what they are looking at. The slightest nuance of change in a plant's vigor is a signal to you of its response to its growing conditions. There may be a hundred different climates within your own property!

The most frequently asked question regarding trees and shrubs is, "How big will it get?", says Marie Orlin of Neils Lunceford Nursery in Silverthorne, Colorado. Her answer can only be approximate, for soil type, amount of water, aspect*, and altitude are only part of the qualities of micro-climate. A single evergreen branch may shield a gentian at the right moment in its life that turns it into a cushion of blue in September. The loss of that branch may mean the gentian is headed for the compost next year.

Container Growing

High country dwellers are experts in container growing. The window boxes, hanging baskets, and porch pots burst with color every summer. Ingenious methods were discovered to protect containers from adverse weather conditions, including putting containers of plants on wheels. Wheeled tubs of tomato plants spend their sunny days on decks and patios, but are not uncommon dinner partners in the high country dining room.

Because mountain air can alternate quickly from very wet to very dry, soils for container grown plants should be mixed, according to directions on the package, with a polymer gel. This substance will aid in maintaining a turgidity in the plants as well as aeration of the root zone.

■ *One side of the mountain is different from the other side as if it were a continent away.*

Locating the best place for the container grown plant is different for each site. Experiment with the heat-collecting site of porch ceilings and deck overhangs. Baskets hung just slightly under the roof overhang over a deck or entry, just slightly under the roof facia, and in areas where morning sun will warm the plants slowly are tested to be the best locations. Plan on turning the containers frequently to face the sun.

Greenhouse, Sunpit, and Coldframe

When cabin-fever sets in for real in January, there is no more pleasant respite for the high country gardener than owning a greenhouse or sunpit. The greenhouse, though expensive to operate, can become therapy. The sunpit, though not quite as comfortable, has virtually no cost to operate. Only your vigilance in keeping snow removed from the sunny side of the insulated south-facing glass is needed to keep this a low-cost method of growing or wintering-over tender plants. Even the insulation of the glass is cost free. The insulating plastic bubble wrap that comes with every "handle with care" package in the mail is sprayed with water on one side and the wet side stuck to the inside of the glass of the greenhouse, sunpit, or

* *See Glossary*

coldframe. For extra insurance, you may want to install a thermostatically controlled heater in the sunpit for insurance against the occasional extremely cold night. Set the thermostat for forty degrees.

Weather records show that hail of a size to break glass seldom occurs in the mountains. Glass, rather than fiberglass or plastic, is recommended for greenhouse, sunpit, and coldframe windows. Ultraviolet light at high altitude makes quick work of glass substitutes, breaking them down within a very few years.

The coldframe is for anyone who has three boards, an old window frame and a southern exposure next to their home. Give the boards for the sides a slanting cut to make the attached window frame shed snow and rain. Excavate the soil inside the frame to about thirty inches; for you will, inevitably, want to store a large, tender shrub at some future date. Line the inside of the frame with styrofoam boards. Tack old carpet around the top edge so that the glass won't break should you accidentally drop the lid. Amend the excavated soil and replace some of it in the sections of the frame you wish to grow early or late crops of spinach, lettuce, radishes, etc. Electric heat tape can be installed to make the coldframe become a hotbed for growing seedlings for transplant. Cold frame management is another step in the ladder of becoming a gardener.

■ *Cold frame management is another step in the ladder of becoming a gardener.*

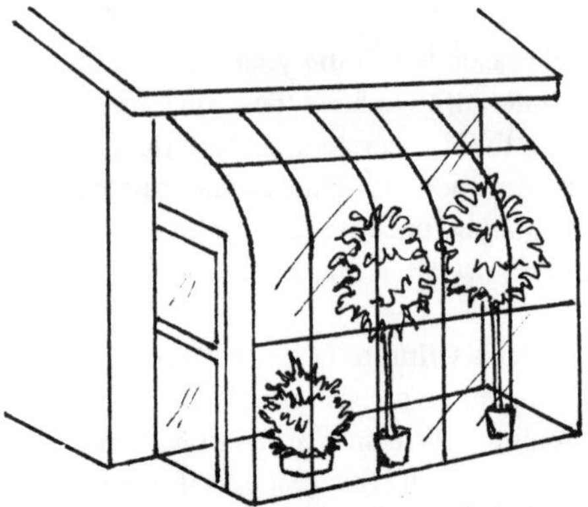

The greenhouse attached to the south-facing side of the home will dispel cabin fever.

After installation, the sunpit window snow removal chore is its only upkeep.

A coldframe is attached to a south-facing wall and insulated with styrofoam boards. Electric heat tape will protect spring seedlings.

Suggested Plants for Greenhouse or Sunpit Culture

Annuals will be the easiest of your under-glass regime. Climbing sweet peas (*Lathyrus odoratus*) are strung up on string in the center of a bench where they will receive light from both sides. Their fragrance is light, not cloying; colors are pastels with claret and purple added for zest.

Ten-Week Stock (*Matthiola incana*) comes into flower about ten weeks after sowing and lasts about a month. Sow it in succession, keeping a pot or two in flower at all times.

Calendula is available with such enticing names as "Apricot Bon Bon" or "Stormy Sunset." Its cousin Godetia has a satin finish to papery petals.

The forcing of bulbs can become your specialty. With a spot under a bench for placing pots of bulbs for the cooling period, you have all the rest of the growing conditions needed for bulb culture. Tulips and daffodils seem to be the most successful. Try planting some of the major and minor bulbs in the same pot, such as daffodils faced down* with porcelain 'Blue Spike' grape hyacinths (*Muscari spp.*). Freesia and paper-white narcissus can furnish fresh flowers for the dining table.

The citrus group will thrive in the cool glass house. The big Meyer Lemon (*Citrus limon cv. 'meyer'*) becomes a very acceptable tree with enormous, seedy fruits, while the Persian Lime (*Citrus aurantiifolia cv. 'Tahiti'*) furnishes fruits for drinks and Key Lime pie. The little kumquats and oranges will not overwhelm you with fruit, but they bloom and fruit at the same time; so you will always have fragrance and fruit.

Gardenias are not for beginners, but Camellias furnish long-lasting blooms in shades of pink, rose, and red. They set buds in late summer, and always too many. Thin the buds to one for each branch; otherwise, they all drop. Feed them only when they are in their growth stage.

A vine in the glass house takes up little room, and can become an heirloom. If *Bougainvillea* is too common for you, think what a feather in your gardener's cap it would be to furnish *Stephanotis* for a bride's bouquet.

Complete your cool glasshouse growing with chrysanthemums at any season. Grow herbs and kitchen vegetables that prefer cool temps. Save a little space in March for starting seed flats of the plants that will be transplanted in beds and borders outdoors in June.

■ *. . . think what a feather in your gardener's cap it would be to furnish Stephanotis for a bride's bouquet.*

The Hoop House for Vegetables

Vegetables grow quickly and robustly in high altitude, but nothing is more discouraging than a frost in midsummer. All efforts are lost and there is no time remaining in the growing season to start new plants.

The hoop house is a half-round structure of minimum strength that is covered with clear plastic of medium weight. It covers the vegetables all summer and is dismantled in winter for storage. Or the plastic is removed and the frame is left standing.

The vegetables are grown in the ground, not in raised benches as in a greenhouse. The soil is prepared and a drip irrigation system is laid down before planting. Often the ends of the house are left open in midsummer for good air circulation and for bees to fly in to pollinate the flowers. A flap of plastic is tied down so that it can be released to cover the ends quickly in the event of an imminent freeze.

* *See Glossary*

Suggested Trees, Shrubs, & Flowers for High Country Gardens

Evergreens hardy to 10,000 ft. elevation:

Note: Many of the following are described in Chapters 11, 12, 14, and 15, and description will be omitted here. When more than one species of the same genus is listed, the genus will be abbreviated for those following.

■ *Abies lasiocarpa*,
SUBALPINE FIR, 30'. A native tree of timberline. Needs a cool, moist soil.

■ *Picea engelmanni*,
ENGELMANN SPRUCE. 40'. A handsome native that will tolerate wet soils where oxygen is present in fast-running streams.

■ *Picea pungens*,
COLORADO SPRUCE. 60'.

■ *Pinus aristata*,
BRISTLECONE PINE. 40'.

■ *P. contorta latifolia*,
LODGEPOLE PINE. 50'.

■ *P. flexilis*,
LIMBER PINE 25'.

Deciduous trees hardy to 10,000 ft. in elevation:

■ *Alnus tenuifolia*,
THIN-LEAF ALDER. 20'.

■ *Populus angustifolia*,
NARROWLEAF COTTONWOOD. 45'. A native of moist soils that is often mistaken for a willow because of the narrow leaves.

■ *P. balsamifera*,
BALSAM POPLAR. 30'. A native with handsome, thick-textured foliage and fragrant buds. Moist soil. Difficult to locate in nurseries.

■ *P. tremuloides*,
QUAKING ASPEN.

Evergreen trees hardy up to 8.500 ft. in elevation. All of the above plus:

■ *Pinus ponderosa*,
PONDEROSA PINE.

Deciduous trees hardy up to 8.500 ft. in elevation. All of the above plus:

■ *Acer negundo*,
BOX ELDER.

■ *Fraxinus pennsylvanica lanceolata*,
GREEN ASH.

☐ *Malus baccata*,
CRAB APPLE. Look for cultivars at high-country nurseries with proven ability to be hardy in protected locations.

☐ *M. x hybrida*,
APPLE.
CULTIVARS:
'Lodi' and 'Haralson' have proved to be hardy for protected locations.

☐ *Prunus virginiana*,
CHOKECHERRY.
CULTIVAR:
'Shubert' has deep brown/purple leaves and orange fall color.

■ *Ulmus pumila*,
SIBERIAN ELM.

Evergreen trees hardy up to 7.500 ft. in elevation. All of the above plus:

☐ *Abies concolor*,
WHITE FIR.

☐ *Picea glauca 'Densata'*,
BLACK HILLS SPRUCE.

☐ *Pinus edulis*,
PINYON PINE.

☐ *P. nigra*,
AUSTRIAN PINE.

☐ *Thuja occidentalis*,
WESTERN ARBORVITAE.

Deciduous trees hardy up to 7,500 ft. in elevation. All of the above plus:

■ *Acer platanoides*,
NORWAY MAPLE.

■ *A. saccharum*,
SUGAR MAPLE.

■ *A. saccharinum*,
SILVER MAPLE.

■ *Crataegus mollis*,
DOWNY HAWTHORN.

■ *Elaeagnus angustifolia*,
RUSSIAN OLIVE.

■ *Gleditsia triacanthos inermis*,
HONEYLOCUST.

■ *Prunus ameniaca*,
MANCHURIAN APRICOT.

■ *P. canescens*,
SHRUB CHERRY. 6'. Pink flowers before leaves. Fruit attractive to birds.

■ *P. cerasifera*,
CHERRY PLUM. 12'.
CULTIVAR:
'Newport' has white flowers appearing before dark maroon leaves unfold.

■ *P. Cerasus*,
SOUR CHERRY. 15'.
CULTIVARS:
'Montmorency' and 'Early Richmond' have proven ability to produce.

■ *P. nigra*,
CANADA PLUM. White flowers aging to pink. Ornamental only.

■ *Rhus typhina*,
STAGHORN SUMAC.

■ *Robinia pseudoacacia*,
BLACK LOCUST.

■ *Sorbus aucuparia*,
EUROPEAN MOUNTAIN ASH.

Culture

■ *Getting trees to establish at high altitude takes some doing.*

Getting trees to establish at high altitude takes some doing. Very early spring is the best planting time because it will give a tree the longest possible time to establish roots before the ground freezes in the fall. However, digging into wet or frozen soil is not often a possibility in early spring. Early in the fall before the contemplated planting, dig the hole wide and shallow. Set aside the backfill and mix it with sphagnum peatmoss or weathered manure. Cover the backfill soil with a tarp held down with tent stakes threaded through the grommets. Line the hole with a plastic tarp and fill with leaves or straw. Leave it to wait out the winter. In spring, the leaves will be a frozen mass, but you can lift them out by the corners of the plastic tarp and have a dry hole in which to plant. As you fill in around the roots with the pre-mixed backfill, water it gently to drive out air pockets. Mulch with a sheet of clear plastic which will be a heat collector to start root hairs growing immediately. Water as needed, but take care not to overwater. Remove the plastic only if the soil temperature rises above seventy degrees.

Clear plastic sheet over the top of pole peeling mulch will be a heat collector to start root hairs growing in cold soil.

Wrap the trunks of all trees with commercial tree wrap. Begin the wrap at the bottom and wind upward through some of the lower-most branches. If rodents and rabbits are a problem, use cylinders of hardware cloth anchored into the soil at least three inches and extending up above the expected snow line. The wire cylinder should have interstices small enough so that teeth and paws cannot reach through it.

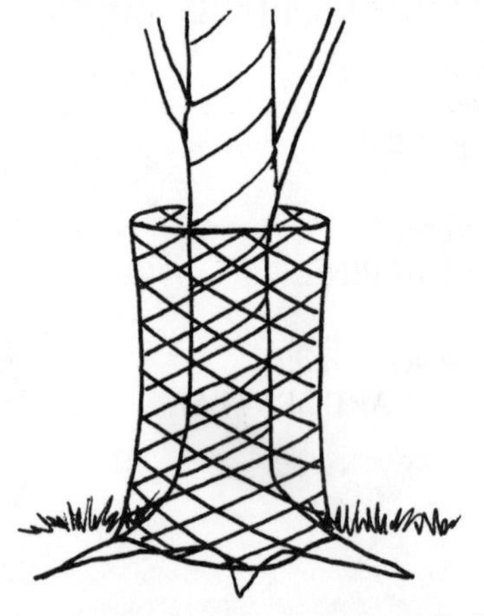

Tree wrapped and with a protective cylinder of wire is ready to face the winter.

In late summer the hardening-off process is even more important for high-country trees and shrubs than at lower altitudes. Water must be withheld from August 15 until the first sign of autumn leaf color. This will give soft new-growth tissue time to harden to corky, freeze-resistant cells.

In fall before the first snow, mulch the soil heavily around the newly planted tree(s) to prevent the soil from freezing. Many years the snow arrives while the soil is still warm, and the soil remains at a cold, but not frozen, temperature all winter. This is the best of both worlds. The areas of very heavy snow where icy crusts form in late winter are a danger to trees. The snow below the crust melts first, leaving the heavy crust sagging against limbs that are under the snow surface. These limbs are almost certain to break unless supported. Use heavy forked limbs saved from pruning operations to support them. If you do not have any forked limbs, make your own from 2"x4" lumber.

Forked limbs or 2"x4" braces will keep limbs from breaking under a heavy snow load.

Snow fence is of help to trap wind-driven snow and to ameliorate high winds. Since powder snow is the best of mulches, erect the snow fence windward of the plants to be protected.

Help Lies Ahead

A new device coming on the market is called a Tubex tube. It is a slender tube about six inches in diameter and twenty inches high made of wire-reinforced plastic that is protected against UV light. It is placed over newly planted seedlings, either woody or herbaceous. It has proved to be a great benefit in the growth of plants under adverse conditions.[1] Watch for it at your local nursery.

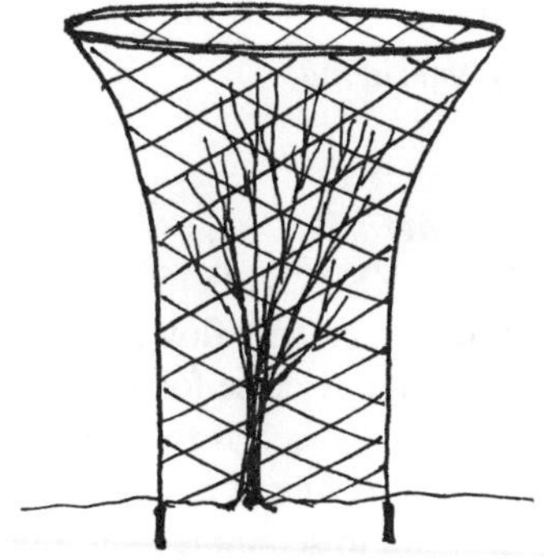

A Tubex protects a seedling tree or shrub for its first year.

Shrubs hardy to 10,000 ft. elevation : Evergreen

■ *Juniperus sabina*,.
SAVIN JUNIPER.

Deciduous

■ *Amelanchier alnifolia*,
SERVICEBERRY.

■ *In late summer the hardening-off process is even more important for high country trees and shrubs that at lower altituded.*

[1] *Research of Scott Skogerboe, 500 W. Prospect #22C, Fort Collins, CO 80520.*

■ *Betula glandulosa*,
BOG BIRCH. 3'. A dwarf native for moist soils. Showy buds, serrated leaves; brilliant red fall foliage. Hardy above timberline.

■ *Caragana arborescens*,
SIBERIAN PEASHRUB.

■ *Cercocarpus montanus*,
MOUNTAIN MAHOGANY.

■ *Cotoneaster acutifolius*,
PEKING COTONEASTER. Closely set small dark green leaves. Inconspicuous flowers followed by dry black fruits. Tolerates dry sites.

■ *Holodiscus dumosa*,
ROCK SPIREA.

■ *Jamesia americana*,
JAMESIA.

■ *Lonicera fragrantissima*,
WINTER HONEYSUCKLE. 5'. Abundant, very fragrant, creamy flowers line its stems in late winter. Coarse foliage, no fall color. To cover its graceless form in summer, give it a partner of a climbing Clematis jackmani to scramble over it in summer. Cut the vine to the ground in fall. If you plant two of these shrubs, give the second one an old fashioned rambler (not climbing) rose, such as 'Dorothy Perkins'. Lay the rose down in winter, scatter mothballs around the canes; then cover with cut brush.

■ *L. involucrata*,
BEARBERRY HONEYSUCKLE. 6'. A native in moist, rich soils. Foliage is glossy green. Black fruit in pairs with showy red bracts.

■ *L. korolkowi*,
ZABEL HONEYSUCKLE. 6'. Not bothered by the honeysuckle aphid at this altitude. Tolerates some shade; bright red fruit.

■ *Mahonia repens*,
CREEPING HOLLY GRAPE. Native hill-holder for sun or shade. Yellow flowers, blue fruits.

■ *Potentilla fruticosa*,
CINQUEFOIL.

■ *Ribes spp.*,
GOOSEBERRY, CURRANT. 3'. Arching stems of small, lobed leaves. The gooseberry cultivar 'Welcome' is sweeter than the species. The currant 'Jonkeer von Tets' is a heavy bearer. Both have red fall foliage.

■ *Rhododendron spp.*,
2-3'. Snow cover and protection is the secret to the ability to grow this group. Select only those that will be covered by the average snow cover in your area. Begin your selection with cultivars 'Ramapo' and 'PJM'. See Chapter 18 "Azaleas and Rhododendrons".

■ *Salix spp.*,
WILLOW. If you have a stream running through your property where willow shrubs would thrive, choose from the many native species available at high country nurseries, plus Bluestem Willow (*S. purpurea nana*).

■ *Sambucus canadensis*,
AMERICAN ELDER. 5'. Compound light green foliage. Flat-topped clusters of flowers (cymes) that become edible black berries. Good for wine, jelly, pies.

■ *Sheperdia canadensis*,
CANADA BUFFALOBERRY. 3'. Low native with brown-dotted leaves. Red berries on female plants. Shade tolerant.

■ *Sorbaria sorbifolia*,
URAL FALSE-SPIREA. 2'. Summer-flowering, creeping shrub; useful for soil erosion control. Flowers are white on stiffly upright stems. Cut to 6-inch stubble in early spring.

■ *Syringa persica*,
PERSIAN LILAC.

■ *S. vulgaris.*,
COMMON LILAC.

■ *Viburnum opulus*,
HIGHBUSH CRANBERRY.

Shrubs hardy to 9,000 ft. elevation: All of the above plus:

Evergreen

■ *Juniperus sabina tamariscifolia*,
TAMY JUNIPER.

Deciduous

■ *Acer glabrum*,
MOUNTAIN MAPLE. 15'. Tall native with brilliant red fall color. Useful on north-facing sites.

■ *Betula fontinalis*,
WATER BIRCH. 20'. For moist places where its red, cherry-like bark shines in winter.

■ *Cornus sericea*,
RED OSIER DOGWOOD.

■ *Prunus americana*,
AMERICAN PLUM. Purschia tridentata, ANTELOPE BRUSH. 5'. Native of dry, rocky hillsides. Brouse for deer.

■ *Rubus spp.*,
RASPBERRY. The native *R. strigosus* is useful in rocky, moist, disturbed ground. The domestic cultivar 'Boyne' has proven ability to produce abundantly under a regime of rabbit manure compost and 3" of water weekly.

Shrubs hardy to 8,000 ft. elevation: All of the above plus:

Evergreen

■ *Juniperus communis*,
CREEPING JUNIPER. 3'. A native for dappled shade, rich, moist soil. Does not transplant well.

Deciduous

■ *Acer ginnala*,
AMUR MAPLE.

■ *Artemisia abrotanum*,
WORMWOOD SAGE. 2'. Low hedge useful for dry sites. Many other native sages need wider distribution as ornamentals.

■ *Berberis thunbergi*,
JAPANESE BARBERRY.

■ *Chrysothamnus nauseosus*,
RABBITBRUSH. 4'. A hill-holder of merit for its burst of golden blooms in early September, heralding the autumn season. Combine with blue fall asters.

■ *Euonymus vegetus*,
WINTERCREEPER EUONYMUS. 2'. A shrubby creeper that is a broadleaf evergreen. For north or east exposures with consistent moisture.

■ *Ligustrum vulgare*,
COMMON PRIVET. 5'. An unclipped screen hedge with inconspicuous flowers; black berries are poisonous.

■ *Rhus trilobata*,
LEMONADE SUMAC.

■ *Rosa harrisoni*,
HARRISON'S YELLOW ROSE. 5'. The old traditional shrub rose in bloom at Memorial Day. Fragrant; suckers freely; no insects or disease.

■ *R. rubrifolia*,
RED LEAF ROSE. 5'. A graceful shrub of deep maroon foliage if grown in sun; pale gray in shade. Pale pink, single flowers. Somewhat drought tolerant.

■ *Rubus deliciosus*,
BOULDER RASPBERRY. 3'. Large single white flowers ; tasteless black berries. Prefers dappled shade and spring moisture.

■ *Spirea bumalda cvs.*,
FROBEL SPIREA.

■ *S. vanhouttei*,
BRIDALWREATH SPIREA.

■ *Syringa villosa*,
LATE LILAC. 6'. Tough, leathery leaves withstand late frosts. Blooms small but sweetly scented. Blooms three to four weeks later than other lilacs.

■ *Viburnum lantana*,
WAYFARING TREE.

■ *V. lentago*,
NANNYBERRY. 6'. Cymes of white flowers in June; clusters of black berries in August; brilliant red fall foliage.

Flowers for 6,000 to 10,500 in elevation:

If a flower listed below is not described, you will find its description in Chapter 15 "Annuals" or Chapter 14 "Perennials."

ANNUALS

BOTANIC NAME	COMMON NAME
*Antirrhinum majus**	SNAPDRAGON
Brachycome iberidifolia	SWAN RIVERDAISY
Brassica oleracea	ORNAMENTAL CABBAGE
Calendula officinalis	CAPE MARIGOLD
Catharanthus x hybrida	VINCA
Centaurea cyanus	BATCHELOR BUTTON
Chrysanthemum paludosum	ANNUAL CHRYSANTHEMUM
Consolida ambigua	LARKSPUR
Dianthus cultivars	PINK
Dimorphotheca aurantiaca	AFRICAN DAISY
Gomphrena globosa	GLOBE AMARANTH
Helichrysum bracteatum	STRAWFLOWER
Hesperis matronalis	SWEET ROCKET
Ibiris umbellata	CANDYTUFT
Lathyrus odoratus	SWEET PEA
Limnanthes douglasii	FRIED EGGS
Lobelia erinus	LOBELIA
Lobularia maritima	SWEET ALYSSUM
Matthiola, spp.	TEN-WEEK STOCK
Moluccella laevis	BELLS OF IRELAND
*Portulaca grandiflorum**	MOSS ROSE
Viola hybrids	PANSY

*Needs very warm growing conditions.

Flowers for 6,000 to 10,500 in elevation:

If a flower listed below is not described, you will find its description in Chapter 15 "Annuals" or Chapter 14 "Perennials."

PERRENIAL FLOWERS

BOTANIC NAME	COMMON NAME
Achillea x taygetea 'Moonshine'	YARROW
A. ptarmica	SNEEZEWEED
Aconitum napellus	MONKSHOOD
Anaphalis margaritacea	PEARLY EVERLASTING
Anchusa officinalis	BUGLOSS
Anemone pulsatilla	PASQUE FLOWER

Aquilegia x hybrida	COLUMBINE
A. caerulea	COLUMBINE
A. canadensis	COLUMBINE
Arabis caucasica	ROCKCRESS
Aster nova-belgi	MICHAELMAS DAISY
Aurinia saxatilis	BASKET-OF-GOLD
Campanula spp.	BLUEBELL
Centranthus ruber	VALERIAN
Centaurea montana	CORNFLOWER
Chrysanthemum leucanthemum	OX-EYE DAISY
C. x morifolium	GARDEN CHRYSANTHEMUM
C. x superbum	SHASTA DAISY
Delphinium grandiflorum	DELPHINIUM
Dianthus spp.	PINK
Doronicum cordatum	LEOPARD'S BANE
Echinacea purpurea	CONE FLOWER
Erigeron x hybridus	FLEABANE
Erysimum allionii	WALLFLOWER
Euphorbia polychroma	CUSHION SPURGE
Gentian spp.	GENTIAN
Clematis spp.	SHRUB CLEMATIS
Gaillardia aristata	BLANKET FLOWER
Gypsophila repens	BABY'S BREATH
Heuchera x brizoides	CORAL BELLS
Iris x germanica	GERMAN IRIS
I. orientalis	ORIENTAL IRIS
I. sibirica	SIBERIAN IRIS
Linum perrene	BLUE FLAX
Lupinus x hybrida	LUPINE
Lychnis chalcedonica	MALTESE CROSS
Meconopsis spp.	ASIATIC POPPY
Mertensia	CHIMING BELLS
Myosotis alpestris	FORGET-ME-NOT
Paeonia lactiflora	PEONY
Papaver spp.	POPPY
Penstemon spp..	BEARD TONGUE
Phlox subulata	CREEPING PHLOX
Platycodon gradiflorus	BALLOON FLOWER
Polemonium caeruleum	JACOB'S LADDER
Primula spp.	PRIMROSE
Ranunculus aconitifolius	BUTTERCUP
Sempervivum	HEN AND CHICKS

Bulbs for 6,000 ft. to 10,000 ft. elevation:

BOTANIC NAME	COMMON NAME
Crocus	CROCUS
Daffodil	DAFFODIL
Hyacinthus amethystinus	ALPINE HYACINTH
Muscari	GRAPE HYACINTH
Tulipa	TULIP

Many more herbaceous perennials are available to the high country gardener. Use the general lists in Chapter 14 "Perennials." Nurseries will have their own lists that reflect their own experience and that of their clients. You will find gardening columns in high country newspapers written by Cooperative Extension as well as other experienced gardeners.

Grass Planting in the High Country

Whether preparing home grounds for the planting of turfgrass or revegetating large areas of disturbed ground, the soil problems will be many and discouraging. Mountain meadow soils can be highly alkaline. Desirable building sites near streams are almost always rocky or underlain with gravel and with very little soil present. Steep sites are better candidates for rock gardens instead of grass.

Saving topsoil is paramount. No matter how bad it looks, it is better than what lies beneath. It can be amended easily before replacing it after construction is finished.

Probing With An Iron Bar

Strange as it may seem at first, an iron bar is a good investment if you live in the mountains. If you prefer electronic equipment, invest, instead, in equipment appropriate to probing with a beam. As you walk over your property before planting grass, use the bar (or beam) to probe for boulders. Small rocks and "donies" will be turned up during cultivation, but auto-sized boulders are not uncommon a foot or two under the surface. If they are found now, they can be excavated and shattered with dynamite into movable-sized boulders. If left in place, the grass will be forever sparse and burned out in that area. Hire an expert for blasting.

A few areas in the Mountain West are pocked with caves and sink-holes, known as *karst topography*. A large boulder can be the signal for a subsidence that would require heavy equipment, thus destroying turf or other areas of landscaping.

A soil test will give you recommendations as to amendments needed. It is not wise to fracture the soil deeply as was recommended in Chapter 4. Adding organic matter and missing nutrients revealed by the soil test will give you the balance needed. If topsoil is added, once again, ask for a pH test or make the test yourself.

Transplanted Californians who encounter a hard soil under the surface assume it to be hardpan, an impervious subsoil layer they are accustomed to dealing with in California. This is probably not a true hardpan, but, nevertheless, may require chiseling or ripping with heavy equipment to penetrate.

If no artificial watering is planned, fall seeding at about the time the Quaking Aspen are turning yellow is a good time.

■ *Saving topsoil is paramount. No matter how bad it looks, it is better than what lies beneath.*

■ *Crimping of straw is the most sucessful method to keep the mulch in place.*

There will be no germination prior to freezing weather and the seeding will go into the winter with protective snow cover. The first days of spring and the thawing will see the first spears of grass appear.

Summer seedings are successful if they are artificially watered to promote germination and growth of deep roots all during the summer.

Seedings should be mulched to prevent washing of the seed. Crimping of straw is the most successful method to keep the mulch in place. If you can't locate a farmer/rancher who has a disc to crimp the straw, cover it with cut brush until spring. A third method is to engage specialists who own hydro-seeding equipment. This equipment will mix a tacky asphaltum substance with the seed, when is then blown onto a hillside. As the grass seed germinates, it pushes through the substance and is in no danger of washing away. Ski slopes are prepared in this manner.

Crimping straw mulch into the soil holds it in place. Discing a mountain meadow planted with a pure stand of Smooth Brome is necessary when it becomes sod-bound. A mixed species grass meadow is seldom sod-bound.

■ *A pure stand of Smooth Brome, for example, will quickly become sod-bound and gradually kill itself.*

Mixing of grass species is recommended, with the following available as both single and as mixed seeds sold by the pound. Seeding at a rate of 2 lbs. per 1,000 ft_2 will give an adequate cover with a good germination rate.

Tall Fescue	Bunch grass, persistent, bluegreen color.
Red Fescue	Dark green persistent, bunch grass, but sod-forming, depending on variety.
Chewings Fescue	Bunch, shade tolerant.
Kentucky Bluegrass	Persistent, spreads by stolons; less seedling vigor than above.
Perennial Rye	Fast starter, bunch, shade tolerant, but not reliably hardy.

Seeding for Erosion Control

Areas of extensive disturbance require immediate attention. Erosion can lead to mass wasting (mud slide) very quickly in the high country. It can be as devastating as a snow avalanche.

Drilling seed under the surface, using a specialized drilling device is the best method. Ranchers and farmers will often do this work for you on a custom basis if you advertise in the local newspaper. The hydro-seeding method described above is also appropriate, for a price. Once again, a mixture of seed species is recommended. A pure stand of Smooth Brome, for example, will quickly become sod-bound and gradually kill itself. It must be sliced deeply, using a disc drawn by a vehicle.

Use ten to fifteen pounds per acre of a mixture of the following seed

Smooth Brome	Sod former, very persistent, good seedling vigor.
Timothy	Bunch, persistent on moist site.
Meadow Foxtail	Persistent at higher elevations, very fluffy seed.
Pubescent Wheatgrass	Does well on drier sites; not adaptable above 10,000'.
Slender Wheatgrass	Good seedling vigor, produces fast cover; short-lived.

Suggested Viewing
Vail Botanic Garden,
Vail, Colorado. Exit 176 from Hwy I-70. Turn left on South Frontage Road. Park at the tennis courts and walk down the asphalt path past the Gerald Ford Amphitheatre. The rock-alpine garden and the Betty Ford Alpine Garden are directly in front of the Amphitheatre entrance.

Suggested Visits
Neills Lunceford Nursery,
P.O. Box 2130, Silverthorne, Colorado. (303) 468-0340. Exit 205 from I-70 to Silverthorne. Drive one mile north on Hwy 9, also known as Blue River PArkway. The nursery will be on the right.

Colorado Alpines, Inc. Nursery, P.O. Box 2708, Avon, Colorado. (303) 949-6464). Parkway Exit 171 from I-70 ; left at the base of the on-ramp. The nursery will be on the left.

Suggested Reading
"Building a Solar-Heated Pit Greenhouse" A-37, Storey's Books for Country Living, Dept. A42, Schoolhouseroad, Pownal, Vermont 05261.

"Building and Using Coldframes" - A-39. Same publisher as above.

CHAPTER 21

Turf - The Lawn is the Stage

A lawn has been a status symbol in the suburban subdivisions of the Mountain West, just as it has been in almost every other area of the country. However, the total area a lawn covers in a home landscape is changing drastically, and it's about time! Ordinances are showing up on city council agendas to limit the amount of quality turf for each city lot. Restrictions of amounts of water used for turf have effectively cut the total square footage as well. It is now generally accepted that not more than one thousand square feet of turf is needed for most homes, with two thousand square feet for the grandest of mansions in a country setting. A large lawn will decrease the value of your property. It is a detriment because of the cost of water and maintenance. Let there be enough turf for game-playing by children and adults and enough to set the stage for the foundation planting. The remainder is more attractive planted in a broad border of trees and shrubs, both evergreen and deciduous. The border of your property that adjoins the sidewalk or drive is omitted from the planting of turf as well. This area (usually about five feet wide) is one of radiated heat that would take five times as much water as the area

■ *A large lawn will decrease the value of your property.*

beyond. Plant it in shrubs or groundcover instead. Let the broad vistas of bluegrass remain in public parks and on the playing fields.

Before beginning soil preparations for seeding or sodding turfgrass, ask the following questions of yourself and others in your family:

1. What will the turf be used for? Is it being planted strictly to set off the home, or will it be played on heavily and frequently?
2. Will the turf receive a high level of maintenance, or will it receive only minimal amounts of water and fertilizer and little or no pest control?
3. What is the desired level of visual quality?
4. Is there a ready supply of inexpensive, good quality water? If not, are you willing to pay the price of the water for the desired level of quality turf?
5. How hard are you willing to work? A little, just medium, or a lot?
6. Is the lawn area sunny or shady?
7. What is the altitude?
8. Is there a history of insects, mites, or turf disease in the neighborhood?
9. Are you willing to use pesticides, or are they totally out of the question?
10. If you will be using well water, has the water been tested for salts?
11. Is the soil sandy, clay, or loam?
12. Hilly or level?

Seed or Sod?

There are points in favor of both seed and sod. Sod is never as smooth a walking or playing surface as the seeded lawn. No matter how skillful the sod-layer, the seams where each sod roll abuts the next are always slightly discernible. On the other hand, sod gives immediate good looks. The soil preparation for sod is exactly the same as that of a seeded lawn. Its installation ends the work of putting it down and begins the process of getting it to knit together into a smooth surface. Its cost will always be higher than seeding. Sod almost eliminates the possibility of weeds. The knitting together of the sod rolls is almost immediate. Weeds are crowded out if the sod is of good quality. Sod is recommended in spring between April 10 and June 10 because spring wind would destroy a seeding.

Seeding a lawn results in a smoother surface for the life of the lawn. It means more work, but less expense. Seeding is recommended for the middle of August until September 20 when nights are cool, but days hot and sunny. Later seeding is risky, for early freezing weather is not uncommon. Lack of sunlight and cold, wet weather can make a late fall seeding fail very quickly. A seeded lawn will always have a few weeds, but seeding in late summer means that annual weed seeds will germinate and grow a little, but will be killed by the first frost. Both a seeded and sodded lawn should be carefully monitored during the first winter because the roots have not yet pushed deeply into the soil. Winter watering, by hand if necessary, is a chore to consider when snow is not covering the lawn surface.

Choice of Seed

The turf type Tall Fescues have rocketed to fame in the last few years, and they deserve their status, especially in the Mountain West. From humble beginnings as a pasture grass, turf type Tall Fescue has been selected from tiny promising seedlings to display the impressive vigor of deep roots, insect and disease resistance, and heat and drought tolerance.

Kentucky bluegrass is still the most popular throughout the northern tier of states. Its fine texture, good green color and complete hardiness make it a favorite where water, weather, and owner-friendliness occur. There is no doubt that bluegrass is more prone to diseases and insects, and takes more care than other grasses. Proper management can change that, however. Bluegrass can become as a spoiled child. The poorer the consistency in upbringing, the more intolerant it is of change. When soil preparation has been complete and watering and fertilization practices consistent, bluegrass can become docile, well-behaved, and a general, all-around good buddy.

Perennial ryegrass is used widely in grass mixes, and rarely as a pure stand. Its performance is excellent in close-knitting, and fair in drought and heat tolerance. It's main problem is that no one is absolutely certain that it is winter-hardy in the Mountain West. When the minus forty degree winter with no snow comes along, will there be grass to green up in spring?

Examine closely the advantages and disadvantages of the different turf grasses from the research of Dr. Anthony Koski, turf specialist, Colorado State University.

Tall Fescue (Festuca arundinacea), Seeding Rate: 6-8 lbs/l000ft^2

ADVANTAGES	**DISADVANTAGES**
+ establishes quickly	- slow recuperation from damage
+ drought resistant	- can become clumpy (deep rooted)
+ wear tolerant	- susceptible to brown patch and net blotch under very low maintenance
+ few insect problems	- must be mowed often
+ few disease problems	- poor quality of cut unless mower is sharp
+ excellent heat and cold tolerance	- often unavailable in pure sod form
+ slow thatch former	
+ performs well in shade	
+ good salt tolerance (6-12 mmhos)	

Commercially available cultivars:

Adventure	Mojave
Apache	Monarch
Arid	Mustang
Bonanza*	Olympic
Bonsai	Pacer
Chesapeake	Rebel II
Cimarron	Tempo
Falcon	Titan
Finelawn I	Trailblazer*
Finelawn 5GL	Tribute
Jaguar	Trident
Maverick	Williamette
Mesa	Wrangler

* *low growth habit*

Avoid the folowing for high quality turf:
K-31
Johnstone
Barcel
Kenhy

Kentucky Bluegrass (*Poa pratensis*) Seeding Rate: 3-4 lbs/1000 ft^2

ADVANTAGES	**DISADVANTAGES**
+ sod-forming by rhizomes	- thatch-former
+ high recuperative potential and rate	- disease-prone
+ high quality color and density	- insect problems
+ readily available in sod form	- lack of salt tolerance
+ good drought resistance (goes dormant)	- higher irrigation requirements because of shallow roots
+ easy to mow	
+ excellent heat and cold tolerance	- generally poor shade tolerance

Commercially available cultivars for expected high maintenance:

Adelphi	Classic	Midnight	Princeton 104
Alpine	Connie	Miranda	Suffolk
Barsweet	Indigo	Nobelesse	Glade - shade tolerant
Broadway	Limousine	Platini	

Commercially available cultivars for expected low maintenance:

Barmax	NuStar
Bartitia	Opal
Barzan	Park
Miracle	Washington

Perennial Ryegrass (*Lolium perenne*) Seeding Rate: 6-8 lbs/1000 ft^2

ADVANTAGES	DISADVANTAGES
+ quick establishment	- poor recuperative potential
+ wear tolerant	- dull mower blade results in poor quality cut
+ good color and density	
+ does not form thatch	- poor shade tolerance
+ good heat, drought tolerance	- unavailable as pure sod
+ moderate salt tolerance	- poor cold, flood tolerance

Commercially available cultivars:

Citation	Cowboy	Fiesta	Pennfine	Manhatten II
Derby	Elka	Pennant	Yorktown II	Premier
Ranger	Palmer	Tara	Dasher	Saturn
Diplomat	Repell	Blazer	Prelude	
Omega	Birdie II	Gator	Allstar	

■ *If turf is not for you, consider intsead a front yard of flowers, ornamental grasses, and shrubs.*

The above cultivars may seem more than numerous - bordering on over-abundant. However, the business of introducing turfgrass cultivars is very large and lucrative. Each company has its own. If you walk into a nursery armed with the above list, the chance is good that you may find one or two available. Nurseries cannot afford to carry every brand name. They are usually more than willing to make a special order for you. If you would prefer a mixture of several of the turf-type grasses, your dealer can make those mixtures also. A few mixtures are available off the shelf.

The Grasses for Unusual Situations

The Mountain West gardener has been bombarded with publicity about Buffalograss (*Buchloe dactyloides*) with the emphasis on it as a native grass. This fact is not always in its favor. Examine the following chart, and add to its disadvantage that if you are the only one on the block with a Buffalograss lawn, you will not be thought of as a good neighbor. The early browning in September and late green-up in May will make your property look out of place. If turf is not for you, consider instead a front yard of flowers, ornamental grasses, and shrubs. If, however, you have a large back lot that does not adjoin your neighbor's bright green bluegrass, by all means choose Buffalograss as a low-maintenance solution to keeping a large area good looking and weed free with only establishment water* necessary for its maintenance.

Buffalograss (*Buchloe dactyloides*) [1] Seeding rate: 1-3 lbs / 1000 ft_2

ADVANTAGES	DISADVANTAGES
+ excellent heat, drought tolerance	- warm season grass: straw-colored
+excellent low temperature tolerance	- between first frost and late May
+ few disease and insect problems	- not shade tolerant
+ sod-former (strongly stonoliferous)	- not salt tolerant
+ low fertility requirement	- seed is expensive
+ requires only infrequent mowing	- becomes less agressive if over-fertilized or over-watered
+ can be established from seed, sod, plugs	- not recommended for elevations over 6,000 feet.
+ a native species	- easily set afire during its dormant season
+ can withstand 4 days of flooding	

[1] *Dr. Anthony Koski, Turf Specialist, Colorado State University, Fort Collins, CO*

Commerically available cultivars: 'Texoka' and 'Sharp's Improved' are available as seed. New cultivars 'Buffalawn', 'Highlight 15', and three cultivars that bear only numbers thus far have superior performance ratings and will be available soon. 'Prairie' and '609' are commerically available vegetative types sold only as sod or plugs.

Crested Wheat (*Agropyron spp.*), Blue Grama (*Bouteloua spp.*), and Smooth Brome (*Bromus inermis*) are excellent choices for rough areas beyond the manicured turf areas of the country property. They can be watered three or four times in summer, mowed, or allowed to set their seed heads for a beautiful fall and winter scene of waving grain.

* *See Glossary*

Seeding rates: Crested Wheat - 5 lbs/1000 ft_2; Blue Grama - 1-3 lbs 1000 ft_2; Smooth Brome - 10-12 lbs/1000 ft_2. None of the above grasses should be seeded directly adjoining a manicured turf area, for they will quickly invade it and make it very unsightly. Instead, plan a wide (10-25') border of flowering trees and shrubs around the turf area. Install a drip irrigation system under the tree-and-shrub border and cover it with a fabric weed barrier and a pole peeling mulch for the ultimate in low maintenance and beauty.

Edging

After choosing the seed or sod, edging is the next decision. Keeping a sharp edge on the turf at the points where it touches the tree-shrub-and-flower border with an edging tool has been promoted by the British. If this kind of acitivity is not for you, shop for the edging that suits your budget. Steel edging is long-lasting and stays in place. It is extremely sharp and should have a grooved plastic top to prevent a serious accident. Black plastic edging comes in various grades. It is difficult to install and does not stay in place unless buried to its top edge. Redwood benderboard is an old and still popular method to prevent turf from spreading into the shrub and flower border. It splinters easily if stepped on.

Choice of Water Application Methods

Automatic sprinkler systems can be expensive for the large turf area, but for one thousand square feet - even two thousand - the expense is not great. Let the seller of name-brand systems design your system. They want you to succeed with their product, and have been trained in designing its use. Make sure they have done a good job by taking your design plan to your Cooperative Extension agent for horticulture in your county for assessment.

If you prefer to drag hoses, and many people do, buy good quality hose of a dimension that moves easily, but does not kink. Lightweight, cheap hose will be the frustration of your summer gardening activities. Sprinkler nozzles vary every year. The "sweep" sprinkler is to be avoided because it sprays water high in the air, and more is evaporated than reaches the soil. The low-arc sprinkler with large droplets is more economical of water and better for the soil after germination is complete. Use a fine mist sprinkler head when watering before germination and while seedlings are very weak.

The sprinkler with a low-arc spray will save water.

Steep Grades An Error

Forty inches of annual precipitation in the East make a steep grade away from the house foundation a necessity. But in the Mountain West, we coddle every ounce of moisture by making turf surfaces more level. The contractor often grades a slope to three inches of slope to every ten feet. This is still too steep to adequately hold moisture in the soil. Three inches of drop in twenty feet is more amenable to a good lawn.

If a precipitous slope falls away naturally from your home, investigate terraces, rock gardens, a deck, anything but turf!

"Where shall we put the lawn, dear?"

Soil Preparation and the Finish Grade

The directions for soil preparation will not be repeated here, and will be found in Chapter 4, "Soil." The finish grade is the place where the hurried lawnmaker cuts corners and will forever regret it. After the rotary tilling is finished, there are many hills and valleys (pillows and cradles to the Easterner). Unless these are filled and leveled, there will be uneven growing conditions. The little hills, however imperceptible now, will be dry and sparsely covered. The valleys will be ideal for weedy bunch grasses to take hold and to become ankle-sprainers as well. Sharpen a stake and attach a cord. Drive the stake into the soil at the highest point of gravity and sweep the cord over the soil. Where it touches, a "hill" must be raked level. The valleys will show up as soon as you begin the next step - settling.

Using a series of sprinklers or your automatic sprinkler system, thoroughly wet down the soil surface. The valleys will now become puddles. After waiting for several days for the surface to dry, you can fill in easily the places where puddles developed. At this point you may elect to use a light-weight roller to roll the surface smooth. Many lawnmakers use a roller after seeding, but this practice leads to erosion, for water does not enter a rolled surface easily.

Seeding

Seeding is the easiest part of the process. Use the rate directed by the package of seed you have selected. The hand-held whirling device is one of the easiest and most efficient to use. After seeding, scuff the surface slightly with a broom rake. Grass seed requires some light for good germination; so don't bury it.

Mulching is difficult in spring when winds sweep the area. You may want to use a collection of brush from your spring pruning operations. It won't be a thing of beauty, but will stay in place on a windy day and allow the seedlings protection until they are established. Mulching in the late summer or fall is usually with clean wheat straw - four straws deep. Depending upon temperature, germination is complete within two weeks. Watering the newly seeded surface if an automatice sprinkler system is not in place can be a job to do by hand.

One hour of drying and the seed germination is greatly diminished! On the other hand, too much water leads to lack of oxygen and germination failure as well.

Four Season Care

Spring is the season everyone wants to spring into action and do something about the lawn. Actually there is very little to do. The best March activity is to put the catcher on the lawn mower and lower the blades to as low as possible and mow the lawn. Save the dry brown clippings you have collected to protect flower and vegetable seedlings later on. The removal of the dead leaves will give you a very neat and trim-looking lawn, and it will open the crowns of the grass plants to spring sun and rain. Turfgrass de-thatching is a practice that will die hard in the Mountain West. The resultant piles of dead grass give the owner a good-housekeeping seal of disapproval by turf specialists, however. The new blades of grass that are just greening up are easily torn by the monster machine, making the turf thin and sparse, and inviting a weed invasion. Chances are slim that you have any thatch. It seldom occurs in the Mountain West, and if it does, will be found in low-lying areas where drainage is poor.

Mow in March to give the grass blades sun, air, water, and nutrients.

Purchasing your first lawn mower may leave you with big question marks over your head. The reel versus the rotary - that is the question. The rotary is the biggest seller. It has a horizontally moving, high-speed blade which cuts by impact, as would a scythe or sickle. A reel mower has fixed blades that are part of a turning cylinder (reel), which moves down and back against a stationary bedknife at the base of the mower. Reel mowers, if they are sharp and well-adjusted, cut the cleanest. The reel mower, having only two wheels, can cut cleanly down into depressions; while the rotary mower tends to move across a depression, leaving the grass growing long and lank. Nevertheless, the rotary is more versatile for cutting many types of areas, such as rough grass, tall weeds, and over small twigs without jamming. The blade of a rotary is more lethal in an accident, but both are hazardous.

Mowing often begins as early as April 15. Put your grass catcher bag away and raise the blades of the mower to two inches, and count on mowing twice a week during May and June - the season of fast growth. As soon as the grass grows to three inches, cut off one inch. Leave the clippings on the grass, for they will sift down to become added nutrients for the continued growth of the grass. They also are useful in soil insulation against summer heat and in moisture retention.

Summer begins with the watering season and will probably not occur until early May, but let your old and trusted screwdriver tell you when to begin. Use a long (12") screwdriver to push into the soil. If the push is easy, the soil does not need water. If the push is hard, water until the push is easy! As warm weather approaches, the watering schedule will settle down to about every three days. Watering at night is an excellent plan. Don't be misled by the scare tactics of those who say night watering promotes turf disease. Mountain West's dry air does not promote disease.

In July the growth slows, but picks up again in August. If dry spots show up, use a spading fork to loosen the soil; then use a hand-held hose daily until the spots green up again.

Many municipalities measure and publish the amount of water needed by the turf each day, listing it as the evapotranspiration rate. This is usually correct, but in the Mountain West, rainfall can be spotty. The shower your neighbor's property received may not have blessed yours. Keep this in mind when you read the evapotranspiration rate, and keep the trusted, old screwdriver handy.

Kentucky bluegrass typically requires 1.5 inches of water weekly, applied .5 inch, three times per week in the hot weather season.

To determine how much water your sprinkler delivers to your grass, set tuna or cat food cans at varying distances from the sprinkler head and within the sprinkler coverage pattern. Turn on the sprinkler for fifteen minutes; then measure the amount of water in the cans. Add them up and divide the total by the number of cans you used. You now know the average amount of water delivered in fifteen minutes. If you found your average to be .25 inches in fifteen minutes, you know your sprinkler delivers one inch per hour. (4 x 15 = 60 minutes).

The following weekly watering amounts are suggested for Kentucky bluegrass:

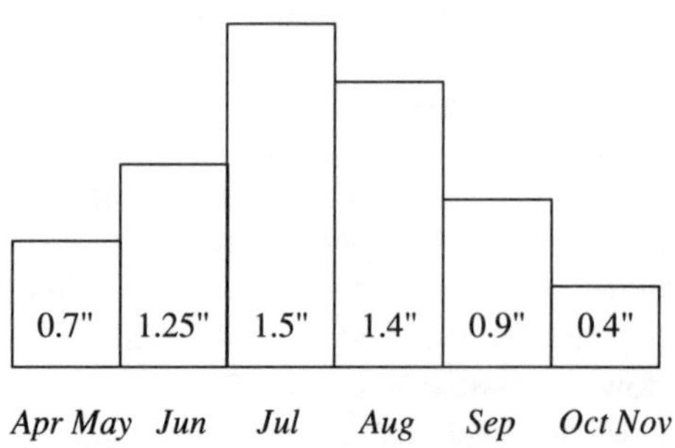

Water-stressed grass will have a bluish color and footprints can be seen. Over-watered turf, on the other hand, is usually infested with three tell-tale weeds: Bentgrass (*Agrotis tenuis*), annual bluegrass (*Poa annua*) and nimblewill (*Muhlenbergia schreberi*). Light, frequent sprinklings encourage crabgrass.

In early May the turf will signal that nutrients are needed. There is a fading or lightening of the green color. This is the best time of year to use a complete fertilizer, such as 20-10-5. Many fertilizers sold in the Mountain West contain added iron. Lack of available iron, known as iron chlorosis, may be responsible for the light yellow color in turf. It is common in soils with a pH of 7.2 or above. It can be corrected with fertilizer that contains added iron, or with a foliar or soil application of iron sulfate or iron chelate. Iron sulfate is most effective if applied to the foliage as a spray. Apply a two percent solution (.33 pound of iron sulfate in two gallons of water with a surfactant such as dish detergent). Apply at a rate of one-half gallon per 1,000 square feet. Apply an iron chelate to foliage at a rate of .1 to .3 pounds of actual iron per 1,000 square feet. Follow label instructions. Iron sources can stain clothing, sidewalks, drives, siding, and almost everything else!

If you have weeds, such as dandelions, spray each individual plant with a 2,4-D solution, mixed as directed on the bottle. Other broadleaf weeds will succumb to this treatment as well, except for Prostrate Spurge. To get this one, consider a product containing pendimethylin. This is a pre-emergent chemical that will kill the seed so that it will not germinate. This product is also useful for crabgrass. Study the label carefully before buying. The timing of application is critical.

If you are uncertain as to the identity of the weeds in your lawn, pick examples of each, making sure you have the bloom and/or seed head and some of the foliage. Place all in water and make a trip to your county Cooperative Extension Office for identification and control measure recommendations.

Aeration with a plug-type aerator is a once or twice yearly operation that allows air, water, and fertilizer to get down deep into the soil. These machines can be rented, or you can choose a lawn-care company to do the job. There is a foot-powered aerator that is also useful. It takes out two plugs at each push of the foot. Use it in small, compacted areas, such as those near a corner or where bicycle wheels have strayed.

About the middle of August, it's time to begin the fall fertilization program. Use one pound of actual nitrogen per one thousand square feet in August, and again in September and October. Measure you lawn area to get an accurate number to use to determine the number of pounds you will need.

Add a zero to the nitrogen (first number) number of the analysis on the fertilizer bag. Divide this number into 1000. The answer will be the number of pounds to apply to 1000 ft_2.

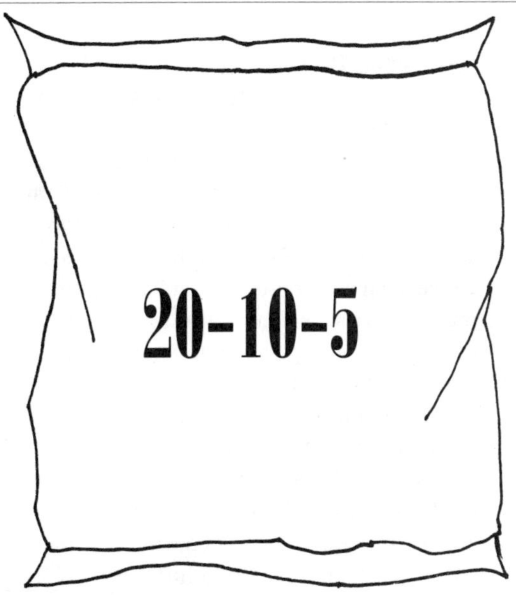

Add a zero to the nitrogen number.
20 + 0 = 200
1000 divided by 200 = 5 lbs/1000 ft_2

Continue mowing through the leaf-fall season, catching the leaves and small amount of grass by vacuum action in the catcher bag. This will keep the leaves from smothering the turf; provide chopped leaves and grass for an excellent compost pile; and leave your turf looking neat and clean and ready for the first snow fall. There is no advantage to lowering the cutting blades of your mower in the fall. In truth, if a snowless winter occurs, your lawn will need the insulation and protection of long, matted turf. It won't win prizes for neatness, however.

Water turf once monthly during all the months of winter when there is no snow except March. Enough natural precipitation usually falls in March to keep the soil damp. Keep foot traffic away from frozen turf. Avoid paths through the snow that will leave ice in its wake. Snow is the friend of turf; ice is its enemy.

Insects and Disease

There are only four turf insects of much consequence in the Mountain West: Sod Webworm, Billbug, White Grub, and Mites. Sometimes the Ataenius beetle is a problem in urban areas, but mostly it is a pest of the Midwest. Except for mites, the difference between an insect problem and a disease problem in turf is determined by a tug on the turf. If you tug on it and it comes up in your hand without much effort, it is a bug problem. If not, chances are good that it is a disease. Take a six-inch square of diseased turf (roots and all) to your Cooperative Extension Office for identification and recommendations for control. For the insect problem, it may be a little more difficult to flush out the culprit. Mix a bucketful of pyrethrin according to directions and pour it on the affected area. Usually the insects will surface in a few minutes and you can collect a few for the trip, once again to your Cooperative Extension Office.

The Thin, Sparse Lawn

There is an urge to tear up and start over when a new homeowner is confronted with a thin, sparse, weed-infested lawn. If the surface is smooth, if the grade correctly drains water away from the house, and if there is at least four hours of full sun, save yourself a headache by upgrading. This means frequent, light applications of fertilizer - usually monthly beginning in early May through September. Use different types of fertilizer, such as a chemical 20-10-5 fertilizer one month. The following month, use an organic poultry waste product; then a slow-release product the third month. Along with the fertilization program, copious watering will be needed. This does not mean drowning. Fertilizer is a salt that draws water out of plants. If there are spots that are totally bare, rake them over to scarify the surface; then seed with a spot-seeding mix. The bluegrass will gradually send out stolons and by fall you will have a thick, resilient turf.

If the sparseness of your lawn is due to shade, begin the above process by scarifying the entire area with a rake; then overseed with a shade-tolerant bluegrass species, such as "Glade." Proceed as above, but take care that the new seeding does not dry. Examine closely after three weeks to see if new shoots are appearing; then slack off on the water.

Replacing a Lawn

If your lawn is a mass of weeds; if the lawn was planted on subsoil clay; if you want to change turf species to take advantage of the new water-saving cultivars; if the grade is a tumble of hills and valleys; if you want to change the design of the amount of turf — replacement is the answer. It is time to kill the existing lawn with glyphosate and get on with it. Read the directions carefully. You will need to spray only once on a calm day. If it rains within six hours, you must spray over again. Wait about three weeks until all the grass appears dead. You may have to respray some tough, stubborn weeds. Then plow the whole area under deeply. A rotary tiller does not have tines long enough to do a good job. Find a farmer who does custom plowing. The chemical will dissipate with the deep plowing. Then add six inches of sphagnum peatmoss plus ten to fifteen pounds of triple super-phosphate per one thousand square feet to the plowed surface and go over the area with a tiller to break up the clods, incorporate the peat, and begin leveling. Proceed as directed above for seeding.

Lawn Care Guidelines With Impending Water Restrictions

- Raise the height of the mower blade as high as you can. Longer blades of grass help shade the soil, thereby reducing moisture evaporation.
- Watering evenly and deeply with a sprinkler is preferred to a light watering with a hose and nozzle. The deep watering ensures that the water reaches the soil, which encourages deep root growth.
- Apply a weed control to actively growing weeds, which steal water from grass plants. If weeds are dormant, weed control treatment should be suspended until you can water your lawn thoroughly.
- Fertilize your lawn only if there is enough rainfall or opportunity to water to start the grass growing again. When you do fertilize, use a controlled-release fertilizer.
- To avoid moisture loss, do not aerate or dethatch lawn during drought.
- Avoid seeding your lawn until fall, when more rainfall is expected.

Bluegrass will recover from drought. Buffalograss will not recover until the following spring, once it has browned out.

Turfgrass Is A Way of Life

There is still a place for turfgrass in the way of life of the Mountain West. Crowding has not reached the point that we must wall ourselves in or give up parks, playgrounds, or golf courses. If we continue to be wary of water use, the oxygen-providing grasses will set off our view of the mountains and separate spaces within space.

Part IV

The Garden Necessities

CHAPTER 22

Garden Furnishings and Structures

When planning a landscape design, it is natural to think of the living materials first - trees, shrubs, flowers, and the lawn. But no garden is complete without appropriate inanimate materials and objects. Often these materials give character and interest to a garden in winter, as do the living plants in summer. The four-season livability and beauty of the garden also depends on building materials.

stone	brick	steel	pottery	glass
wood	gravel	plastics	wicker	copper
concrete	tile	iron	basketry	bamboo

The construction work you will learn to do yourself can be completed in winter or during the cold days and weekends of very early spring or fall. It is very difficult for a gardener to remain indoors in bad weather. Keep a supply of materials on hand and a list of projects needing completion.

planter boxes, pool covers, tables, chairs, swings

Moderately heavy construction work is enjoyable during cool weather. Save these projects for the cool crisp days.

patio	walks	screens	rockery	barbeque
deck	fences	walls	fountain	statuary
porch	gates	pool	gazebo	firepit

■ *Search for ways to use the family's found art.*

Search for ways to use the family's found art. This is the driftwood you picked up at the beach, the old wagon wheel you unearthed while enjoying a memorable day in the mountains, a child's brightly colored pebble collection, and on and on. These are the things that make the garden your own.

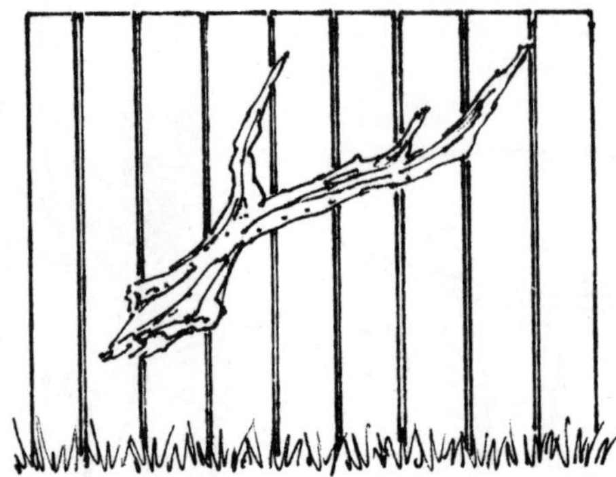

"Found Art" mounted on a fence that screens the vegetable garden.

Stone

Inanimate garden accessories may be made of many materials, both natural and synthetic, but of all the possiblities, the sandstone that is cut from the many native formations in the Mountain West seems to fit the greatest number of construction features. It has good color and texture. In the hands of a skilled stonemason, patios, steps, walls, and other objects are created. If you are strong and have even the slightest of artistic talent, you can learn to cut and fit the stone yourself. There is a thrill to piecing together irregular pieces of stone to make a pattern. The end result is of greater satisfaction and much longer lasting than the jigsaw puzzle it resembles. An added benefit in the Mountain West is that stone is very inexpensive compared with the stone in other states. There is probably a quarry within driving distance of your home. Investigate it and begin learning to use stone.

■ *It is the ha-ha, named becuase it fools the eye.*

Flagstone is a natural for a patio. Make sure the earth is tamped level before you begin laying. The flags must be large enough not to tip when stepped upon. If you use concrete or sand between the flags, bring it up even with the edge of the stone to keep stumbling over a slight imperfection at a minimum.

Flagstone is often used in walks. Somehow, the tendency is to break the stones in half, laying them side by side. The result is a hopscotch course, not a walk. Keep the walk wide enough so that two people can walk together. Set the stones into turf high enough so that the turf won't grow over them.

Boulders are discussed in Chapter 17 "Rock Gardens." The so-called "moss rock" is often used in gardens. It is covered with lichen, not moss. It is said that a dime-sized area of lichen is about fifty years old.

Using moss rock in indoor construction is always a mistake because it takes only two or three years for it to die and flake off. In the outdoor situation, it grows slowly as long as it does not receive any traffic or covering. Various substances are said to make it grow faster, such as buttermilk, urine, and tea, but none have proved to be successful in giving it a growth spurt. Leave it alone and it will increase at its own speed.

Laying Up A Ha-Ha

The pastoral views of rolling hills, grazing animals, blue skies, puffy clouds are all valued views in Great Britain as they are here. The Brits long ago devised an ingenious method to enjoy the view from their broad terraces without interrupting it with a fence to keep the farm animals from straying onto the terrace. It is the ha-ha, named because it fools the eye. A trench with one vertical wall is dug across the area where animals are to be kept in bounds. On the vertical portion of the trench, stones are laid up in a dry wall. The animals may wander into the trench, but the wall side is too high for them to jump and the opposite side is too shallow to cause them any harm. Those persons sitting on the terrace enjoying the view still see the grazing animals, but the trench is invisible and it appears as though the land continues in a rolling hillside.

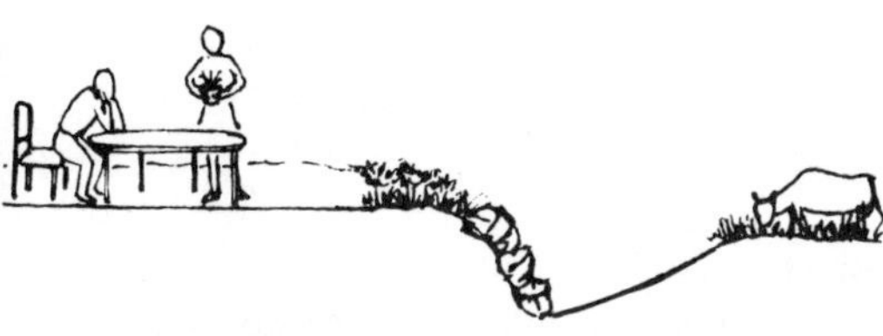

The British ha-ha is as adaptable to the country scene today as it was two centuries ago.

Wood

Wood is a popular construction material, with redwood being the more long-lasting. Cedar is less expensive and easily available because it is native to the Mountain West. Douglas fir is harvested from the forests and tree farms of the west; therefore, shipping costs are minimal. The hardwoods of the tropics are offered for sale in garden furniture. Being gardeners, you may wish to refrain from purchasing this valuable world resource until these woods can be grown and harvested from a treefarm. If you watch public television or travel in the tropics, you have seen the mass destruction of the rain forest and know what it means. You may also have seen small samples of unknown tropical hardwoods in the floors of the native huts. Let us hope these remain undiscovered.

Redwood or white-wood lattice is very effective in landscape construction. More sturdy than it looks, it can be nailed to furring strips on tall privacy fences to soften the visual height and to serve as support for vines. Redwood weathers to a soft gray.

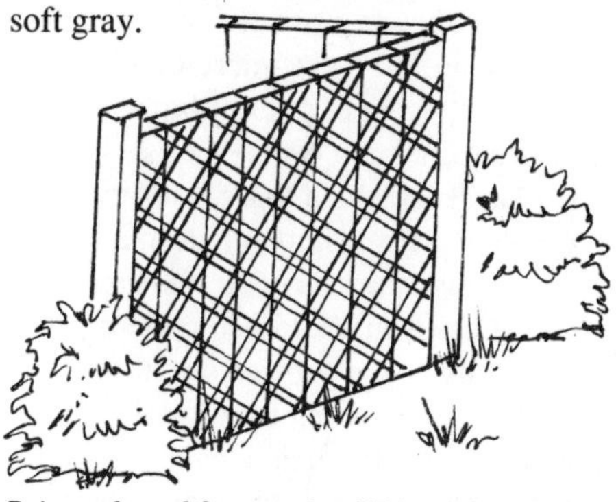

Privacy board fence gains distinction with the addition of redwood or whitewood lattice.

A summer house design.

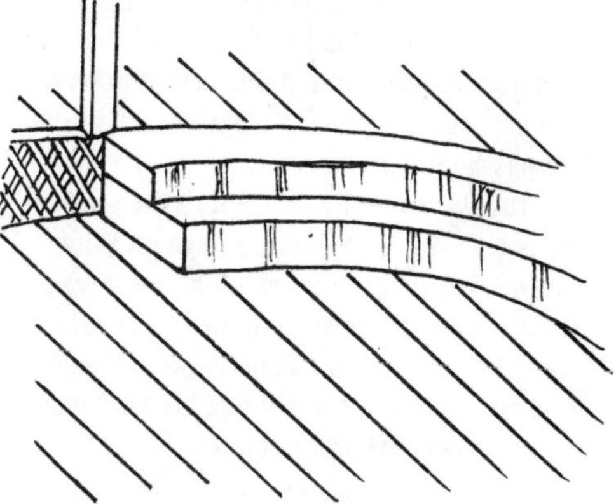

A redwood deck is long-lasting and easy to maintain.

■ *It stands there proclaiming its utilitarian glory for all to see, and through it, everyone can see you!*

Steel and Iron

Fences of steel chain-link seem to be despised by everyone, yet there is much in their favor. They last forever. No painting. No digging up and replacing rotting wood posts and disposing of piles of broken boards after fifteen to twenty years. The properly installed chain link fence attached to steel alloy posts is impervious to all except the trash truck or other misdirected driver that backs into it. The problem with the chain-link is that you can see it. It stands there proclaiming its utilitarian glory for all to see, and through it, everyone can see you! The solution is to plant it out, meaning that you design a broad (at least five feet) border of deciduous and evergreen shrubs to be planted next to the offending fence, and within three years the shrubs will grow together and you won't see the fence at all, nor will anyone be able to see you. The interstices of this fence also allow for good air movement, which is non-existent with a board fence. There will be summer breezes and less powdery mildew on your roses!

Ornamental wrought iron fences and gates must be painted occasionally but remain the choice of many for security and permanence. No one is likely to cut it to gain entry; no one is likely to climb it if it is six feet or more in height. Yet it does not give the appearance of a bastion and allows free passage of air.

Wrought iron may be used in the garden to design a distinctive lamp to mark your entrance. A plant bracket for a blank wall transforms both the wall and accents the plant. Wrought iron has no connotation of an historic period; thus, it can be used with modern or period architecture.

Concrete

Construction with concrete is at a minimum today. This material is hot in summer, cold in winter, and the glare is unbearable when the sun is on it. The day is gone of the little tract house with its postage stamp patio of concrete. Those that remain are easily enlarged and covered with stone or warm-colored pavers as described in Chapter 2 under "The Townhouse and Condominium Garden." Mortar and concrete are still the base of garden construction project, for no other material is more malleable or inexpensive.

Brick

If the home is of brick construction, it follows that the patio and walks, and sometimes the drive are also of brick. It is a warm but formal material. Laying brick dry on a tamped soil base with sand swept between the bricks is seldom successful. In the Mountain West frost will heave each brick at a different rate, and it becomes the hapless gardeners job to re-lay the brick each spring. Set them in concrete in the first place and enjoy your brick patio without further to-do. A drawback to point out is that it is difficult to shovel snow from brick. Using a snowbrush solves the problem.

Tile

We think of tile as those colorful squares you could not resist on your trip to Mexico. Tile as a building material is useful for the gardener as a patio planter. They are heavy enough not to tip over in an inadvertent bump against them; they are heat and cold resistent, making good root development material; they are pleasing rosy or beige in color. Give each a base of wood. Use the Mexican tiles as insets in a wall or to brighten a plain planter.

Tile planters are not tipsy; plants grow well in them; they are pleasing in color.

Gravel

Gravel is another behind-the-scenes material like concrete. Use it behind the stones of a stone wall to prevent frost heave and provide good drainage. Use it as a base for the brick, concrete, or asphalt drive. Use it as a base for setting flagstones in a path. Use is in soil mixes for the rock garden. Use it as a mulch in areas where high winds would blow away organic materials such as pole peelings. Don't use it as a substitute for lawn, thinking you are saving your nations' resources. The increase in air-conditioning costs will offset your saving.

The Screen Fence

Screens are different than the perimeter fence. They are designed as an ornament that disguises their use as a method to screen from view a neighbor's yard, a utility area, or to prevent wind in the patio area, or create intimacy to an area. In the design of the screen fence you can use plastics, fiberglass, leftover building materials, or any of a hundred other different materials. Keep the overall general design of your landscape plan in mind, but let your imagination be your guide.

Firepits and Barbeques

The evening air at high altitude cools quickly as the day's heat rises. The firepit is the refined bonfire of the Mountain West. It is a square or circular pit dug into the patio, eight or ten inches deep, and lined with fire brick. The camaraderie it creates is the same as the old camping-trip campfire; the warmth is more than welcome and makes a cool evening bearable. A grate can be fitted over it for cooking, and the ashes can be cleaned easily with a small shovel.

The portable barbeque has largely taken the place of the built-in outdoor fireplace. Bottled propane is the fuel of choice rather than charcoal briquettes. A better design might be using a manufactured barbeque built into a simple stone structure.

Garden Furnishings

The chairs, tables, benches, or lounges are available in such bewildering array that the gardener can make mistakes in fitting the furniture to the style of the landscape. There is no substitute for trying out different styles before you buy. Often a dealer will allow you to take home a chair and small table of different styles. Expect to leave an imprint of your credit card, which is safe in the hands of a reliable dealer. You will be more certain of which furniture style complements your patio if you look at each style in the different light cast on it in morning, high noon, late afternoon and early evening. With the price of garden furniture nowdays, it pays to make the right choice the first time.

■ *. . . let your imagination be your guide.*

CHAPTER 23

Tooling Up

Buying tools is a satisfying task for a gardener. Each one that is selected is sure to do the best job and make the garden more successful than last year. Eternal optimism is a trait all gardeners share.

A minimum of tools may satisfy a few gardeners, but most succumb to alluring displays in the garden center sooner or later. But let us assume you are starting out with buying your first tools. Acquiring one of each of the following will be your aim, with gradual build-up of the tool arsenal as you gain experience.

Hand Tools

■ The shovel or spade is necessary to begin preparing soil, and it is your misfortune to step right into a controversy right off. There are proponents of the long-handled, round blade shovel, called the "irrigating shovel", and those who insist that the short-handled square bladed spade is the only one to have. Since you are a new Mountain Westerner, you would be wise to go with the flow and buy a shovel. There aren't many spades sold in these parts. The specialists in orthopedic medicine approve as well. It seems that the long handle gives leverage that allows one to lift and throw the load with greater ease. Two sizes are wise. The small one, known as Mother's Teaspoon in the author's family, is useful for both men and women in digging small holes and for getting into tight places.

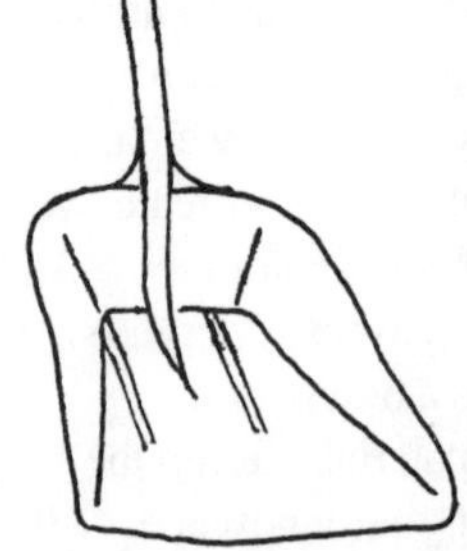

■ Another shovel - the scoop shovel - is used by rock gardeners to roll a heavy stone onto its flat surface and drag it by the handle to its permanent location. Country dwellers will also find the scoop useful in cleaning animal stalls.

■ Spading forks are much the same. About the third year of your gardening efforts you will invest in a second one to use with the first one in prying apart clumps of perennials. A fork is useful in the fall as you fork over the soil in the vegetable garden to leave it rough and humpy for the winter.

■ The pry-bar or crow-bar's usefulness is too long to list. For the gardener, it pays to purchase a heavy one of steel.

■ The foot-powered aerator takes two cores about three inches long from the soil when the foot is pushed on the bar. With the following push, the cores from the first push are ejected from the top. It is useful in aerating small areas where heavy foot traffic has compacted the turf.

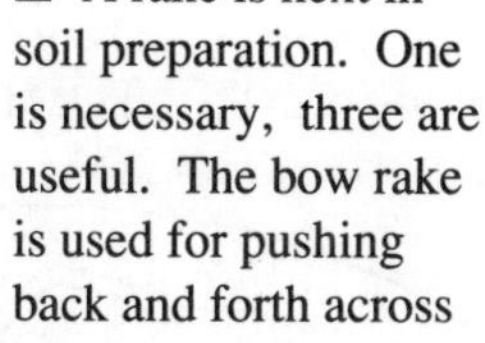

■ A rake is next in soil preparation. One is necessary, three are useful. The bow rake is used for pushing back and forth across roughly spaded soil to break clods and smooth the surface.

■ The broom rake is used in raking autumn leaves and general clean-up tasks.

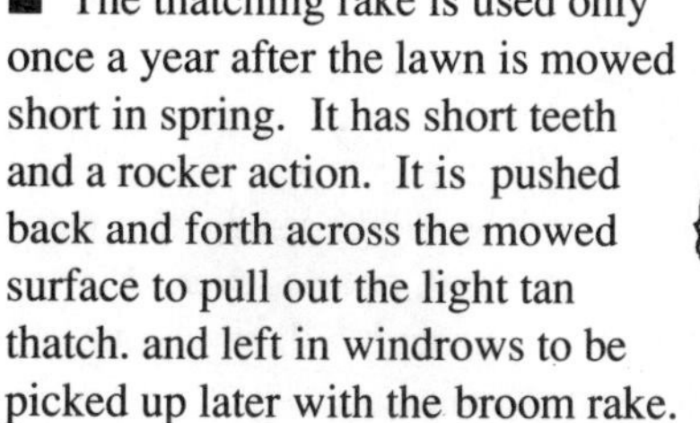

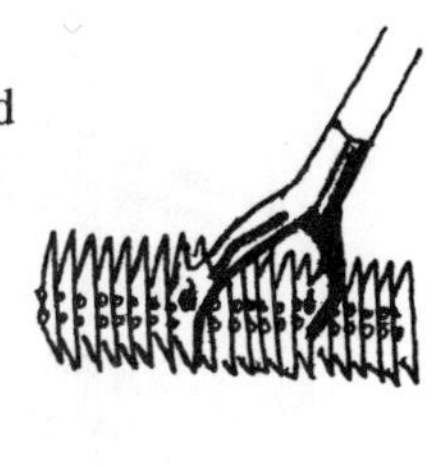

■ The thatching rake is used only once a year after the lawn is mowed short in spring. It has short teeth and a rocker action. It is pushed back and forth across the mowed surface to pull out the light tan thatch. and left in windrows to be picked up later with the broom rake.

The various hoes will find many uses, primarily to open rows for planting seeds.

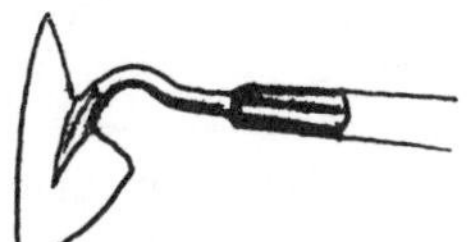

■ The Warren hoe will see the most duty. Its triangular tip opens the row, and the "ears" on the opposite end pull the soil over the newly planted seeds.

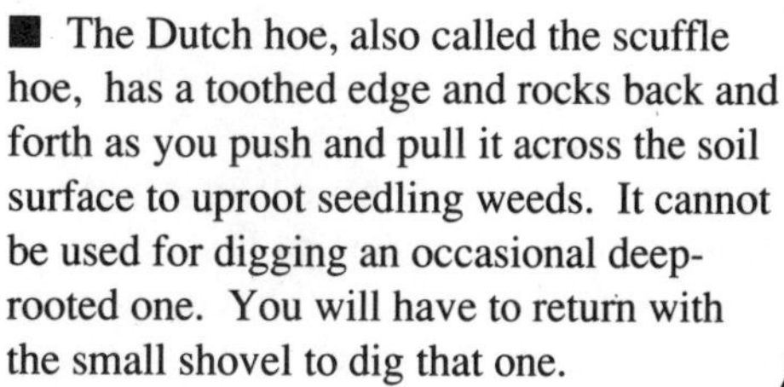

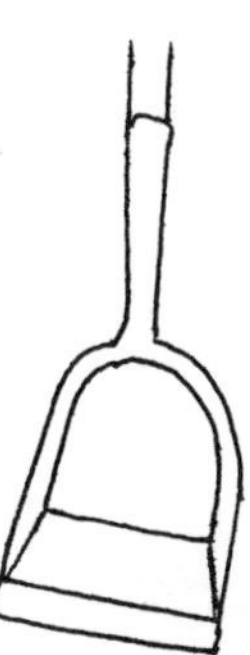

■ The Dutch hoe, also called the scuffle hoe, has a toothed edge and rocks back and forth as you push and pull it across the soil surface to uproot seedling weeds. It cannot be used for digging an occasional deep-rooted one. You will have to return with the small shovel to dig that one.

■ The three-pronged cultivator falls into the "hoe" category, for its diamond-shaped tines stir the soil surface to cut weeds and prevent crusting. When purchasing, make sure the center prong is beneath and back of the other two for the best cultivating action.

■ The mattock hoe will be used when there is a root to be dug out, or as a lever. You won't need it often, but it will save your back many times over.

Small hand tools include

■ A trowel of sufficient strength that you won't bend it in half with the first thrust is the best buy. The strongest is often referred to as the "No Blister." It is made of aluminum alloy and has a red cushion-grip handle that makes it easy to locate in tall grass.

■ An asparagus knife has a long straight shank with a notch at the tip. It's used for cutting asparagus, of course, but its most frequent use is in weeding.

■ The Japanese Hori-Hori is a very strong broad blade with one sharp edge and one serrated edge. It is useful in digging holes for transplants as well as sawing divisions from a clump of perennials.

Cutting tools will serve you long and well if they fit your hand. Try out every sort before buying pruning shears. The two types of blade are: the anvil which has one sharp blade that squeezes off the branch against a solid broad blade: and the by-pass which has two sharp blades that pass each other as they cut through the branch. Of the two, the by-pass probably gives a cleaner cut.

■ Lopping shears are long-handled by-pass or anvil shears with the ability to cut larger limbs. As with all pruning blades, good construction will allow you to take the blades apart for sharpening.

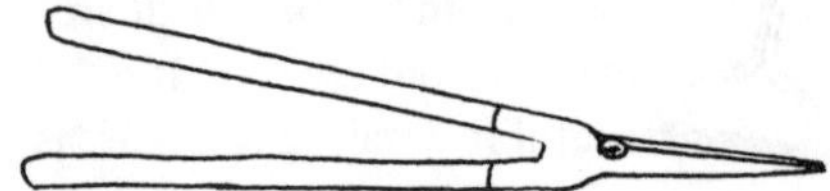

■ If you have a hedge, a hedge shear will be needed even though you will do the bulk of the work with a power tool. Pointed blades will get in between twigs more easily than the standard blunt-tipped blades.

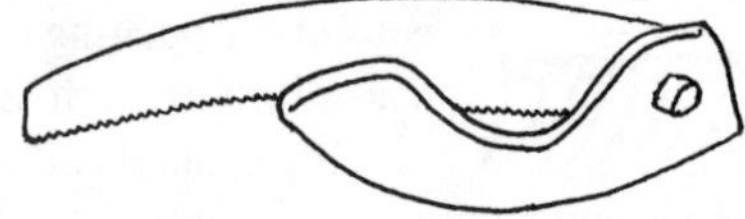

■ Saws will be needed by the third year of your gardening endeavor. Both six and twelve-inch folding saws will be used many times because the eye-bolt holding the blade can be loosened to angle the blade around a branch for sawing a branch in a tight space.

■ The bow saw is indispensable in sawing large limbs where space is not cramped. They are inexpensive. The blade is replaceable. Keep and extra on hand.

■ A pole saw can be useful if you own older trees or for mature dwarf fruit trees. Leave the pole pruner to be used by the professional unless you live beyond the area where professional tree-care people are available.

■ You may have never used a sharpening device, but you will need at least one to keep your spades, shovels, and hoes sharp. The bastard file is the most useful.

■ The Arkansas oilstone is needed by the country dweller where sharpening shops are not available. You will need both a hard and soft stone, plus the honing oil. Follow the directions that come with the kit and you will soon be proficient in its use.

Carrying Devices

■ Carts versus wheelbarrows - each has their champion. The cart has the advantage of better balance. The wheelbarrow can be directed around tighter corners. Most gardeners will have both as they begin to acquire more tools.

■ More useful than either the cart or the wheelbarrow is the plastic tarp. When cutting down large quantities of perennials in the fall or pruning in the spring, it can hold three times more than a cart or wheelbarrow. There is no need to handle the trash twice because you simply drag the tarp to the trash container or compost bin, lift and dump. With a cart or wheelbarrow you must load and unload. In addition, when you spread the tarp near where you will be working, you don't have to aim the material. Just toss it in the general direction and you will hit the tarp.

■ A wheeled or hand-carried fertilizer spreader is an inexpensive item that some gardeners prefer not to use. Actually, holding a basket of fertilizer under one arm and tossing handfuls with the other is the preferred method by most. It is much less trouble than pouring, setting dials, trying to adjust the hopper openings, pacing around the area, then cleaning the hopper before putting it away.

■ Tool carriers eliminate many trips to the tool shed. If your property is large, invest in the carrier that carries rakes, hoes, shovels, etc., in an upright carrier. The gardener of a smaller plot will appreciate a canvas bag with sturdy handles and many pockets.

■ The come-along is not a carrying tool. It most often eliminates carrying. It is also called a "power mule', though it is not a tool using electric or gas-fired power. It is more a winch or an old-time block-and-tackle, using leverage to move objects weighing one ton (the small size) or two tons (the large size) by moving a handle back and forth. There are few households that would not find a use for this tool. The rock gardener will use it to move boulders; the water gadener will use it to lift lily tubs out of the water; the country dweller will use it to pull downed trees to the wood pile for cutting. It will also find use in lifting the canoe to the rafters; Grandma's sofa into the attic, and on and on. As indicated, this tool comes in two sizes, each for less than fifty dollars.

Pesticide Applicators

■ The knapsack pressure tank is touted as the most accurate pesticide applicator. Pressure is pumped into the tank after filling; continuous action spraying operates between forty and sixty pounds of pressure.

■ The hose-bottle spray gun is the most convenient. There is no need to measure the amount of pesticide. The bottle is filled; then the correct number of teaspoons or tablespoons of concentrate is dialed on the top of the applicator. After attaching to the hose, trigger action with the thumb activates the spray. The correct amount of water is mixed with the concentrate to deliver the spray about twenty to thirty feet.

■ The one-quart spray bottle with trigger action has a place in the tool shed for the small amounts of spray sometimes needed on a few plants.

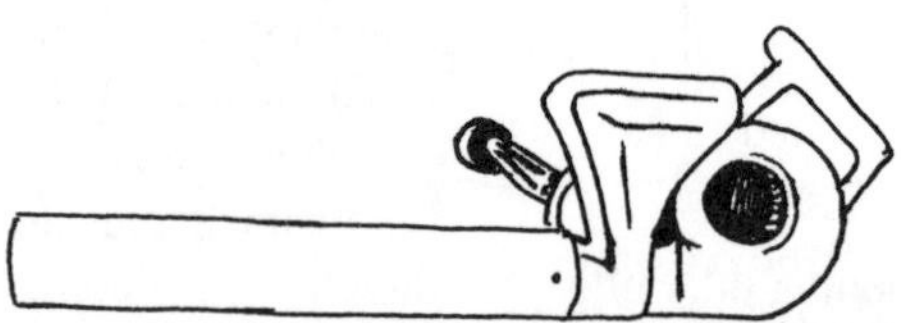

■ The duster is used more and more because dust is easier to use and can be stored in the device for instant access. All parts are non-corrosive and the dust is dispersed evenly.

Protection Devices

■ A gardener's knees are usually the first to go. Take care of yours by buying the best device possible to cushion the knees. Test the kneeling bench which allows you to rise from your knees easily by using the hand-holds. The device is difficult to remember to carry around, however. Easier to remember is the inexpensive foam plastic kneeler.

■ Safety glasses are a nuisance, but you won't think so when the first flying object hits your safety lenses and you realize that the object would have seriously damaged your eye.

■ Gloves are a very personal part of the gardener's attire. More than hats, pants, or jackets. Every gardener is very particular about the gloves he likes best, and sings their praises loud and long. A few of the most-praised are: The split cowhide with a tight wrist to prevent soil from sliding inside; the nylon-coated cotton mesh for coolness and extra thickness when moving rock; the heavy cowhide gauntlet for protection when pruning thorny trees or shrubs; the plastic gauntlet for use around pesticides; the tight-fitting unlined rubber glove used when transplanting seedlings.

You might like to know that only amateurs are gloveless in the garden. Your hands are your most important tool. Protect them - tetanus is out there waiting to attack!

Power Tools

■ Your biggest investment is your lawn mower. Please see Chapter 21 "The Lawn Is the Stage" for advice in choosing a lawn mower.

■ The power blower has largely taken the place of the push broom because it does a better job in a shorter time. You may also want to investigate one that has a bag attachment for vacuum action.

■ The string trimmer, also called weed wacker, is no longer for parks employees. Lightweight electric models give everyone a chance to use this versatile tool. When you get very good at its control, you will be able to slow the speed and selectively nick an unwanted plant in among desirable plants. You will also be able to tilt the head of the trimmer to direct the flow of waste in the direction you want it to go. Remember to wear your safety glasses, heavy shoes, or sturdy boots.

The string trimmer is a danger to trees when they are grown in the turf with no island around them for protection. The whirling nylon strings effectively girdle a tree when the operator is trying to trim grass around the trunk. The tree may survive a few whacks, but eventually growth slows and it dies after a few years of this treatment.

■ Electric hedge clippers are needed by those with lengthy hedges. Use a professional service to have them sharpened annually and they will serve you a long time.

■ The power edger is an unnecessary tool because you live in the Mountain West where water is in short supply. You should not be growing turf next to the sidewalk, drive, or patio where radiated heat makes grass growing difficult and where it uses five times more water than in other areas.

■ A chain saw is needed by the country dweller, but is best rented when there is need of one in the city. Small saws are easily operated, even by a woman, when taking down trees or shrubs. keep in mind that they are not used to make the final cut on a large limb. There is too much danger in cutting into the bark ridge or branch collar. See Chapter 9 "Pruning."

■ The chipper-grinder is a high-ticket item that every gardener aspires to owning. Its use is valuable in making short work of limbs, branches, twigs, leaves, sod, and clods. The resulting organic mulch material may be enough for your needs throughout the year.

■ The rotary tiller is the workhorse of the large vegetable garden and home fruit orchard. Each year new models supersede those of previous years. Check the many buyer's guides at your public library before buying.

■ The small tiller is seen in many city and town backyards as a device for tilling small areas, cultivating weeds in the perennial border, and for digging trenches, such as those needed when planting asparagus. Each model has its attributes and drawbacks. Don't hesitate to stop and ask about a tiller when you see a gardener using one. Most are willing to tell you what they like or don't like about their model.

■ The mini-tractor, like the riding mower, is for the country dweller. They are a bargain because so many attachments are available: gang-reel mower, cart, disc, seed-hopper, fertilizer spreader, and many more.

Many power tools will be rated in the consumer-guides at your public library. Consult these documents before you make a major purchase.

Suggested catalogs

A.M. Leonard, Inc.
P.O. Box 816
Piqua, Ohio 45356
1-800-433-0633

Mellinger's
2310 W. South Range Rd.
North Lima, Ohio 44452-9731
1-800-321-7444

CHAPTER 24

Records are Important

The keeping of garden records is both difficult and necessary. You may think you will keep the location of a new plant in mind, but it seldom happens. Devising a record-keeping system has driven botanic garden executives to the wall and it will do the same for you.

If throwing receipts into a shoebox is all you can manage at first, so be it. It's a start. For incentive, realtors tell us documented evidence of the price paid for a shrub or tree can be multiplied by FIVE to reach the increase in the selling price of your home when the trees and shrubs reach maturity. Additionally, if you should decide to sell off the excess seedlings you grew this spring, or go into the horticulture business seriously, there is a tax deduction for a portion of your expense in buying seeds, fertilizer, cuttings, lining-out stock, etc. You will need a record of expenses.

The plan you made at the beginning of this book is good only for the long-lived plants. You aren't likely to change tree species unless an unforeseen catastrophe occurs. Flower borders never remain the same year after year. Your tastes change. You see the possibilities of a different color combination or new species comes on the market that you want to try.

Record Books

Each successive year new record books will be on the market because gardening is a fast-growing hobby and the more advanced a gardener becomes, the more need for records will be recognized. You will probably buy several before you devise your own according to your needs. If you have a small corner of your tool shed, a kitchen desk , or, luxury of all luxuries, a home office where your garden plan can be

■ *. . . white plastic labels are dubbed "tombstones for mice."*

mounted for easy reference on the wall, you will be at ease in changing the records as you move out old plants, plant new plants, and add structures to your garden.

Your rock garden will be the most difficult to keep track of. Those with long experience prefer 3x5" cards for each plant kept in a box with alphabetical index tabs. Each card has a notation of the common and Latin names, date of aquisition, geographical origin, culture notes, and approximate location in the garden. The latter is the problem. It is considered bad form among rock gardeners to use a conspicuous label on a plant. The little white plastic labels are dubbed "tombstones for mice." Inconspicuous labels are regarded as prized possessions of squirrels and children. The plants themselves often overgrow a label that is inserted flat with the soil surface. If your note card gives the location of the plant as "in the middle section three inches north of the rock with the orange lichen," you will be seen counting orange-lichened rocks in the middle section forevermore. If you don't find it, you assume that it died, but don't be too sure. It may have thrown seed explosively when your head was turned and all the little strangers are not weeds. Count on at least a dozen occasions of major confusion once a year. Fellow rock gardeners who are visiting can be pressed into identification service, and you will be given the same opportunity to aid in identifying their nameless orphans when you visit their gardens.

The Sturdy File Cabinet

Gardening magazines and plant society journals will enter your home with regularity as soon as you are genuinely hooked on gardening. "Paper in" and "Paper out" will be justified as your motto to prevent inundation. A file cabinet of medium proportions is called for, together with a gigantic box of file folders. As each magazine and journal is read, it is torn apart. Not later, now. No need to meticulously snip out the ads on the side of the page for discard. Remove the entire page(s) for filing. One day a year is set aside for "purging the files." Horticulture is a swiftly moving science. No need to keep that clipping about the plant introductions of 1992. They are obsolete, and if they aren't, they are readily available in the catalogs that will come in the mail by the tons.

Catalogs are pretty picture books to be perused on long winter evenings. Except for seeds, your local nursery can often supply you with the same plant at the same or lower cost, considering the cost of shipping today. Mark your seed orders with the words "Send seeds or send money." This admonition will give the order-taker notice that you won't stand for being sent a voucher to be used in a later order. If the item ordered it not in stock, you should be refunded your money; not given a voucher. Keep records of orders sent because names of plants, dates of the order, and dates of the arrival of shipment are important if something goes awry.

Keeping track of catalogs is another job for your file cabinet and a set of index separators. Purging this file drawer can be a bonanza for your child's teacher, an artist friend, or your fellow garden club members. Exchanging catalogs is a favorite coffee-time activity.

The Computer Age

When the personal computer comes into your home, sly thoughts will enter your head as you become proficient in this device. Each year, nay, each month brings new programs for gardeners. Computer software related to gardening, at present, seem to fall in three basic categories: (1) drawing and design, (2) plant finder database and (3) miscellaneous. None are perfect. The majority are for growers of vegetables, which is difficult to fathom since the Gallup Poll taken each year by National Gardening shows the number of vegetable gardeners declining rapidly.

For a comprehensive review of twenty-one computer programs for the gardener, check at your library or your own edition of the March/April 1992 National Gardening magazine for "Floppy-Disking the Garden" by judywhite. A postcard to the each of the sources below will access you to information.

Abracadata Ltd.,
P.O. Box 2440, Eugene, OR 97402
(800)451-4871; (503)342-3030

Accu-Weather, Inc.
619 W. College Ave.,
State College, PA 16801, (814)237-0309

Autodesk,
11911 N. Creek Pkwy, South,
Bothell, WA 98011

Birdbrain Software,
574 W20800 Field Dr., Muckego, WI 53150

Compu-Gro,
RR2, Box 2731, Ozark, MO 65721

Compugarden, Inc.,
1006 Highland Dr.,
Silver Spring, MD 20910, (301)587-7995

CompuServe Gardening Forum
5000 Arlington Centre Blvd, P.O.
Box 20212, Columbus, OH 43220
(800)848-8199 (operator 334)

Double-Pawed Software,
432 Bigelow Hollow Rd.,
Eastford, CT 06242

Elemental Software,
P.O. Box 919, Emigrant, MT 59027
(406)333-4472

Expert Software,
P.O. Box 143376,
Coral Gables, FL 33134, (800)759-2562

Gardenfind Magazine Index,
P.O. Box 2703, Lynnwood, WA 98036
(206)743-6605

Green Thumb Software,
P.O. Box 18442, Boulder, CO 80308
(303)460-8384

Green Scape Sytems,
P.O. Box 857,
Blacksburg, VA 24063-0857,
(703)552-3755

Infopoint Software,
Box 83, Arcola, MD 65603,
(417)424-3424

J. Mendoza Gardens,
18 E. 16th St., New York, NY 10003
(212)989-4253

Mindsun,
RD2, Andover, NJ 07821
(201)398-9557

Public Brand Software Shareware Cat.,
P.O. Box 51315, Indianapolis, IN 46251,
(800)426-3475

Robert W. Boufford, Ohio State Univ.,
Agricultural Technical Institue,
1328 Dover Rd.,
Wooster, OH 44691-4000

Ron McCauley,
P.O. Box 982, Temiscaming, Que.,
Canada JOZ-3R0

Shannon Software Ltd.,
P.O. Box 6126,
Falls Church, VA 22046
(703)573-9274

Software Toolworks,
60 Leveroni Ct., Novato, CA 94949
(415)883-3000

Terrace Software,
P.O. Box 271, Medford MA 02155
(617)396-0382

Glossary of Horticultural Terms

Abcission Layer - A layer of thin-walled cells which are formed at the base of the leaf petiole to facilitate leaf fall.

Acid - In reference to soil that is below the pH rating of 7.0 neutral.

Adventitious buds - Latent buds along a stem that will be stimulated when other buds are destroyed.

Alkaline - In reference to soil that is above the pH rating of 7.0 neutral.

Allelopathic - The ability of certain plants to prevent the growth of another.

Alpine - The region higher in altitude than the sub-alpine region or at the point of 47° constant isotherm. Also a reference to the plants that grow in this region.

Alternate - The arrangement of plant parts on a stem, usually of leaves.

Annual - A plant that grows from seed, blooms, and sets seed in one season.

Apical - The point or tip, e.g. of a stem.

Armed - A plant with sharp defense such as thorns, spines, prickles or barbs.

Aspect - The exposure facing a particular direction.

B & B - Balled and Burlapped - a procedure for wrapping the rrot ball of the tree with burlap for shipping and transport to the planting hole.

Biennial - A plant that grows from seed and dies down with the first frost; grows, blooms and sets seed the second season before dying.

Bloom - The flower of a plant. The gray coating on a leaf or fruit that can be wiped away.

Bole - The stem or trunk of a tree.

Broadleaf evergreen - A plant having evergreen leaves that have a midrib and veins, as opposed to needled (pine) or scale-leafed (juniper) evergreens.

Bud - The rudimentary state of a stem or branch. Also used as a term for an unexpanded flower.

Bulb - A subterranean leaf-bud with fleshy scales. Example, an onion.

Callus - Wound tissue which develops from cambium or other exposed meristem.

Calyx - The sepals of a flower as a group.

Cambium - The cylinder of meristematic (growth) tissue between the wood and the bark.

Chelate - An organic compound containing metallic elements necessary for plant growth. They are useful in supplying deficient minerals.

Coniferous - A cone-bearing woody plant. Examples, Spruce, Fir, Pines. Most coniferous plants are evergreens, but the Larch is deciduous.

Corm - A thickened, vertical solid underground stem.

Crown - The portion of a herbaceous plant at the soil level. The portion of a woody plant that is topmost.

Cutting - Any portion of a plant having meristematic tissue that is used to star a new plant.

Dappled Shade - Moving overhead shade from trees that allows sun to reach the soil for a short time as it moves in its arc.

Day-neutral - A plant without floral or vegetative response to length of day.

Deciduous - A plant that drops its leaves, once a year.

Dicot - Plant with two cotyledons or seed leaves in its seed, e.g., bean, oak.

Dioecious - A plant have unisexual flowers, each sex confined to a separate plant.

Division - A portion of a plant having roots and the potential of stems and leaves that is separatedfrom the mother plant to start a new plant.

Doer - A term describing a plant that performs exceptionally well.

Dormant - A restive condition of a plant, usually in winter.

Drainage - A condition of soil that allows water to flow freely through it. A natural geographical formation or man-made structure to allow air or water to flow to a lower elevation.

Dripline - The line at ground level where water dripping from the outermost branches of a tree will fall.

Ecology - The relationship of plants to their environment and each other.

Establishment water - Water required for a plant to become established before it can grow on its own with natural precipitation.

Exotic - A plant that is not native to the area in which it is growing.

F_1 - The first generation progeny of a cross.

Faced down - A plant with an ultimate height lower than the one growing directly behind.

Fastigiate - Upward growing, closely parallel stems or limbs.

Fertilization - (in sexual propagation) Fusion of male and female germ cells following pollination.

Flare - The portion of a tree's trunk at the soil line.

Fortified Leaves or Sawdust - Sawdust that has a chemical or organic fertilizer added to make up for the nitrogen lag when decomposition organisms remove nitrogen before returning it with the death and decomposition of their bodies.

Genus - A biological classification of plants ranking between the family and the species. The plural is genera.

Hardening Off - Subjecting plants to adverse conditions to hasten tissue maturation for increasing hardiness.

Hardy - The reference to the ability of a plant to withstand a severe climate.

Heading Back - A pruning term meaning to cut terminal growth back.

Herbaceous - A plant with no woody overwintering parts above the soil level.

Heeling in - temporarily planting plants in a protected until they can be planted in their permanent position.

Humus - Partly decomposed organic matter.

Hybrid - A plant resulting from a cross between two or more species of plants which are more or less alike.

Imbibition - The taking up of water by a seed.

Indigenous - A native plant.

Limbing Up - A pruning procedure in which lower limbs are removed from a tree to allow a person to walk underneath.

Meristem - The portion of a plant capable of cell division.

Monecious - A plant species having unisexual flowers on the same plant. Example = corn.

Monocot - (monocotyledonous) Plant with one cotyledn in its seed, e.g., sweet corn, coconut.

Mossy - A matted growth habit with leaves overlapping.

Mulch - Various organic or inorganic material used to cover soil to prevent weeds, preserve moisture, maintain soil temperature and eliminate cultivation.

Naturalize - A process of establishing plants in an environment where they will continue to grow and to propagate themselves unaided as would native plants.

Node - A point on a stem where a leaf or flower bud originates, sometimes represented by a leaf scar or swelling.

Ovary - The flask-shaped female organ of the flower which contains ovules. The undeveloped fruit.

Parthenocarpic - Seedless as in some fruits.

Perennial - A plant with viable roots for three growing seasons. Stems and leaves die down each fall.

Perfect - Referring to a flower containing both male and female parts.

Photoperiodism - Response of plants to the daily duration of light.

Pinching back - Pruning the soft succulent tip of a shoot to stimulate lateral growth.

Pistillate - Refers to the female part of the flower which produces the seed or fruit.

Pole Peeling Mulch - The organic mulch created when woody plants are run through a chipper/grinding machine. The resulting thin slivers knit together quickly so as not to blow away.

Potting on - Repotting a plant to a pot the next size larger.

Restrictive Covenant - An agreed-upon restriction to the deed of real property disallowing certain items, such as high fences, dogs, or the keeping of goats and chickens.

Rhizome - A thickened underground root. Example is Iris.

Ringing - Removing a narrow strip of bark around the periphery of the stem to prevent downward translocation of food beyond that point. Often used to stimulate a fruit to bear.

Scarification - Injuring or scratching the seed coat to aid in imbibition and germination.

Scion - The shoot inserted into another plant in grafting.

Seeding Around - An expression denoting the plant that self-sows its seed into the surrounding area.

Slip - A herbaceous softwood cutting.

Sport - A sudden and unusual variation of a plant's growth. This can occur within any portion of a plant.

Spur - Short, woody, fruiting stem attached to a branch.

Staminate - Refers to the male part of a flower which produces the pollen to fertilize the female flower.

Stolon - A horizontal stem that roots at its tip and there gives rise to a new plant.

Stooling out - A horticultural term referring to the shoots rising from the crown of a plant that become new plants. Usually referring to grass species.

Successive Plantings - Varied planting dates of the same crop or a different crop to extend the growing season.

Succulent - Referring to the soft and tender portions of a plant. Also referring to a class of plants having thick, juicy stems, able to store water in stems and leaves.

Sucker - A soft shoot of new growth originating from limbs or roots. Those suckers originating from limbs are loosely attached. Also refers to the adhering discs of a vine.

Sub-soil - That portion of soil lying under the topsoil. Subsoil may be located only inches or many feet below the topsoil. It is often low in organic matter but high in mineral nutrients.

Taper - An increase in girth of the branches and trunk of a tree.

Template - An overlay used as a pattern, such as in drawing the shape of a tree or shrub.

Tender - A reference to a plant that is susceptible to damage from cold, heat, drought or any other restrictive condition.

Timberline - A western term meaning the alpine region where trees fail to grow. This is the 47° constant isotherm.

Translocation - Movement of water, minerals, and nutrients within the plant.

Transpiration - Water loss by evaporation from internal leaf surfaces.

True Leaves - The first pair of leaves to emerge after the cotyledon leaves that are contained in the seed

Tuber - A short thickened underground organ, usually, but not necessarily, a stem.

Tubex tube - A UV light protected, wire-reinforced plastic tube used to protect seedling woody plants in windbreaks, country landscapes, and public plantings. Cost varies from $2-$3 each. Fact sheets available from 1-800-248-8239.

Utility Easement - That portion of your property containing the sewer, water, electric and gas lines. The municipality has the right to remove any structures or plantings in this area in order to service the lines.

Water-logged - A soil without aeration due to poor aeration and overwatering.

Watersprouts - Rapidly growing shoots that arise from adventitious or latent buds on branches or trunks.

Warty - A plant part marked with rounded tubercles, rougher than granules.

Watery - Sap that is thin and clear.

Whorl - Arrangement of three or more structures, such as leaves, from a single node.

Wood - The dead hard xylem tissue.

Woolly - A plant having long, soft, matted hairs, like wool.

x - Indicates a hybrid.

Xylem - A complex tissue of tough, fibrous, elongated cells forming vessels and woody tissue. Responsible for upward movement of water and minerals from roots to leaves.

Zone - An area restricted by a range of annual average minimum temperatures, used in describing hardiness.

Bibliography

American Rock Garden Society and Denver Botanic Garden 1986. *Rocky Mountain Alpines*, Timber Press, Portland, OR.

Archibald, David and Mary Patton. 1990. *Water Gardens*, Camden House Willowdale, Ontario, Canada M2H 2S4.

Bailey, Liberty Hyde. 1949. *Manual of Cultivated Plants.* Macmillan Co., N.Y.1116 p.

Bailey Hortorium, 1976. *Hortus III.* Macmillan Co. New York. 1290 p.

Bennett and Forsyth,1990 *The Harrowsmith Annual Garden*, Camden House, Camden East, Ontario, Canada

Bloom, Adrian. 1972 *Conifers in Your Garden.* American Garden Guild.

Borland, James, *Paradise Lost*, 1987 Colorado Green, Spring.

Brooklyn Botanic Gardens' Plants and Gardens Handbooks covering many subjects. Booklet list available from Brooklyn Botanic Garden, 1000 Washington Ave., Brooklyn, New York 11225.

Butler, George D. 1958. *Recreation Areas, Their Design and Equipment*, The Ronald Press Co., New York.

Chronic, Halka, 1984, *Pages of Stone, Geology of the Rocky Mountains & Western Great Plains*, The Mountaineers, Seattle, WA.

Church, Thomas D. 1955. *Gardens Are For People*, Reinhold, New York.

Crockett, James Underwood 1971, *Evergreens*, Time-Life Series.

Crockett, James Underwood 1972, *Flowering Shrubs*, Time-Life Series.

Crockett, James Underwood 1972, *Trees*, Time-Life Series.

Denver Botanic Garden 1990, 1991, *Mountain, Plains and Garden*

Dirr, Michael A., *Manual of Woody Landscape Plants*, 4th edition, Stipes Pub. Co.

Everett, Thomas H. 1980 T*he New York Botanical Garden Illustrated Encyclopedia of Horticulture*, Garland STP Press. New York.

Foley, Daniel J. 1972; *Ground Covers for Easier Gardening*, Dover Inc., N.Y.

Forest Service, USDA. 1974. *Seeds of Woody Plants in the United States*, Agriculture Handbook No. 450, Sup't of Documents, U.S. Government Printing Office., Washington D.C.

Freestone, Doris, Len Freestone, John Mirgon, Mary Mirgon, Ellen Westbrook, Gayle Weinstein, *Ornamental Water Gardening*, 1991, The Shereth Group, Denver, CO.

Hersey, Jean, 1961, *The Woman's Day Book of Annuals & Perennials*, Simon and Schuster, N. Y.

Hill, Lewis, 1987, *Cold-Climate Gardening*, Storey Communications, Inc., Pownal, Vermont 05261.

Hyde, Barbara J., 1977 *Homescaping*, Colorado State University.

Ingwersen, Will 1981, *Alpine Garden Plants*, Blandford Press, Dorset, U.K.

Judywhite, Floppy-Disking the Garden, National Gardening magazine, March/April 1992.

Kelaidis, Gwen and Panayoti, 1988, *Rock Garden Plants for the Denver, Colorado Area*, Rocky Mountain Chapter of American Rock Garden Society.

Kelly, George W. 1970, *Woody Plants of Colorado*, Pruett.

Kelly, George W. 1967, *Rocky Mountain Horticulture*, Pruett.

Klaber, Doretta 1959, *Rock Garden Plants*, Holt and Company, New York.

Loewer, Peter, 1988, *The Annual Garden*, Rodale Press

Lima, Patrick, 1987, *The Harrowsmith Perennial Garden*, Camden House, 7 Queen Victoria Rd., Camden East, Ontario KOK 1J0

Pirone, P.P., 1988, *Tree Maintenance*, 6th ed. Oxford Univ. Press, Oxford, U.K.and New York.

Phillips, Roger and Martyn Rix 1989. *Shrubs*, Random House, New York.

Rehder, Alfred, *1940 Manual of Cultivated Trees and Shrubs*, Macmillan Co., N.Y.

Rogers,Ruth and Nicolas Ekstrom, 1989, *Perennials for American Gardens*, Random House, New York.

Sabuco, John J. *The Best of the Hardiest*, 1985, Good Earth.

Strauch, Jr., J.G., and J.E. Klett, 1989, *Flowering Herbaceous Perennials for the High Plains*, Colorado State University, Ft. Collins, CO. 80523

Sunset Garden Dept. Staff, 1971, *Rhododendrons and Azaleas*, Lane Books, Menlo Park, CA

Tisdale, Samuel L. and Werner L. Nelson, 1966, *Soil Fertility and Fertilizers*, 2nd ed. Macmillan, N. Y.

Van Melle, P.J., 1943, *Shrubs and Trees for the Small Place*, American Garden Guild.

Wilder, Louise Beebe 1918 & 1990, *Color In My Garden*, Atlantic Monthly Press.

Wilkinson, Elizabeth, and Majorie Henderson, 1985, *The House of Boughs,* Yolla Bolly Press, Japan.

Wyman, Donald, 1954, *The Arnold Arboretum Garden Book*, D. Van Nostrand Co., Inc.

Wyman, Donald, 1961, S*hrubs and Vines for American Gardens*, Macmillan.

Wyman, Donald, 1951, *Trees for American Gardens*, Macmillan.

Index

B

C

D

N

O

P

Q

R

S

T